Convection Oven Cookbook

Learn to make 500+ Easy and Healthy Recipes with the amazing Appliance and Enjoy your meals

KARA HERSEY

Table of Content

INTRODUCTION: 11

CHAPTER 1: EVERYTHING ABOUT CONVECTION
OVEN   11

1.1 Types of convection oven   12
1.2 Settings of convection and how to use them   14
1.4 Why choose a convection oven instead of a normal one:
                                                                 15

CHAPTER 2: BREAKFAST AND BRUNCH RECIPES   17

2.1 Best breakfast toast with egg and cheese   17
2.2 Breakfast Apple omelet   18
2.3 Brunch Bacon Pizza   18
2.4 Chevre And Roasted Veggies Quiche   19
2.5 Brunch Baked Strawberry Rolls   19
2.6 Feta And Roasted Pumpkin Tarts   20
2.7 Farmer's Breakfast Casserole   20
2.8 Caramelized Onion, Spinach, And Bacon Strata   21
2.9 Baked tater tots   21
2.10 Classic Egg Casserole   22
2.11 Egg Cheese And Bacon Breakfast Bread   22
2.12 Tasty Snickers Flavored Croissants   23
2.13 Tasty Streusel Blueberry Coffee Cake   23
2.14 Ham And Broccoli Cheese Quiche   24
2.15 Easy And Yummy Brunch Reuben Bake   24
2.16 Egg And Potato Cheesy Bake   25
2.17 Southern Style Pastry Puff For Brunch   25
2.18 Baked French Toast With Stuffed Apples   26
2.19 Blueberry Breakfast French Toast   26
2.20 Southwest-Style Bake Sausage   27
2.21 Baked Breakfast Apple Butter Biscuit   27
2.22 Brunch Onion Tart   28
2.24 Classic And Simple Oven Omelet   28
2.23 Egg Sausage-Vegetable Bake   29
2.25 Cranberry Garlic And Cheddar Mini Breads   29
2.26 Tasty Cheese And Ham Croissant   30
2.27 Brunch Florentine Pizza   30
2.28 Crumpet Butter And Caramel Pudding   31
2.29 Low-Carb Garlic Bread   31
2.30 Breakfast Danish Buns   32
2.31 Quiche Brunch Cups   32
2.32 Apple Caramel French Toast Casserole   33
2.33 Pumpkin Cookies Sandwich With Frosting Of Maple Cream Cheese 33
2.34 Easy Pumpkin Breakfast Bread   34
2.35 Simple And Classic Breakfast Pizza   34
2.36 Baked Zucchini Slice (Gluten-Free)   35
2.37 Breakfast Egg In A Hole Bagel   35
2.38 Quick And Tasty Peanut Butter Bread   36
2.39 Date And Walnut Quick Bread   36
2.40 Baked Peach French Toast   37
2.41 Baked Mixed Berries Oatmeal   37
2.42 Baked Banana and Nuts French Toast   38

2.43 Healthy And Tasty Oatmeal Blueberry Bread   38
2.44 Baked Breakfast Italian Eggs   39
2.45 Breakfast Cranberry and Orange Bread   39
2.46 Crescent Sausage Rolls   40
2.47 Potato, Egg, and Beef Bake   40
2.48 Quick And Easy Pistachio Bread   41
2.49 Egg And Bacon Breakfast Lasagna   41
2.50 Breakfast Baked Oatmeal   42
2.51 Cocoa Peanut Butter Granola   42
2.52 Pecan cookies with rye and barley flakes   43
2.53 Breakfast Burrito Casserole   43
2.54 Bacon and Eggs Dutch Baby Pancakes   44
2.55 Quick breakfast Pizza slices with quail eggs   45
2.56 Scrumptious bacon and egg cupcake omelet   46
2.57 Apple Granola Crisp   46
2.58 Brunch Bake   47
2.59 Cheesy Sausage & Egg Bake   47
2.60 Easy Breakfast Bake   48
2.61 Scrambled Egg Muffins   48
2.62 Sausage Bites   49

CHAPTER 3: APPETIZERS AND SNACKS RECIPES   51

3.1 Baked Parmesan Chicken Slider   51
3.2 Corn Mini Muffins with Cheddar Spicy Filling   52
3.3 Pepperoni Pizza Bread Loaf   52
3.4 Chicken Cheese Puffs   53
3.5 Classic Sausage Italian Bruschetta   53
3.6 Simple and Easy Pinwheels   54
3.7 Easy Chicken Buffalo Dip   54
3.8 Cheese 'n' Ham Biscuit Stacks   55
3.9 Bean And Tuscan Sausage Dip   55
3.10 Pecan,Pear and Pancetta Puffs   56
3.11 Artichoke And Hot Collards Dip   56
3.12 Pepperoni Pizza Rolls   57
3.13 Easy and Quick Broiled Tomatoes   57
3.14 Tasty Pizza Bagels   58
3.15 Mac And Cheese Jalapeno Bites   58
3.16 Wrapped Bacon Scallops   59
3.17 Tasty Stuffed Mushrooms (Stuffed Sausage Mushrooms)
                                                                 59
3.18 Tasty Pizza Bubble   60
3.19 Mini Brie And Cranberry Bites   60
3.20 Easy And Quick Crostini   61
3.21 Cheese Bread Sticks   61
3.22 Mini Zucchini Bites   62
3.23 Classic Giant Pretzels   62
3.24 Loaded Nachos Tater Tot   63
3.25 Yummy And Easy Pizza Rolls   63
3.26 Party Savory Bread   64
3.27 Tasty Grilled Pineapples   64
3.28 Banana Bread Inspired Brownies   65
3.29 Cheeseburger Bacon Bombs   66
3.30 Oven-Baked Zucchini Fries   66
3.31 Pineapple And Carrot Muffins   67

3.32 Jalapeno Crescent Cups 67
3.33 Tasty Potato Skins Baked 68
3.34 Grilled Chicken Hawaiian Pizza 68
3.35 Tasty Cheese And Ham Sliders 69
3.36 Pistachio Puff Pastry Twists 69
3.37 Cheesy Easy Pizza Flavored Dip 70
3.38 Popper Cups With Jalapeno 70
3.39 Cheddar Chile Cornbread 71
3.40 Bacon And Cheese Round Potatoes 71
3.41 Easy Granola Cookies 72
3.42 Broiled Crab Snacks 72
3.43 Pepperoni Pizza Cheesy Puffs 73
3.44 Stuffed Baked Cherry Peppers 73
3.45 Squares Cheese Appetizer 74
3.46 Asparagus Cheesy Snack 74
3.47 Cheese Olives Baked 75
3.48 Cheddar Bacon Garlic Bread 75
3.49 Stuffed Pizza Mushrooms 76
3.50 Best Artichoke And Spinach Dip 76
3.51 Roasted Mixed Nuts 77
3.52 Crispy Baked French Fries 77
3.53 Homemade Chicken Nuggets 78
3.54 Homemade Fish Sticks 78
3.55 Buffalo chicken bites with spinach and parmesan cheese 79
3.56 Beet and goat cheese appetizers 80
3.57 Cinnamon Roll Smokies 80
3.58 Bacon Wrapped, Stuffed Mini Peppers 81
3.59 Bbq Chicken Wings 82
3.60 Cinnamon Sweet Potato Chips 82
3.61 Spinach Chips 83
3.62 Seasoned Oyster Crackers 83
3.63 Crispy Tofu Bites 84

CHAPTER 4: VEGETABLE RECIPES 85

4.1 Cabbage Wedges Roasted 85
4.2 Dijon Crispy Smashed Potato 86
4.3 Vegetable Cheesy Casserole 86
4.4 Roasted Brown Sugar Rutabaga 87
4.5 Classic Italian Parmesan Eggplant 87
4.6 Tasty Vegetable Lasagna 88
4.7 Root Vegetables Roasted 88
4.8 Oven-Baked Parmesan Tomatoes 89
4.9 Crispy And Tasty Brussels Sprouts 89
4.10 Roasted Parmesan Garlic Potatoes 90
4.11 Tasty And Quick Vegetable Pasta Salad 90
4.12 Simple And Tasty Vegetable Frittata 91
4.13 Easy and Delicious Mushrooms Roasted 91
4.14 Delicious Zucchini Casserole 92
4.15 Tasty Vegetable Casserole 92
4.16 Roasted Yams with Ginger, Miso and Scallions 93
4.17 Delicious Mediterranean Vegetable Sandwich Grilled 93
4.18 Tasty And Easy Cheesy Vegetable pizza 94
4.19 Delicious Vegetable Pot Pie 94
4.20 Cauliflower Mac And Cheese Baked 95
4.21 Baked California Vegetable 95

4.22 Cornish Vegetable Pasties 96
4.23 Grilled Potato Packets (Potato in A Foil) 96
4.24 Pattypan Squash Roasted 97
4.25 Cheese And Mushroom Strata 97
4.26 Delicious Rutabaga Gratin 98
4.27 Cucumber And Tomato Bruschetta 98
4.28 Vegetable Egg Muffins 99
4.29 Tasty Baked Duchess Potatoes 99
4.30 Butternut Squash Roasted 100
4.31 Mushrooms With Marinara And White Beans 100
4.32 Spinach And Cheese Stuffed Mushrooms 101
4.33 Cheesy Spinach Lasagna 101
4.34 Tasty And Easy Carrot Cake 102
4.35 Roasted Cauliflower With Cheese Sauce 102
4.36 Mexican Style Stuffed Peppers 103
4.37 Acorn Squash Stuffed 103
4.38 Carrot And Broccoli Lasagna 104
4.39 Mushrooms Leeks and Sweet Potatoes Quiche 104
4.40 Simple And Delicious Broccoli Casserole 105
4.41 Crispy Onion Rings Baked 105
4.42 Red Peppers With Basil Roasted 106
4.43 Blue Cheese Courgette Pizza 106
4.44 Oven Roasted Italian Style Vegetables 107
4.45 Easy And Tasty Potato Gratin 107
4.46 Classic French Vegetable Loaf 108
4.47 Vegetable Enchilada Pie 108
4.48 Leek And Cauliflower' Cheese' Herb-Crusted 109
4.49 Roasted Spicy Okra 110
4.50 Crispy Potato Wedges Baked 110
4.51 Salt and Vinegar Roasted Potatoes with Feta and Dill 111
4.52 Maple Balsamic Roasted Vegetables 111
4.53 Homemade pizza in a convection oven 112
4.54 Huevos Rancheros Bake 113
4.55 Artichoke Pie 113
4.56 Greek Stuffed Peppers with Feta & Mizithra Cheeses 114
4.57 Roasted Carrots 114
4.58 Lentil and roast vegetables salad 115
4.59 Spiced cauliflower 115
4.60 Cabbage Rolls 116
4.61 Zucchini Boats 117
4.62 Mexican Style Eggplant 117

CHAPTER 5: FISH AND SEAFOOD RECIPES 119

5.1 Simple And Delicious Seafood Pizza 119
5.2 Baked Herb-Crusted Salmon 120
5.3 Easy And Tasty Tuna Noodles Casserole 120
5.4 Delicious Seafood Stuffing 121
5.5 Crusted Parmesan Tilapia 121
5.6 Stuffed Crab Mushrooms 122
5.7 Tasty Fish Croquettes Baked 122
5.8 Seafood Cottage Cheese Lasagna 123
5.9 Tasty Baked Cod Fish 123
5.10 Easy And Quick-Roasted Salmon 124
5.11 Delicious Seafood Salad Baked 124
5.12 Tasty Broiled Scallops 125
5.13 Scallops. Flounder And Shrimp Lasagna 125

5.14 Grilled Sriracha Shrimps 126
5.15 Cheesy Crabmeat Dip 126
5.16 Tasty Tuna Cheesy Melts 127
5.17 Baked Trout Fish in A Foil 127
5.18 Butter Lemon Baked Salmon Fettuccine Pasta 128
5.19 Delicious Grilled Garlic Shrimp 128
5.20 Simple Crab Tart With Avocado 129
5.21 Shrimp And Crabmeat Enchiladas 129
5.22 Baked Salmon With Honey Glazed 130
5.23 Watercress And Crab Mini Soufflé Tarts 130
5.24 One-Pan Ginger Sesame Salmon 131
5.25 Delicious Seafood Gratin 131
5.26 Crab Filled Crescent Cups 132
5.27 Tasty Seafood Stuffed Peppers 132
5.28 Haddock And Seafood Baked 133
5.29 Fish Nuggets Baked 133
5.30 Easy And Quick Baked Shrimp Dip 134
5.31 Baked Garlic Butter Lobster Tails 134
5.32 Crabmeat and Shrimp Loaf 135
5.33 Shrimp And Broccoli Alfredo Bake 135
5.34 Crab Stuffed Muffins 136
5.35 Baked Teriyaki Salmon 136
5.36 Cheesy Seafood White Sauce Pizza 137
5.37 Tasty Seafood Ravioli Baked 137
5.38 Simply Baked Seafood Potatoes 138
5.39 Quick And Simple Sea Bass Oven-Baked 138
5.40 Spicy Seafood Penne Pasta 139
5.41 Mayo-Cheese Mussels Dynamite 139
5.42 Garlic Mayonnaise-Parmesan Topping Halibut 140
5.43 Tasty Baked Tilapia Pecan-Crusted 140
5.44 Delicious Spinach And Seafood Mornay 141
5.45 Classic Baked Catfish Fillets 142
5.46 Crabmeat Roll-Ups Lasagna 142
5.47 Broiled Steelhead Trout With Lemon Garlic And Rose-mary 143
5.48 Crabmeat And Prawns Southwestern Thin Crust Pizza 143
5.49 Crispy Lobster And Crab Stuffed Mushrooms 144
5.50 Italian Style Baked Oysters 144
5.51 Lemon-herb Baked Rainbow Trout 145
5.52 Parmesan Herb Baked Tilapia 145
5.53 Grilled Garlic Salmon 146
5.54 Ginger Soy Mahi Mahi 146
5.55 Oven-Baked Sea Bass 147
5.56 Cajun Tilapia 147
5.57 Broiled Swai with Salsa 148
5.58 Parmesan-Crusted White Fish 148
5.59 Crunchy Oven Fried Fish 149
5.60 Honey Dijon Salmon 149
5.61 Parmesan Basil Salmon 150
5.62 Smokin' Mahi Mahi 150

CHAPTER 6: 30 MINUTES RECIPES 151

6.1 Quick And Easy Roasted Vegetables Tortillas 151
6.2 Easy Baked Apple-Sugar Puff Pastry 152
6.3 Easy And Quick Cheesy Baked Gnocchi 152
6.4 Quick Baked Red Potatoes With Butter And Sour Cream Topping 153
6.5 Lime Scallion Flavored Sea Bass 153
6.6 Classic Chicken And Pineapple Casserole 154
6.7 Quick Parsley And Dill Rolls 154
6.8 Beef And Cheese Taco Pies 155
6.9 Simple And Quick Tortilla Crust Pizza 155
6.10 Chocolate Chips and Butterscotch Bars 156
6.11 Tasty And Quick Meatloaf 156
6.12 Cheesy Salsa Bean Burritos 157
6.13 Banana Oat And Cinnamon Muffins 157
6.14 Quick Baked Artichoke And Brie 158
6.15 Tasty Dijon-Crusted Fish Fillets 158
6.16 Cinnamon, Butter And Sugar Stuffed-Apples 159
6.17 Beef And Broccoli Braided Bread 159
6.18 Classic Peanut-Butter Flavored Cookies 160
6.19 Crispy Pork Chops Baked 160
6.20 Tasty Apple Sauce Flavored Cornbread 161
6.21 Crispy And Tasty Turkey Burgers Baked 161
6.22 Classic Shepherd's Pie 162
6.23 Baked Eggplant Layered With Seasoning 162
6.24 Classic Baked Pineapple Butter Casserole 163
6.25 Italian Style Simple Baked Chicken 163
6.26 Quick Nut And Banana Bread 164
6.27 Tasty Garlic And Cheddar Biscuits 164
6.28 Cheddar And Cream Cheese Stuffed Jalapeno Poppers 165
6.29 Parmesan And Butter Chicken 165
6.30 Quick Classic Chocolate Cake 166
6.31 Tasty Meatballs Cheesy Pizza 166
6.32 Baked Beef And Cheese Cups 167
6.33 Quick And Crunchy Raisin Oatmeal Cookies 167
6.34 Delicious Baked Jalapeno Cranberry Dip 168
6.35 Quick Cheese Spicy Bread 168
6.36 Tasty Baked Chicken Mushroom 169
6.37 Baked Banana Cinnamon Fritters 169
6.38 Baked Cheesy Leeks 170
6.39 Baked Steelhead Trout Croquettes 170
6.40 Tasty And Quick Caesar Chicken Baked 171
6.41 Quick And Easy Herb Bread 171
6.42 Baked Beans, Tomato And Bacon 172
6.43 Baked Caramel Oatmeal bars 172
6.44 Baked Asparagus With Italian Seasoning Cheese Sauce 173
6.45 Quick Cheesy Potato Pizza 173
6.46 Tasty Baked Cheese Breaded Squash 174
6.47 Baked Butter Cream Onions 174
6.48 Easy and Quick Chicken With Guacamole And Salsa 175
6.49 Quick And Tasty Cheesy Baked Grits 175
6.50 Baked Mushroom Bread With Parmesan And Italian Sea-soning 176
6.51 Baked Quinoa Chicken Nuggets 176
6.52 Roasted Red Potatoes 177
6.53 Roasted Vegetables 177
6.54 Lemony garlic tilapia 178
6.55 Salmon with Rosemary 178
6.56 Coconut Crusted Mahi Mahi 179

6.57 Breaded Lemon Chicken 179
6.58 Cinnamon roll apple pie 180
6.59 Oven Roasted Corn 180
6.60 Asparagus Fries 181
6.61 Marinated Prawns 181
6.62 4 Cheese Fresh Garden Stuffed Jalapeno 182

CHAPTER 7: POULTRY, BEEF, LAMB AND PORK RECIPES 183

7.1 Beef Crostini With Blue Cheese 183
7.2 Ground Pork Shepherd's Pie 184
7.3 Armenian-Style Lamb And Beef Pizza 184
7.4 Greek-Style Pork Chops 185
7.5 Baked Buttermilk Spicy Chicken 185
7.6 Classic Turkey Stuffing 186
7.7 Beef And Pork Stuffed Pasta Shells 186
7.8 Baked Beef Mixture Under A Bun 187
7.9 Grilled Sweet And Sour Chicken Thighs 187
7.10 Grilled Marinated Beef Ribeyes Steaks 188
7.11 Grilled Pork Barbecued Kebabs 188
7.12 Spicy Beef And Bean Pie 189
7.13 Chicken And Stuffing Muffin Cups 189
7.14 Cheesy Beef Steak Pizza 190
7.15 Baked Garlic And Butter-Flavored Pork Steaks 190
7.16 Cheesy Baked Chicken Penne Pasta 191
7.17 Baked Creamy Mushroom Chicken 191
7.18 Classic Lamb Gratin 192
7.19 Tasty And Simple Meatball Casserole 193
7.20 Baked Turkey And Potato Croquettes 193
7.21 Russian-Style Baked Beef 194
7.22 Butter Lemon Baked Chicken Tenders 194
7.23 Tasty Lamb Meatballs Baked 195
7.24 Classic Pork Chops Baked With Mushroom Sauce 195
7.25 Chicken Cheese Taco Casserole 196
7.26 Delicious Lamb Stuffed Peppers 196
7.27 Tasty Duck Rillettes 197
7.28 Spinach Beef And Rice Baked 198
7.29 Baked Lamb Moroccan Kebabs 198
7.30 Baked Honey-Mustard Flavored Chicken 199
7.31 Roasted Beef Tenderloin Salt-Crusted 199
7.32 Classic And Simple Lamb Loaf 200
7.33 Baked Italian-Style Breaded Pork Chops 200
7.34 Beef And Salsa Baked Taquitos 201
7.35 Baked Teriyaki Pineapple Chicken 201
7.36 Baked Meatballs Stuffed With Mac And Cheese 202
7.37 Baked Cheese Stuffed Chicken Breasts With Sauce 202
7.38 Baked Beef Potato Pie 203
7.39 Baked Maple Flavored Pork Loin Roast 203
7.40 Cheesy Chicken Roll-Ups Baked 204
7.41 Classic Chicken Parmesan Meatloaf 204
7.42 Roasted Beef Teriyaki Shish Kebabs 205
7.43 Beef And Egg Noodles Bake 205
7.44 Baked Pesto-Flavored Chicken 206
7.45 Baked Swiss Cheese And Corned Beef Dip In Bread Bowl 206
7.46 Greek-Style Stuffed Lamb Leg 207

7.47 Baked Chicken Cheesy Potatoes Ranch 207
7.48 Roasted Avocado And Dijon Rubbed Beef Tenderloin 208
7.49 Beef Cheese Spaghetti Pie 208
7.50 Oven-Roasted Stuffed Duck 209
7.51 Skillet Roast Chicken with Schmaltzy Potatoes 209
7.52 Roasted Chicken with Garlic and Herb Butter 210
7.53 Lemon Garlic Roasted Chicken and Potato Wedges 211
7.54 Cracker Barrel Meatloaf 211
7.55 Dijon Herb Chicken Breasts 212
7.56 Roast Turkey 212
7.57 Honey Lime Chicken Breasts 213
7.58 Crispy Honey Garlic Chicken 213
7.59 Old Meatloaf 214
7.60 Sheet Pan Chicken Pot Pie 215
7.61 Creamy Chicken and Corn Burritos 215
7.62 Yummy spicy coconut chicken 216

CHAPTER 8: 5 INGREDIENTS RECIPES (TASTY RECIPES WITH NO MORE THAN 5 INGREDIENTS) 217

8.1 Easy Cocktail And Shrimp Dip 217
8.2 Easy Chocolate Chip Cookies With 5-Ingredient 218
8.3 Baked Bacon-Wrapped Chicken 218
8.4 Cheesy Cauliflower Crackers 219
8.5 Quick And Easy Peanut Butter Cookies With 3-Ingredient 219
8.6 Party Mini Beef Burgers Baked 220
8.7 Baked Chicken With Lemon-Pepper Seasoning 220
8.8 Tasty Cabbage Baked Steaks 221
8.9 Pineapple Casserole Baked 221
8.10 Ukraine-Style Potato Baked 222
8.11 Barbecue-Style Chicken Bacon Bake 222
8.12 Baked Apple And Sausages 223
8.13 Baked Cheese Sausage Biscuits 223
8.14 Garlic Parmesan Roasted Carrots 224
8.15 Caramelized Pecan Bacon Baked 224
8.16 Muffin With A Meal 225
8.17 Avocado Flavored Cloud Bread 225
8.18 Tater-Tot Beef Casserole 226
8.19 Baked Onion Chicken 226
8.20 Parmesan Green Beans Roasted 227
8.21 Prosciutto-Wrapped Pesto Chicken 227
8.22 Ham And Cheddar Baked Omelet 228
8.23 Chocolate-Peanut Marshmallow Bars 228
8.24 Oven-Baked Rosemary Parmesan Potato Chunks 229
8.25 Easy And Classic Meyer Lemon Pie 229
8.26 Buttermilk Flavored Mac And Cheese Baked 230
8.27 Tasty Fries And Cheeseburger Casserole 230
8.28 Delicious Picante And Cheese Omelet Pie 231
8.29 Mini Garlic-Herb Cheese Quiches 231
8.30 Tasty And Creamy Scalloped Potatoes 232
8.31 Cinnamon-Flavored Strawberry Biscuits 232
8.32 Delicious Chicken Gratin 233
8.33 Sausage Stuffed Jalapenos Wrapped In Bacon 233
8.34 Tasty Ranch-Parmesan Bread Rolls 234
8.35 Quick And Easy Ham Steaks Baked 234
8.36 Baked Chicken Parmesan Nuggets 235

8.37 Tasty Hash Browns Baked 235
8.38 Classic Rice And Chicken Casserole 236
8.39 Baked Seasoned Jicama Fries 236
8.40 Creamy Quick Biscuits 237
8.41 Baked Eggs In An Avocado hole 237
8.42 Baked Oatmeal Stuffed Apples 238
8.43 Barbecue Chicken Tenders Baked 238
8.44 Simple Ravioli Cheese Casserole 239
8.45 Tasty Fresh Blueberry Cobbler 239
8.46 Baked Egg And Bacon Bundles 240
8.47 Buffalo Cheese Chicken Pockets 240
8.48 Southern-Style Tasty Buttermilk Biscuits 241
8.49 Chive-Garlic Oven-Baked Fries 241
8.50 Easy Chicken Barbecued Pizza 242
8.51 Crispy Roasted Artichokes 242
8.52 Baked Sweet Potato Fries 243
8.53 Crispy Smashed Potatoes 243
8.54 Easy Roasted Red Potatoes 244
8.55 Fish with Parsley Pesto 244
8.56 Roasted Garlic Mahi Mahi 245
8.57 Salmon and Asparagus 245
8.58 Flounder Dijon 246
8.59 Brown Sugar and Garlic Chicken 246
8.60 Baked Chicken Thigh 247
8.61 Baked Salmon 247
8.62 Baked Chicken Teriyaki 248

CHAPTER 9: CAKES, COOKIES AND DESSERTS RECIPES 249

9.1 Cream Cheese And Strawberry Cobbler 249
9.2 Classic Molasses Cookies With Coffee-Glazed 250
9.3 Walnut And Cranberry Loaf 250
9.4 Basic Oatmeal And Peanut Butter bars 251
9.5 Simple And Crispy Sugar Cookies 251
9.6 Cake Mix Cheesecake Dessert With Raspberry Topping 252
9.7 Pumpkin Pie Mini Muffins 252
9.8 Coconut Pineapple Cake With Lime Frosting 253
9.9 Easy And Quick Oatmeal Banana Cookies 253
9.10 Double Chocolate And Macadamia Biscotti 254
9.11 Tasty Poppy Seeds Lemon Cake 254
9.12 Crisps Almond Coffee Cookies 255
9.13 Raspberry Jam Dessert Bars 255
9.14 Orange-Zest Blackberry Cake 256
9.15 Basic And Soft Raisin Apricot Cookies 256
9.16 Classic Banana Chocolate Cake 257
9.17 Irish-Style Cupcakes With Irish Cream Frosting 257
9.18 Tasty Pecan Butter Cookies 258
9.19 Easy And Delicious Gingerbread Cake 258
9.20 Cherry Cracker Dessert 259
9.21 Tasty And Soft Baked Lemon Cheesecake Bites 259
9.22 Mexican-Style Sugar Chocolate Crisps 260
9.23 Pecan And Chocolate Pie Dessert Bars 260
9.24 Baked Croissant Creamy Pudding With Delicious Kahlua Sauce 261
9.25 Zucchini-Flavored Chocolate Cookies 261
9.26 Caramel Apple Cinnamon Crisps 262
9.27 Delicious Pumpkin Cake With Cream Cheese And Butter Frosting 262
9.28 Date And Pecan Cookies 263
9.29 Marshmallow Butterscotch Brownies 263
9.30 Soft Fruit Cocktail And Nut Cookies 264
9.31 Classic Coconut Macaroons With Chocolate Glaze 264
9.32 Moist And Tasty Basic Chocolate cake 265
9.33 Persimmon And Walnuts Cookies 265
9.34 Lemon And Ricotta Cheese Dessert Cake 266
9.35 Cream Cheese Chocolate Chip Brownies 266
9.36 Lemon-Flavored Buttermilk Pie 267
9.37 Chia Seeds And Oatmeal Cookies 267
9.38 Tasty And Moist Lime-White Chocolate Muffins 268
9.39 Simple And Crunchy Cornmeal Cookies 268
9.40 Apricot And Nut Square Bars 269
9.41 Delicious And Chewy Chocolate Chip Cookies 269
9.42 Tasty And Moist Red Velvet Cheesecake 270
9.43 Butter Bars With Baked Lemon Curd Filling 270
9.44 The Best Banoffee Pie 271
9.45 Starbucks Inspired Swirl Raspberry Pound Loaf With Frosting 271
9.46 Lemon-Honey Glaze Cheesecake Baklava 272
9.47 Best-Ever Plum Pudding Dessert Baked 272
9.48 Easy And Moist Red Velvet Cookies 273
9.49 The Perfect Baked Raisin Rice Pudding 273
9.50 Almond Chocolate And Coconut Cake 274
9.51 Toaster Oven Peanut Butter Cookies 274
9.52 Strawberry Pie with Strawberry Crust 275
9.53 Chocolate Chip Cookie for Modern Times 276
9.54 Christmas Magic Cookie Bars 276
9.55 Chocolate Chip Cookies 277
9.56 Meringue cookies. 278
9.57 Lemon Squares 278
9.58 oven chocolate fudge cake 279
9.59 Oven Chocolate Cookies 279
6.60 Easy Cinnamon Sugar Baked Apples 280
9.61 Oven Baked Pears 280
9.62 Marble cake with cacao and turmeric 281
9.63 Fresh Homemade Peach Pie 282
9.64 Orange Butter Cookies 282
9.65 Easy cinnamon rolls with homemade jam 283

CONCLUSION **284**

Hello dear reader!

I hope you will enjoy this book.

I want to let you know how important your purchase and judgment can be to me.

To give you a brief introduction: I'm a small writer, I write for passion, and I think that the recipes of this book can help people deepen into the topic, create new dishes, and get the basis of your knowledge about the ideas inside this book. Writing a book is a great challenge that keeps you busy for hours on end, trying to create the best you can do.

Like the other independent writers, I don't have the big advertising budget that many other publishers and businesses spend online.

So, one way you can support my work is by leaving me a review of this book.

You can do it by using this QR code:

If you liked the book, leave a good review, perhaps with some pictures, so that everybody can see the book's contents. I've spent many hours on it, and I'd like to see your appreciation.
Maybe you can also leave some pictures of the dishes prepared with these recipes; it will be great!
You can leave a rating if you don't have much time. It will only take you 2 seconds.
For an independent writer like me, getting ratings and reviews means submitting my book for advertising.

So, every review and rating means a lot to me.

I can't THANK YOU enough for this!

Kara

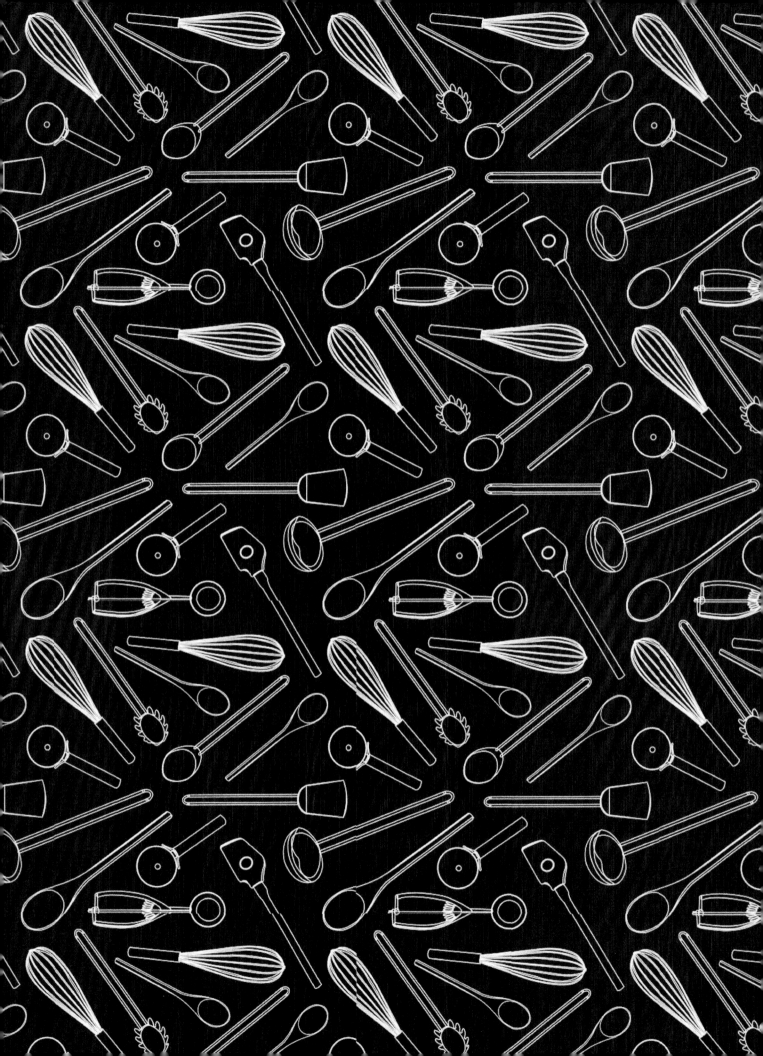

Introduction:

From antiquity to present times. An oven is an important appliance in almost every household. In regards to cooking, an oven is invaluable. It can use for baking, stovetop cooking, broiling different kinds of steaks, or roasting a chicken or vegetables. The oven history goes back to 29,000 BC in central Europe, where people used a non-commercial oven for roasting and boiling. Since then, the oven is a widely used tool professionally and domestically worldwide for different purposes.

The term oven refers to a very hot environment in which different kinds of food substances are cooked, baked, grilled, roast, or even heated. The term oven was used first, during the Second World War, and became a very popular word by that time. Ovens come in a range of shapes and sizes since they are used for a variety of purposes. Depending on their intended motives and how they produce heat, these forms vary.

The different kinds of ovens used for cooking are convection ovens, conventional ovens, microwave, or oven toaster grill (OTG) oven.

Moreover, the most suggested and favored type of oven is a convection oven. This is not surprising because using a convection oven has many advantages that are not typically provided by a traditional(conventional)oven.

Will you like to intensify your cooking game? Then choose a convection oven. Convection ovens heat up faster and cook food more evenly than traditional ovens. Thanks to some easy modifications to the appliance. All this adds up to delicious baked items, meats, and more. Here is everything you need to learn about convection ovens, types of convection ovens, how they work, and how they are better than other types of ovens, etc.

Chapter 1: Everything About Convection Oven

A convection oven is an oven that comes up with a built-in fan. In simple words, a convection oven has an exhaust and fan structure, unlike traditional ovens through which it circulates air all over the food resulting in even heat distribution.

In 1914, the first oven with the built-in fan was invented but never commercially introduced. The convection oven for commercial purposes was invented in 1945, was the first commonly used convection oven.

A built-in fan oven cooks a lot faster than a regular non-fan oven, which relies solely on natural convection to circulate hot air around the food.

The built-in fan oven temperature is normally decreased compared to a non-fan oven, often by 20 to 25 °C (40 °F).in order to prevent overcooking the food's exterior. Radiant heat suppliers at the top and bottom of convection ovens boost heat transfer and speed cooking from a cold start. On the other hand, many ovens have all the heating components placed in an outer enclosure and hidden from the food. This lessens the impact of radiant heat on the food. However, the oven walls will still be heated by the circulating warm air. Although the resulting temperature is much weaker than that of a radiant heat source, it is still hot enough to give some heat source to the food from wall radiation.

The convection oven special mechanism makes it a favorite kitchen gadget. Faster cooking times, uniformly cooked food, and less energy used when cooking are all benefits of using a convection oven.

1.1 TYPES OF CONVECTION OVEN

Convection ovens come in several shapes and sizes, but the two most common forms are classified into two types. The first type is called regular and true convection ovens. They are distinguished by fan positioning and additional heating component's location.

The second type is known as the countertop convection oven and floor model convection ovens, and they are differentiated by their location and arrangement in the kitchen.

Regular convection oven:

A regular convection oven also known as "American Version" is a regular oven with an extra fan situated at the back of the oven to assist with air circulation within the oven's interior.

The fan in this form of convection oven circulates both hot and cold air inside the oven. The food may not be as uniformly cooked as expected due to the difference in the air being blown.

True convection oven:

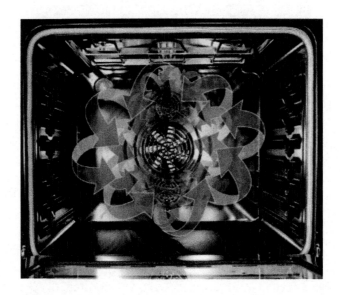

A true convection oven is one that has both a fan and a third heating component at the back of the oven. Often the term "European convection oven" is used to describe a true convection oven.

Unlike a standard convection oven, which circulates pre-heated air, a true convection oven uses its fan to disperse heated air. As a consequence, the food is uniformly cooked, the interior temperature is stabilized, and cooking time is reduced.

Countertop convection oven:

Countertop convection ovens can be settled on counters, tables, and other open areas. Countertop convection ovens are suitable for tiny spaces because they are moveable, smaller, and lighter.

When it is about food, this sort can only carry a small amount of it. This type of convection oven has the advantage of being simple to install and remove.

If you run a snack bar, food truck, convenience shop, or quick-serve restaurant, countertop convection ovens are likely to meet your cooking needs. These ovens' performance, which can have wattage ratings up to 7700, is unaffected by a lack of floor space. They're simple to set up and come in quarter-, half-, and full-size sizes.

Floor Model Convection Ovens:

A floor model convection oven is considerably larger than a countertop convection oven and can cook more food at once. It's available in half and full sizes, depending on the capacity you have.

Restaurants and other food establishments prefer a floor model convection oven because it allows for concurrent cooking of large quantities of food faster.

Floor model convection ovens are flexible pieces of equipment that come in various configurations to suit your needs. Half-size models are ideal for kitchens with minimal room or low-performance requirements, while full-size models are ideal for high-volume kitchens with no space constraints. When it comes to size and performance, you can choose between single-deck and double-deck. There are also many programmable functions, such as "cook and keep," which allows you to set the temperature lower than in a standard oven for slow-cooking roasts and other meat dishes.

There are many types of convection ovens, but the one best for your kitchen depends on your particular needs, considering the appliance's function, the amount of food to be cooked, and the location where the convection oven to be kept.

When do you use the setting of convection?

Your oven's convection setting activates a fan and an exhaust device that circulates hot air in the oven. As a result, the exterior edges of dishes are cooked more uniformly. Furthermore, the exhaust system eliminates moisture from the oven, allowing foods to dry quickly. Knowing when to use the convection setting and taking steps to improve your oven's performance will allow you to cook with the convection setting with ease.

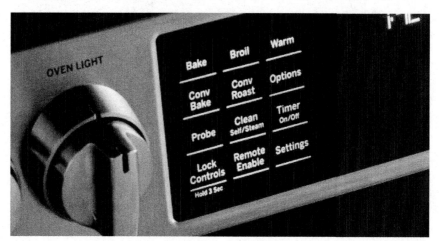

1. When roasting food, select the convection setting. The convection environment is suitable for roasting food because it helps in fat rendering and provides a more evenly browned surface. Convection cooking also speeds up the caramelization of natural sugars in fruits and vegetables, and you will get creamy middle and crispy edges as a result. The following are some examples of foods that can be roast with the convection setting on

- Turkey
- Potatoes
- Chicken
- Apples
- Numerous vegetables etc.

2. When you want flakier baked goods, use the convection settings. Your baked goods would be lighter, crisper, and flakier due to the way hot air travels in a convection oven. They can also cook more quickly. Furthermore, you won't have to spin them as often. Cookies, Brownies, pies, pastries, various kinds of bread and crust are some baked goods you can cook with the convection setting.

3. If you want to toast or dry food, use the convection setting. The convection setting will hasten the drying process and ensure that your food is toasted evenly. In fact, a convection oven might be better than a dehydrator for drying jerky. Think of toasting or drying, Fruit, Jerky, Nuts, etc.

4. When it comes to delicate foods like Soufflés and custards that start as batter and set while cooking, the fan becomes a liability. Blowing air on these foods will result in a lopsided outcome. When making these dishes, avoid using the convection setting.

5. For fried and crunchy foods, Turn on the convection setting. If you're cooking or warming something that needs to stay crunchy. The convection oven works best in this way by removing moisture and crisping the food because it circulates hot air around the food.

- For reheating the fried chicken, if you want to operate a convection oven, you can do so.
- Cook your French fries in the convection oven if you like them crispy.

What is the safest and best way to operate a convection oven?

1.Converting Recipes for Convection Ovens: Go through the recipe to see if you required to change the time or temperature using a convection oven. While most recipes are made for regular ovens, some do provide times and temperatures for convection cooking and baking.

2.Adjusting the Temperature: When using fan convection, a reasonable rule is to deduct 25°F from the specified temperature. Although time and temperature changes differ by oven cavity, if your favorite brownie recipe asks for a 325°F preheating, reduce the temperature to 300°F.

3.Making Time Changes: Multiply the described period by 0.75.2 for true convection. If your brownie recipe requires for 40 minutes of baking time, decrease it to around 30 minutes. Check your owner's manual for precise guidance about how to change the time and temperature. Since ovens differ, it's a good idea to keep your eye on what's cooking.

4.Preheating the oven: Preheat your convection oven to the temperature you've selected. Convection ovens in fact, preheat faster, which is an added advantage.

5.Cooking, roasting, or baking: Position your timer for the new time and arrange your baking dishes on the oven racks for even cooking and steady heat. For a crispy and brown outer layer on meats, use the convection roast setting.

Dos and Don'ts of convection oven cooking:

Dos:

- If you want your dish to remain moist, add more liquid.
- To boost air circulation, use cooking and baking dishes with lower sides.
- For the best results, change recipe times and temperatures.
- For the browning, roasting, and crisping, use the convection roast setting.

Don'ts:

- The convection mechanism circulates hot air in the oven, so don't use tall cookware. It will block the convection fan.
- Please don't overload your oven; doing so will reduce its efficiency.
- For delicate, moist, baked goods and desserts like cheesecake and flan, avoid using the convection setting.

1.3 Kitchen tools needed to make the recipes in the book:

If you enjoy cooking with your oven and want to develop your skills, now is the time. But, before you put on your baker's hat, bear in mind that you'll need the right kitchen tools to produce the best treats.

- Convection oven
- Mixing bowls in different sizes
- Wooden spoons
- Hand beater
- Hand and electric mixer
- Food scale
- Cookie scoops
- Cooling racks
- Different kinds of spatulas and whisks
- Knives
- Cutting board
- Flour sifter
- Measuring cups
- Weighing scale
- Donuts and biscuits cutter
- Puff pastry cutter
- Measuring spoons
- Baking sheets (for different purposes)
- Low-sided Pizza pan
- Low-sided cake pans in different shapes
- Pie pan
- Tart pan
- Pastry brush
- Casserole dishes

- Cupcakes pan
- Rolling pin
- Dough scraper

You can use utensils made of glass, silicon, and metal in a convection oven. Whereas plastic, paper, or wood utensils are not compatible with convection oven and cannot be used.

1.4 WHY CHOOSE A CONVECTION OVEN INSTEAD OF A NORMAL ONE:

In a regular oven, heat directly rises to the top. Items that are on the top rack cook faster than those on the bottom rack due to this. If you're baking dozens of muffins for sale or dinners at home, for example, and want to use every rack, you'll run into some issues. The cookies or cupcakes on the bottom rack will still be underdone when the top rack ones are perfectly cooked.

On the other hand, Inside the convection oven, a fan circulates the hot air. Everything cooks more evenly because the air doesn't just stay at the top.

While this seems like a slight detail, it makes a significant difference. Your pies' tops will not overcook while the bottoms will remain soggy. The roast chicken has a uniform browning. Even better, you can rest assured that items on the bottom rack will take the same amount of time to cook as those on the top.

Other benefits of choosing a convection oven over a regular one:

- Equal heat distribution and even baking
- Minimal rotating
- Browning, crisping, and roasting have all improved.
- Quick baking and roasting
- Faster preheating
- Cooking for multiple dishes at once has never been easier.
- Bake for long periods of time without allowing food to dry out.
- Cooking on multiple racks gives you more options.
- Suitable for cooking a vast range of dishes, including meats, vegetables, cookies, and casseroles.

These are most of the benefits of a convection oven, which regular ovens lack, and this is why you should opt for a convection oven over a regular oven.

2.1 BEST BREAKFAST TOAST WITH EGG AND CHEESE

Time of cooking
22 minutes
Prep time 10 minutes
Cook time 12 minutes

Servings
4

Nutrition facts
(Per serving)
Calories 230
Total Fat 9g
Protein 11g
Carbs 29g

Ingredients:
- 4 thick bread slices
- 4 slices of bacon
- 4 eggs large
- 1 cup of shredded cheddar
- 2 tablespoons of chopped chives

Instructions:
Follow the instructions below to make breakfast toast with egg and cheese.
1.Preheat the oven at 350°F (175°C)
2.Put all the slices of bread on a baking sheet lined with parchment paper.
3.With the back of the spoon, make a well on the middle of each bread slice, place bacon slices around the bread and crack an egg in the center. On the top of the egg, sprinkle cheddar cheese—Bake for 8 to 12 minutes.
4.Remove toast from the oven, top up with salt, pepper, and chives and serve.

2.2 BREAKFAST APPLE OMELET

Time of cooking
25 minutes
Prep time 10 minutes
Cook time 15 minutes

Servings
2

Nutrition facts
(Per serving)
Calories 253
Total Fat 5g
Protein 9g
Carbs 44g

Ingredients:
* 3 tablespoons of all-purpose flour
* 2 eggs at room temperature
* 3 tablespoons of sugar
* 3 tablespoons of milk
* 1 tablespoon of lemon juice
* 1/8 teaspoon of salt
* 1/2 teaspoon of baking powder

For topping:
* 1 sliced apple (peel if you like)
* 1 1/2 teaspoons of sugar
* 1/4 teaspoon of cinnamon (ground)

Instructions:
Follow the instructions below to make breakfast apple omelet.
1.Preheat the oven at 350°F (175°C). Combine flour, baking powder, salt in a bowl and set aside. In another separate mixing bowl, add egg yolks, milk, and lemon juice, whisk well, and add flour mixture into it and mix until well combined.
2.Using an electric hand beater on medium speed, beat egg whites. Slowly add sugar into egg whites mixture one table-spoon at a time. Beat on high speed after each insertion. Then fold the egg batter into the flour mixture.
3.Coat the 9 inches deep-dish pie pan with baking spray pour the mixture into it. Place slices of apple on the top of the pie and sprinkle cinnamon and sugar.
4.Bake for 15 minutes without covering the top and check by inserting the wood skewer. If it comes out dry, it's done.
5.Serve straightaway.

2.3 BRUNCH BACON PIZZA

Time of cooking
25 minutes
Prep time 10 minutes
Cook time 15 minutes

Servings
8

Nutrition facts
(Per serving)
Calories 352
Total Fat 20g
Protein 20g
Carbs 24g

Ingredients:
* 1 tube of refrigerated pizza crust(13.8ounces)
* 6 eggs large
* 1 cup of shredded cheddar cheese
* 3 ounces of bacon bits
* 1 cup of Monterey jack cheese shredded
* 2 tablespoons of olive oil
* 2 tablespoons of water

Instructions:
Follow the instructions below to make bacon brunch pizza.
1.At 375°F (190°C), preheat the oven.
2.Unroll pizza dough spread evenly on a 15x10 greased pizza pan, press the dough onto the bottom of the pan, and prick holes with a fork. Brush the dough's surface with one table-spoon of olive oil and bake for 6 to 7 minutes until light golden brown.
3.Meanwhile, on a nonstick frying pan, heat one tablespoon of olive oil on medium heat. Whisk eggs and water in a bowl. Add eggs to a pan and cook until it gets thicken and no liquid remains.
4.Pour eggs over the baked crust, sprinkle bacon bits and cheeses, bake until cheese is fully melted for around 7 to 8 minutes.
5.Serve hot.

2.4 CHEVRE AND ROASTED VEGGIES QUICHE

Time of cooking
55 minutes
Prep time 10 minutes
Cook time 45 minutes

Servings
6

Nutrition facts
(Per serving)
Calories 219
Total Fat 14g
Protein 3g
Carbs 19g

Ingredients:
- 1 sheet of refrigerated pie crust
- 2 eggs large and 2 egg yolks
- 3/4 cup of cream (half and half)
- 4 ounces of crumbled goat cheese
- 2 minced garlic cloves
- 1 tomato (cut into pieces)
- 1 eggplant (cut into pieces)
- 1 poblano (cut into pieces)
- 1 tablespoon of olive oil
- 1 teaspoon of salt
- 1 teaspoon of pepper

Instructions:
Follow the instructions below to make roasted chevre and veggies quiche.
1.At 400°F (205°C), preheat the oven.
2.Unroll pie crust and spread into 9 inches tart pan and refrigerate the crust for around 30 minutes.
3.Remove from refrigerator and bake the crust in the oven for 8 to 10 minutes until golden brown. Remove once done and transfer the crust into a cooling rack.
5.In a mixing bowl, add tomato, pepper, garlic, eggplant, and oil mix and transfer into the greased baking pan, roast for 5 to 10 minutes.
6.Lower the oven temperature to 350°F. Pour roasted veggies into pie crust. In another mixing bowl, add eggs, cream, egg yolks, pepper, salt, and whisk until fully incorporated. Pour over the top of the crust, and sprinkle goat cheese in the end.
7.Place on a baking sheet and bake for around 20 to 25 minutes on oven lower rack. (Wrap the edges of pie with foil if they begin to get darker)
8.Cut into slices and serve.

2.5 BRUNCH BAKED STRAWBERRY ROLLS

Time of cooking
30 minutes
Prep time 15 minutes
Cook time 15 minutes

Servings
6

Nutrition facts
(Per serving)
Calories 210
Total Fat 3.5g
Protein 4g
Carbs 40g

Ingredients:
For the roll:
- 1 sheet of crescent rolls
- 1 cup of fresh strawberries (chopped)
- 1 cup of strawberry preserves
- 2 tablespoons of melted butter
- sugar to sprinkle
For the glaze of strawberry rolls:
- 1 cup of powdered sugar
- 4 oz. softened cream cheese
- 4 tablespoons of softened butter
- 1 1/2 tablespoons of milk
- 1 teaspoon of lemon zest
- 1 teaspoon of vanilla extract

Instructions:
Follow the instructions below to make baked strawberry rolls.
1.At 350°F (175°C), preheat the oven. coat 8x8 inches pan with cooking spray.
2.On a floured surface, Unroll the crescent roll dough and cut it into four rectangles. To close the perforations, pinch them together. Spread the strawberry preserve and cover all rectangles, then topped with chopped strawberries. Roll up each rectangle, starting with one short side, and pinch the edges to seal. Each roll should cut into 4 to 5 slices. Place in a baking pan side by side, cut side up.
3.With melted butter, brush the tops of rolls and sprinkle sugar all over.
4.Bake for 15 minutes or until it turns golden brown in color.
5.Meanwhile, ready the glaze for strawberry rolls: in a mixing bowl, beat butter, cream cheese, and powdered sugar using a hand beater until fully incorporated. Add vanilla, milk, and lemon zest and mix until creamy.
6.Drizzle the top of baked strawberry rolls with glaze and serve.

2.6 FETA AND ROASTED PUMPKIN TARTS

Time of cooking
35 minutes
Prep time 10 minutes
Cook time 25 minutes

Servings
6

Nutrition facts
(Per serving)
Calories 144
Total Fat 10g
Protein 4.5g
Fiber 0.5g

Ingredients:
• 275g of pumpkins (seeded, peeled, and cut into cubes)
• 1 (25x25) thawed butter puff pastry
• 60g feta crumbled
• 10 to 12 halved black olives
• 180g of fresh ricotta
• 2 tablespoons of pine nuts
• 1 tablespoon of olive oil
• 1 tablespoon of fresh thyme
• Thyme sprigs to sprinkle

Instructions:
Follow the instructions below to make feta and roasted pumpkin tarts.
1.At 350°F warm up the oven.
2.In a nonstick baking sheet, place pumpkin top up with oil and season with salt and pepper, toss and bake for 15 minutes and then set aside.
3.Change the temperature of the oven to 375°F. Lined a baking sheet with parchment paper. Cut 12 rectangles of 6 cm each from pastry, place in a baking sheet. Prick holes with a fork in each rectangle.
4.Add ricotta and chopped thyme in a small mixing bowl. Sprinkle salt and pepper and combine. Spread the mixture evenly onto each pastry. At the top, pour pumpkin, olives, nuts, and feta. Bake for around 10 minutes. Remove and sprinkle thyme sprigs all over the pastry and serve.

2.7 FARMER'S BREAKFAST CASSEROLE

Time of cooking
1 hour
Prep time 10 minutes
Cook time 50

Servings
6

Nutrition facts
(Per serving)
Calories 252
Total Fat 14g
Protein 17g
Carbs 14g

Ingredients:
• 3 cups of frozen hash brown potatoes shredded
• 1 cup of fully cooked ham cubed
• 1/4 cup of green onions chopped
• 3/4 cup of Monterey jack cheese shredded
• 4 eggs large
• 1 can of evaporated milk (12 ounces)
• 1/2 teaspoon of salt
• 1/4 teaspoon of pepper

Instructions:
Follow the instructions below to make Farmer's breakfast casserole.
1.In 8 inches baking dish, Spread potatoes and sprinkle ham, onions, and cheese on the top. Take a medium mixing bowl, whisk milk, eggs, salt, and pepper, pour the egg mixture on top of the potatoes, cover, and place in the refrigerator for some hours or preferably overnight.
2.Approx 30 minutes before baking, remove from refrigerator, remove the cover and bake at 325°F, in the warmed-up oven for 45 to 50 minutes until casserole turns golden brown in color.
3.Serve straightaway.

2.8 CARAMELIZED ONION, SPINACH, AND BACON STRATA

Time of cooking
1 hour 10 minutes
Prep time 35 minutes
Cook time 35 minutes

Servings
6

Nutrition facts
(Per serving)
Calories 391
Total Fat 22g
Protein 17g
Carbs 31g

Ingredients:
- 8 cups of Italian bread cubed
- 2 chopped onions
- 1-3/4 cups of half and half cream
- 1 cup of fresh spinach
- 1/4 cup of gorgonzola cheese crumbled
- 1/2 cup of fontina cheese shredded
- 6 chopped bacon strips
- 2 tablespoons of melted butter
- 1 tablespoon of mustard
- 1/2 teaspoon pepper
- 1/2 teaspoon salt

Instructions:
Follow the instructions below to make caramelized onion, spinach, and bacon strata.
1.Cook bacon in a large skillet over medium-low heat, stirring periodically, until crispy. Drain on paper towels after removing them with a slotted spoon. Keep two tablespoons of the drippings in the pan and throw out the remaining drippings.
2.Add onions to drippings and cook for 2-4 minutes, constantly stirring, over high heat. Now reduce heat to medium-low and cook for 20-30 minutes, stirring occasionally, or until onion turns golden brown.
3.Whisk together eggs, milk, melted butter, mustard, salt, and pepper in a large mixing bowl until fully incorporated. Add the pizza, kale, cheeses, caramelized onions, and bacon. Place in an 8-inch greased square baking dish. Cover the top of the dish and refrigerate for 1 hour or overnight.
4.At 300°F, preheat the oven. Remove from refrigerator while the oven heats up, remove the cover and bake for 30 to 35 minutes.
5.Before serving, let it cool for at least 10 minutes.

2.9 BAKED TATER TOTS

Time of cooking
45 minutes
Prep time 10 minutes
Cook time 35 minutes

Servings
6

Nutrition facts
(Per serving)
Calories 443
Total Fat 29g
Protein 22g
Carbs 23g

Ingredients:
- 6 ounces bacon (cut into strips)
- 6 eggs large (slightly beaten)
- 4 cups of tater tots frozen(thawed)
- 1 1/2 cups of cheddar cheese
- 1 chopped onion
- 1/2 cup of cream (half and half)
- 1/2 cup of sour cream
- 1 tablespoon of canola oil
- 1 tablespoon of dried parsley
- 1/2 teaspoon of pepper
- 1/2 teaspoon of garlic powder
- 1/2 teaspoon of salt

Instructions:
Follow the instructions below to make baked tater tots.
1.Warm up the oven at 325°F.
2.Put oil and heat in a skillet over low-medium heat. Cook, frequently stirring, about 2 to 3 minutes until the onion is tender. Now add bacon, cook, occasionally stirring, until bacon is lightly browned, For 1 to 2 minutes. Remove the pan from the heat.
3.Spread Tater Tots on the bottom of a greased 11x7-inch baking dish, then top with the onion and bacon mixture. In a bowl, add and whisk together the eggs, cream, sour cream, and seasonings until well mixed. Add the cheese and pour it over the top. Bake for 30-35 minutes, until golden brown.

2.10 CLASSIC EGG CASSEROLE

Time of cooking
50 minutes
Prep time 15 minutes
Cook time 35 minutes

Servings
12

Nutrition facts
(Per serving)
Calories 286
Total Fat 19g
Protein 14g
Carbs 16g

Ingredients:
- 12 ounces chopped bacon
- 8 eggs large
- 6 English muffins cut into cubes
- 4 egg yolks
- 2 cups of milk
- 1/2 cup of heavy whipping cream
- 1/2 cup of melted butter
- 2 tablespoons of lemon juice
- 1 teaspoon of mustard
- 1 teaspoon of onion powder
- 1 teaspoon of paprika

Instructions:
Follow the instructions below to make a classic egg casserole.
1.In a greased 13x9 baking dish, spread half of the bacon; top with English muffins and the remaining bacon. Whisk together the eggs, onion powder, and milk in a large mixing bowl; pour over the end. Cover the baking dish and refrigerate overnight.
2.At 350°F, preheat your oven. While the oven heats up, remove the casserole from your refrigerator. Sprinkle paprika on the top. Bake with cover for 25 minutes in the oven, remove the cover and bake for another 10 minutes.
3.Whisk milk, egg yolks, lemon juice, and mustard in a double boiler or a metal bowl over hot boiling water until totally combined; cook, keep whisking until mixture becomes thick enough to cover a metal spoon and temperature reaches 160°. Bring down the heat to lower. Drizzle in the warm melted butter slowly over the casserole.
4.Serve right away and enjoy.

2.11 EGG CHEESE AND BACON BREAKFAST BREAD

Time of cooking
40 minutes
Prep time 10 minutes
Cook time 30 minutes

Servings
8

Nutrition facts
(Per serving)
Calories 230
Total Fat 13g
Protein 11g
Carbs 17g

Ingredients:
- 3 cans of refrigerated biscuits
- 6 slices of bacon
- 1 1/3 cups of shredded Monterey jack cheese
- 1 1/2 cups of skim milk
- 4 eggs large
- 1/2 teaspoon of black pepper
- 1/2 of salt

Instructions:
Follow the instructions below to make egg cheese and bacon breakfast bread.
1.At 350°F, warm up the oven and grease a Bundt pan with baking spray. In a nonstick pan, cook bacon over medium heat until crisp, around 6 minutes. Shift to drain on a paper towel-lined plate before crumbling.
2.In the mixing bowl, add milk, eggs, salt, and pepper and mix to combine. 3.Dip quarter biscuits into the egg mixture, then add a layer of biscuits to the bottom of the bundt pan. Now add cheese layer, then bacon layer, then again continue with biscuits layer until the pan is three-quarters loaded. Place the remaining egg mixture on top of the bundt pan.
4.Bake for 25 to 30 minutes until the egg is fully cooked and the bread turns golden brown in color.
5.Transfer to a dish and cool down for a while before serving.

2.12 TASTY SNICKERS FLAVORED CROISSANTS

Time of cooking
35 minutes
Prep time 15 minutes
Cook time 20 minutes

Servings
8

Nutrition facts
(Per serving)
Calories 358
Total Fat 23.2g
Protein 6.7g
Carbs 32.4g

Ingredients:
- 2 sheets of ready-rolled frozen puff pastry
- 1/2 of cup peeled almonds
- 1 egg slightly beaten
- 3 bars of snicker (150g) chopped
- 1/2 cup of caramel spread

Instructions:
Follow the instructions below to make tasty snickers flavored croissants.
1. At 350°F, Preheat your oven and line 2 different baking sheets with baking paper.
2. Cut each sheet of puff pastry into halves. Sprinkle one-eighth of the Snickers on one pastry square, beginning in one corner. To make a log, roll it up diagonally. Form a crescent shape with your hands. Place on a prepared baking sheet. To make eight croissants, repeat with the remaining pastry and Snickers.
3. With egg wash, brush the top of each croissant and sprinkle almonds all over. Bake for 20 minutes, or until golden and puffy. Cool it down for a while before eating.
4. In a small saucepan over low heat, melt the caramel for 1-2 minutes or until it gets smooth.
5. Drizzle the caramel sauce on top of croissants before serving.

2.13 TASTY STREUSEL BLUEBERRY COFFEE CAKE

Time of cooking
50 minutes
Prep time 15 minutes
Cook time 35 minutes

Servings
9

Nutrition facts
(Per serving)
Calories 476
Total Fat 26g
Protein 6g
Carbs 57g

Ingredients:
- 2 cups of all-purpose flour
- 1 cup of pecan chopped
- 1 cup of blueberries fresh
- 1/2 cup of softened butter
- 1/2 cup of whole milk
- 3/4 cup of sugar
- 1 egg at room temperature

For topping:
- 1/3 cup of all-purpose flour
- 1/2 cup sugar
- 1/4 cup of cold butter

Instructions:
Follow the instructions below to make a tasty streusel blueberry coffee cake.
1. At 350°F, Preheat your oven. Add all-purpose flour, salt, and baking powder in a mixing bowl and whisk. Cream the sugar and butter together in a separate bowl until fluffy. Mix in the egg and milk with the dry ingredients. Combine the blueberries and pecans in a mixing bowl. Fill a greased 9-inch square baking pan halfway with the batter.
2. Combine sugar and flour in a mixing bowl; break in butter until crumbly. Sprinkle on top of the batter. Bake for 30-35 minutes. Check by placing a toothpick in the middle of the cake; if the toothpick comes out dry, your cake is done.
3. Allow cooling for some time on a wire rack before serving.

2.14 HAM AND BROCCOLI CHEESE QUICHE

Time of cooking
18 minutes
Prep time 10 minutes
Cook time 8 minutes

Servings
4

Nutrition facts
(Per serving)
Calories 283
Total Fat 17g
Protein 22g
Carbs 11g

Ingredients:
- 2 cups of frozen hash brown potatoes shredded
- 1 cup of cooked ham diced
- 1/2 cup of milk
- 1 cup of cheddar cheese shredded
- 1/2 cup of broccoli chopped
- 4 eggs large
- 1 teaspoon of minced onion dried
- 1 teaspoon of salt
- 1 teaspoon of garlic powder
- 1 teaspoon of black pepper

Instructions:
Follow the instructions below to make a ham and broccoli cheese quiche.
1.In a greased 9-inches baking pie pan, put hash browns. Bake for 2 minutes, uncovered, at 300°F in a preheated oven. Push into the plate's bottom and halfway up the edges: spread cheese, ham, and broccoli on top.
2.Whisk together the eggs, milk, and seasonings in a large mixing bowl; pour over the ham mixture. Bake for 5 minutes, or until a wooden skewer inserted in the middle comes out clean.
3.Before eating, allow to cool down.

2.15 EASY AND YUMMY BRUNCH REUBEN BAKE

Time of cooking
55 minutes
Prep time 10 minutes
Cook time 45 minutes

Servings
8

Nutrition facts
(Per serving)
Calories 290
Total Fat 20g
Protein 17g
Carbs 10g

Ingredients:
- 2 cups of swiss cheese shredded
- 8 eggs large slightly beaten
- 1 can (14 ounces) of sauerkraut
- 1 package (2 ounces) of the corned beef deli(cut into pieces)
- 3 slices toasted rye bread chopped
- 1/2 cup of milk
- 1/2 cup of green onions chopped
- 1/4 cup of butter melted
- 1 tablespoon of mustard
- 1 teaspoon of pepper
- 1/2 teaspoon of salt

Instructions:
Follow the instructions below to make a brunch Reuben bake.
1.Combine eggs, sauerkraut, cheese, onions, milk, corned beef, mustard, salt, pepper, and mix. Spread into 11x7 inches baking dish. Cover and refrigerate overnight.
2.30 minutes before baking, remove the casserole from your refrigerator—Preheat the oven to 300°F. Toss the rye bread crumbs with the butter and sprinkle on top of the casserole. Bake for 40-45 minutes, uncovered until a wooden skewer inserted in the middle comes out clean. Leave for 10 minutes to rest before serving.

2.16 EGG AND POTATO CHEESY BAKE

Time of cooking
50 minutes
Prep time 10 minutes
Cook time 40 minutes

Servings
12

Nutrition facts
(Per serving)
Calories 315
Total Fat 20g
Protein 20g
Carbs 16g

Ingredients:
- 1 pound of breakfast sausages
- 6 cups of potato crowns frozen
- 4 cups of chopped fresh spinach
- 2 cups of cheddar cheese shredded
- 1 3/4 cups of mushrooms chopped
- 1 cup of milk
- 6 eggs large
- pinch of salt

Instructions:
Follow the instructions below to make an egg and potato cheesy bake.
1.At 350°F, Preheat the oven. Cook sausages in a frying pan until it changes its color, splitting it into crumbles around 5-7 minutes. Cook, stirring periodically, until spinach is wilts and mushrooms are soft, about 2-4 minutes more.
2.Fill a coated 13x9-inch baking dish halfway with sausage mixture. Whisk together the eggs, milk, and salt in a large mixing bowl; pour over the sausage mixture—spread potato and cheese layer on the top.
3.Bake for 35 to 40 minutes until the top turns golden brown and crispy.

2.17 SOUTHERN STYLE PASTRY PUFF FOR BRUNCH

Time of cooking
45 minutes
Prep time 15 minutes
Cook time 30 minutes

Servings
12

Nutrition facts
(Per serving)
Calories 587
Total Fat 39g
Protein 18g
Carbs 43g

Ingredients:
- 2 cups+1 tablespoon of water
- 7 eggs large
- 1 package puff pastry frozen(17.3 ounces)
- 1 cup of cheddar cheese shredded
- 1/2 cup of cooking grits quick
- 1/2 pound of pork sausage
- 1/4 cup of cubed butter
- 1/4 cup of a sweet red pepper chopped
- 1/2 teaspoon of black pepper
- 1/2 teaspoon of salt

Instructions:
Follow the instructions below to make a southern-style pastry puff.
1.At 350, warm up your oven. Bring water to a boil in a saucepan. Stir in the grits slowly. Cook and reduce the heat to medium-low, covered, for five minutes or until the sauce thickens. Remove the pan from the stove. Combine the butter, cheese, pesto, salt, and black pepper until well mixed.
2.Meanwhile, cook red pepper and sausages in a large skillet over medium heat, for 4 to 6 minutes or until sausage change its color and red pepper is soft; splitting up sausage into crumbles, then drain.
3.In a mixing bowl, beat eggs and the remaining pepper and salt until fully incorporated. Return the sausage to the pan. Pour in the egg mixture and cook, constantly stirring, until the eggs thicken.
4.Onto a parchment sheet of 12x10 inches, unfold each pastry sheet. Spread the grits within 1/2 inch of the edges. Place sausage mixture on each pastry over half of the grits. Surround puff pastries over sausage mixture Press and seal the edges with a fork—place in a baking sheet.
5.Brush egg wash over the top of puff pastries. Sprinkle some ground pepper on top if you like. Bake until golden brown, about 30 minutes. Allow for a 10-minute to cool down. Cut each pastry into four parts.

2.18 BAKED FRENCH TOAST WITH STUFFED APPLES

Total time of cooking
40 minutes
Prep time 10 minutes
Cook time 30 minutes

Servings
6

Nutrition Facts
(Per serving)
Calories 854
Total Fat 46g
Protein 14g
Carbs 102g

Ingredients:
- 12 slices of Italian bread
- 6 eggs large
- 2 large apples peeled and sliced
- 1 1/2 cups of milk
- 1 cup of pecans chopped
- 1 cup of brown sugar packed
- 1/2 cup of cubed butter
- 2 tablespoons of corn syrup
- 1 1/2 teaspoons of cinnamon ground
- 1 teaspoon of vanilla extract
- 1/4 teaspoon of nutmeg ground
- 1/4 teaspoon of salt

Caramel sauce:
- 1/4 cup of cubed butter
- 1/2 cup of brown sugar packed
- 1 tablespoon of corn syrup

Instructions:
Follow the instructions below to make a baked French toast with stuffed apples.

1. Combine the brown sugar, butter, and corn syrup in a small saucepan; stir and cook over medium heat until thickens. Fill a greased 13x9-inch baking dish halfway with pecans, then a single layer of bread and the remaining pecans. Arrange the apples and the rest of the bread on top.

2. Whisk together the eggs, milk, vanilla, cinnamon, nutmeg, and salt in a big mixing bowl. Pour the sauce over the rolls. Keep in the refrigerator overnight with a cover.

3. Remove around 30 minutes before baking from your refrigerator. Uncover the baking dish and bake at 350°F for 25 to 30 minutes.

4. Combine the ingredients of the sauce listed above in a saucepan. Cook, constantly stirring until the sauce thickens. Serve the sauce with toast.

2.19 BLUEBERRY BREAKFAST FRENCH TOAST

Total time of cooking
1 hour
Prep time 15 minutes
Cook time 35 minutes

Servings
8

Nutrition Facts
(Per serving)
Calories 621
Total Fat 31g
Protein 19g
Carbs 68g

Ingredients:
- 12 slices of crust removed old white bread
- 2 cups of milk
- 1 cup of fresh blueberries
- 1/3 cup of honey or maple syrup
- 12 slightly beaten eggs
- 16 ounces of cream cheese

For Sauce:
- 1 cup of fresh blueberries
- 1 cup of water
- 1 cup of sugar
- 2 tablespoons of cornstarch
- 1 tablespoon of butter

Instructions:
Follow the instructions below to make a blueberry breakfast French toast.

1. Cut the 1 inches cubes out of bread. Spread half in 13x9 inches greased pan. Make 1 inches cubes of cream cheese and place them on the top of the bread—Layer the top of the pan with the remaining bread cubes and blueberries.

2. Whisk together the milk, eggs, and syrup in a mixing bowl. Pour the mixture over the bread. Refrigerate for around 8 hours or overnight, covered.

3. Remove 30 minutes before baking from your refrigerator— Bake with cover for 20 minutes at 340°F. Uncover the pan and bake for additional 15 minutes, or until a wooden skewer placed in the toast comes out clean.

4. Whisk together the sugar, water, and cornstarch in a saucepan, until creamy. Bring the mixture in a saucepan to a boil; cook for 3 minutes, or until thickened. Bring to a boil after adding the blueberries. Reduce the stove's heat to very low and cook for 8-10 minutes more, or till berries burst. Remove from the stove and add the butter. Serve sauce with French toast.

2.20 SOUTHWEST-STYLE BAKE SAUSAGE

Total time of cooking
1 hour
Prep time 10 minutes
Cook time 50 minutes

Servings
12

Nutrition Facts
(Per serving)
Calories 329
Total Fat 19g
Protein 16g
Carbs 19g

Ingredients:
- 6 (10 inches flour tortillas), cut into 1/2-inch strips
- 2 sliced tomatoes
- 2 cups of Monterey Jack cheese shredded
- 1-pound cooked pork sausage
- 10 slightly beaten eggs
- 16 ounces canned green chilies chopped
- 1/2 cup of milk
- 1/2 teaspoon of salt
- 1/2 teaspoon of paprika
- 1/2 teaspoon of onion salt
- 1/2 teaspoon of garlic salt
- 1/2 teaspoon of pepper
- 1/2 teaspoon of ground cumin
- Salsa and sour cream

Instructions:
Follow the instructions below to make a southwest-style bake sausage.

1. In a 13x9 greased baking pan, add a layer of half of the tortillas, sausages, chilies, and cheese. Repeat the procedure.

2. Whisk together the eggs, milk, onion salt, garlic salt, pepper, and ground cumin in a big mixing bowl; pour over the cheese. Sprinkle the paprika on the top. Cover and refrigerate overnight.

3. Remove 30 minutes before baking from your refrigerator. Bake for 40 minutes at 325°F, uncovered. Arrange the tomato slices on top—Bake for an additional 10 minutes. Allow resting for 10-minute before cutting. Serve with salsa and sour cream.

2.21 BAKED BREAKFAST APPLE BUTTER BISCUIT

Total time of cooking
1 hour
Prep time 10 minutes
Cook time 50 minutes

Servings
12

Nutrition Facts
(Per serving)
Calories 331
Total Fat 15g
Protein 16g
Carbs 31g

Ingredients:
- 6 eggs large
- 10 to 12 leftover biscuits
- 2 1/2 cups of reduced-fat milk
- 2 cups of cheddar cheese shredded
- 1 1/2 cups of cooked ham
- 3/4 cup of apple butter
- 1/4 cup of fresh minced parsley
- 1 teaspoon of salt
- 1/4 teaspoon of mustard
- 1/2 teaspoon of pepper

Instructions:
Follow the instructions below to make a breakfast apple butter biscuit.

1. Cut biscuits into half crosswise. On the cut sides of the biscuits, spread apple butter. Displace the tops. Slice each biscuit into quarter and position in a greased 13x9 inch baking dish in a single layer. Make a top layer of cheese, parsley, and ham.

2. Whisk together the eggs, milk, salt, mustard and pepper in a big bowl. Pour the mixture over the biscuits. Cover and leave overnight in a refrigerator.

3. At 300°F warm up the oven, Remove the strata from your refrigerator. Uncover the dish and bake for around 45 to 50 minutes until puffed and the top turns golden brown. Allow resting for 10 minutes before eating.

2.22 BRUNCH ONION TART

Total time of cooking
55 minutes
Prep time 15 minutes
Cook time 40minutes

Servings
6

Nutrition Facts
(Per serving)
Calories 361
Total Fat 23g
Protein 11g
Carbs 26g

Ingredients:
- 1 (9 inches) unbaked pastry shell
- 6 thinly sliced green onions
- 3 eggs large
- 2 thinly sliced sweet onions
- 1/2 cup of whole milk
- 1/3 cup of Parmesan cheese shredded
- 3/4 cup of cream (half and half)
- 1/2 cup of feta cheese crumbled
- 2 tablespoons of olive oil
- 2 tablespoons of chives minced
- 1 tablespoon of mustard
- 1/2 teaspoon of salt
- 1/8 teaspoon of ground nutmeg
- 1/4 teaspoon of ground pepper
- 1/8 teaspoon of hot pepper sauce

Instructions:
Follow the instructions below to make a brunch onion tart.
1.At 425°F, preheat the oven. With a double layer of heavy-duty foil, line a pastry shell and bake for 5 to 6 minutes. After 6 minutes, remove foil and bake 5 minutes more—transfer on a cooling rack.
2.Sauté onions in oil in a small skillet until tender. Combine the eggs, feta cheese, pepper, salt, nutmeg, and hot pepper sauce in a food processor; cover and process until creamy. Gradually drizzle in the cream and milk, and process until completely mixed.
3.Brush mustard on the inside of the crust. Place chives, green onion, and sautéed onions, slowly pour the egg mixture on onions, sprinkle parmesan cheese on the top.
4.Bake for 25 to 30 minutes at 350°F.

2.24 CLASSIC AND SIMPLE OVEN OMELET

Total time of cooking
40 minutes
Prep time 5 minutes
Cook time 35 minutes

Servings
6

Nutrition Facts
(Per serving)
Calories 313
Total Fat 19.4g
Protein 26.1g
Carbs 7.3g

Ingredients:
- 2 cups of milk
- 10 eggs of large size
- 1 cup of cooked ham
- 1 cup of Parmesan cheese shredded
- 1/4 cup of fresh leaf parsley chopped
- 1 teaspoon of salt
- 1/2 teaspoon of black pepper

Instructions:
Follow the instructions below to make a classic and simple oven omelet.
1.At 325°F, preheat your convection oven. Using olive oil or nonstick cooking spray, lightly coat a 9x13-inch baking dish.
2.In a big mixing bowl, whisk together the eggs and milk. Combine the ham, cheese, and parsley in a mixing bowl. Season with salt and pepper before pouring into the pan. (You can cover the pan and refrigerate for up to 24 hours at this point.)
3.Bake for 35 minutes, or until it turns golden from the top. Keep an eye so it doesn't get burned. Allow 5 minutes to cool before slicing. Serve immediately.

2.23 EGG SAUSAGE-VEGETABLE BAKE

Total time of cooking
1 hour
Prep time 15 minutes
Cook time 45 minutes

Servings
8

Nutrition Facts
(Per serving)
Calories 248
Total Fat 15g
Protein 21g
Carbs 6g

Ingredients:
• 1 package (19-1/2 ounces) of Italian turkey sausage (casings removed)
• 9 eggs large
• 3 cups of Swiss chard sliced
• 1 1/4 cups of reduced-fat milk
• 1 cup of mozzarella cheese shredded
• 1/4 cup of white wine
• 1/4 cup of Parmesan cheese grated
• 1/4 teaspoon of pepper
• Fresh parsley mushrooms sliced
• 3 cloves of garlic, minced
• 1 tablespoon of butter
• 1/2 teaspoon of salt
• 1/4 teaspoon of parsley

Instructions:
Follow the instructions below to make an egg sausage-vegetable bake.

1. Preheat the oven to 325°F. Cook sausage in a skillet for 5 to 7 minutes, or until it changes color, splitting it up into crumbles. Move sausage to a 13x9 inch greased baking dish and spread uniformly with a slotted spoon. Drain the drippings from the pan.
2. Melt butter in the same skillet. Pour the mushrooms and cook until its soft and tender, around 3 to 5 minutes. Now mix in the Swiss chard, wine, and garlic until the chard is tender and there is no liquid left about 1 to 2 minutes more—place in a baking dish.
3. Whisk together the eggs, milk, pepper, and salt in a big mixing bowl; pour over the vegetable mixture. Top up with mozzarella cheese.
4. Bake for 45 minutes, add parmesan cheese on top. Allow 5 minutes to cool down before serving. At the time of eating, garnish parsley on top.

2.25 CRANBERRY GARLIC AND CHEDDAR MINI BREADS

Total time of cooking
30 minutes
Prep time 10 minutes
Cook time 20 minutes

Servings
6

Nutrition Facts
(Per serving)
Calories 276
Total Fat 18g
Protein 6g
Total Carbs 21g

Ingredients:
• 1/4 cup of cranberry sauce
• 1/4 cup of cheddar smoked
• 1/4 cup of sage chopped
• 1/4 cup of mozzarella grated
• 18 to 20 sage leaves
• 80g of softened unsalted butter
• 200g Bake At Home White Dinner Rolls
• 2 cloves of garlic crushed
• 1 tablespoon of olive oil

Instructions:
Follow the instructions below to make cranberry garlic and cheddar mini breads.

1. At 350°F, preheat your convection oven.
2. Using the baking paper, line a baking tray. In a mixing bowl, combine the garlic, butter, chopped sage, cheddar, and mozzarella. To mix, stir all together. Fold in the cranberry sauce until it is well combined.
3. Cut three equally spaced slits crosswise into each roll with a small sharp knife. Spread the cheese mixture through each slit. Toss in a few sage leaves. Place the rolls on a tray that has been lined. Brush with some oil and season.
4. In a warmed-up oven, bake for 15 to 20 minutes, or until the cheese melts down and the rolls turn golden brown. Serve and enjoy.

2.26 TASTY CHEESE AND HAM CROISSANT

Total time of cooking
25 minutes
Prep time 5 minutes
Cook time 10 minutes

Servings
4

Nutrition Facts
(Per serving)
Calories 410
Total Fat 13g
Protein 18g
Total Carbs 25g

Ingredients:
- 4 butter croissants
- 4 slices of cheddar cheese
- 100g of shaved ham
- 20g of spinach leaves
- 2 teaspoons of mustard

Instructions:
Follow the instructions below to make cheese and ham croissants.

1.At 350°F, warm up your convection oven. Cut the croissants horizontally with a serrated knife. Apply mustard to the bases. Add the cheddar and ham on top. Cover with the tops of croissants—place croissants on a baking sheet.

2.Bake for 8 to 10 minutes in a warmed-up oven or until croissants turn golden brown and cheese melts down completely.

3.Remove the tops of the croissants. Arrange the spinach on top of the ham. Replace the tops and serve right away.

2.27 BRUNCH FLORENTINE PIZZA

Total time of cooking
25 minutes
Prep time 10 minutes
Cook time 15 minutes

Servings
4

Nutrition Facts
(Per serving)
Calories 730
Total Fat 31.2g
Protein 47.5g
Total Carbs 61.8g

Ingredients:
- 2 pizza bases of 30cm each
- 280g of spinach leaves (baby spinach)
- 250g of cherry tomatoes
- 300g of bacon
- 250ml jar of mild Mexican sauce
- 6 eggs
- 2 cups of mozzarella grated

Instructions:
Follow the instructions below to make brunch Florentine pizza.

1.At 375°F, warm up your convection oven. In a nonstick frying pan over medium heat, cook the bacon for 2 minutes on each side or until golden brown. Transfer to a paper towel-lined tray.

2.Put spinach in the pan and cook, occasionally turning, for 2 to 3 minutes or until the spinach is wilted. Remove the pan from the stove.

3.Spread pizza bases in two baking trays. Cover the bases with sauce. Sprinkle cheese on top. Toss the bacon and spinach on top of the pizza. Crack and lightly beat 1 egg into a cup, pour on pizza. Continue with the remaining eggs. Serve with cherry tomatoes on top. Bake in the preheated convection oven for 12 to 15 minutes, or until the eggs are set and the tomatoes soften.

4.Place the pizza on a clean surface. Serve with the existing spinach, cut into wedges.

2.28 CRUMPET BUTTER AND CARAMEL PUDDING

Total time of cooking
1 hour
Prep time 20 minutes
Cook time 40 minutes

Servings
6

Nutrition Facts
(Per serving)
Calories 763
Total Fat 42g
Protein 14g
Total Carbs 81g

Ingredients:
- 300ml of thick cream
- 620g of crumpet toast or fresh crumpets (crusts removed)
- 120g of butter
- 2 cups of milk
- 1/2 cup of caster sugar
- 1/2 cup of brown sugar
- 4 eggs
- Mixed berries for serving

Instructions:
Follow the instructions below to make crumpet butter and caramel pudding.
1.At 300°F, preheat your convection oven. Grease an oval deep-dish pudding pan.
2.In a saucepan, add brown sugar, cream, and half of the butter. Stir occasionally and cook for 10 to 12 minutes, or until fully melted and smooth. Allow cooling properly.
3.In a bowl, combine and whisk the milk and eggs. Spread the existing butter on one side of each crumpet slice. Split in half diagonal shape. Assemble overlapping in prepared dish. Pour the milk mixture on top. Leave and allow to absorb for 15 minutes.
4.In a large baking dish, position the pudding dish. Put boil water in the baking dish until it reaches halfway up the side of the smaller dish—Bake in preheated oven for 40 minutes, or until golden and firm. Allow 10 minutes for cooling.
5.In a nonstick cooking pan over medium heat, melt the caster sugar. Cook caster sugar for 4 to 5 minutes, or until sugar turns golden in color and fully melted. Keep shaking the pan periodically. Drizzle over the pudding right away. Allow 5 minutes to pass. Serve with berries on the side.

2.29 LOW-CARB GARLIC BREAD

Total time of cooking
30 minutes
Prep time 15 minutes
Cook time 15 minutes

Servings
8

Nutrition Facts
(Per serving)
Calories 283
Total Fat 25.8g
Protein 10g
Total Carbs 1.6g

Ingredients:
- 1 1/2 cups of almond meal
- 1 cup of mozzarella cheese grated
- 1/3 cup of warm water
- 3 lightly beaten eggs
- 2 tablespoons of olive oil
- 2 tablespoons of psyllium husk
- 1 tablespoon of pouring cream
- 1 tablespoon of ground flaxseed
- 2 teaspoons of apple cider vinegar
- 1 teaspoon of baking powder
- 1/2 teaspoon of table salt
- 3 cloves of garlic
- 7g sachet of instant yeast
- Chopped parsley for serving

Instructions:
Follow the instructions below to make low-carb garlic bread.
1.Grease and, using the baking paper, line a 20cm square cake pan. In a small cup, combine the yeast, cream, and water. To mix the ingredients, whisk them together. Leave for about 10 minutes or until it becomes foamy.
2.Whisk together the psyllium husk, almond meal, flaxseed, baking powder, and salt in a large mixing bowl. In the center, dig a well. Combine the yeast mixture, olive oil, egg and vinegar in a mixing bowl. To mix, whisk all together thoroughly. Transfer to the pan that has been prepared. Cover using plastic wrap loosely and let stand for around 1 hour, or until the mixture rises.
3.Warm up your convection oven at 350°F, bake for 10 minutes. Drizzle olive oil all over the bread, then seasons with garlic and cheese. Bake for another 5 minutes, or until the cheese melts. Sprinkle parsley over the top of garlic bread before serving.

2.30 BREAKFAST DANISH BUNS

Total time of cooking
 25 minutes
Prep time 10 minutes
Cook time 15 minutes

Servings
10

Nutrition Facts
(Per serving)
Calories 274
Total Fat 8g
Protein 8g
Total Carbs 41g

Ingredients:
- 3 cups+2 tablespoons of flour
- 1 cup of milk
- 75g of softened butter
- 42g of fresh yeast
- 2 tablespoons of sugar
- 1 teaspoon of salt
- 1 egg

Instructions:
Follow the instructions below to make breakfast Danish buns.
1.Hot the milk over low heat in a medium-sized saucepan, then mix in the yeast until it dissolves. Whisk in the salt and sugar until well combined.
2.In a mixing bowl, combine flour, soft butter, and egg. Knead the dough using a hand mixer until smooth, adding milk and yeast mixture, and beat until fully mixed. Wrap with a kitchen cloth and set aside for around 1 hour to proof.
3.Shape small buns with the dough after it has been proofed and leave for 15 minutes again for proofing.
4.At 300°F preheated oven, bake buns for 15 minutes approximately.

2.31 QUICHE BRUNCH CUPS

Total time of cooking
25 minutes
Prep time 10 minutes
Cook time 15 minutes

Servings
12

Nutrition Facts
(Per serving)
Calories 216
Total Fat 15g
Protein 9g
Total Carbs 10g

Ingredients:
- 1 package of puff pastry
- 1 cup of cheddar cheese shredded
- 3 1/2 tablespoons of cream
- 250g of ham
- 4 eggs
- 1 1/8 teaspoons of chives
- 1/2 teaspoon of salt
- 1/2 teaspoon of pepper

Instructions:
Follow the instructions below to make quiche brunch cups.
1.Warm up the convection oven to 350°F. Coat the muffin pan with baking spray. Cut the squares of puff pastry and place them into a muffin pan. Cut the ham into cubes and shred cheddar cheese. Make fine ring slices of chive.
2.In a bowl, beat the eggs until the eggs turn frothy. Then add pepper, salt, and cream and whisk well to mix.
3.When you are finished, transfer the cheese, cubed ham, and chives between the muffin cups. Spread the mixture of egg on the top of each muffin cup. Bake in preheated oven for 15 minutes or until puff pastry turns golden brown in color. Serve and Enjoy!

2.32 APPLE CARAMEL FRENCH TOAST CASSEROLE

Total time of cooking

55 minutes

Prep time 10 minutes

Cook time 45 minutes

Servings

12

Nutrition Facts

(Per serving)

Calories 333

Total Fat 4g

Protein 8g

Total Carbs 68g

Ingredients:

*   1 French bread loaf
*   6 peeled and sliced apples
*   1 1/2 cups of milk
*   1 jar of caramel topping
*   1/3 cup of sugar
*   1/2 cup of sugar
*   1/2 cup of brown sugar
*   1 tablespoon of vanilla
*   Pinch of nutmeg
*   Pinch of cinnamon

Instructions:

Follow the instructions below to make apple caramel French toast casserole.

1.Split the bread slices (widthwise) 3 inches broad and assemble in a greased 13 x 9-inch pan.

2.Beat together the eggs, sugar, and vanilla together in a large bowl until the mixture is light and foamy. Spread the mixture on bread slices and arrange the apples over the top of the bread.

3.Season with nutmeg, cinnamon, and sugars (brown sugar as well) over the apple layer.

4.Refrigerate with cover overnight.

5.Bake for around 40 to 45 minutes in the morning at 325°F.

6.Top with Caramel topping and serve.

2.33 PUMPKIN COOKIES SANDWICH WITH FROSTING OF MAPLE CREAM CHEESE

Total time of cooking

25 minutes

Prep time 10 minutes

Cook time 15 minutes

Servings

24

Nutrition Facts

(Per serving)

Calories 309

Total Fat 14g

Protein 3g

Total Carbs 43g

Ingredients:

*   1 package of pumpkin spice pudding mix
*   2 1/4 cups of flour
*   1-2 cups of semi-sweet chocolate chip cookies
*   1/4 cup of sugar
*   3/4 cup of brown sugar
*   3/4 cup of softened butter
*   2 eggs
*   1 teaspoon of baking soda
*   1 teaspoon of pumpkin pie spice
*   1 teaspoon of vanilla
*   1/2 teaspoon of salt

For Frosting:

*   8 oz of cream cheese
*   2 cups of powdered sugar
*   1/4 cup of butter
*   3 tablespoons of pure maple syrup
*   1/2 teaspoon of cinnamon

Instructions:

Follow the instructions below to make a pumpkin cookies sandwich with a frosting of maple cream cheese.

1.Mix in a bowl the butter, brown sugar, sugar. Then add pumpkin spice instant pudding mix and whisk until completely mixed.

2.Pour in eggs and vanilla mix, then add pumpkin pie spice, salt, soda, and flour, beat until fully incorporated.

3.Roll dough with a rolling pin into 1 inches ball, place them on a non-stick baking sheet, and bake for around 10 to 15 minutes at 325°F.

For the frosting:

1.Beat together the butter, cream, cinnamon, and maple syrup. Slowly pour in the powdered sugar and blend until all the sugar is completely dissolved in the mixture.

2.Spread the cream cheese frosting between the cookies. And keep them in the refrigerator.

2.34 EASY PUMPKIN BREAKFAST BREAD

Total time of cooking
50 minutes
Prep time 10 minutes
Cook time 40 minutes

Servings
20

Nutrition Facts
(Per serving)
Calories 176
Total Fat 2g
Protein 3g
Total Carbs 36g

Ingredients:
- 3 cups of all-purpose flour
- 2 cups of granulated sugar
- 2 cups of solid pack pumpkin
- 1 cup of canola oil
- 3 eggs large
- 2 teaspoons of baking powder
- 2 teaspoons of vanilla extract
- 2 teaspoons of pumpkin pie spice
- 2 teaspoons of cinnamon
- 1 teaspoon of baking soda
- 1 teaspoon of salt

Instructions:
Follow the instructions below to make a pumpkin breakfast bread.

1. In a mixing bowl, Add together the oil, eggs, sugar, pumpkin, and vanilla in a bowl. Keep it aside.
2. In another mixing bowl, mix the flour, baking soda, baking powder, salt, pumpkin spice, and cinnamon.
3. Fold in the wet ingredients into dry ingredients and mix until incorporated. (avoid over mixing)
4. Coat two loaf pans of 9×5 with baking spray. Distribute the batter between the pans equally.
5. Bake for 40 minutes at 300°F. Once the bread is baked, allow the bread to cool down for some time.
6. Sprinkle with powdered sugar upon serving if you like.

2.35 SIMPLE AND CLASSIC BREAKFAST PIZZA

Total time of cooking
25 minutes
Prep time 10 minutes
Cook time 15 minutes

Servings
4

Nutrition Facts
(Per serving)
Calories 586
Total Fat 28g
Protein 38g
Total Carbs 26g

Ingredients:
- 2 large pizza bases or whole meal pita bread
- 1 cup of Pizza Blend Shredded Cheese(100g)
- 100g of cherry tomatoes
- 100g of sliced brown mushrooms
- 1/2 cup of tomato passata(125ml)
- 60g of Baby Spinach
- 6 bacon rashers
- 6 Eggs
- 2 Classic Pork Sausages (remove casings)
- Baby rocket leaves for serving

Instructions:
Follow the instructions below to make a classic breakfast pizza.

1. At 350°F, preheat your convection oven. Turn on the stove and heat a large nonstick pan. Cook the bacon for 2 to 3 minutes until browned. Transfer to a paper towel-lined plate. In the same nonstick pan, add sausage and cook. Keep mixing. Break up into lumps with a wooden spoon's help until sausage turns golden for around 5 minutes. Transfer to the bacon plate. Now add mushroom in the pan and stir until tender for just 1 to 2 minutes.
2. Grease two large baking sheets. Place the pizza bases or pita bread on the sheet. Evenly spread the passata, sprinkle half amount of pizza cheese and top up with spinach, sausage, mushroom, and tomatoes. Spread the remaining pizza cheese. Onto each pizza, bread cracks three eggs.
3. On preheated oven, bake for 10 to 15 minutes. Sprinkle rocket at the top of pizza cut into slices before serving.

2.36 BAKED ZUCCHINI SLICE (GLUTEN-FREE)

Total time of cooking

40 minutes

Prep time 10 minutes

Cook time 30 minutes

Servings

12

Nutrition Facts

(Per serving)

Calories 133

Total Fat 6.8g

Protein 9.1g

Total Carbs 8.3g

Ingredients:

- 150g of gluten-free smoked bacon
- 2/3 cup of gluten-free self-raising flour
- 2 grated zucchini (380g)
- 5 eggs
- 80g gluten-free grated cheddar
- 1 chopped onion
- 2 teaspoons of extra virgin olive oil plus 1/4 cup extra
- 1 teaspoon of baking powder gluten-free
- Rocket leaves for serving

Instructions:

Follow the instructions below to make a gluten-free baked zucchini slice.

1. Preheat your convection oven at 350°F. Grease a 20x30cm slice baking pan and line it with baking paper.

2. In a nonstick pan, heat the oil. Cook Onion and bacon, occasionally stirring for 7 to 8 minutes or until the bacon turns crispy and onion is tender. Allow cooling for a while.

3. In a bowl, whisk eggs with a fork. Then add in the flour and baking powder and mix well until smooth. Put the zucchini, bacon mixture, cheese, and extra oil. stir to mix. Spread the mixture into the prepared slice pan and bake until the slice turns golden for around 25 to 30 minutes.

4. Cut the baked slice into 12 pieces, serve and enjoy.

2.37 BREAKFAST EGG IN A HOLE BAGEL

Total time of cooking

18 minutes

Prep time 10 minutes

Cook time 8 minutes

Servings

2

Nutrition Facts

(Per serving)

Calories 892

Total Fat 51.7g

Protein 44.4g

Total Carbs 64.4g

Ingredients:

- 2 bagels
- 4 bacon rashers
- 2 eggs
- 2 peeled avocados
- 1x 8oz of Halloumi (divided into 6)
- 2 heaping teaspoons of chili jam
- 1 teaspoon of butter
- Fresh lemon juice for taste
- Extra virgin olive oil for drizzle
- Fresh chives for garnishing
- Pinch of salt and pepper

Instructions:

Follow the instructions below to make a breakfast bagel.

1. Start by blending an avocado in lemon juice, sprinkle with salt and fresh ground pepper, drizzle over olive oil. Keep it aside.

2. Cut your bagel from the center so you will have top and base slice. Make a large enough hole in the top part of the bagel to fit an egg.

3. Fry bacon rashers on medium heat until it turns crispy. Then fry halloumi slices in the same pan until they turn golden from both sides.

4. Make a layer of smashed avocado, bacon, Halloumi, and chili jam on the bagel base. Close the bagel with and crack an egg in the hole of the top bagel and sprinkle chives on the egg— place in a butter greased baking tray.

5. Bake at 300°F for 5 minutes and put under the grill for 3 minutes.

6. Serve straightaway.

2.38 QUICK AND TASTY PEANUT BUTTER BREAD

Total time of cooking
1 hour
Prep time 10 minutes
Cook time 50 minutes

Servings
12

Nutrition Facts
(Per serving)
Calories 181
Total Fat 7g
Protein 6g
Total Carbs 25g

Ingredients:
- 2 cups of flour
- 1 cup of whole milk
- 1/2 cup of peanut butter
- 1/3 cup of brown sugar
- 2 teaspoons of baking powder
- 1 egg large
- 1 teaspoon of salt

Instructions:
Follow the instructions below to make a quick peanut butter bread.
1.At 325°F, preheat your convection oven and coat 9x4 inches loaf pan with baking spray.
2.For 45 seconds, microwave the peanut butter to softens it, then in a bowl, mix it with the brown sugar, milk, and egg until it becomes smooth and creamy.
3.Add and whisk together flour, salt, and baking powder and mix it with the wet ingredients. Blend the dry and wet ingredients until fully incorporated. Pour the batter into your greased loaf pan lined with baking paper.
4.Bake for around 45 to 50 minutes.
5.Let it cool before serving.

2.39 DATE AND WALNUT QUICK BREAD

Total time of cooking
1 hour 5 minutes
Prep time 10 minutes
Cook time 55 minutes

Servings
12

Nutrition Facts
(Per serving)
Calories 203
Total Fat 7g
Protein 4g
Total Carbs 33g

Ingredients:
- 1 3/4 cups of all-purpose flour
- 1 cup of walnuts chopped
- 1 cup of dates chopped
- 1 cup of brown sugar
- 1 cup of boiling water
- 1 egg
- 3 tablespoons softened butter
- 1 teaspoon of baking soda
- 1/4 teaspoon of salt

Instructions:
Follow the instructions below to make a date and walnut quick bread.
1.Combine water and dates in a bowl, do not drain the water; keep it aside for 15 minutes. In another bowl, add and mix butter and brown sugar, add egg, and whisk well. Gather flour, salt, and baking soda, add to the egg mixture along with dates and liquid. Fold in the walnuts.
2.In an 8x4 inches loaf pan, pour in the batter. Bake at 350°F in a convection oven for 50 to 55 minutes.
3.When baked, remove and transfer to a cooling rack. Serve and enjoy.

Total time of cooking

45 minutes

Prep time 10 minutes

Cook time 35 minutes

Servings

6

Nutrition Facts

(Per serving)

Calories 253

Total Fat 8.5g

Protein 8.8g

Total Carbs 36.4g

Ingredients:

- 6 slices of oatmeal peach bread gluten-free
- 2 large peaches sliced
- 2 whole eggs
- 1/2 cup of fat-free milk
- 2 egg whites
- 1 teaspoon of vanilla
- 1/2 teaspoon of ground ginger
- 1/2 teaspoon of salt
- 1/2 teaspoon of cinnamon
- Maple syrup and fresh raspberries (for garnishing)

Instructions:

Follow the instructions below to make a baked peach French toast.

1.Coat 8 x 8 inches baking pan with cooking spray and spread the layer of oatmeal peach bread slices.

2.In a small-sized mixing bowl, add egg whites, milk, egg, cinnamon, vanilla, salt, and ginger and mix. Pour the mixture in the baking pan over the bread layer.

3.Top with peach slices, cover the pan and keep in refrigerate for overnight.

4.Bake in a 325°F preheated convection oven in the morning without cover for 35 minutes. Serve the toast with maple syrup and fresh raspberries.

2.41BAKED MIXED BERRIES OATMEAL

Total time of cooking

50 minutes

Prep time 10 minutes

Cook time 40 minutes

Servings

6

Nutrition Facts

(Per serving)

Calories 383

Total Fat 20g

Protein 10g

Total Carbs 43g

Ingredients:

- 2 cups of oats
- 2 cups of mixed berries
- 1 3/4 cups milk of any kind
- 1/3 cup of maple syrup
- 3/4 cup of chopped walnuts
- 2 eggs large
- 3 tablespoons of unsalted butter
- 1 teaspoon of cinnamon
- 1 teaspoon of vanilla
- 1 teaspoon of baking powder
- 1/2 teaspoon of salt
- 1/2 teaspoon of nutmeg
- Greek yogurt for serving

Instructions:

Follow the instructions below to make baked mixed berries oatmeal.

1.Preheat your convection oven to 350°F.cover a 9×9-inch baking pan with cooking spray. Heat the walnuts in a pan until fragrant, about four to five minutes. Remove the walnuts from the pan and roughly chop them.

2.In a medium-sized bowl,mix walnuts,oats,nutmeg,cinnamon,salt and baking powder.

3.Take another small-sized bowl and whisk milk, eggs, maple syrup, butter, and vanilla together. Mix the mixture into the bowl with oats. Fold in the berries, then pour into the baking dish evenly.

4.Bake in a preheated convection oven for 35 to 40 minutes until the top turns golden brown. Serve with Greek yogurt.

2.42 BAKED BANANA AND NUTS FRENCH TOAST

Total time of cooking

40 minutes
Prep time 10 minutes
Cook time 30 minutes

Servings

8

Nutrition Facts

(Per serving)
Calories 375
Total Fat 16g
Protein 15g
Total Carbs 44g

Ingredients:

- 1 loaf of crusty sliced whole grain bread
- 1 cup of walnuts
- 1 cup of low-fat milk
- 3 large sliced bananas
- 8 eggs large
- 2 teaspoons of vanilla
- 1 teaspoon of cinnamon
- 1/2 teaspoon of salt
- 1/2 teaspoon of nutmeg
- Maple syrup for serving

Instructions:

Follow the instructions below to make baked banana and nuts, French toast.

1. Coat with baking spray a 9 x 13 inches oblong baking dish and spread a single layer of bread slices into the baking pan. (cut the bread slices into half)

2. Mix milk, eggs, cinnamon, vanilla, nutmeg, and salt in a bowl. Place 1/3 of the egg mixture over the top of a single layer of bread.

3. Top the egg-soaked bread layer with half slices of banana and 1/3 of the walnuts, spread the remaining slices of bread, pour in the remaining egg mixture, and make sure all slices are fully soaked. Spread the remaining slices of banana and top up with walnuts. Cover the baking dish with a lid and keep it in the refrigerator overnight (or at least 2 hours).

4. Remove lid and bake at 325°F at preheated convection oven for 25 to 30 minutes. Top up with maple syrup or any syrup of your preference.

2.43 HEALTHY AND TASTY OATMEAL BLUEBERRY BREAD

Total time of cooking

1 hour
Prep time 10 minutes
Cook time 50 minutes

Servings

14

Nutrition Facts

(Per serving)
Calories 194
Total Fat 6.7g
Protein 5.6g
Total Carbs 29.1g

Ingredients:

- 1 1/2 cups of white whole wheat flour or whole wheat pastry flour
- 1 1/2 cups of plain yogurt low fat
- 1 cup of blueberries
- 1 cup of oats
- 1/2 cup of Flaxseed meal
- 1/3 cup of vegetable oil
- 3/4 cup of sugar
- 2 eggs large
- 2 teaspoons of baking powder
- 2 teaspoons of vanilla
- 1 teaspoon of cinnamon
- 1/2 teaspoon of salt
- 1/2 teaspoon of baking soda

Instructions:

Follow the instructions below to make healthy oatmeal blueberry bread.

1. At 325°F, warm up your convection oven. And with baking spray or butter, grease a bread baking pan.

2. In a medium-sized bowl, Add and whisk whole wheat flour, oats, flaxseed, sugar, cinnamon, baking powder, salt, and baking soda.

3. Beat Yogurt, eggs, oil, and vanilla on medium speed using an electric mixer. Gradually add dry ingredients until fully incorporated. Fold in the blueberries slowly, then spread the batter into the baking pan.

4. Bake in the preheated convection oven for 45 to 50 minutes.

5. Let the bread cool down completely. Slice and enjoy.

2.44 BAKED BREAKFAST ITALIAN EGGS

Total time of cooking
15 minutes
Prep time 5 minutes
Cook time 10 minutes

Servings
4

Nutrition Facts
(Per serving)
Calories 121
Total Fat 1.9g
Protein 7.2g
Total Carbs 1.4g

Ingredients:
- 10 sliced grape tomatoes
- 4 eggs large
- 4 teaspoons of extra virgin olive oil
- 4 teaspoons of fresh basil
- 4 teaspoons of grated Parmigiano-Reggiano cheese
- 1/4 teaspoon of black pepper ground
- 1/4 teaspoon of salt

Instructions:
Follow the instructions below to make baked Italian eggs.
1. At 300°F, preheat your convection oven.
2. By adding 1 teaspoon oil to each ramekin, grease 4 ramekins with a pastry brush.
3. Place on the bottom of each ramekin 5 to 6 slices of tomatoes.
4. Into each ramekin, pour 1 teaspoon of basil.
5. Crack one egg into each ramekin one by one.
6. Sprinkle 1 teaspoon of cheese, pepper, and salt into each ramekin.
7. On the baking sheet, arrange ramekins and bake for 10 minutes. Serve right away.

2.45 BREAKFAST CRANBERRY AND ORANGE BREAD

Total time of cooking
1 hour
Prep time 10 minutes
Cook time 50 minutes

Serving
2 loaves (16 slices each)

Nutrition facts
(Per serving)
Calories 98
Total Fat 2g
Protein 2g
Carbs 19g

Ingredients:
- 2 3/4 cups of all-purpose flour
- 2 cups of fresh or frozen cranberries chopped
- 1 cup of reduced-fat milk
- 2/3 cup of brown sugar
- 1/2 cup of orange juice
- 2/3 cup of sugar
- 1 peeled and chopped apple
- 1 egg at room temperature
- 3 tablespoons of canola oil
- 3 1/2 teaspoons of baking powder
- 1 teaspoon of salt
- 1/4 teaspoon of ground nutmeg
- 1/2 teaspoon of ground cinnamon

Instructions:
Follow the instructions below to make breakfast cranberry and orange bread.
1. Combine the flour, sugars, baking powder, salt, cinnamon, and nutmeg in a big mixing bowl. In another medium-sized bowl, whisk together the egg, milk, orange juice, oil, and orange zest; mix into the dry ingredients until just combined. Add in the cranberries and apple in a mixing bowl and fold.
2. Spread into two 8x4-inch greased loaf pans. At 325°F, bake for 45 to 50 minutes in a preheated convection oven or check by placing a wooden skewer in the middle. If it comes out clean, your bread is done. Allow cooling for 10 minutes before slicing.

2.46 CRESCENT SAUSAGE ROLLS

Total time of cooking
25 minutes
Prep time 10 minutes
Cook time 15 minutes

Serving
36

Nutrition facts
(Per serving)
Calories 165
Total Fat 9g
Protein 5g
Carbs 18g

Ingredients:
- 36 fully cooked frozen sausages
- 5 cups of all-purpose flour
- 3 eggs at room temperature
- 1 cup of warm water
- 3 eggs at room temperature
- 1/2 cup of butter melted
- 1/2 cup of sugar
- 1 teaspoon of salt
- 1/4 ounce of active dry yeast

For Topping:

- 1 egg white
- 3 tablespoons of toasted sesame seeds
- 1 tablespoon of water

Instructions:
Follow the instructions below to make crescent sausage rolls.
1.Put sausage in a skillet and cook until it turns brown. Keep turning. cool down for some time and refrigerate.
2.In a bowl of hot water, dissolve the yeast. Add-in 2 cups flour, sugar, butter, eggs, and salt Using a hand mixer on medium speed, blend until smooth. To build a soft dough, stir in enough remaining flour. Cover and leave in the refrigerator overnight.
3.Place dough on a floured surface. Divide dough into six parts; every section should be rolled into a 10-inch circle, and cut each circle into six wedges. Place a sausage at each wedge's wide end and roll up from the wide ends. Place on greased baking sheets points sides down, 2 inches. Apart. Cover with a kitchen towel and set aside to grow until doubled in size, around 1 hour.
4.At 325°F, preheat your convection oven. Whisk egg white and water together; brush on top of rolls. Spread with sesame seeds on top. Bake until light brown and crispy, 12-15 minutes. Serve straight away.

2.47 POTATO, EGG, AND BEEF BAKE

Total time of cooking
55 minutes
Prep time 10 minutes
Cook time 45 minutes

Serving
12

Nutrition facts
(Per serving)
Calories 218
Fat 11g
Protein 20g
Carbs 9g

Ingredients:
- 1 pound of ground beef
- 10 ounces of chopped frozen spinach
- 14 eggs large
- 4 cups of frozen hash brown potatoes shredded
- 1 1/3 cups of halved tomatoes
- 1 cup of ricotta cheese
- 3/4 cup of Monterey Jack cheese shredded
- 1/3 cup of milk
- 2 teaspoons of onion powder
- 1 1/2 teaspoons of salt

- 1 teaspoon of pepper
- 1 teaspoon of garlic powder
- 1/2 teaspoon of red pepper flakes
- 1/2 teaspoon of rubbed sage

Instructions:
Follow the instructions below to make potato, egg, and beef bake.
1.At 325°F, warm up your convection oven.
2.Cook beef, onion powder, salt, garlic powder, sage, and pepper flakes in a large skillet over normal heat for 6 to 8 minutes, or until it changes color, splitting up beef into crumbles; drain. Add the spinach and mix well. Remove the pan from the stove.
3.In a greased 13x9 inch baking dish. Spread the potatoes and cover with the beef mixture. Whisk eggs, ricotta cheese, milk, pepper, and the remaining salt together in a large mixing bowl; pour over the top—sprinkled cheese. Make a layer with tomatoes on top.
4.Bake in a convection oven for 40 to 45 minutes or until it turns golden brown from the top. Cool for some time before eating.

2.48 QUICK AND EASY PISTACHIO BREAD

Total time of cooking
45 minutes
Prep time 10 minutes
Cook time 35 minutes

Serving
2 loaves (12 slices each)

Nutrition facts
(Per serving)
Calories 169
Total Fat 7g
Protein 2g
Carbs 24g

Ingredients:
• 1 package of regular size white cake mix
• 1 package (3.4 ounces) of instant pistachio pudding mix
• 1 cup of sour cream
• 1/3 cup of sugar
• 1/4 cup of canola oil
• 1/4 cup of water
• 4 eggs large
• 3/4 teaspoon of ground cinnamon

Instructions:
Follow the instructions below to make pistachio bread.
1.Gather cake and pudding mixes in a bowl. Add in eggs, water, sour cream, and oil; beat until completely mixed (batter should be thick).
2.Combine cinnamon and sugar. Spread half batter into two 8x4 inches greased loaf pans; top up with 2 tablespoons of cinnamon sugar on each loaf—layer the remaining batter and sprinkle again with the remaining cinnamon sugar.
3.In a convection oven, bake for 30 to 35 minutes at 325°F. Keep checking during bake time, so the bread doesn't get burnt. Cool down on the wire rack before serving.

2.49 EGG AND BACON BREAKFAST LASAGNA

Total time of cooking
35 minutes
Prep time 10 minutes
Cook time 25 minutes

Serving
12

Nutrition facts
(Per serving)
Calories 386
Fat 20g
Protein 23g
Carbs 28g

Ingredients:
• 1 pound of diced bacon strips
• 4 cups of milk
• 2 cups of swiss cheese shredded
• 12 boiled eggs (sliced)
• 12 cooked lasagna strips
• 1 onion chopped
• 1/3 cup of Parmesan cheese shredded
• 1/3 cup of all-purpose flour
• 2 tablespoons fresh parsley minced
• 1 teaspoon of salt
• 1/4 teaspoon of black pepper

Instructions:
Follow the instructions below to make egg and bacon breakfast lasagna.
1.At 325°F, warm up your oven.
2.Cook bacon until crisp in a large-sized skillet. With a slotted spoon, transfer to paper towels. Set aside 1/3 cup of the drippings. Sauté onion until it becomes tender in the drippings. Add salt, flour and pepper into onions until all is well combined. Stir in the milk gradually. Bring in to a boil, then reduce to low heat and simmer, constantly stirring, for about 2 minutes, or until the sauce has thickened. Switch off the stove.
3.In 13x9-inch greased baking dish, pour 1/2 cup of sauce. 4 lasagna strips, a third of the bacon, eggs, Swiss cheese, and remaining sauce on top. Repeat the procedure of layers twice. Sprinkle Parmesan cheese on top.
4.Bake, without cover, for 25 minutes. If you like, sprinkle parsley on top. Let wait for 15 minutes before cutting.

2.50 BREAKFAST BAKED OATMEAL

Total time of cooking
30 minutes
Prep time 5 minutes
Cook time 25 minutes

Serving
6

Nutrition facts
(Per serving)
Calories 235
Fat 4g
Protein 5g
Carbs 31g

Ingredients:
- 1-1/2 cups of cooking oats
- 1/2 cup of milk
- 1/2 cup of sugar
- 1/4 cup of melted butter
- 1 egg large
- 1 teaspoon of vanilla extract
- 3/4 teaspoon of salt
- Fresh fruits
- Warm milk

Instructions:
Follow the instructions below to make baked breakfast oatmeal.
1.At 350°F, preheat your oven. Gather the first eight ingredients from the list on a large bowl and mix until fully incorporated. Pour evenly on 13x9 inches coated baking pan.
2.Bake for 25 minutes or until the corners are golden brown. Straightaway spoon into bowls. Add milk top with fruits. If you like, sprinkle brown sugar as well.

2.51 COCOA PEANUT BUTTER GRANOLA

Total time of cooking
1 Hr 40 minutes
Prep time 55 minutes
Cook time 45 minutes

Servings
15

Nutrition facts
(per serving)
Calories 333kcal
Fat 20g
Protein 9g
Carbs 37g

Ingredients
- A third of a cup of cocoa powder
- 4 cups oats, old fashioned
- 1/3 cups of honey
- 3/4 cup smooth peanut butter, with a little more to serve
- 1 1/2 tablespoons vanilla extract (pure)
- A third of a cup of peanuts oil
- 6 oz. Dark chocolate, chopped
- 1/2 cup of cocoa nuts

Instructions
1.Preheat the oven to 300 degrees Fahrenheit. Using a nonstick spray, lightly oil the baking pan.
2.Combine the oats and cocoa powder in a large mixing basin. In a medium saucepan, combine the peanut butter, honey, and oil; cook over medium heat until the mixture is fluid, approximately 2 minutes. Mix in the vanilla extract.
3.Toss the oats with the peanut butter mixture and whisk to incorporate on the baking sheet, spread into an equal layer.
4.Bake for 45 minutes, stirring every 5 minutes until the granola is golden brown. On the baking sheet, cool fully. Combine the cocoa nibs and dark chocolate in a mixing bowl.
5.Drizzle with peanut butter before serving.

2.52 PECAN COOKIES WITH RYE AND BARLEY FLAKES

Total time of cooking
23 minutes
Prep time: 10 Minutes
Cook time: 13 Minutes

Servings
10

Nutrition facts
(per serving)
Calories 283kcal
Protein 6g
Fat 14g
Carbs 37g

Ingredients
- Rye flakes (150 g)
- 100 g flakes of barley
- 100 g pecans, chopped
- A single huge egg
- 100 grams of flour
- A half teaspoon of baking soda
- 70 g softened butter
- 50 ml organic coconut blossom nectar
- 1/4 teaspoon salt
- Brown sugar, 60 g

Instructions
1.Gather all of the materials and preheat the oven to 180 degrees Celsius/350 degrees Fahrenheit. Two baking sheets should be greased or lined with parchment paper.
2.Whisk together the dry ingredients together in a large bowl: flour, rye, and barley flakes, the majority of the chopped and roasted nuts, baking soda, and salt. Leave a handful of nuts on top of each cookie to garnish.
3.Using an electric hand mixer, combine the soft butter and cane sugar in a separate large mixing dish. Combine the egg and the coconut blossom nectar in a mixing bowl. Continue mixing/beating until everything is lovely and smooth.
4.Stir in dry ingredients until they are well combined with the butter mixture. Scoop equal quantities of dough with an ice cream scoop and arrange on a baking sheet, allowing about 1 inch between each cookie.
5.Slightly flatten the cookies/batter and sprinkle with the remaining chopped pecans.
6.Bake for 13 minutes in the oven. You may need to bake them in more times, so take them out of the oven and let them cool somewhat before transferring them to a cooling rack to cool entirely.

2.53 BREAKFAST BURRITO CASSEROLE

Total time of cooking
60 minutes(Prep time: 15 minutes/Cook time: 45 minutes)

Servings
8-10

Nutrition facts
Calories 334.5
Fat 10.4g,
Proteins 29.3g
Carbs 40.1g

Ingredients
- Flour tortillas (eight)
- 1/2 cup onions
- 2 russet potatoes, chopped
- A dozen eggs
- 1/2 cup chopped red bell peppers
- 32 oz salsa
- Half c shredded cheddar cheese
- Sour cream, 12 ounces
- 15 bacon slices
- A tablespoon of olive oil
- Jimmy dean sausage, 1 pound (12 oz)
- 1/8 teaspoon of pepper
- 1/8 teaspoon of salt

Instructions
1.Grease a 9x13 baking dish lightly. Bacon should be cooked. Allow cooling. Set aside after chopping into bits.
2.Cook the sausage and leave it aside, dividing it up into tiny parts.
3.Peel and cut potatoes into cubes. Heat the olive oil and toss in the potatoes. Cook for about 8 minutes. Combine the peppers and onions in a large mixing bowl. Cook until the potatoes are fork-tender. Remove the item and place it away.
4.In a mixing dish, whisk together all of the eggs. Season with salt and pepper. Fill a big frying pan halfway with water and cook until done.
5.Place one flour tortilla on a chopping board. Scoop some eggs, sausage, potato mixture, salsa, and cheese in that order.
6.Roll the tortilla tightly closed, including both ends, to completely include all of the contents. Place in a casserole dish and bake. Carry on with the rest of the tortillas in the same manner.
7.Combine the sour cream and the second jar of salsa in a blender or with a mixer. Pour the sauce over the burritos. Any leftover cheese and bacon should be sprinkled on top of the sauce.
8.Bake for 15-20 minutes at 350 degrees. Cut each tortilla in half and serve.

Total time of cooking
30 minutes
Prep time: 12 Minutes
Cook time: 18 Minutes

Servings
6

Nutrition facts
(per serving)
Calories 380kcal
Fat: 24g
Protein: 14g
Carbs: 26g

Ingredients
For the dutch batter:
- 2 huge eggs or 3 little eggs
- all-purpose flour (125 g)
- 2 tbsp sugar
- 240 mL semi-skimmed milk (2 percent fat)
- 1 teaspoon vanilla extract
- 1 teaspoon of Rum (if desired)
- 1 teaspoon of salt

For cooking:
- 3 tbsp butter or oil

For toppings:
- 4 eggs (tiny)
- 4 rashers perfectly cooked bacon
- 1 tablespoon freshly chopped fresh herbs (optional)
- 1 tbsp honey to sprinkle over the top when serving (optional)

Instructions
Making the batter:

1.In a blender or food processor, combine the eggs, milk, flour, sugar, vanilla, and salt, depending on which you want to use to mix your batter. For around 10-15 seconds, whizz or combine. You'll end up with a somewhat liquidy batter.

2.Allow the batter to rest for a few minutes. Enable for at least 20 to 30 minutes of resting time to allow the flour to absorb the liquid. If you just have 10 minutes to rest it, it's not a huge deal.

3.While your batter rests, preheat the oven by placing the skillet you're using on the center shelf. Preheat the oven to 425° F.

4.When the oven and skillet are hot and ready to create the pancakes, take the skillet from the oven (using oven gloves, of course) and set it on top of the stove. Pour in the oil or butter (if using butter) and swirl the pan to evenly cover the bottom and sides.

5.Pour the batter onto the pan, turning it slightly to properly distribute the batter on all sides. Preheat the oven to 350°F. Place the skillet in the oven.

Baking the dutch baby:

1.Bake until the Dutch baby is attractively puffed up and golden brown on top and edges. The baking time is about 15 to 20 minutes.

2.Prepare the topping by cooking bacon rashers and eggs in a big pan while the pancake is baking. It's best if they are fried separately.

3.The Dutch baby may be served right out of the pan or transferred to a wide serving platter for sharing. Toss in the toppings (bacon and eggs). Cut into hefty wedges and serve with a drizzle of honey or maple syrup and a sprinkling of fresh herbs, if desired

Serving the pancakes:

1.The Dutch baby may be served right out of the pan or transferred to a large serving platter for sharing. Toss in the toppings (bacon and eggs).

Total time of cooking

50 minutes

Prep time: 10 Minutes

Cook time: 40 Minutes

Servings

4

Nutrition facts

(per serving)

Calories: 370kcal

Protein 13g

Fat 17g

Carbs 44g

Ingredients

For The Tomato Sauce:

- 1 chili pepper
- 1 onion, shredded or chunked
- 1 teaspoon of salt
- 1 chopped tomato can
- 1 celery stick, chopped or grated
- 1 teaspoon of tomato paste
- tomato sauce (200 mL)
- 1 garlic clove, smashed and chopped
- 1 tbsp soy sauce (sweet)
- tbsp extra virgin olive oil
- 1 teaspoon dried or fresh thyme
- 1 teaspoon of Worcestershire sauce

For the topping:

- 24 olives (black)
- 16 eggs from quail
- optional red chili
- 5-6 tbsp chopped fresh parsley

Instructions

1.Put the Olive oil in a skillet and heat over medium heat, then add the onions, garlic, pepper, salt, celery, and pepper. Sauté them for a good 10 minutes, stirring periodically and adding a sprinkle of water if needed.

2.Add the tomato sauce, chopped tomatoes, tomato paste, Worcestershire sauce, sweet soy sauce, and thyme when the veggies are tender. From the boiling point, cook uncovered for 15 minutes on low heat. It must be cooked down completely, with no juices flowing. Set aside and let to cool once completed.

3.Preheat the oven to 350° F.

4.Line a baking pan with parchment paper.

5.Toast 8 pieces of bread and spread a dollop of tomato sauce on top.

6.In the tomato sauce, make two wells and crack the quail eggs into them. Add 2-3 olives and season with salt and pepper to suit.

7.Bake for 5-8 minutes, or until the quail eggs are tender or extremely well done, depending on your preference.

8.Remove it from the oven, sprinkle with parsley and red chilies if desired, and serve while still warm. Later on, this may be served chilled.

2.56 SCRUMPTIOUS BACON AND EGG CUPCAKE OMELET

Total time of cooking
35 minutes
Prep time: 10 Minutes
Cook time: 25 Minutes

Servings
4

Nutritional facts
(per serving)
Calories 708kcal
Protein: 19g
Fat: 68g
Carbs 3g

Ingredients
- 30 ml organic milk, full fat
- eggs (organic)
- 100-gram egg whites
- 150 g cheese mozzarella
- 80 grams of spinach
- 200 g prosciutto or bacon
- Cream cheese, 1 tbsp
- Sunflower seeds or pine nuts, 1 tbsp
- Finely ground chili pepper (red or green) to taste

Instructions
1. Preheat the oven to 180 degrees Fahrenheit.
2. Combine the eggs, egg whites, pepper, a little milk, half of the cheese, and the wilted spinach in a mixing dish.
3. Cut the bacon into long strips by halving it lengthwise. If you like, you may trim some of the fat.
4. Place a bacon strip on the edge of a silicone muffin pan (thinner if the bacon has not been de-salted). Half-fill the container with the egg mixture. Place in the oven with a few sunflower seeds and extra shredded mozzarella cheese on top.
5. Heat oven at 425° F and bake for 20-25 minutes.

2.57 APPLE GRANOLA CRISP

Total time of cooking
65 minutes
Prep time: 20 minutes
Cook time: 45 minutes

Servings
4-5

Nutrition facts
(per serving)
Calories 250kcal
Fat 12g
Protein 5g
Carbs 34g

Ingredients
- Apples (four)
- 1/2 cup sugar (white)
- A half teaspoon of cinnamon
- Flour (1/2 tbsp)
- 1/2 cup granola (flavour of choice)
- 1/4 cup of water
- A half-cup of brown sugar
- Flour (1/2 cup)
- 1/8 teaspoon bicarbonate of soda
- A quarter teaspoon of baking powder
- A tablespoon of flour
- A quarter cup of melted butter

Instructions
1. Preheat the oven to 350°F and peel and core the apples before slicing them into slices. Place in a stainless-steel mixing bowl.
2. Combine white sugar, 1 tablespoon flour, and cinnamon in a mixing bowl.
3. Finally, stir in the granola. Then add the water and stir it in again to moisten the granola and allow it to absorb the liquid.
4. Toss the apples with the granola mixture and fully combine. Fill a 1 1/2-quart casserole dish halfway with the mixture.
5. Combine brown sugar, baking powder, baking soda, flour and melted butter in a separate basin. To produce a crumble topping that falls apart, mix everything with your hands.
6. Scatter the mixture on top of the apple-granola mixture. Make sure to cover the whole area.
7. Preheat oven to 350°F. 45 minutes or check it until desired tenderness is reached.
8. Tip: If using granola with nuts, remove the nuts and cut or mince them before adding to the mixture. Almonds and walnuts were found in mine. It's entirely up to you how crispy you want your apple granola crisp to be.

2.58 BRUNCH BAKE

Total time of cooking
50 minutes
Prep time: 20 minutes
Cook time: 30 minutes

Servings
12

Nutrition facts
(per serving)
Calories 183kcal
Fat 9g
Protein 4g
Carbs 18g

Ingredients
- A third of a cup of sour cream
- A dozen eggs
- 1 pound cheddar cheese, finely shredded
- 1 pound of pork sausage
- 1 medium chopped onion
- 1 cup sliced mushrooms
- 1 cup chopped tomatoes

Instructions
1. Preheat the oven to 400 degrees Fahrenheit.
2. Whisk the sour cream and eggs until well combined. Bake for 10 minutes or until the egg mixture is softly set in a buttered 13 by 9 baking dish.
3. Meanwhile, sauté sausage, mushrooms, and onions for 6 to 8 minutes in a large pan over medium heat, or until sausage is cooked through; drain.
4. Lower the oven temperature to 325°F. Spread tomatoes on top of the egg layer, then top with sausage and cheese. Heat oven till 350°F and bake for 30 minutes, or until center is set.

2.59 CHEESY SAUSAGE & EGG BAKE

Total time of cooking
1 hour 25 minutes
Prep time: 25 minutes
Cook time: 1 hour

Servings
12

Nutrition facts
(per serving): Calories 5428 kcal, Fat 403g, Protein 282g, Carbs 161g

Ingredients
- 1 1/2 cup fresh mushrooms, sliced
- 1 pound cooked and drained bulk pork sausage
- medium chopped tomatoes
- sliced medium green onions
- 12 eggs
- 1 1/4 cup Bisquick mix (original)
- A cup of mozzarella cheese, shredded
- 1 1/2 teaspoons of salt
- 1 quart of milk
- 1 1/2 teaspoon pepper
- 1 1/2 teaspoon oregano leaves, minced

Instructions
1. Preheat the oven to 350 degrees Fahrenheit. 13x9x2 inch rectangle baking dish, greased In a baking dish, layer sausage, onions, mushrooms, tomatoes, and cheese.
2. Mix in the remaining ingredients. Pour the sauce over the cheese.
3. Bake for 30–35 minutes, uncovered, or until golden brown and set.
4. Kitchen Tip: Start your day with a nutritious breakfast! Instead of pork sausage, use turkey sausage and low-fat mozzarella cheese. Serve with a side salad of fresh spinach and berries.

2.60 EASY BREAKFAST BAKE

Total time of cooking
1 hr 30 minutes
Prep time: 20 minutes
Cook time: 1 Hr 10 minutes

Servings
12

Nutrition facts
(per serving)
Calories190kcal
Fat 11g
Protein 13g
Carbs 6g

Ingredients
- 1 cup chopped bell pepper
- 1cup frozen hash brown potatoes
- 1/2 cup chopped onion
- c cheddar cheese, shredded (8 oz)
- quarts milk
- 1 cup Bisquick original mix eggs
- A quarter teaspoon of pepper

Instructions
1.Preheat the oven to 400 degrees Fahrenheit. 13x9x2 inch rectangle baking dish, greased In a 10-inch skillet, brown the sausage, bell pepper, and onion over medium heat. Drain after stirring periodically until the sausage is no longer pink. In a baking dish, combine the sausage mixture, potatoes, and 1 1/2 cups of cheese.
2.Combine Bisquick mix, milk, pepper, and eggs in a mixing bowl. Pour the mixture into a baking dish.
3.Bake for 42 minutes, uncovered, or until a knife inserted in the middle comes out clean. Sprinkle on top the remaining cheese. Bake for other 2 minutes, or until the cheese has melted. Allow cooling for 5 minutes.

2.61 SCRAMBLED EGG MUFFINS

Total time of cooking
40 minutes
Prep time: 15 minutes
Cook time: 25 minutes

Servings
12

Nutrition facts
(per serving)
Calories 133 kcal
Fat 10g
Protein 9
Carbs 2g

Ingredients
- A dozen eggs
- 1 pork sausage, 1/2 pound
- A half-cup of shredded cheddar cheese
- A half teaspoon of salt
- 1/2 cup onion, chopped
- A quarter teaspoon of garlic powder
- 1 tsp black pepper, ground

Instructions
1.Preheat the oven to 350° F,12 muffin cups should be lightly greased or lined with paper muffin liners.
2.Melt the butter and add the sausage; cook and stir until crumbled, uniformly browned, and no longer pink, about 10 to 15 minutes; drain.
3.In a large mixing basin, whisk together the eggs. Combine the green pepper, pepper, salt, onion, and garlic powder in a mixing bowl. Combine the sausage and Cheddar cheese in a mixing bowl. Fill muffin cups 1/3 cup at a time.
4.Bake for 20 to 25 minutes in a preheated oven or until a knife inserted near the middle comes out clean.

Total time of cooking

35 minutes
Prep time: 15 minutes
Cook time: 20 minutes

Servings

10

Nutrition facts

(per serving)
Calories 120kcal
Fat 10g
Protein 6g
Carbs 2g

Ingredients

- 1 pound cream cheese (8 ounces)
- 1 pound sausage
- A pinch of garlic powder
- A pinch of salt and pepper

Instructions

1.Brown sausage in a frying pan; drain. Season with pepper and salt,and garlic powder.
2.Blend in the cream cheese until it is completely melted.
3.Place one crescent roll packet on a baking pan and unroll it. To seal the seams, gently press them together with your fingertips. Cover the crescent roll dough with the sausage mixture, leaving a 1/2-inch border around the edges. Place the remaining crescent rolls on top of the sausage mixture after unrolling them. To seal the edges, press them together. Press the seams together gently.
4.Bake for approximately 22 minutes at 375° F, or until the crescent roll dough is golden brown. Serve by cutting into tiny squares.

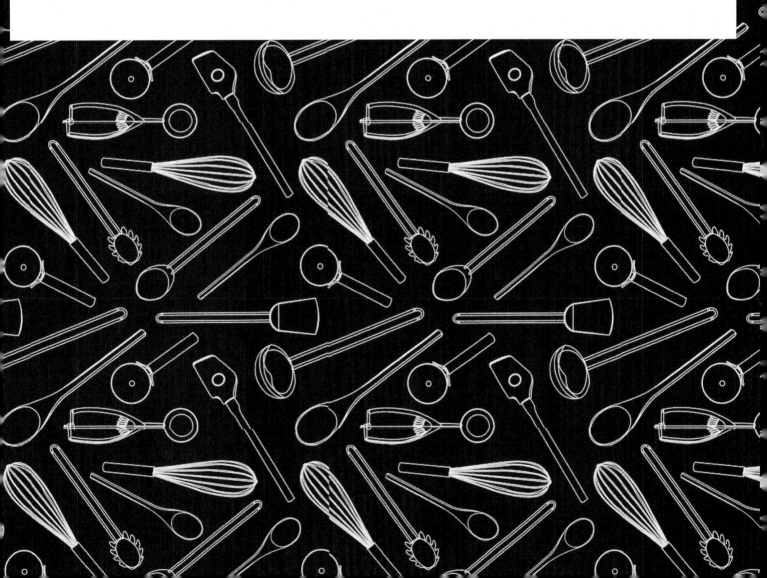

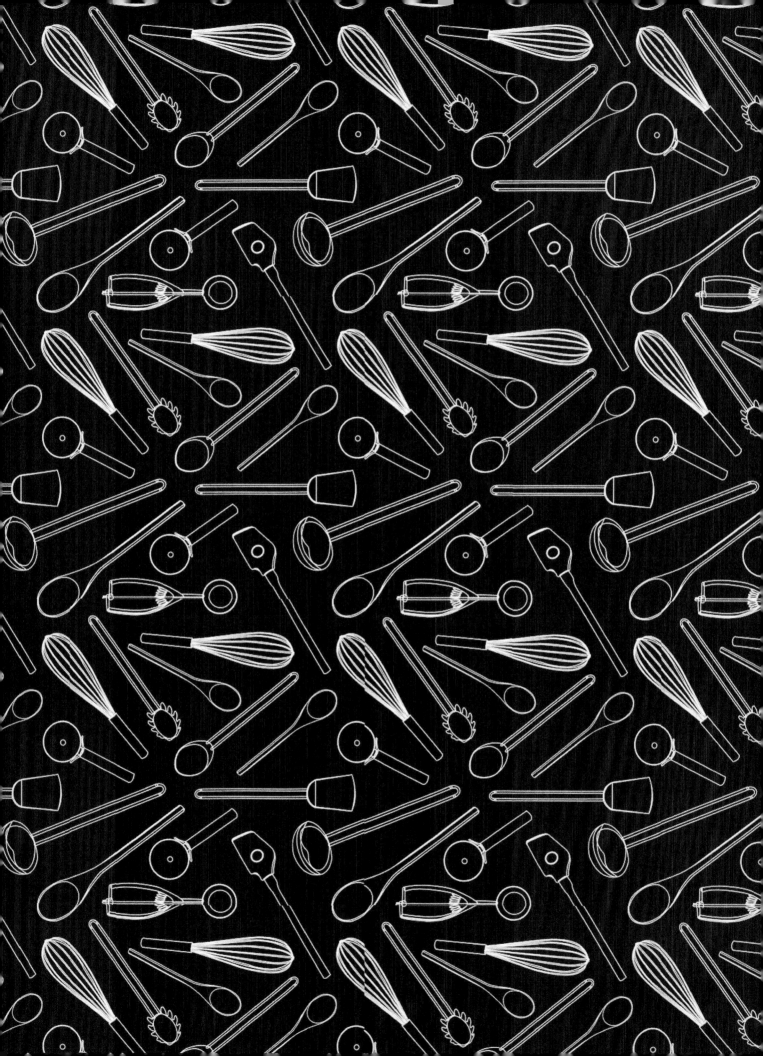

3.1 BAKED PARMESAN CHICKEN SLIDER

Total time of cooking
35 minutes
Prep time 10 minutes
Cook time 25 minutes

Serving
12

Nutrition facts
(Per serving)
Calories 402
Fat 23g
Protein 17g
Carbs 34g

Ingredients:
- 1 package of Hawaiian sweet rolls (12 ounces)
- 1 jar of marinara sauce (24 ounces)
- 24 ounces of frozen chicken tenders breaded
- 1 package of sliced provolone and mozzarella cheese blend (7-1/2 ounces)
- 1/4 cup of Parmesan cheese grated
- 1/2 cup of cubed butter
- 2 tablespoons of fresh basil minced
- 1 teaspoon of red pepper flakes
- 1 teaspoon of garlic powder

Instructions:
Follow the instructions below to make a baked parmesan chicken slider.
1. Preheat your convection oven at 350°F.
2. Make chicken tenders following your package details. Meanwhile, cut rolls horizontally in half without separating them; layer bottoms of roll in a 13x9 inches greased baking pan half cheese slices on top of the roll bottom. Spread m layer. Bake for 4 to 5 minutes until cheese melts down.
3. Spread half of the sauce and chicken tenders over rolls, then spread existing sauce and cheese slices. Cover with the top layer of rolls.
3. For the topping of rolls, melt butter, red pepper flakes, and garlic powder. Mix them well and pour on rolls; top up with parmesan cheese. Bake for 15 to 20 minutes until rolls turn golden brown—season with basil before serving.

Total time of cooking
35 minutes
Prep time 10 minutes
Cook time 25 minutes

Serving
48

Nutrition facts
(Per serving)
Calories 67
Fat 3g
Protein 2g
Carbs 8g

Ingredients:
- 1 1/2 cups of all-purpose flour
- 3/4 cup of reduced-fat milk
- 1 cup of cornmeal
- 1/4 cup of canola oil
- 1 egg at room temperature
- 1 can of cream-style corn (14-3/4 ounces)
- 2 teaspoons of sugar
- 1/4 teaspoon of salt
- 3/4 teaspoon of baking powder

For filling:
- 2 cups of cheddar cheese(shredded)
- 1/4 cup of pimientos diced
- 1/4 teaspoon of hot pepper sauce
- 1 teaspoon of chili powder

Instructions:
Follow the instructions below to make corn muffins with cheddar spicy filling.

1.Preheat your convection oven at 300°F.

2.In a large-sized bowl, Mix all-purpose flour, cornmeal, sugar, baking powder, and salt. In another medium-sized bowl, whisk milk, oil, and egg until fully combined. Mix in with flour mixture and fold corn in the mixture.

3.Pour mixture to coated mini muffins pan 3/4 full. Bake corn muffins for 15 to 20 minutes in a convection oven. Leave it aside for cooling.

4.Meanwhile, in a large-sized bowl, gather filling ingredients and mix well. Using a spoon, scoop out the middle from all muffins, put filling in the middle of each muffin, and bake for 5 minutes more.

3.3 PEPPERONI PIZZA BREAD LOAF

Total time of cooking
35 minutes

Serving
12

Nutrition facts
(Per serving)
Calories 296
Fat 17g
Protein 13g
Carbs 24g

Ingredients:
- 1 loaf of bread dough frozen (1 pound)
- 8 ounces of pepperoni sliced
- 1 can of sliced olives (2-1/4 ounces)
- 1 can of mushroom pieces (4 ounces)
- 1 can of pizza sauce (15 ounces)
- 2 cups of mozzarella cheese shredded
- 1/2 cup of pickled pepper rings
- 2 eggs, separated
- 1 diced green pepper
- 1 tablespoon of olive oil
- 1 tablespoon of parmesan cheese grated
- 1 teaspoon of dried oregano
- 1 teaspoon of fresh parsley minced
- 1/2 teaspoon of garlic powder
- 1/4 teaspoon of pepper

Instructions:
Follow the instructions below to make pepperoni pizza bread loaf.

1.Preheat your convection oven to 325°F.On a greased baking tray, spread and roll out the pizza dough into a rectangle of 15x10 inches.

2.In a small-sized bowl, gather the egg yolks, oil, parmesan cheese, oregano, garlic powder, parsley, and pepper. Brush all over the dough evenly.

3.Top with pepperoni, mushrooms, mozzarella, pepper rings, olives, and green pepper. Beginning with a long side, roll up in jelly-roll style. Pinch the seam to wrap and tuck the ends under

4.Place the pizza loaf on a baking sheet seam side down; Brush the top with egg. Bake until dough cooks and turns golden brown, about 30 to 35 minutes.

5.Slice the loaf and serve with warm pizza sauce.

3.4 CHICKEN CHEESE PUFFS

Total time of cooking
25 minutes
Prep time 10 minutes
Cook time 15 minutes

Serving
32

Nutrition facts
(Per serving)
Calories 67
Fat 4g
Protein 2g
Carbs 6g

Ingredients:
- 2 tubes of refrigerated crescent rolls (8 ounces each)
- 4 ounces of softened cream cheese
- 1/2 cup cooked chicken shredded
- 1/2 teaspoon of garlic powder

Instructions:
Follow the instructions below to make chicken cheese puffs.
1. In a small-sized bowl, mix garlic powder and cream cheese until creamy. Fold in the chicken.
2. Roll out the dough into a floured surface. Divide into 16 triangles. Two triangles split each triangle in half lengthwise; spread 1 teaspoon of chicken mixture in the center of each dough. Fold the short side of dough over the filling. Press sides to close and roll-up.
3. Place with the distance of 1 inch on coated baking sheets. Bake in a convection oven at 350° until it turns golden brown, 12 to 15 minutes. Serve hot.

3.5 CLASSIC SAUSAGE ITALIAN BRUSCHETTA

Total time of cooking
25 minutes
Prep time 15 minutes
Cook time 10 minutes

Serving
24

Nutrition facts
(Per serving)
Calories 131
Fat 11g
Protein 4g
Carbs 5g

Ingredients:
- 1 pound of Italian sausage
- 24 (1/2-inch-thick) slices French bread baguette
- 8 ounces softened mascarpone cheese
- 3/4 cup of seeded plum tomatoes chopped
- 3 tablespoons of Parmesan cheese shredded
- 3 tablespoons of fresh parsley chopped
- 3 tablespoons of olive oil
- 3 tablespoons of prepared pesto

Instructions:
Follow the instructions below to make Italian sausage bruschetta.
1. Turn on heat to medium, in a large-sized skillet, cook sausages for 6 to 8 minutes or until it changes in color, break into crumbles and drain. In a small-sized bowl, gather mascarpone cheese and pesto.
2. Preheat the broiler of your oven, Place bread on non-stick baking sheets, and brush one side of bread with oil, Broil 4 to 5 inches from heat until the bread turns light brown, for around 30 to 45 seconds on each side; spread the mascarpone mixture. Top up with sausage, tomatoes, parmesan cheese, and parsley, serve right away.

Total time of cooking
25 minutes
Prep time 10 minutes
Cook time 15 minutes

Serving
16

Nutrition facts
(Per serving)
Calories 118
Fat 7g
Protein 4g
Carbs 8g

Ingredients:
- 1 package of crescent rolls (8 ounces)
- 1 jar of pizza sauce, warmed (14 ounces)
- 1/2 cup of mozzarella cheese shredded
- 1/4 cup of Parmesan cheese grated
- 1/2 cup of ricotta cheese
- 1/4 cup of fresh mushrooms chopped
- 1/2 cup of pepperoni diced
- 1/4 cup of green pepper chopped
- 3 tablespoons of chopped onion
- 1/4 teaspoon of salt
- 1 teaspoon of Italian seasoning

Instructions:
Follow the instructions below to make pinwheels.

1.Preheat the convection oven to 350°F. In a small-sized bowl, mix the mozzarella cheese, ricotta cheese, parmesan cheese, onion, pepperoni, green pepper, mushrooms, Italian seasoning, and salt

2.Roll out the dough and divide it into four rectangles. Spread cheese mixture on rectangles inside 1/4 inch of edges. Roll up the jelly-roll style rectangles, begin with a shorter side, pinching the seam to seal.

3.Cut each roll in four slices, using a knife; place on a non-stick baking sheet and cut the side down. Bake for 12 to 15 minutes until it turns golden brown in color. Serve the pinwheels with pizza sauce.

Total time of cooking
25 minutes
Prep time 5 minutes
Cook time 20 minutes

Serving
2 cups

Nutrition facts
(For 2 tablespoons)
Calories 152
Fat 13g
Protein 7g
Carbs 2g

Ingredients:
- 2 cups of Monterey Jack cheese shredded
- 1 package of cream cheese (8 ounces)
- Slices of French bread baguette
- 1 cup of cooked chicken breast chopped
- 1/2 cup of salad dressing (ranch or blue cheese)
- 1/2 cup of Buffalo wing sauce

Instructions:
Follow the instructions below to chicken buffalo dip.

1.Preheat the convection oven to 325°F. Into Shallow 1-qt baking dish spread cream cheese.Place layer of chicken, buffalo wing sauce, and salad dressing. Top up with cheese.

2.Bake in a convection oven for 15 to 20 minutes until cheese fully melts down, serve the dip with baguette slices.

3.8 CHEESE 'N' HAM BISCUIT STACKS

Total time of cooking
20 minutes
Prep time 10 minutes

Serving
40 appetizers

Nutrition facts
(Per serving)
Calories 121
Fat 7g
Protein 4g
Carbs 11g

Ingredients:
• 4 tubes of (6 ounces each) small flaky biscuits (5 counts each)
• 1/4 cup of stone-ground mustard
For Assembling:
• 10 thick slices of quartered deli ham
• 20 ripe olives, patted dry and drained
• 10 slices of quartered Swiss cheese
• 20 olives pimiento-stuffed, patted dry and drained
• 2 1/2 cups of romaine shredded
• 40 pieces of frilled toothpicks
• 1/2 cup of softened butter

• 1/4 cup of mayonnaise
• 1/4 cup of green onions chopped
• 1/4 cup of honey
• 1/2 cup of stone-ground mustard

Instructions:
Follow the instructions below to make cheese and ham biscuit stacks.
1. Preheat the convection oven to 375°F. To make half circles cut biscuits in half. Place on nonstick baking sheets with 2 inches distance. Over tops spread the mustard. Bake until it turns golden brown, about 8 to 10 minutes. Let it cool down completely on the oven rack.
2. Combine butter and green onions. In another medium-sized bowl, add mayonnaise, mustard, and honey and mix. Break each biscuit into two layers.
3. Spread butter mixture in biscuits bottom and layer up with ham, cheese romaine, and biscuit tops. Put the mustard mixture over the tops. Add one olive into each toothpick. And place into stacks. Serve and enjoy.

3.9 BEAN AND TUSCAN SAUSAGE DIP

Total time of cooking
30 minutes
Prep time 10 minutes
Cook time 20 minutes

Serving
16

Nutrition facts
(per 1/4 cup)
Calories 200
Fat 14g
Protein 10g
Carbs 7g

Ingredients:
• 1 package of fresh baby spinach chopped
• 1 pound of Italian sausage
• 1 can of cannellini beans (15 ounces)
• 1 package of cream cheese (8 ounces)
• 1 cup of seeded tomatoes chopped
• 1 medium chopped onion
• 1 cup of shredded mozzarella cheese
• 4 minced garlic cloves
• 1/2 cup of Parmesan cheese shredded
• 1/2 cup of chicken broth or dry white wine

• 1/4 teaspoon of salt
• 1/2 teaspoon of dried oregano
• 1/4 teaspoon of dried thyme
• Toasted French bread baguette slices or assorted crackers

Instructions:
Follow the instructions below to make bean and Tuscan sausage dip.
1. Preheat the convection oven to 350°F. Cook onion, sausage, and garlic in a large-sized skillet, over the medium temperature of heat until sausage changes its color. Break up the Italian sausage with a spoon into crumbles; Mix in wine, thyme, oregano, and salt. Let it boil and cook until no liquid remains.
2. Put cream cheese and stir well until it melts down. Add in beans, spinach, and tomatoes; cook and occasionally stir until spinach wilts. Transfer to square 8 inches greased baking dish. Top up with cheeses.
3. Bake for 20 minutes in convection or until bubbly, serve with baguette or crackers.

3.10 PECAN, PEAR AND PANCETTA PUFFS

Total time of cooking
20 minutes
Prep time 10 minutes
Cook time 10 minutes

Serving
24

Nutrition facts
(Per serving)
Calories 105
Fat 7g
Protein 2g
Carbs 8g

Ingredients:
- 1 sheet of puff pastry frozen
- 1/4 cup of fresh goat cheese crumbled (1 ounce)
- 6 ounces of softened cream cheese
- 3 tablespoons of peeled ripe pear finely chopped
- 3 tablespoons of crumbled cooked bacon or crumbled crisp pancetta
- 2 tablespoons of toasted pecans finely chopped
- 2 tablespoons of honey
- 1/8 teaspoon of pepper
- 1/8 teaspoon of salt

Instructions:
Follow the instructions below to make pecan, pear, and pancetta puffs.
1. Preheat the convection oven to 375°F. Unfold pastry dough on a floured surface, cut pastry dough into 24 circles with a 1-3/4 inches cookie cutter.
Transfer to baking paper-lined baking sheets. Bake until it turns light golden brown, for 8 to 10 minutes, remove and let it cool down on a wire rack.
2. Meanwhile, Beat together honey, cream cheese, salt, and pepper until fully blended. Fold in pancetta, cheese, pecans, and pear.
3. Cut each baked pastry into half. Layer cream cheese mixture onto the bottom of half pastry and cover with the top half. Serve and enjoy.

3.11 ARTICHOKE AND HOT COLLARDS DIP

Total time of cooking
30 minutes
Prep time 10 minutes
Cook time 20 minutes

Serving
24 servings (1/4 cup each)

Nutrition facts
(For 1/4 cup)
Calories 190
Fat 17g
Protein 6g
Carbs 2g

Ingredients:
- 12 ounces of frozen chopped collard greens frozen chopped, thawed, and squeezed dry
- 10 thick-sliced bacon strips peppered, crumbled, and cooked
- 2 jars of marinated quartered artichoke hearts, chopped and drained (7-1/2 ounces each)
- 1 package of garlic-herb spreadable cheese (6-1/2 ounces)
- 1 1/2 cups of mozzarella cheese
- 1 cup of sour cream
- 1 cup of Parmesan cheese grated
- 3/4 cup of mayonnaise
- Warmed garlic flatbreads (cut into wedges)

Instructions:
Follow the instructions below to make artichoke and hot collards dip.
1. In a large-sized bowl, mix collard greens, artichoke, sour cream, garlic herb cheese, parmesan cheese, bacon, and mayonnaise, and 1 cup of mozzarella cheese until fully incorporated. Transfer to 11x9 inches greased baking pan and sprinkle remaining mozzarella on the top.
2. Bake at 325°F in a convection oven until cheese melts down for around 20 minutes, serve with garlic flatbread.

3.12 PEPPERONI PIZZA ROLLS

Total time of cooking
20 minutes
Prep time 10 minutes
Cook time 10 minutes

Serving
8

Nutrition facts
(Per serving)
Calories 172
Fat 12g
Protein 6g
Carbs 12g

Ingredients:
- 1 can of crescent rolls
- 24 slices of pepperoni
- 4 string mozzarella cheese
- 1 cup of pizza sauce (for dipping)
- 1 tablespoon of parmesan cheese grated
- ¼ teaspoon of garlic powder

Instructions:
Follow the instructions below to make pepperoni pizza rolls.
1.Preheat the convection oven to 350°F.Line a baking sheet with baking paper.
2.Split each string cheese into halves, and lay a layer of crescents, and spread 3 pepperoni slices overlapping and a piece of string cheese.
3.Fold the wide end of the wrap over the ingredients and pinch the sides to seal the bag. Continue to roll the dough and place it seam side down on the baking sheet. Sprinkle the parmesan cheese and garlic powder over the top of pizza rolls.
4.Bake in a convection oven for about 8 to 10 minutes or until it turns golden. Serve the pizza rolls with pizza sauce dipping.

3.13 EASY AND QUICK BROILED TOMATOES

Total time of cooking
8 minutes
Prep time 5 minutes
Cook time 3 minutes

Serving
4

Nutrition facts
(Per serving)
Calories 145
Fat 10g
Protein 8g
Carbs 6g

Ingredients:
- 1 pound of large ripe tomatoes at room temperature
- 1 ounce of parmesan cheese
- 1 clove of garlic minced
- 3 ounces of mozzarella cheese
- 1 tablespoon of olive oil
- 1 teaspoon of Italian seasoning

Instructions:
Follow the instructions below to make easy and quick broiled tomatoes.
1.Cut tomatoes into 3/4 thick slices.
2.Add and mix olive oil, Italian seasoning, and garlic in a bowl. Brush over all sides of tomatoes, transfer to a baking sheet, and top up with cheeses.
3.Place the convection oven rack on the top rack and preheat the broiler to 450°F.
4.For 2 to 3 minutes, broil the tomatoes or until cheeses turn brown and bubbly.

3.14 TASTY PIZZA BAGELS

Total time of cooking

15 minutes
Prep time 5 minutes
Cook time 10 minutes

Serving

6

Nutrition facts

(Per serving)
Calories 276
Fat 11g
Protein 14g
Carbs 30g

Ingredients:

- 3 full-size bagels plain and halved
- 24 slices of pepperoni
- 6 ounces of pizza sauce
- 6 ounces of mozzarella cheese shredded

Instructions:

Follow the instructions below to make pizza bagels.
1.Preheat your convection oven to 350°F.
2.Cut bagels into halves and spread with pizza sauce, pepperoni slices, and mozzarella cheese equally.
3.Place in oven and bake for around 10 minutes or until cheese melts and turns slightly brown.

3.15 MAC AND CHEESE JALAPENO BITES

Total time of cooking

30 minutes
Prep time 10 minutes
Cook time 20 minutes

Serving

24 bites

Nutrition facts

(Per serving)
Calories 83
Fat 5g
Protein 3g
Carbs 7g

Ingredients:

- 1 cup of cheddar cheese(shredded)
- 1 cup of bread crumbs
- 2 eggs
- 1/4 cup of flour
- 1 package of Mac and Cheese
- 1/4 cup of jalapenos
- 3 tablespoons of butter
- 2 tablespoons of bacon bits

Instructions:

Follow the instructions below to make mac and cheese jalapeno bites.
1.Preheat convection oven at 350°F.
2.In a medium-sized bowl, combine flour, cheddar, and 1/2 cup of bread crumbs. Slowly stir in jalapenos and macaroni. Add eggs and fold in until well mixed. Scoop out into coated mini muffin pan.
3.In a small-sized bowl, gather remaining bread crumbs, bacon bits, and melted butter. Spread over jalapeno bites.
4.Bake in a convection oven for 15 to 20 minutes. Serve straight away.

3.16 WRAPPED BACON SCALLOPS

Total time of cooking

20 minutes
Prep time 10 minutes
Cook time 10 minutes

Serving

4

Nutrition facts

(Per serving)
Calories 196
Fat 16g
Protein 10g
Carbs 2g

Ingredients:

- 12 of large sea scallops
- 6 slices of bacon
- 1 tablespoon of melted butter
- 1/2 teaspoon of lemon pepper
- 1 clove of garlic minced
- 1 teaspoon of parsley
- Salt and pepper to season

Instructions:

Follow the instructions below to make wrapped bacon scallops.
1. Soak wooden sticks in water for 30 minutes.
2. Cook bacon in a medium-sized frying pan from each side for 4 to 5 minutes. (do not crisp)
3. With paper towels, dab scallops dry and sprinkle salt and pepper over it.
4. Around bacon, wrap the scallops and arrange 3 scallops onto each wooden stick.
5. Mix melt butter, parsley, garlic, and lemon pepper and brush on the scallops' tops.
6. Adjust the oven rack 6" from the broiler. Place scallops on a nonstick baking sheet and broils for 8-10 minutes, flipping over the scallops after three minutes. Cook until the bacon turns crispy and scallops are cooked, do not overcook.

3.17 TASTY STUFFED MUSHROOMS (STUFFED SAUSAGE MUSHROOMS)

Total time of cooking

25 minutes
Prep time 10 minutes
Cook time 15 minutes

Serving

24 mushrooms

Nutrition facts

(Per serving)
Calories 64
Fat 5g
Protein 3g
Carbs 1g

Ingredients:

- 24 mushrooms
- 4 ounces of cream cheese
- 1/4 cup of parmesan cheese shredded
- 2 ounces of cheddar cheese
- ½ pound of sausage(optional)
- 2 tablespoons of minced onion
- 2 cloves of garlic

Instructions:

Follow the instructions below to make stuffed mushrooms.
1. Preheat convection oven at 375°F.
2. Remove stems from mushrooms and clean. Scoop out the center of the mushrooms to make a hole for filling.
3. Dice the stems finely and put stems, sausage, onion, and garlic in a small-sized pan. Cook until color changes. Drain out fat.
4. Mix the parmesan and cheddar cheese and keep 1/4 cup for topping out of it.
5. Gather cheese mixture and cream cheese and sausage mixture in a small-sized bowl. Fill in the hole of each mushroom with the filling.
6. Top with 1/4 cup reserved cheese and bake for around 10 to 15 minutes or until cheese melts down.

3.18 TASTY PIZZA BUBBLE

Total time of cooking
30 minutes
Prep time 10 minutes
Cook time 20 minutes

Serving
6

Nutrition facts
(Per serving)
Calories 347
Fat 13g
Protein 15g
Carbs 40g

Ingredients:
- 1 roll of biscuits dough
- 1 1/2 cups of mozzarella of cheddar cheese shredded
- 1 cup of pizza sauce
- 1/4 cup of parmesan cheese shredded
- Toppings as desired

Instructions:
Follow the instructions below to make a pizza bubble.
1.Preheat convection oven at 350°F.Cut each biscuit into four pieces with the help of a knife or kitchen scissors.
2.In a large-sized bowl, toss in pizza sauce, biscuit pieces,1/2 cup of cheese, and toppings.
3.Into A greased pan of 9x9 inches, spoon biscuit pieces, and spread toppings. Bake until it turns light brown in color for around 15 to 20 minutes.

3.19 MINI BRIE AND CRANBERRY BITES

Total time of cooking
25 minutes
Prep time 10 minutes
Cook time 15 minutes

Serving
24 bites

Nutrition facts
(Per serving)
Calories 79
Fat 5g
Protein 3g
Carbs 5g

Ingredients:
- 1 package of crescent rolls
- 1 cup of cranberry sauce
- 12 ounces of brie cheese
- 24 pecans
- Rosemary for garnishing

Instructions:
Follow the instructions below to make mini brie and cranberry bites.
1.Preheat the convection oven to 350°F.Finely grease 24 mini muffin baking pan.
2.Spread and roll out crescent rolls into a floured surface, pinching seams to seal. Cut the rolled dough into 24 pieces.
3.Fit each piece of dough into a muffin pan. Place brie cheese and add two teaspoons of cranberry sauce into each roll.
4.Bake in a convection oven until the muffin turns golden, for 15 minutes.

3.20 EASY AND QUICK CROSTINI

Total time of cooking
15 minutes
Prep time 5 minutes
Cook time 10 minutes

Serving
20 slices

Nutrition facts
(Per serving)
Calories 60.15
Fat 3.27g
Protein 1.3g
Carbs 6.37g

Ingredients:
- 1 large baguette
- 2 tablespoons of parmesan cheese grated
- 1/4 cup of olive oil
- 2 cloves of garlic minced
- 1/2 teaspoon of salt
- Parsley for garnishing

Instructions:
Follow the instructions below to make easy and quick crostini.
1.Preheat the convection oven to 350°F.
2.Cut the baguette into 1/4-inch slices.
3.With olive oil, brush each slice and Arrange it in a single layer on a baking sheet. Sprinkle the top of the baguette with parmesan cheese and salt.
4.Bake until slightly toasted for 8 to 10 minutes. Remove and rub slices with garlic and spread with parsley on top.

3.21 CHEESE BREAD STICKS

Total time of cooking
20 minutes
Prep time 5 minutes
Cook time 15 minutes

Serving
6

Nutrition facts
(Per serving)
Calories 132
Fat 9g
Protein 9g
Carbs 1g

Ingredients:
- 1 can of prepared pizza dough
- 1 cup of mozzarella cheese
- 1/4 cup of parmesan cheese
- 1/2 cup of cheddar cheese
- 3 tablespoons of butter
- 1 tablespoon of fresh parsley
- 1 teaspoon of Italian seasoning
- 1 clove of garlic minced

Instructions:
Follow the instructions below to make cheese breadsticks.
1.Preheat the convection oven to 375°F.Roll and spread the dough to fit in the greased 12 inches pizza pan.
2.Add garlic, butter, and Italian seasoning in a small-sized bowl and microwave for 30 seconds to melt it down.
3.Brush the top of pizza dough with butter and sprinkle cheeses and parsley over the top. Bake until cheese turns light brown and bubbly for 12 to 15 minutes.
4.Cut the pizza bread vertically into sticks. Serve with sauce of your choice.

3.22 MINI ZUCCHINI BITES

Total time of cooking
30 minutes
Prep time 10 minutes
Cook time 20 minutes

Serving
24 to 36 bites

Nutrition facts
(Per serving)
Calories 51.3
Fat 3.2 g
Protein 2.3 g
Carbs 3.6 g

Ingredients:
- 3 slices of bacon, finely sliced
- 1 large grated zucchini
- 1 chopped onion
- 1 large grated carrot
- 3 eggs
- 1 cup of cheese grated
- 1/2 cup of self-rising flour
- 1/4 cup of cream
- 1 tablespoon of olive oil

Instructions:
Follow the instructions below to make mini zucchini bites.
1. Heat oil in a large-sized pan and cook onion until translucent. Add the bacon and cook until it changes color; put the zucchini and carrot and cook for 2 to 3 minutes. Let it cool down for a while.
2. In a different bowl, add and beat together the cream, eggs, and cheese together; mix the egg mixture into zucchini mixture and mix in the flour.
3. Grease and flour the little muffin pans. Spoon the zucchini bites mixture into each cup.
4. Bake in a convection oven to 325°F for around 15 to 20 minutes.

3.23 CLASSIC GIANT PRETZELS

Total time of cooking
20 minutes
Prep time 10 minutes
Cook time 10 minutes

Serving
8

Nutrition facts
(Per serving)
Calories 192.7
Fat 0.5 g
Protein 5.2 g
Carbs 41.2 g

Ingredients:
- 2 tablespoons of water plus 1 cup of water (at 80 degrees)
- 1/2 cup of baking soda
- 3 cups of all-purpose flour
- 2 quarts of water
- 3 tablespoons of brown sugar
- 1 1/2 teaspoons of dry yeast active
- 1 teaspoon of salt

Instructions:
Follow the instructions below to make pretzels.
1. Preheat convection oven at 400°F. Add water, flour, sugar, and yeast in a large-sized bowl. Mix well and knead the dough using your hands or with the machine for 5 to 10. (check and add two tablespoons of flour after few minutes if required)
2. Spread the dough on a floured surface. Divide into eight equal balls. Roll out each ball and make 20-inch ropes and form a pretzel shape.
3. In a large-sized saucepan, Add water and baking soda and wait for a boil.
4. Pour pretzels into water one by one and boil for 10 to 20 seconds.
5. Remove and drain.
6. On a greased baking sheet, transfer pretzels and bake for 10 minutes or until it turns golden brown in color in a convection oven.
7. Lightly brush the top with water, sprinkle salt, and serve.

Total time of cooking
35 minutes
Prep time 10 minutes
Cook time 25 minutes

Serving
6

Nutrition facts
(Per serving)
Calories 640
Fat 44g
Protein 20g
Carbs 41g

Ingredients:
- 1 (32 oz) bag of tater tots
- 6 slices of bacon crumbled and cooked
- 1/2 cup of smoked sausage chopped and cooked
- 2 cups of shredded cheddar cheese

Toppings:
- 4 sliced green onions
- 1/2 cup of sour cream
- 1 cup of diced tomatoes

Instructions:
Follow the instructions below to make nachos tater tot.
1. At 400°F, preheat your convection oven.
2. With parchment paper, line a large-sized baking dish. Spread tater tots in a baking dish in a single and bake for around 15 to 20 minutes.
3. Put bacon, sausage, and cheddar on tater tots and bake for additional 5 minutes or until cheese melts and turns bubbly.
4. Remove from the convection oven and top with tomatoes, sour cream, and green onion. Serve right away.

3.25 YUMMY AND EASY PIZZA ROLLS

Total time of cooking
25 minutes
Prep time 10 minutes
Cook time 15 minutes

Serving
12 rolls

Nutrition facts
(Per serving)
Calories 193
Fat 10g
Protein 9g
Carbs 17g

Ingredients:
- 1 pound of pizza dough
- 1 1/2 cups of mozzarella shredded
- 1 cup of pizza sauce
- 2/3 cup of chopped pepperoni
- 1/3 cup of parmesan cheese grated
- 2 teaspoons of fresh parsley
- 1/2 teaspoon of garlic powder

Toppings:
- 2 tablespoons of olive oil
- fresh parsley for garnishing
- 2 tablespoons of grated parmesan cheese

Instructions:
Follow the instructions below to make yummy pizza rolls.
1. At 375°F, preheat your convection oven. Roll out the pizza dough at the floured surface in 16x14 inches square.
2. Mix garlic powder and parsley with 1/2 cup of pizza sauce and place a layer over the dough. Sprinkle parmesan cheese, mozzarella, and chopped pepperoni on top and roll up the dough in cinnamon roll style.
3. Split into 12 slices and transfer to a greased muffin pan.
4. Pour parmesan cheese on top and bake for around 12 to 15 minutes.
5. Cool down for a while and serve with 1/2 cup remaining pizza sauce.

3.26 PARTY SAVORY BREAD

Total time of cooking
30 minutes
Prep time 10 minutes
Cook time 20 minutes

Serving
8

Nutrition facts
(Per serving)
Calories 481
Fat 31g
Protein 17g
Carbs 32g

Ingredients:
- 1 round sourdough bread loaf (unsliced 1 pound)
- 1/2 cup of green onions chopped
- 1 pound of Monterey Jack cheese
- 1/2 cup of butter melted
- 2 to 3 teaspoons of poppy seeds
- Salt and pepper to season

Instructions:
Follow the instructions below to make party savory bread.
1.Warm-up convection oven at 325°F.
2.Mark cuts on bread widthwise into 1 inches slices to inside 1/2 inches of the bottom loaf. Rehearse the same cuts in the opposite direction. Cut slices of cheese and cut small cheese cubes out of it. Arrange the cheese cubes into bread cuts.
3.In a small-sized bowl, mix green onions, butter, and poppy seeds, season with salt and pepper. Spread over bread. Place on a non-stick baking sheet. Bake for 15 to 20 minutes. Serve with your favorite dipping and enjoy.

3.27 TASTY GRILLED PINEAPPLES

Total time of cooking
10 minutes
Prep time 5 minutes
Cook time 5 minutes

Serving
6 slices

Nutrition facts
(Per serving)
Calories 132
Fat 5g
Protein 1g
Carbs 24g

Ingredients:
- 1 pineapple (whole)
- 2 tablespoons of brown sugar
- 2 tablespoons of olive oil
- ¼ teaspoon of salt
- ¼ teaspoon of ground ginger

Instructions:
Follow the instructions below to make grilled pineapple.
1.Preheat convection oven grill to medium.
2.Peel off the pineapple's skin and cut it into 1/2-inch disks each.
3.Gather brown sugar, olive oil, and ginger in a small-sized bowl. Add pineapple to the mixture, toss to coat well, and marinate for at least 40 minutes.
4.Remove from marinade and sprinkle salt over pineapple disks Grill for 3 to 4 minutes from each side or until sugar caramelizes.

Total time of cooking

35 minutes
Prep time 10 minutes
Cook time 25 minutes

Serving

15 brownies

Nutrition facts

(Per serving)
Calories 436
Fat 16.3g
Protein 3.4g
Carbs 70.8g

Ingredients:

- 3 to 4 mashed bananas
- 2 cups of all-purpose flour
- 1 1/2 cups of sugar
- 2 eggs
- 1 cup of sour cream
- 1/2 cup of chopped walnuts
- 1/2 cup of softened butter
- 2 teaspoons of vanilla extract
- 1 teaspoon of baking soda
- 3/4 teaspoon of salt

Frosting:
- 4 cups of powdered sugar
- 3 tablespoons of milk
- 1/2 cup of butter
- 1 1/2 teaspoons of vanilla extract

Instructions:

Follow the instructions below to make banana bread-inspired brownies.

1.Warm up your oven to 350°F.Grease And flour jelly roll pan for 15x10 inches. In a large-sized bowl, mix and beat butter, sugar, sour cream, and eggs until it turns creamy. Stir in bananas and vanilla extract. Add in flour, salt, baking soda, and salt blend for one minute. Fold in chopped walnuts.

2.Pour in batter evenly into prepared pan. Bake for 20 to 25 minutes in a convection oven or until it is completely cooked and turns golden brown.

3.Meanwhile, heat butter in a medium-sized saucepan for frosting over medium heat until it boils. Cook the butter until it turns to delicate brown in color, then remove from the stove immediately.

4.Add powdered sugar, milk, and vanilla extract into butter and whisk well
until it becomes smooth and creamy. Using a spoon, pour the brown butter frosting over the warm brownies and serve.

3.29 CHEESEBURGER BACON BOMBS

Total time of cooking
30 minutes
Prep time 15 minutes
Cook time 15 minutes

Serving
10

Nutrition facts
(Per serving)
Calories 389
Fat 24g
Protein 17g
Carbs 25g

Ingredients:
- 1 can of Pillsbury Biscuits (10 biscuits)
- 5 ounces of cheddar cheese (cut into 10 squares)
- 1 pound of lean ground beef
- 3 slices of chopped bacon
- 1 egg white
- 1/3 cup of cream cheese
- 1/2 finely chopped onion
- 2 tablespoons of barbecue sauce
- 1 tablespoon of ketchup
- 1 teaspoon of Worcestershire sauce
- 1 teaspoon of mustard
- sesame seeds

Instructions:
Follow the instructions below to make cheeseburger bacon bombs.
1.Preheat convection to 350°F.In a large-sized pan, brown ground beef, onion, and bacon until completely cooked, drain out any grease, then add cream cheese, ketchup, mustard, barbecue sauce, and Worcestershire sauce. Stir on low-medium heat until cream cheese melts down completely. Allow cooling for some time.
2.Roll out each biscuit thinly. Fill out two tablespoons of the beef mixture and place 1 square of cheese on each biscuit. Wrap the biscuit around the cheese and beef and close the edges tightly.
3.Arrange biscuits on a non-stick baking sheet seam side down and brush egg white on top of biscuits, top up with sesame seeds.
4.Turn down the temperature of the convection oven to 325°F and bake for 13 to 15 minutes. Serve hot.

3.30 OVEN-BAKED ZUCCHINI FRIES

Total time of cooking
30 minutes

Serving
6

Nutrition facts
(Per serving)
Calories 59
Fat 2g
Protein 3g
Carbs 6g

Ingredients:
- 2 zucchinis large
- 1 cup of bread crumbs
- 1 egg
- 1/2 cup of parmesan Cheese
- 1 tablespoon of fresh parsley
- 1 tablespoon of milk
- 2 teaspoons of olive oil
- 1/2 teaspoon of pepper
- 1/2 teaspoon of garlic powder
- 1/2 teaspoon of seasoning salt

Chipotle Mayonnaise:
- 1/3 cup of mayonnaise
- 1 adobo chipotle
- 1/4 cup of sour cream
- 1 teaspoon of lime juice

Instructions:
Follow the instructions below to make baked zucchini fries.
For chipotle mayonnaise, add together all the ingredients and blend until creamy and smooth.
1.Preheat the convection oven to 375°F.Combine in a bowl bread crumbs, parmesan cheese, olive oil, and pepper, mix well and keep it aside.
2.Wash and cut zucchini into fries; do not peel off the skin.
3.Beat milk and egg and toss zucchini fries in the milk and egg mixture.
4.Coat each zucchini into bread crumbs.
5.Place on a spray-coated baking sheet lined with baking paper. Bake for 15 to 20 minutes until fries turn crispy.
6.Serve with chipotle mayonnaise dipping.

3.31 PINEAPPLE AND CARROT MUFFINS

Total time of cooking

30 minutes

Prep time 10 minutes

Cook time 20 minutes

Serving

12

Nutrition facts

(Per serving)

Calories 259.2

Fat 13.1g

Protein 2.9g

Carbs 33.3g

Ingredients:

- 1 1/2 cups of all-purpose flour
- 1 cup of sugar
- 1 cup of crushed pineapple
- 1 cup of grated carrot
- 2/3 cup of vegetable oil
- 2 teaspoons of baking powder
- 2 eggs
- 1 teaspoon of cinnamon
- 1 teaspoon of vanilla
- 1 teaspoon of baking soda
- 1/2 teaspoon of salt

Instructions:

Follow the instructions below to make pineapple and carrot muffins.

For chipotle mayonnaise, add all the ingredients and blend until creamy and smooth.

1. Stir together oil, sugar, eggs, and vanilla until fully incorporated.
2. In another medium-sized bowl, Gather flour, baking soda, baking powder, salt, and cinnamon. Mix in with sugar mixture until fully combined.
Fold in carrots and pineapple.
3. Place the mixture into the greased muffin pan.
4. Bake in warmed up convection oven at 350°F for 20 minutes.
5. Cool down before serving.

3.32 JALAPENO CRESCENT CUPS

Total time of cooking

20 minutes

Prep time 10 minutes

Cook time 10 minutes

Serving

18 crescent cups

Nutrition facts

(Per serving)

Calories 128

Fat 9g

Protein 4g

Carbs 6g

Ingredients:

- 1 package of crescent rolls
- 6 ounces of jalapenos diced
- 8 ounces of softened cream cheese
- 1/4 cup of bacon bits
- 1/2 cup of mozzarella cheese
- 3/4 cup of shredded cheddar cheese
- 2 tablespoons of chopped green onions
- 2 tablespoons of sour cream
- cooking spray

Instructions:

Follow the instructions below to make jalapeno crescent cups.
1. Preheat your convection oven to 350°F. Coat muffin pan with cooking spray.
2. Separate 1/3 cup of cheddar cheese. Except for crescent rolls, mix all the remaining ingredients in a medium-sized bowl.
3. Open and roll crescent rolls and split into 18 squares evenly. Place roll squares in a coated muffin pan and softly press into the muffin cups. Spoon the filling in each cup. Sprinkle reserved 1/3 cup of cheddar cheese on the top of cups.
4. Bake in a preheated convection oven for 8 to 10 minutes. Cool and serve.

3.33 TASTY POTATO SKINS BAKED

Total time of cooking
30 minutes
Prep time 10 minutes
Cook time 20 minutes

Serving
8

Nutrition facts
(Per serving)
Calories 263.9
Fat 18.3g
Protein 9.6g
Carbs 15.6g

Ingredients:
- 4 large baked baking potatoes
- 2 cups of cheddar cheese shredded (8 ounces)
- 4 sliced green onions
- 8 cooked and crumbled bacon slices
- 1/2 cup of sour cream
- 3 tablespoons of vegetable oil
- 1 tablespoon of parmesan cheese grated
- 1/4 teaspoon of paprika
- 1/2 teaspoon of salt
- 1/8 teaspoon of pepper
- 1/4 teaspoon of garlic powder

Instructions:
Follow the instructions below to make tasty potato skins baked.
1. Split potatoes into half lengthwise; spoon out the potato pulp and discard, leave at least 1/4 inches shell.
2. Transfer to a greased baking sheet.
3. Mix oil, salt, parmesan cheese, garlic powder, pepper, and paprika and spread all over the potato skins.
4. Bake in a convection oven to 400°F for about 8 minutes and then turn over. Bake for another 7 minutes, and now turn the right side of the potato up, inside potato skins, sprinkle cheddar and bacon evenly.
5. Bake around 2 more minutes or until the cheese melts completely.
6. Top up with onions and sour cream upon serving.

3.34 GRILLED CHICKEN HAWAIIAN PIZZA

Total time of cooking
25 minutes
Prep time 15 minutes
Cook time 10 minutes

Serving
6

Nutrition facts
(Per serving)
Calories 343
Fat 19g
Protein 18g
Carbs 25g

Ingredients:
- 1 Hawaiian thin crispy pizza crust
- 2 sliced green onions
- 3 boneless and skinless chicken thighs
- 1/2 thinly sliced green pepper
- 1/4 cup of thick teriyaki sauce
- 1/2 thinly sliced red pepper
- Extra cheese if you desired

Instructions:
Follow the instructions below to make grilled chicken Hawaiian pizza.
1. Preheat the convection oven grill to 350°F.
2. Spread teriyaki sauce over the chicken pieces and grill for 4 to 5 minutes on each side until cooked.
3. Make slices out of chicken and spread all over the frozen pizza crust, top with peppers and 1/2 of the green onion and cheese if you are using.
4. Transfer directly on the grill with a close lid and cook for 10 minutes or until the crust turns golden and cheese melts down.
5. Cool 2 to 3 minutes after removing pizza from oven grill; sprinkle remaining green onions on top and serve.

3.35 TASTY CHEESE AND HAM SLIDERS

Total time of cooking

30 minutes
Prep time 10 minutes
Cook time 20 minutes

Serving

12 sliders

Nutrition facts

(Per serving)
Calories 272
Fat 15g
Protein 13g
Carbs 21g

Ingredients:

- 12 dinner rolls
- 8 ounces of swiss cheese
- 12 slices of ham
- 6 tablespoons of melted butter
- 1 1/2 teaspoons of grainy mustard
- 1 teaspoon of dried minced onion
- 1 teaspoon of Worcestershire sauce
- 1 teaspoon of poppy seeds

Instructions:

Follow the instructions below to make cheese and ham sliders.
1.Preheat the convection oven to 325°F.In a small-sized bowl, combine four tablespoons of mustard, butter, Worcestershire sauce, poppy seeds, and dried onion.
2.Separate the rolls into half by cutting the top and bottom. Brush the inside of the rolls with 2 tablespoons of the remaining butter.
3.Arrange the bottom of rolls in a baking sheet and layer with ham and cheese. Place with the other half of the roll on the top and evenly spoon the butter mixture on top of sliders.
4.Bake for 20 minutes in a convection oven or until cheese melts and the tops turn light brown. Serve straight away.

3.36 PISTACHIO PUFF PASTRY TWISTS

Total time of cooking

25 minutes
Prep time 10 minutes
Cook time 15 minutes

Serving

36

Nutrition facts

(Per serving)
Calories 82
Fat 5.7g
Protein 1.3g
Carbs 6.5g

Ingredients:

- 1 package of puff pastry frozen (17.5 ounces)
- 1/3 cup of finely chopped pistachios
- 1 beaten egg white
- Salt to taste

Instructions:

Follow the instructions below to make pistachio puff pastry twists.
1.Preheat the convection oven to 325°F.
2.Unroll the puff pastry sheets and brush with egg white all over; pour pistachios and salt over the egg white layer. Flip over the puff pastry sheet, brush the layer of egg white and sprinkle salt and pistachios.
Using a knife, Split pastry into strips around 3 inches long and about 3/4 inches broad. Twist the puff pastry strips twice with your hands, then transfer to a baking paper-lined baking sheet.
3.Bake around 15 minutes in the preheated convection oven until browned.

3.37 CHEESY EASY PIZZA FLAVORED DIP

Total time of cooking
35 minutes
Prep time 10 minutes
Cook time 25 minutes

Serving
8

Nutrition facts
(Per serving)
Calories 246
Fat 20g
Protein 11g
Carbs 3g

Ingredients:
- 8 oz of softened cream cheese
- 2 cups divided shredded mozzarella
- 1 cup of pizza sauce
- 1/2 cup of shredded cheddar cheese
- Pepperoni slices (approx. 1/4 cup)
- 1/4 cup of parmesan cheese
- 1 loaf of sourdough bread or tortilla chips for serving
- 1/4 teaspoon of dried basil
- 1/2 teaspoon of dried oregano

Instructions:
Follow the instructions below to make a pizza-flavored dip.
1.Preheat the convection oven to 325°F.Mix cream cheese, basil, cheddar cheese, oregano,3/4 cup of mozzarella cheese.
2.Pour the cream cheese mixture into a casserole dish and layer pizza sauce on top of the cream cheese mixture. Sprinkle the remaining amount of cheeses finished with pepperoni on top of a casserole dish.
3.Bake until bubbly and cheese turn brown around 25 minutes.
4.Serve warm with Sourdough bread or tortilla chips.

3.38 POPPER CUPS WITH JALAPENO

Total time of cooking
30 minutes
Prep time 10 minutes
Cook time 20 minutes

Serving
12

Nutrition facts
(Per serving)
Calories 81
Fat 6.2g
Protein 3.2g
Carbs 3g

Ingredients:
- 12 mini tart shells
- 2 jalapeno peppers, chopped and seeded
- 4 ounces of softened cream cheese
- Bacon bits
- 1/2 cup of shredded Cheddar cheese
- 1 tablespoon of hot pepper sauce

Instructions:
Follow the instructions below to make popper cups with jalapeno.
1.Preheat the convection oven to 325°F.Arrange tart shells onto a baking sheet.
2.Mix cheddar cheese, cream cheese, hot sauce, and jalapenos in a medium-sized bowl. Spoon mixture into tart shells equally. Sprinkle the top of each tart with bacon bits. Bake in preheated convection for 15 to 20 minutes until golden brown. Serve and enjoy.

3.39 CHEDDAR CHILE CORNBREAD

Total time of cooking
40 minutes

Serving
10

Nutrition facts
(Per serving)
Calories 273
Fat 13g
Protein 8g
Carbs 32g

Ingredients:
- 1 cup of defrosted frozen corn
- 1 cup of cornmeal
- 1 cup of buttermilk
- 1 cup of flour
- 1 cup of cheddar cheese
- 1 can of mild green chiles
- 1/4 cup of sugar
- 1/4 cup of diced red pepper
- 1/3 cup of melted butter plus 1 tablespoon extra for greasing
- 1 teaspoon of baking powder
- 1/2 teaspoon of salt
- 1/2 teaspoon of baking soda
- 2 eggs

Instructions:
Follow the instructions below to make cheddar chile cornbread.
1.Preheat the convection oven to 350°F.In a bowl, gather flour, baking powder, cornmeal, baking soda, sugar and salt.
2.In another bowl, whisk egg, melted butter, and buttermilk. Then place the buttermilk mixture in cornmeal mixture and mix until the mix is completely incorporated and moist. Fold in corn, chiles, peppers, and 1/2 cup of cheddar cheese.
3.Great 10 inches cast iron skillet with one tablespoon of melted butter
and Pour the mixture into the pan. Sprinkle the top with the remaining cheese.
4.Bake in a convection oven for 25 to 30 minutes and serve.

3.40 BACON AND CHEESE ROUND POTATOES

Total time of cooking
45 minutes
Prep time 10 minutes
Cook time 35 minutes

Serving
4

Nutrition facts
(Per serving)
Calories 806
Fat 54.2g
Protein 39.8g
Carbs 39.7g

Ingredients:
- 4 baking potatoes, cut into slices of 1/2 inches
- 8 slices of bacon - crumbled and cooked
- 1/4 cup of melted butter
- 1/2 cup of green onions chopped
- 8 ounces of cheddar cheese shredded

Instructions:
Follow the instructions below to make bacon and cheese round potatoes.
1.Preheat the convection oven to 375°F.
2.Brush butter all over the potato slices and transfer them into an ungreased cooking sheet. Bake at 375°F preheat convection oven for 30 to 35 minutes until potatoes turn light brown from both sides
3.When potatoes are done, sprinkle with bacon, cheese, and green onion and bake for few more minutes until cheese melts down.
4.Serve.

3.41 EASY GRANOLA COOKIES

Total time of cooking
25 minutes
Prep time 10 minutes
Cook time 15 minutes

Serving
24

Nutrition facts
(Per serving)
Calories 229
Fat 11.6g
Protein 3.3g
Carbs 29g

Ingredients:
- 1 1/2 cups of all-purpose flour
- 1 3/4 cups of granola
- 1 cup of dates, chopped and pitted
- 1 cup of softened butter
- 3/4 cup of brown sugar packed
- 1/2 cup of peanuts chopped, dry-roasted and unsalted
- 3/4 cup of white sugar
- 1 egg
- 1 teaspoon of baking soda
- 1 teaspoon of vanilla extract
- 1 teaspoon of salt

Instructions:
Follow the instructions below to make granola cookies.
1.Preheat the convection oven to 350°F.Coat cookies sheet with baking spray.
2.In a bowl, cream together the brown sugar, white sugar, and butter. Add and beat in egg and vanilla and combine in the flour, baking soda, and salt. Stir them into creamed mixture. Finally, fold in the granola, peanuts, and dates. Place heaping teaspoonfuls of dough into a greased cookie sheet—place cookie dough with two inches of distance.
3.Bake in a convection oven until cookies turn light brown from the edges for 12 to 15 minutes. Once done, transfer to cooling racks and cool completely before serving.

3.42 BROILED CRAB SNACKS

Total time of cooking
15 minutes
Prep time 10 minutes
Cook time 5 minutes

Serving
20

Nutrition facts
(Per serving)
Calories 139
Fat 7g
Protein 9g
Carbs 9.9g

Ingredients:
- 1 package of English muffins (12 ounces)
- 1 jar of processed cheese spread (16 ounces)
- 1 pound of fresh crab meat
- 2 tablespoons of softened butter
- 1 tablespoon of mayonnaise
- ½ teaspoon of paprika

Instructions:
Follow the instructions below to make broiled crab snacks.
1.Preheat the convection oven to broil.
2.In a mixing bowl, mix crab meat, mayonnaise, cheese, and butter. Pour a heaping tablespoon of mixture on muffins one by one. Sprinkle paprika on top. Split muffins into quarters and transfer onto a cookie sheet
3.Broil in a convection oven for 3 to 5 minutes until the crab mixture turns golden brown and bubbly. Serve straight away.

Total time of cooking
30 minutes
Prep time 10 minutes
Cook time 20 minutes

Serving
10 puffs

Nutrition facts
(Per serving)
Calories 160
Fat 9g
Protein 9g
Carbs 10g

Ingredients:
- 1 cup of cheese shredded (cheddar or mozzarella)
- 4 strings of mozzarella cheese
- 3/4 cup of flour
- 3/4 cup of mini pepperoni
- 1/2 cup of readymade pizza sauce
- 3/4 cup of milk
- 1/2 diced red or green pepper
- 1 teaspoon of baking powder
- 3/4 teaspoon of oregano
- 1/2 teaspoon of garlic powder
- 1/2 teaspoon of basil
- 1 lightly beaten egg

Instructions:
Follow the instructions below to make pepperoni pizza cheesy puffs.
1.Preheat the convection oven to 350°F. Grease a muffin pan with cooking spray. Combine in a bowl flour, spices, and baking powder. Pour in milk and egg and stir until fully incorporated.
2.Fold in shredded cheese, pepperoni, and red pepper and leave the mixture to stand for 10 minutes.
3.Pour the mixture equally into each muffin cup. Split each cheese string into three pieces and place one piece into each muffin center, and press.
4.Bake in a preheated convection oven for about 20 minutes.
5.Serve hot with pizza sauce.

3.44 STUFFED BAKED CHERRY PEPPERS

Total time of cooking
40 minutes
Prep time 10 minutes
Cook time 30 minutes

Serving
25 pieces

Nutrition facts
(Per serving)
Calories 46
Fat 3.5g
Protein 1.9g
Carbs 1.2g

Ingredients:
- 1 jar of cherry peppers (14 ounces)
- 1/4 pound of sausage
- 1/4 cup of Parmesan cheese grated
- 1/4 pound of ground beef
- 1 egg

Instructions:
Follow the instructions below to make stuffed baked cherry peppers.
1.Preheat the convection oven to 375°F. Remove all seeds from peppers and drain.
2.In a large-sized bowl, combine sausage, ground beef, cheese, and egg. Mix well and stuff peppers with meat mixture.
3.Bake for 30 minutes in a preheated convection oven. Serve at room temperature.

3.45 SQUARES CHEESE APPETIZER

Total time of cooking
40 minutes
Prep time 10 minutes
Cook time 30 minutes

Serving
16

Nutrition facts
(Per serving)
Calories 133
Fat 10.7g
Protein 8.7g
Carbs 0.6g

Ingredients:
- 1 pound of Cheddar cheese shredded
- 2 jalapeno peppers, chopped and seeded
- 4 eggs
- 1 teaspoon of onion minced

Instructions:
Follow the instructions below to make squares cheese appetizer.
1.Preheat the convection oven to 325°F.
2.Crack eggs into a food processor and process until eggs turn frothy.
Now add cheddar cheese, jalapeno peppers, and onion and again process until creamy and smooth. Spread the batter into 8x8 inches baking dish.
3.Bake in the preheated convection oven until set,25 to 30 minutes, cool for 5 minutes, cut into squares and serve.

3.46 ASPARAGUS CHEESY SNACK

Total time of cooking
25 minutes
Prep time 15 minutes
Cook time 10 minutes

Serving
2

Nutrition facts
(Per serving)
Calories 658
Fat 49.6g
Protein 17.2g
Carbs 39.8g

Ingredients:
- 6 asparagus spears, cut into 1-inch pieces, trims ends
- 1 pizza crust prebaked
- 1/2 cup of mayonnaise
- 2 egg whites
- 2 tablespoons of Parmesan cheese grated
- 1/4 teaspoon of dry mustard

Instructions:
Follow the instructions below to make an asparagus cheesy snack.
1.Preheat the convection oven to 425°F.
2.Boil water in a saucepan and cook asparagus until they turn bright green, for 1 to 2 minutes. Drain and rinse with cold water.
3.Mix parmesan cheese, mayonnaise, and dry mustard in a bowl.
4.Beat egg whites for 4 to 5 minutes; fold the egg whites into a mayonnaise mixture.
5.Spread prebaked pizza crust into a baking sheet, place asparagus on the crust, and spread mayonnaise mixture on top.
6.Bake in the preheated convection oven for around 8 to 10 minutes and serve.

3.47 CHEESE OLIVES BAKED

Total time of cooking
25 minutes
Prep time 10 minutes
Cook time 15 minutes

Serving
9

Nutrition facts
(Per serving)
Calories 110
Fat 8g
Protein 4g
Carbs 5.7g

Ingredients:
- 1 cup of Cheddar cheese shredded
- 24 green olives pimento-stuffed
- 1/2 cup of all-purpose flour
- 2 tablespoons of softened butter
- 1/8 teaspoon of cayenne pepper

Instructions:
Follow the instructions below to make cheese olives baked.
1.Preheat the convection oven to 375°F.
2.In a medium-sized bowl, combine butter and cheese and stir in the flour and cayenne pepper into the butter and cheese mixture. Mix well. Cover each green olive around one table-spoon of dough and give the dough a ball shape with your hands. Transfer the wrapped olives into a baking sheet.
3.Bake in a preheated convection oven for 15 minutes or until it turns light golden brown.

3.48 CHEDDAR BACON GARLIC BREAD

Total time of cooking
25 minutes
Prep time 10 minutes
Cook time 15 minutes

Serving
8

Nutrition facts
(Per serving)
Calories 252
Fat 18g
Protein 6g
Carbs 16g

Ingredients:
- 1 cup of shredded cheddar cheese
- 1 French baguette
- 1/4 cup of chopped green onions
- 1/2 cup of softened butter
- 1/2 cup of cooked bacon
- 2 teaspoons of mustard
- 1 teaspoon of lemon juice
- 1/2 teaspoon of minced garlic

Instructions:
Follow the instructions below to make cheddar bacon garlic bread.
1.Preheat the convection oven to 325°F.
2.Slice the baguette into 1-inch slices and do not cut till the bottom.
3.In a mixing bowl, combine all the other ingredients, and between the slices of baguette, stuff the cheese mixture.
4.Wrap foil around the baguette and bake for 10 to 15 minutes until cheese melts down.
5.Serve warm.

3.49 STUFFED PIZZA MUSHROOMS

Total time of cooking
30 minutes
Prep time 10 minutes
Cook time 20 minutes

Serving
24 mushrooms

Nutrition facts
(Per serving)
Calories 181
Fat 9g
Protein 15g
Carbs 16g

Ingredients:
- 24 mushrooms
- Mini pepperoni
- 1 can of pizza sauce
- Mozzarella cheese
- 2 teaspoons of olive oil
- Basil for serving
- 1 clove of garlic

Instructions:
Follow the instructions below to make stuffed pizza mushrooms.
1. Preheat the convection oven to 350°F.
2. Remove stems from mushrooms and clean them. Scoop out the inside of mushrooms and make room for filling.
3. Chop mushroom stems, and over medium heat, add olive oil, garlic, and chopped mushroom stems to a frying pan. Cook for around 5 minutes and let it cool down.
4. Stuff mushroom caps with mushroom stems. Top each mushroom with one tablespoon of pizza sauce, three mini pepperonis, and one tablespoon of cheese.
5. Bake for around 18 to 20 minutes or until mushrooms are fully done and cheese turned brown. Serve and enjoy.

3.50 BEST ARTICHOKE AND SPINACH DIP

Total time of cooking
40 minutes
Prep time 10 minutes
Cook time 30 minutes

Serving
12

Nutrition facts
(Per serving)
Calories 292
Fat 20g
Protein 12g
Carbs 15g

Ingredients:
- 1 1/2 cups of divided shredded mozzarella cheese
- 14 oz marinated chopped artichoke hearts
- 8 oz of softened cream cheese
- 10 oz of frozen spinach chopped (defrosted)
- 1/2 cup of parmesan cheese shredded
- 2/3 cup of sour cream
- 1/2 cup of gruyere cheese shredded
- 1/3 cup of mayonnaise
- 2 cloves of garlic minced
- 1 baguette and olive oil for serving

Instructions:
Follow the instructions below to make the best artichoke and spinach dip.
1. Preheat the convection oven to 350°F.
2. In a medium-sized bowl, combine sour cream, cream cheese, mayonnaise, and garlic using a hand mixer until creamy.
3. Fold in parmesan cheese, gruyere cheese,1 cup of mozzarella cheese, artichoke, and spinach.
4. Spread into a 9x9 inches casserole dish and sprinkle the top with the remaining 1/2 cup of mozzarella cheese.
5. Bake for around 25 to 30 minutes or until cheese is browned and bubbly.
6. Cut the French baguette into 1/2-inch slices and brush olive oil into one side of each slice. Broil the oil-coated side of the baguette for about 2 minutes.
7. Rub each slice of baguette with a clove of minced garlic and serve with dip.

Total time of cooking
25 minutes
Prep time: 15 minutes
Cook time: 10 minutes

Servings
24

Nutrition facts
(per serving)
Calories 233 kcal
Fat 21g
Protein 6g
Carbs 9g

Ingredients
- cups plain mixed nuts
- tablespoons fresh rosemary, chopped
- 1/3 cup extra-virgin olive oil
- teaspoons fresh thyme, chopped
- 2 tbsp. fresh oregano, chopped
- cayenne pepper (1 teaspoon)
- 1 tablespoon paprika (smoked)
- Sea salt with a flaky texture, to taste
- 2 tablespoons powdered garlic

Instructions
1.Preheat oven to 350 degrees Fahrenheit. Using parchment paper, line a baking sheet.
2.Toss the nuts in a large mixing basin to blend. Whisk together the olive oil, herbs, and spices in a medium mixing basin. Toss the nuts in the seasoned oil and toss well to mix.
3.Arrange the nuts equal on the prepared baking sheet, then season with flaky sea salt evenly.
4.Bake for 12 minutes, or until the nuts smell toasted. Allow cooling fully before storing in an airtight container until ready to serve (up to three weeks).

Total time of cooking
1 hour
Prep Time: 30 minutes
Cook Time: 30 minutes

Servings
4

Nutrition facts
(per serving)
Calories 115kcal
Protein 2g
Fat 4g
Carbs 19g

Ingredients
- 1 tsp coarse salt
- medium russet potatoes
- 1 tbsp oil

Instructions
1.Begin by chopping up a couple of medium russet potatoes. This will serve four people. Preheat the oven to 425 degrees Fahrenheit with convection. If you don't have convection, try 450° or 425°. However, it will take a little longer.
2.If desired, peel the potatoes. Cut your fries in half. Place in cold water for 15 to 20 minutes to soak. Place the fries on a towel to dry after rinsing them with cold water. After drying the bowl, return the fries to it and stir in roughly a tablespoon of oil.
3.Using aluminium foil and a rack, prepare a baking sheet. PAM is sprayed over the surface.
4.Place the fries on a rack that has been prepared. They should not overlap. However, they may brush up against one other. A small sprinkling of coarse salt will be enough.
5.Bake until golden brown, about 30 minutes. It takes around 30 minutes.

3.53 HOMEMADE CHICKEN NUGGETS

Total time of cooking
25 minutes
Prep Time: 10 minutes
Cook Time: 15 minutes

Servings
12

Nutrition facts
(per serving)
Calories 54kcal
Fat 1g
Protein 6g
Carbs 5g

Ingredients
- chicken breasts, skinless and boneless, trimmed
- tbsp. grated Parmesan cheese
- bread crumbs (eight teaspoons)
- 1/2 teaspoon salt
- 1/4 teaspoon pepper

Instructions
1.Preheat the oven to 375 degrees convection.
2.Prepare a baking sheet. To make clean up easier, line the pan with foil. The nuggets will be crispy all over if you use a rack. Then a nice squirt of PAM. If you don't have a rack, you'll have to turn in the nuggets after 8-10 minutes if you don't have one.
3.2 medium skinless, boneless chicken breasts, pat dry and trim (about 1 pound). Cut the breasts into 1 to 12-inch nuggets, about 6-7 nuggets each breast. Pat dry once more.
4.In a small pan or basin, whisk together two egg whites or one whole egg. Combine 8 tablespoons bread crumbs and 2 tablespoons grated Parmesan cheese in a second shallow pan. Season with salt and pepper to taste.
5.Stir the chicken in the egg mixture to coat it. With a fork, pick up the nuggets and shake off any extra egg. Place the nuggets on the rack after thoroughly coating them in the bread crumb mixture.
6.To keep the coated nuggets from drying out too much in the oven, lightly spray them with PAM.
7.Bake for 13 minutes until golden brown, and the thickest part reaches 165°F.

3.54 HOMEMADE FISH STICKS

Total time of cooking
20 minutes
Prep Time: 10 minutes
Cook Time: 10 minutes

Servings
4

Nutrition facts
(per serving)
Calories 309.5kcal
Fat: 10.1g
Protein: 51.1g
Carbs 6.8 g

Ingredients
- A single egg
- 1 tablespoon melted butter
- 1 pound fillets of fish
- 1/3 cup parmesan cheese, grated
- 1/2 teaspoon paprika
- Bread crumbs, 1/3 cup
- 1 tsp parsley (dry)

Instructions
1.Preheat the oven to 450 degrees Fahrenheit.
2.Beat the egg in a small dish. Combine the bread crumbs, Parmesan cheese, paprika, and parsley in a separate shallow dish.
3.Cut the fish into strips (about 3" long and 1/2 inch broad).
4.Each strip should be dipped in the egg, then into the crumb mixture.
5.Put the fish on a baking sheet that has been oiled.
6.Over the fish, drizzle the melted butter.
7.7-10 minutes in the oven, or until salmon flakes readily with a fork.

3.55 BUFFALO CHICKEN BITES WITH SPINACH AND PARMESAN CHEESE

Total time of cooking

40 mins
Prep time: 20 minutes
Cook time: 20 minutes

Serving

6

Nutrition facts

(per serving)
Calories 579kcal
Protein 20g
Fat 20g
Carbs: 80g

Ingredients

For the filling:
- Blue cheese (95 g)
- 280 g cooked chicken, shredded
- Optional: 1 tbsp barbeque sauce
- 25 g parmesan cheese, shredded
- spinach, 75 g
- a tbsp of spicy sauce sriracha

For the dough:
- 210 g wholemeal flour
- 1 egg
- 340 g flour
- 450-500 mL full milk
- 1 teaspoon salt
- 25 g yeast, fresh
- 1 tsp freshly ground pepper
- 1 tbsp olive oil
- 1 tbsp sugar

Instructions

1.Begin by creating the dough by combining all of the flour types and the salt and pepper in a large mixing basin. To homogenize them, give everything a thorough mix. In the middle, make a well and put it aside.

2.Combine the yeast, sugar, and part of the warm milk or warm water in a cup or small basin. Mix the yeast and sugar until they are completely loose. Pour this into the well and let it for 10-15 minutes, or until the yeast begins to bubble.

3.While you're waiting for the yeast to bubble up, shred the chicken and combine it with the stilton cheese, grated Grana Padano, barbecue sauce, and spicy sauce in a mixing bowl. Combine all ingredients and put them aside.

4.Start kneading the flour, salt, yeast, and milk into a good dough after the yeast has bubbled up and is ready to use. Knead for a few minutes, then leave it aside. Form the dough into a ball with some oil. Cover with a kitchen towel and cling film. Allow for a good 20 to 1 hour of proofing time, depending on the temperature and atmospheric conditions.

5.Preheat the oven to 190 degrees Celsius (400 degrees Fahrenheit), and prepare a bigger baking pan or baking sheet with parchment paper. For optimal results, place the oven rack in the middle of the oven.

6.Cut the dough into 4 to 5 equal pieces and place it on a floured surface. Each piece of dough should be rolled and stretched into a 25–30 cm (12in) long rope-like portion.

7.Form the rope-like dough into a rectangle shape with the assistance of a rolling pin. One by one, complete the tasks. Using a small teaspoon and a fork, distribute the filling throughout the whole length of the rectangle strip, more towards one side, leaving a space on edge.

8.Fold the dough in half, gently overlapping the edges. Carry on with the remaining three ropes/rectangular stips in the same manner. Cut the ropes into 11-12 pieces using a knife (less if you want them larger).

9.As you cut the buffalo bits, place them on the prepared tray/ sheet, leaving a finger's width between them. Bake them for 18 minutes at 375°F, until well browned on top.

10.When they're done, take them out of the oven and brush them with melted butter just before serving.

3.56 BEET AND GOAT CHEESE APPETIZERS

Total time of cooking
60 minutes

Serving
6-8

Nutrition facts
(per serving)
Calories 290kcal
Fat 3g
Protein 10g
Carbs 26g

Ingredients
- 1 can beets, sliced
- 1/3 cup of canola oil
- 1 can Pillsbury biscuits (homestyle)
- A quarter cup of apple cider vinegar
- tbsp water
- 1/2 red onion, thinly sliced
- 1 tablespoon dried oregano
- 1 cup extra virgin olive oil for brushing
- 1 goat cheese log, tiny

Instructions
1.In a large mixing basin, combine canola oil, apple cider vinegar, 3 tablespoons water, and 1 tablespoon oregano. Season with salt and pepper to taste. Mix thoroughly. Add the beets and red onion slices. Place something aside.
2.Preheat the oven to 375 degrees Fahrenheit. Open the Pillsbury biscuits and cut each one in half. Each half should be pressed into the muffin pan. Brush with olive oil and a little dusting of oregano. Bake for 10 minutes, or until gently browned.
3.While the biscuits are baking, cut the beets in a tiny chopper a spoonful at a time (about half) until you have small pieces.
4.Take the biscuits out of the oven. Make a tiny depression in the middle of each biscuit with a little spoon. Fill with beet mixture (about 1/2 teaspoon per person). Then sprinkle goat cheese crumbles on top. In addition, a half teaspoon of cheese. Brush with olive oil one more and sprinkle with oregano powder. Bake for a further 13 minutes, until they are golden brown and crispy. More olive oil or olives might be added to the dish. Enjoy!

3.57 CINNAMON ROLL SMOKIES

Total time of cooking
45 minutes
Prep time: 25 minutes
Cook time: 20 minutes

Servings
32

Nutrition facts
(per serving)
Calories 470kcal
Fat18g
Protein 7g
Carbs 68g

Ingredients
- 1 small bag cocktail smokies
- 1 can cinnamon rolls

Instructions
1.Preheat the oven to 350 degrees Fahrenheit.
2.Cut each cinnamon bun into four long pieces and flatten each one with your fingers.
3.In each strip of the cinnamon roll, wrap up a smoke.
4.Place smokies a few inches apart on a baking sheet that has been lightly sprayed. Heat oven till 350°F and bake for 18 minutes, or until golden brown.
5.Remove the cinnamon roll smokies from the oven and set them on a serving platter, iced with the glaze.
6.ENJOY!

Total time of cooking

50 minutes
Prep time: 30 minutes
Cook time: 20 minutes

Servings

4

Nutrition facts

(per serving)
Calories 240kcal
Fat 20g
Protein 11g
Carbs 3g

Ingredients

- 20 tiny peppers (orange and yellow)
- 20 bone-in, skin-on chicken thighs
- mild jalapenos
- ½ cup bacon slices
- ounces cremini mushrooms
- 1-pound applewood bacon
- 1/2-pound Gorgonzola cheese, crumbled
- one red onion
- 1 tablespoon flour (all-purpose)
- 1 cup of half-and-half
- 1 tbsp butter (salted)
- salt and pepper, to taste
- 1/2 teaspoon nutmeg

Instructions

1. Rub chicken with salt, pepper and olive oil on a foil-lined baking sheet and bake at 425° for 30 minutes or until juices flow clear. Allow cooling before serving. Place the applewood bacon on a rack positioned over a cookie sheet and bake for 20 minutes in the same oven. Remove from the oven when it's done but not crispy. Shortly slice into ribbons and layaway.

2. Onions and mushrooms should be thinly sliced. Cook the onions in 1/2 the rendered chicken oil over medium-low heat until they are caramelized but not burnt or crisp. Season with salt and pepper to taste. Remove from the equation. Cook the mushrooms in the leftover chicken grease over medium heat until they are tender. Season with salt and pepper to taste. Remove from the equation.

3. Cook 1 minute over medium heat, constantly stirring until the flour and butter is a light amber colour. 12 and 12 are added together. When the sauce starts to thicken, add approximately a handful of crumbled Gorgonzola cheese at a time, frequently stirring until the cheese is melted. Add roughly a half teaspoon of nutmeg to the mixture.

4. Remove and discard the chicken skin. Add the chicken to the cheese sauce after shredding it with your hands. Toss in the applewood bacon ribbons with the sauce.

5. Cut the tops off each pepper (as little as possible) and scoop out the ribs and seeds as the sauce cools. Fill each pepper with the sauce mixture, cramming it in as tightly as possible.

6. Wrap one piece of bacon around the open end of each pepper the long way, being careful to fill the hole with the bacon. With a little overlap, the bacon should meet. Cut off the extra bacon slice and wrap it around the pepper in the other direction. (It will resemble how you would wrap a ribbon around a gift.) Using a toothpick, secure the bacon to the pepper. Rep with the remaining peppers.

7. Bake the peppers on a rack placed over a baking sheet at 400 degrees for 15 minutes, or until the bacon is crisp.

8. Mini peppers wrapped with bacon and stuffed

9. Serve 5 peppers on a dish as appetizers or with a lovely tossed salad for supper.

3.59 BBQ CHICKEN WINGS

Total time of cooking
60 minutes
Prep time: 15 minutes
Cook time: 45 minutes

Servings
4

Nutrition facts
(per serving)
Calories 472 kcal
Fat 31g
Protein 33g
Carbs 14g

Ingredients
- 1 tablespoon of onion flakes
- 1 cup diet coca-cola
- 1 garlic clove, minced
- 1 teaspoon of lemon juice
- 1 tbsp Worcestershire sauce
- 1-ounce chicken wings
- 1/4 cup tomato paste (no salt)
- 1 salt tube

Instructions
1.Combine cola and tomato paste in a saucepan and stir to combine. Bring all of the ingredients, except the chicken, and boil it.
2.Reduce heat and cook for 5 minutes. In a baking pan, pour the sauce over the chicken wings and let them marinate for 30 minutes at room temperature.
3.Return the sauce to the pan after removing the chicken wings. Heat the oven at 350°F and bake the chicken wings for 40 to 45 minutes.
4.When the chicken wings are done, pour the sauce over them and serve.

3.60 CINNAMON SWEET POTATO CHIPS

Total time of cooking
30 minutes
Prep time: 5 minutes
Cook time: 25 minutes

Servings
4

Nutrition facts
(per serving)
Calories 115kcal
Fat 4g
Protein 2g
Carbs 19g

Ingredients
- 1/2 teaspoon salt
- peeled & thinly sliced sweet potatoes
- 1 tsp brown sugar
- 1/2 tsp cinnamon
- 1 tbsp butter, melted

Instructions
1.Heat the oven to 400° F.Two baking sheets should be greased.
2.Arrange sweet potato slices on baking pans in a single layer. In a small dish, combine the butter, salt, brown sugar, and cinnamon; brush over sweet potato slices.
3.Bake for 20 to 25 minutes in a preheated oven until the edges curl upwards.

3.61 SPINACH CHIPS

Total time of cooking
25 minutes
Prep time: 5 minutes
Cook time: 20 minutes

Servings
4

Nutrition facts
(per serving)
Calories 147kcal
Fat 14g
Protein 3g
Carbs 4g

Ingredients
- 1 tbsp olive oil
- 1 spinach handfuls
- 1/8 teaspoon salt
- A half teaspoon of Italian herb spice

Instructions
1.Combine all ingredients and bake for 9 to 12 minutes at 350°F.

3.62 SEASONED OYSTER CRACKERS

Total time of cooking
1 hr 30 minutes
Prep time: 1 Hr & 10 minutes
Cook time: 20 minutes

Servings
4

Nutrition facts
(per serving)
Calories 233 Kcal
Fat 21g
Protein 6g
Carbs 9g

Ingredients
- Oyster crackers, 12-ounce pkg
- 1 teaspoon dried dill
- 3/4 cup extra virgin olive oil
- 1 pound ranch dressing mix
- A half teaspoon of garlic granules

Instructions
1.Mix all ingredients together
2.Let sit for at least 1 hour
3.Bake at 250F / 121C for 15-20 minutes
Recipes

3.63 CRISPY TOFU BITES

Total time of cooking
2 hrs 10 minutes
Prep Time: 1 hr 40 minutes
Cook Time: 30 minutes

Servings
8

Nutrition facts
(per serving)
Calories 130 kcal
Fat 7g
Protein 9g
Carbs 10g

Ingredients
- 1 tbsp coconut butter
- tbsp. Rice vinegar
- tbsp. Soy sauce
- 1 pound tofu (firm)
- 1 tablespoon sriracha chili sauce
- 1 teaspoon of honey
- A third of a cup of corn starch
- 1 1/2 tbsp garlic powder

Instructions
1. Drain the tofu thoroughly after removing it from the box. Place the tofu on a dish lined with paper towels. Add additional paper towels and a second plate on top. On top of the plate, place a hefty can. Rest for 30 minutes al least.
2. Whisk together the coconut oil, vinegar, soy sauce, Sriracha honey, and garlic powder in a small bowl.
3. Slice the tofu into 1-inch pieces once it has drained. Make 1.5-inch triangles out of the slices. Place the pieces in a big zip-top plastic bag and seal them.
4. Fill the bag with the marinade. Tofu should be marinated for 1 to 1.5 hours.
5. Preheat oven to about 375 degrees Fahrenheit. Using parchment paper, line a baking sheet.
6. Separate the tofu from the marinade and place it on the baking sheet that has been prepared.
7. Sift the corn starch over the tofu in an equal layer. Sprinkle the pieces with salt and pepper once more.
8. Bake it for 25 minutes (at least), until golden brown and crisp. Halfway through baking, flip the tofu over to crisp the other side.
9. Serve the tofu with a sweet spicy or soy dipping sauce while it's still heated. Tofu may be kept in the refrigerator for up to five days if stored in an airtight container

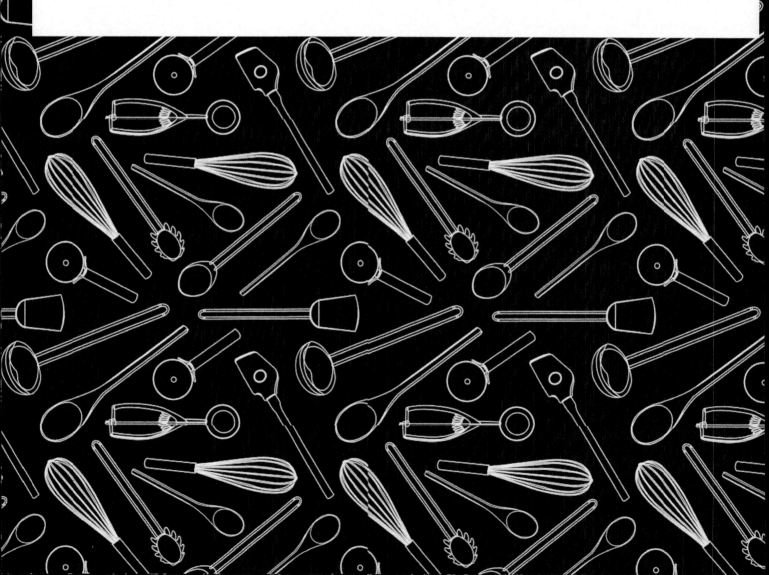

Chapter 4: Vegetable Recipes

4.1 CABBAGE WEDGES ROASTED

Total time of cooking
35 minutes
Prep time 10 minutes
Cook time 25 minutes

Serving
4

Nutrition facts
(Per serving)
Calories 182
Fat 14.4g
Protein 3g
Carbs 13.4g

Ingredients:
- 1 medium green cabbage
- Salt and ground black pepper
- Olive oil for drizzling
- 3 tablespoons of sherry vinegar
- 1 teaspoon of Dijon mustard
- Grated parmesan cheese for garnishing
- 4 tablespoons of olive oil

Instructions:
Follow the instructions below to make cabbage wedges roasted.
1.Preheat the convection oven to 425°F.
2.Cut cabbage into a similar size of eight wedges—place wedges on a baking tray lined with baking paper. Drizzle olive oil on each side of cabbage and sprinkle salt and fresh ground pepper on top and mix lightly with your hands to coat.
3.Roast in the convection oven until it turns brown on the upper side for around 20 to 25 minutes.
4.Meanwhile, take a bowl and whisk the sherry vinegar with Dijon mustard, then add the 3 tablespoons of olive oil and mix well until creamy mixture forms.
5.When cabbage is roasted. Transfer wedges onto a plate and drizzle the vinegar topping and sprinkle with grated parmesan and serve.

4.2 DIJON CRISPY SMASHED POTATO

Total time of cooking

30 minutes
Prep time 10 minutes
Cook time 20 minutes

Serving

6

Nutrition facts

(Per serving)
Calories 135.7
Fat 4.7g
Protein 2.3g
Carbs 21.7g

Ingredients:

- 24 ounces of baby potatoes red
- 3 cloves of minced garlic
- 2 teaspoons of honey
- 2 tablespoons of Dijon mustard
- 1/2 teaspoon of dried thyme
- 1 tablespoon of whole-grain Dijon mustard
- 1/2 teaspoon of dried rosemary
- Salt and ground black pepper to taste

Instructions:

Follow the instructions below to make Dijon crispy smashed potatoes.

1. Preheat the convection oven to 400°F.coat a baking sheet with baking spray.
2. Boil potatoes and drain water.
3. In a small-sized mixing bowl, whisk Dijon mustard, olive oil, whole grain mustard, honey, garlic, rosemary, and thyme, and season with salt and pepper and mix.
4. Place potatoes onto a coated baking tray. Carefully smash the potatoes to flatten but still should remain in one piece with a potato masher. Brush all potatoes with mustard mixture.
5. Bake potatoes for 18 to 20 minutes in a convection oven until they turn golden and crispy. Serve warm.

4.3 VEGETABLE CHEESY CASSEROLE

Total time of cooking

50 minutes
Prep time 10 minutes
Cook time 40 minutes

Serving

4

Nutrition facts

(Per serving)
Calories 513
Fat 35g
Protein 21g
Carbs 29g

Ingredients:

- 1/2 pound of frozen green beans
- 4 ounces of crispy French's onions(divided)
- 1/2 pound of frozen cauliflower and broccoli mixture
- 2 cups of cheddar cheese shredded(divided)
- 1 can of cream of mushroom soup
- 1/4 cup of milk or water
- 1/2 teaspoon of garlic powder

Instructions:

Follow the instructions below to make a vegetable cheesy casserole.

1. Preheat the convection oven to 325°F.Cook green beans and cauliflower, and broccoli according to your package directions until they become crispy.
2. In a medium-sized mixing bowl, mix broccoli, green beans, cauliflower, cream of mushroom soup, garlic powder,1 1/2 cups of cheese, milk, and half of the crispy onions. Pour the mixture into a casserole dish and spread the remaining cheese on the top.
3. Bake in a preheated convection oven for around 30 minutes, spread the remaining crispy onions on top, and bake for another 10 minutes.

4.4 ROASTED BROWN SUGAR RUTABAGA

Total time of cooking

1 hour
Prep time 5 minutes
Cook time 55 minutes

Serving

4

Nutrition facts

(Per serving)
Calories 230
Fat 10g
Protein 4g
Carbs 35g

Ingredients:

- 3 pounds of rutabaga
- 2 tablespoons of brown sugar
- 1 tablespoon of olive oil
- 2 tablespoons of butter
- 1/2 teaspoon of thyme
- Salt and pepper to taste

Instructions:

Follow the instructions below to make roasted brown sugar rutabaga.

1.Preheat the convection oven to 400°F.Peel rutabaga skin and cut into 1-inch cubes. Mix with olive oil, salt, thyme, and pepper.

2.Spread coated rutabaga onto a large-sized roasting pan and roast in convection for 45 to 50 minutes or until they become tender and golden.

3.Take out the pan from the convection oven, spread brown sugar and butter over rutabaga, mix for coating, and roast for more 5 minutes.

4.Serve hot and enjoy.

4.5 CLASSIC ITALIAN PARMESAN EGGPLANT

Total time of cooking

55 minutes

Serving

8

Nutrition facts

(Per serving)
Calories 339
Fat 2g
Protein 31g
Carbs 39g

Ingredients:

- 1 1/2-2 pounds of eggplant sliced (cut into 1/4-inch slices)
- 4 eggs
- 26 ounces of readymade pasta sauce
- 2 cups of bread crumbs
- 16 ounces of shredded mozzarella cheese
- 1/2 cup of flour
- 1/2 cup of shredded parmesan cheese
- 1/4 cup of chopped fresh parsley or basil
- 1/3 cup of shredded parmesan cheese
- 1/2 teaspoon of basil
- 1 lemon zest
- 1/2 teaspoon garlic powder

Instructions:

1.Preheat the convection oven to 400°F.Arrange two baking sheets with parchment paper and keep them aside.

2.Cut eggplant slices with 1/4-inch thickness. And coat with salt and let stand for 20 minutes.

3.In a bowl, whisk together eggs. In another mixing bowl, add the flour, and in the third mixing bowl, mix parmesan, breadcrumbs, lemon zest, basil, and garlic powder and keep all 3 bowls aside.

4.Now rinse salted eggplant under cold water and pat dry eggplant with a kitchen towel.

5.Coat all slices of eggplant one by one, first in the flour, then in egg, and lastly in the breadcrumb mixture. Transfer all the eggplant slices to a prepared baking sheet—spray eggplants with cooking spray.

6.Bake in a preheated convection oven for 10 minutes, then remove the eggplant baking sheet from the oven and lower the temperature to 350°F.

7.Spread a layer of pasta sauce in the bottom of a 9x13 baking dish, then a layer of 1/3 of the eggplant slices, herbs, parmesan cheese, and mozzarella cheese. Repeat the procedure of layers finishing with cheese on top.

8.Bake for 25 to 30 and serve warm.

4.6 TASTY VEGETABLE LASAGNA

Total time of cooking
55 minutes
Prep time 10 minutes
Cook time 30 minutes

Serving
6

Nutrition facts
(Per serving)
Calories 329
Fat 7.2g
Protein 17.2g
Carbs 53.3g

Ingredients:
- 1 package of instant lasagna noodles (16 ounces)
- 1 cup of mozzarella cheese shredded
- 1 can of diced tomatoes (16 ounces)
- 1 head broccoli (cut into florets)
- 2 large diced zucchinis
- 1 large diced eggplant
- 1 cup of ricotta cheese
- 2 summer diced squash
- 2 large shredded carrots
- 1 bunch chopped and washed of fresh spinach

Instructions:
Follow the instructions below to make tasty vegetable lasagna.
1. Preheat the convection oven to 350°F. Grease baking dish of 9x13 inches.
2. Spread a layer of tomatoes at the bottom of a baking dish, followed by a layer of lasagna carrots, spinach, summer squash, zucchini, eggplant, and broccoli. Sprinkle oregano, salt, and pepper on top. Repeat the procedure of layering, finishing with a layer of cheeses on top.
3. Bake in a preheated convection oven for 25 to 30 minutes.

4.7 ROOT VEGETABLES ROASTED

Total time of cooking
55 minutes
Prep time 10 minutes
Cook time 45 minutes

Serving
6

Nutrition facts
(Per serving)
Calories 242
Fat 7g
Protein 3g
Carbs 43g

Ingredients:
- 3 pounds of assorted root vegetables (chopped into 1 1/2-inch piece)
- 4 cloves of minced garlic
- 1 red onion large (chopped into 1 1/2-inch piece)
- 3 tablespoon of olive oil
- 1 teaspoon of dried rosemary
- 1 teaspoon of salt
- Cracked pepper to taste

Instructions:
Follow the instructions below to make root vegetables roasted.
1. Preheat the convection oven to 375°F. With baking paper, line a cookie sheet.
2. Gather all vegetables, onion, and garlic minced in a large-sized bowl. Add olive oil, rosemary, ground pepper, and salt.
3. Mix well until vegetables are fully coated (use your hands to toss the vegetables)
4. Spread on a cookie sheet evenly.
5. Roast at 375°F in a preheated convection oven for 40 to 45 minutes. Turns vegetables halfway through cooking with a spatula.
6. Serve warm and enjoy.

4.8 OVEN–BAKED PARMESAN TOMATOES

Total time of cooking

25 minutes
Prep time 10 minutes
Cook time 15 minutes

Serving

6

Nutrition facts

(Per serving)
Calories 53
Fat 3g
Protein 2g
Carbs 3g

Ingredients:

- 3 large red ripe tomatoes(halved)
- 1/4 cup of parmesan cheese grated
- 3 tablespoons of fresh herbs (oregano, parsley, and basil)
- 3/4 cup of fresh bread crumbs
- 1 clove of minced garlic
- Salt and black pepper (according to taste)
- 1 tablespoon of olive oil

Instructions:

Follow the instructions below to make oven-baked parmesan tomatoes.
1.Preheat the convection oven to 375°F.
2.In a small-sized bowl, combine cheese, breadcrumbs, herbs, olive oil, pepper, and salt. Toss until fully combined.
3.Spread sliced tomatoes in a baking dish, sprinkle with pepper and salt, and spread the breadcrumb mixture on top.
2.Bake in a preheated convection oven for 10 to 15 minutes until crumbs turn light brown. Do not over-bake the tomatoes.

4.9 CRISPY AND TASTY BRUSSELS SPROUTS

Total time of cooking

35 minutes
Prep time 10 minutes
Cook time 25 minutes

Serving

4

Nutrition facts

(Per serving)
Calories 202
Fat 11g
Protein 5.8g
Carbs 25.3g

Ingredients:

- 1 1/2 pounds of Brussels sprouts
- 2 tablespoons of balsamic vinegar
- 3 tablespoons of olive oil
- 2 tablespoons of honey or maple syrup
- 1/4 teaspoon of black pepper
- 1 teaspoon of salt
- 1 teaspoon of hot sauce plus more to drizzle

Instructions:

Follow the instructions below to make crispy and tasty brussels sprouts.
1.Preheat the convection oven to 375°F.
2.Cut off the hard ends of the brussels sprouts. Slice sprouts in half lengthwise and transfer them to a large-sized bowl.
3.Mix sprouts with salt, olive oil, and ground black pepper.
4.Spread the sprouts on a non-stick baking sheet evenly.
5.Roast in a preheated convection oven for around 25 minutes until they become light brown and tender.
6.Meanwhile, whisk balsamic vinegar and maple syrup or honey and 1 teaspoon of hot sauce. When sprouts are roasted, pour the mixture over the top and toss to mix. For a more spicy variation, Drizzle hot sauce on top of roasted sprouts and serve immediately.

4.10 ROASTED PARMESAN GARLIC POTATOES

Total time of cooking
35 minutes
Prep time 10 minutes
Cook time 25 minutes

Serving
6

Nutrition facts
(Per serving)
Calories 259.1
Fat 10.1g
Protein 6.6g
Carbs 36.5g

Ingredients:
- 3 pounds of red potatoes, halved
- 1/3 cup of grated Parmesan
- 5 cloves of garlic(minced)
- 2 tablespoons of unsalted butter
- 2 tablespoons of olive oil
- 2 tablespoons of parsley leaves(chopped)
- 1/2 teaspoon of dried oregano
- Ground black pepper and salt (to taste)
- 1/2 teaspoon of dried basil
- 1 teaspoon of dried thyme

Instructions:
Follow the instructions below to make roasted parmesan garlic potatoes.
1.Preheat the convection oven to 375°F.Coat a baking sheet with cooking spray.
2.Spread potatoes on a prepared baking dish in a single layer. Add olive oil, thyme, garlic, basil, oregano, and parmesan. Sprinkle with salt and black pepper on top. Lightly toss to mix.
3.Roast in a preheated convection oven for 20 to 25 minutes or until potatoes turn crispy. Place butter over Hot potatoes and garnish with parsley.
4.Serve warm and enjoy.

4.11 TASTY AND QUICK VEGETABLE PASTA SALAD

Total time of cooking
30 minutes
Prep time 10 minutes
Cook time 20 minutes

Serving
4

Nutrition facts
(Per serving)
Calories 486
Fat 29.1g
Protein 11.3g
Carbs 49.1g

Ingredients:
- 1 cup of salad dressing Italian-style
- 1 package of rotini/corkscrew pasta (12 ounces)
- 3 ounces of diced feta cheese
- 1 cubed eggplant
- 2 tomatoes chopped
- 1 green chopped bell pepper
- 1 cubed zucchini
- 1 chopped onion
- 2 tablespoons of olive oil
- 1 clove of minced garlic

Instructions:
Follow the instructions below to make a tasty and quick vegetable pasta salad.
1.Preheat the convection oven to 325°F.
2.Combine eggplant, zucchini, bell pepper, onion, and garlic in a baking dish. Coat with olive oil and bake for around 20 minutes, then allow to cool for some time.
3.Boil rotini pasta and drain and rinse with very cold water.
4.In a bowl, combine the vegetable mixture, tomatoes, pasta, feta cubes, and salad dressing. Toss until fully combined and serve.

4.12 SIMPLE AND TASTY VEGETABLE FRITTATA

Total time of cooking
30 minutes
Prep time 15 minutes
Cook time 15 minutes

Serving
6

Nutrition facts
(Per serving)
Calories 315
Fat 18.7g
Protein 18.3g
Carbs 19.2g

Ingredients:
- 1 large chopped leek (white part only)
- 1 1/2 cups of sliced zucchini (cut in 1/2-inch slices)
- 4 ounces of goat-milk feta cheese crumbled, divided
- 12 eggs large
- 1 1/2 cups of sliced potatoes cooked
- 1 jalapeno pepper, diced and seeded
- 1 cup of baby spinach
- 1 1/2 cups of asparagus (cut into 1/2-inch pieces)
- 2 tablespoons of olive oil
- 1 teaspoon of salt
- 1 pinch of cayenne pepper
- 1/2 teaspoon of ground black pepper

Instructions:
Follow the instructions below to make a tasty vegetable frittata.
1.Preheat the convection oven to 325°F.
2.In a medium skillet, heat oil and cook leek along with a pinch of salt, occasionally stirring, until leeks become translucent and soft, for 5 to 6 minutes. Now add zucchini and jalapeno and sprinkle a pinch of salt. Cook until zucchini changes its color to pale green for around 5 minutes. Then add asparagus and cook for about 1 to 2 minutes, add spinach and top with another pinch of salt, cook until spinach turn wilted,1 minute more. Mix in cooked potatoes and let it stay on heat for 5 more minutes.
3.Into a bowl, crack 12 large eggs. Add salt, pepper, and cayenne pepper. Whisk for 1 minute at least. Pour egg mixture into skillet over vegetables on medium heat. Add 3 ounces of goat cheese mix lightly and top with remaining cheese. Turn off the heat.
4.Bake in the preheated convection oven for around 12 to 15 minutes until eggs are nearly done. Then turn on the broiler and broil frittata for 1 to 2 minutes until it turns brown from the top and serves warm.

4.13 EASY AND DELICIOUS MUSHROOMS ROASTED

Total time of cooking
20 minutes
Prep time 5 minutes
Cook time 15 minutes

Serving
4

Nutrition facts
(Per serving)
Calories 85
Fat 7.4g
Protein 3.5g
Carbs 3.7g

Ingredients:
- 1 pound of mushrooms
- 1 tablespoon of chopped fresh herbs (like thyme and chives)
- 2 tablespoons of olive oil
- 1/2 teaspoon of salt
- 1/4 teaspoon of garlic powder

Instructions:
Follow the instructions below to make mushrooms roasted.
1.Preheat the convection oven to 400°F.
2.Clean mushrooms and pat dry with a kitchen towel, Cut mushrooms in half slices. In a large-sized bowl, coat them with garlic powder, salt, and olive oil—spread mushrooms into a baking paper-lined cookie sheet.
3.Roast for 10 to 15 minutes in a preheated convection oven until mushrooms become tender. Sprinkle fresh herbs on top while serving.

4.14 DELICIOUS ZUCCHINI CASSEROLE

Total time of cooking
55 minutes
Prep time 10 minutes
Cook time 45 minutes

Serving
8

Nutrition facts
(Per serving)
Calories 84
Fat 5g
Protein 2g
Carbs 6g

Ingredients:
- 1 pound of Roma tomatoes (cut into 1/4 inches slices)
- 1 1/2 tablespoons of olive oil
- 1 1/2 pounds of zucchini (cut into 1/2 inches slices)
- 1 clove of minced garlic
- 1/2 teaspoon of Italian seasoning
- Fresh basil and parsley for serving

For topping:
- 1/4 cup of bread crumbs
- 2/3 cup of shredded mozzarella cheese
- 1/2 chopped onion
- 1/4 cup of parmesan cheese fresh
- 2 tablespoons of melted butter
- 1 tablespoon of olive oil

Instructions:
Follow the instructions below to make delicious zucchini casserole.

1. Preheat the convection oven to 350°F.
2. For the topping, cook onion in olive oil until it gets tender for around five minutes and keep aside.
3. Cut tomatoes in slices and absorb liquid by placing on paper towels, about 2 to 3 minutes.
4. Gather zucchini, olive oil, Italian seasoning, and garlic in a bowl. Toss to coat well and sprinkle pepper and salt.
5. Arrange tomatoes and zucchini in 9x3 inches dish. Cover with lid and bake in a convection oven for 25 minutes.
6. Combine all ingredients of topping (including onions from step first and mix well).
7. Remove the lid from the casserole dish, spread topping on top, and bake uncovered for another 20 minutes or until zucchini gets tender.
7. Top casserole with fresh herbs and serve warm.

4.15 TASTY VEGETABLE CASSEROLE

Total time of cooking
45 minutes
Prep time 10 minutes
Cook time 35 minutes

Serving
8

Nutrition facts
(Per serving)
Calories 228
Fat 4.9g
Protein 8.5g
Carbs 16.2g

Ingredients:
- 1 grated and peeled zucchini
- 1 chopped onion
- 1 sliced green onion
- 1/2 chopped green bell pepper
- 1 grated and peeled yellow squash
- 1 cup of buttermilk baking mix
- 1 grated carrot
- 1 cup of shredded Cheddar cheese
- 3 beaten eggs
- 1/4 cup of vegetable oil
- 1 teaspoon of salt
- 2 teaspoons of minced garlic
- 1/2 teaspoon of red pepper flakes
- 3/4 teaspoon of Italian seasoning
- 1/2 teaspoon of paprika
- 1 teaspoon of vegetable oil
- Black pepper ground to taste

Instructions:
Follow the instructions below to make a vegetable casserole.

1. Preheat the convection oven to 325°F.Grease square baking dish of 8 inches.
2. In a skillet, heat 1 teaspoon of vegetable oil on medium heat; stir and cook onion, garlic, and bell pepper in hot oil until they turn tender, for around 5 minutes—transfer mixture to a large-sized bowl.
3. Mix eggs, yellow squash, carrot, zucchini, green onion, baking mix, and 1/2 cup of cheddar cheese,1/4 cup of vegetable oil, salt, paprika, Italian seasoning, red pepper flakes, and black pepper into onion mixture
Pout vegetable mixture into a greased baking dish sprinkles the top with the remaining 1/2 cup of cheddar cheese.
4. Bake in a preheated convection oven for around 35 minutes or until it becomes light brown.

4.16 ROASTED YAMS WITH GINGER, MISO AND SCALLIONS

Total time of cooking
1 hour 5 minutes
Prep time 15 minutes
Cook time 50 minutes

Serving
4-6

Nutrition facts
(Per serving)
Calories 271
Fat 9.8g
Protein 2.9g
Carbs 44.5g

Ingredients:
- 2 to 3 yams (sliced them in half, lengthwise)
- 1 large very finely diced shallot
- 3 sliced Scallions
- 1/4 cup of olive oil or coconut oil
- 1 tablespoon of miso
- Salt to taste
- 2 teaspoons of finely minced ginger
- Olive oil for brushing

Instructions:
Follow the instructions below to make roasted yams.
1.Preheat the convection oven to 375°F.Cut yams into half lengthwise and arrange on a non-stick sheet pan, sliced side down, brush yams with olive oil, and roast in a convection oven for 30 to 40 minutes; when they become tender, flip the sides and broil for 10 minutes for more caramelization.
2.Meanwhile, make ginger shallot miso butter. Heat the olive oil on medium-low heat and add the shallot sauté shallot until turn golden, occasionally stirring for 4 to 5 minutes. Add ginger and cook for 2 to 4 minutes, then add the miso and break it up with and mash using a fork into the mixture as much as possible. Sauté 2 more minutes or so until miso bits turn slightly crispy, then remove from stove.
3.When yams are caramelized, transfer them to a platter and spread on to each yam roasted slice evenly. Sprinkle the top of yams with salt and chopped scallions. Serve along with a salad of your choice.

4.17 DELICIOUS MEDITERRANEAN VEGETABLE SANDWICH GRILLED

Total time of cooking
45 minutes
Prep time 20 minutes
Cook time 25 minutes

Serving
6

Nutrition facts
(Per serving)
Calories 356
Fat 14.8g
Protein 9g
Carbs 48.3g

Ingredients:
- 1 eggplant (cut into strips)
- 2 sliced Portobello mushrooms
- 1 loaf of focaccia bread (1 pound)
- 3 cloves of crushed garlic
- 2 red bell peppers
- 4 tablespoons of mayonnaise
- 2 tablespoons of olive oil(divided)

Instructions:
Follow the instructions below to Mediterranean vegetable sandwich grilled.
1.Preheat the convection oven to 375°F.
2.Brush one tablespoon of olive oil on eggplant and red bell peppers; use more if required. Transfer on a nonstick baking sheet and roast in a preheated convection oven for around 25 minutes until vegetables become tender. Once done, let vegetables cool down.
3.Heat on medium heat one tablespoon of olive oil and add mushrooms and cook until tender. Stir mayonnaise with crushed garlic. Cut focaccia into half lengthwise. Spread garlic mayonnaise mixture on both halves of focaccia bread.
4.Spread the layer of eggplant, peppers, and mushrooms on focaccia bread. Wrap a focaccia sandwich with plastic wrap, place a wooden board on it, and weigh it down with some canned foods. Let sandwich sit down for 2 hours before serving.

Total time of cooking

30 minutes

Prep time 20 minutes

Cook time 10 minutes

Serving

16

Nutrition facts

(Per serving)

Calories 196

Fat 12.6g

Protein 4.8g

Carbs 16g

Ingredients:

- 2 packages of refrigerated crescent rolls (8 ounces)
- 1 package of ranch dressing mix (1 ounce)
- 1 package of softened cream cheese (8 ounces)
- 1 1/2 cups of chopped fresh broccoli
- 1 cup of sour cream
- 1/2 cup of halved and sliced radishes
- 1 chopped red bell pepper
- 1 sliced stalk celery
- 1 grated carrot
- 1 chopped small onion
- 1 teaspoon of dill weed dried
- 1/4 teaspoon of garlic salt

Instructions:

Follow the instructions below to make tasty and easy cheesy vegetable pizza.

1.Preheat the convection oven to 325°F.Coat a jelly roll pan with cooking spray.

2.Spread roll dough into jelly roll pan. Prick holes with a fork and let the dough stand for 10 minutes.

3.Bake the dough in a preheated convection oven for 10 minutes. And allow cooling for some time.

4.In a large-sized bowl, mix cream cheese, sour cream, garlic salt, dill weed, and ranch deep mix. Pour this mixture on baked crust evenly. Arrange carrot, onion, celery, bell pepper, and broccoli on top of the mixture. Cover and let chill a few times. Slice into squares, and serve once chilled.

4.19 DELICIOUS VEGETABLE POT PIE

Total time of cooking

50 minutes

Prep time 10 minutes

Cook time 40 minutes

Serving

6

Nutrition facts

(Per serving)

Calories 380

Fat 21.1g

Protein 6.1g

Carbs 40.8g

Ingredients:

- 2 frozen prepared pie crusts (9 inches)
- 1 can of mixed vegetables (15 ounces)
- 1 lightly beaten egg
- 1 can of Campbell's condensed cream of potato soup (10.75 ounces)
- 1/2 cup of milk
- 1/2 teaspoon of ground black pepper
- 1/2 teaspoon of thyme dried

Instructions:

Follow the instructions below to make a delicious vegetable pot pie.

1.Preheat the convection oven to 350°F.

2.In a medium-sized bowl, Mix vegetables, potato soup, milk, black pepper, and thyme.

3.Spread filling in the bottom of the pie crust and cover with top crust and crimp the crust edges to seal. Slit the top of the pie crust. With a beaten egg brush on the top of the pie.

4.Bake in a preheated convection oven for around 40 minutes, allow cooling for 5 to 10 minutes before serving.

4.20 CAULIFLOWER MAC AND CHEESE BAKED

Total time of cooking

35 minutes

Prep time 15 minutes

Cook time 20 minutes

Serving

6

Nutrition facts

(Per serving)

Calories 697

Fat 42g

Protein 32g

Carbs 47g

Ingredients:

- 4 cups of cauliflower (chopped into bite-sized pieces)
- 4 cups of cheddar(divided)
- 2 cups of uncooked elbow macaroni
- 1 1/2 cups of milk
- 1/2 cup of parmesan cheese
- 1 cup of light cream
- 1/4 cup of flour
- 1/4 cup of butter
- 1 teaspoon of garlic powder
- 1/2 teaspoon of salt
- 1/2 teaspoon of onion powder
- 1/2 teaspoon of black pepper

Instructions:

Follow the instructions below to make a cauliflower mac and cheese baked.

1.Preheat the convection oven to 400°F.

2.In salted water, cook macaroni and cauliflower for 5 to 8 minutes. Drain and keep it aside.

3.In a medium-sized saucepan, melt butter on medium heat. Mix in flour and seasonings and cook for 1 minute.

4.Whisk slowly cream and milk, whisking a little bit at a time until mixture turns smooth. Let mixture come to boil while keep stirring once the mixture gets thickens. Remove from stove and stir 3 cups of cheddar cheese and parmesan cheese until melted down. Fold in macaroni and cauliflower and pour into a 9x13 greased pan.

5.Top the mac and cheese with remaining cheddar cheese and bake for around 18 to 20 minutes or until golden browns from the top. Do not overcook.

4.21 BAKED CALIFORNIA VEGETABLE

Total time of cooking

40 minutes

Prep time 10 minutes

Cook time 30 minutes

Serving

10

Nutrition facts

(Per serving)

Calories 471

Fat 39g

Protein 8.5g

Carbs 25.2g

Ingredients:

- 2 bags of California-blend frozen vegetables (20 ounces)
- 1 sleeve of crushed buttery round crackers
- 1 cup of mayonnaise
- 1 cup of onion chopped
- 1 cup of sour cream
- 1 cup of Cheddar cheese shredded
- 1/2 cup of butter melted

Instructions:

Follow the instructions below to make a baked California vegetable.

1.Preheat the convection oven to 325°F.

2.On a double boiler. Steam vegetables with cover until veggies become tender, for 4 to 6 minutes—transfer vegetables into baking dish.

3.Mix sour cream, mayonnaise, cheddar cheese, and onion in a bowl; spread over vegetables. Fold in crushed crackers and melted butter in a separate bowl and pour over the vegetable layer.

4.Bake for around 30 minutes in a preheated convection oven until it becomes bubbly and golden brown in color.

4.22 CORNISH VEGETABLE PASTIES

Total time of cooking
40 minutes
Prep time 10 minutes
Cook time 30 minutes

Serving
4

Nutrition facts
(Per serving)
Calories 687
Fat 44.7g
Protein 17.4g
Carbs 55.4g

Ingredients:
- 1 recipe of whole wheat pastry for a double crust
- 1/4 pound of shredded Cheddar cheese
- 1/4 pound of chopped mushrooms
- 1/4 cup of butter
- 1/4 cup of milk
- 1 large peeled and diced potato
- 1 thinly sliced carrot
- 1 thinly sliced onion
- 1 peeled and diced turnip
- 1 beaten egg
- 2 tablespoons of water
- Salt and pepper to taste
- 1 teaspoon of yeast extract spread
- 1 egg

Instructions:
Follow the instructions below to make Cornish vegetable pasties.
1.Preheat the convection oven to 375°F.
2.Distribute dough into four portions and roll out each portion in a square shape.
3.Add butter to a skillet on medium and melt it down. Add onion and cook for 5 minutes until onion begins to brown. Then add turnip, carrot, mushrooms, potato, and water. Slow down heat and cover with a lid. Let the mixture cook for 10 minutes.
4.In a small-sized bowl, Dissolve yeast in milk. Mix in 1 egg and add this mixture into cooked vegetables. Continue to mix until mixture become thickens, then add cheese, pepper, and salt. Allow cooling for few minutes.
5.Spread 1/4 of filling on each square of pastry. Diagonally fold pastry dough and close edges. Brush with beaten egg on top of the pastry.
6.Arrange pasties on a cookie sheet and bake in a preheated convection oven for around 30 minutes.

4.23 GRILLED POTATO PACKETS (POTATO IN A FOIL)

Total time of cooking
50 minutes
Prep time 10 minutes
Cook time 40 minutes

Serving
4

Nutrition facts
(Per serving)
Calories 280
Fat 9g
Protein 9g
Carbs 44g

Ingredients:
- 3 lbs. potatoes (cut into 1/4-inch slices)
- Mushrooms
- 1 thinly sliced small onion
- 3 tablespoons of butter
- Cheese of your choice
- Salt and pepper to taste

Instructions:
Follow the instructions below to make grilled potato packets (potato in a foil).
1.Preheat the convection oven to 350°F.
2.Spray foil packets with cooking spray: Wash and cut potatoes, onion, and mushrooms into slices. Arrange 1 potato per packet of foil and add any optional toppings if you want. Add butter and Sprinkle salt and pepper on top. Fold each foil packet, tightly close them and transfer them to the cooking sheet.
3.Roast in a preheated convection oven for around 40 minutes and serve warm.

4.24 PATTYPAN SQUASH ROASTED

Total time of cooking
25 minutes
Prep time 10 minutes
Cook time 15 minutes

Serving
12

Nutrition facts
(Per serving)
Calories 63
Fat 5g
Protein 1g
Carbs 5g

Ingredients:
- 1 1/2 pounds of pattypan squash
- 1 clove of minced garlic
- Salt and pepper to taste
- 1 tablespoon of olive oil

Herb oil:
- 2 teaspoons of fresh parsley
- 1 tablespoon of olive oil
- 1/2 tablespoon of fresh basil
- 1/2 teaspoon of lemon zest
- 1/2 teaspoon of fresh dill

- Salt and black pepper to taste

Instructions:
Follow the instructions below to make pattypan squash roasted.
1.Preheat the convection oven to 400°F.
2.Wash and clean pattypan squash and trim from top and bottom. Cut it into 1-inch bite-sized cubes. Mix with olive oil, salt, garlic, and pepper and toss.
3.Roast in a preheated convection oven for 12 to 15 minutes or until it becomes crispy and tender. Also, broil for 1 minute if you like.
4.Meanwhile, chop herbs and whisk herbs with olive oil, lemon zest, and salt.
5.Toss squash with herb oil and serve hot.

4.25 CHEESE AND MUSHROOM STRATA

Total time of cooking
55 minutes
Prep time 10 minutes
Cook time 45 minutes

Serving
8

Nutrition facts
(Per serving)
Calories 343
Fat 19g
Protein 19g
Carbs 25g

Ingredients:
- 8 ounces of cremini mushrooms
- 6 cups of slightly dried bread cubes
- 4 ounces of cubed brie cheese
- 1 cup of shredded mozzarella
- 1 teaspoon of olive oil
- 1 clove of minced garlic
- 1/2 teaspoon of fresh thyme leaves

For egg Mixture:
- 1 1/4 cups of milk
- 4 eggs
- 1/4 teaspoon onion powder
- 1/2 cup of light cream
- 1/2 teaspoon of mustard powder dry
- 1/4 teaspoon of pepper
- 1/2 teaspoon of salt

Instructions:
Follow the instructions below to make cheese and mushroom strata.
1.On medium heat, cook garlic and mushrooms in olive oil until it becomes tender. Keep it aside to cool.
2.Whisk all the egg mixture ingredients in a large-sized bowl, sprinkle with pepper and salt, and put bread cubes, toss. Let stand for 5 minutes and again toss until liquid is totally absorbed in bread cubes. Fold in mushrooms,1/2 of mozzarella, and brie cheese.
3.Spread the mixture to a 9x9 inches greased baking dish, refrigerate with cover for at least 30 minutes or overnight.
4.Preheat the convection oven to 325°F.
5.Bake with lid for 30 minutes. Remove the lid and top with remaining cheese and bake for an additional 10 to 15 minutes.
6.Rest 15 minutes before slicing and serving.

4.26 DELICIOUS RUTABAGA GRATIN

Total time of cooking
45 minutes
Prep time 10 minutes
Cook time 35 minutes

Serving
6

Nutrition facts
(Per serving)
Calories 321.6
Fat 16.72g
Protein 14.08g
Carbs 31.17g

Ingredients:
- 3 1/2 to 4 pounds of cubed rutabaga cubed
- 2 cups of milk
- 1/2 cup of gruyere cheese shredded
- 1/2 cup of chopped onion
- 1 cup of shredded sharp cheddar cheese
- 3 tablespoons of flour
- 1/2 teaspoon of thyme
- 3 tablespoons of butter

Instructions:
Follow the instructions below to make delicious rutabaga gratin.
1.Preheat the convection oven to 350°F.
2.Peel rutabaga and cut into cubes. Pour in a pot of cold water and boil for 10 to 15 minutes, do not overcook. Drain.
3.Meanwhile, on medium-low heat, cook onion in butter for around 5 minutes. Mix flour and thyme and cook for 2 to 3 minutes.
4.Add milk slowly, a little amount at a time, and keep mixing after each addition until the mixture becomes smooth. Cook on medium heat until become bubbly and thick. Remove from stove and fold in cheeses. Sprinkle with pepper and salt.
5.Coat rutabaga in sauce and transfer to a baking sheet. Bake in a preheated convection oven for around 30 to 35 minutes.

4.27 CUCUMBER AND TOMATO BRUSCHETTA

Total time of cooking
15 minutes
Prep time 10 minutes
Cook time 5 minutes

Serving
6

Nutrition facts
(Per serving)
Calories 146
Fat 3g
Protein 4g
Carbs 23g

Ingredients:
- 1 diced English cucumber
- 3 tablespoons of chopped fresh basil
- 1 diced tomato
- 1 tablespoon of olive oil
- 1 clove of garlic minced
- 2 teaspoons of red wine vinegar
- Salt and pepper to taste

For Serving:
- Olive oil
- 1 clove garlic
- 1 baguette

Instructions:
Follow the instructions below to make cucumber and tomato bruschetta.
1.Mix all the topping ingredients in a bowl. Split the baguette into 3/4-inch slices and brush the top of each baguette slice with olive oil.
2.Broil 2 to 3 minutes in a convection oven or until it gets toasted. When done, rub each slice of baguette with a garlic clove. Spoon the cucumber and tomato mixture on top of baguette slices to serve.

Total time of cooking

35 minutes
Prep time 10 minutes
Cook time 25 minutes

Serving

12 muffins

Nutrition facts

(Per serving)
Calories 144
Fat 8g
Protein 10g
Carbs 7g

Ingredients:

• 3 cups of mixed vegetables (mushrooms, broccoli, peppers, spinach, etc.)
• 1 cup of cheddar cheese
• 12 eggs large
• 1/4 cup of parmesan cheese
• 1/4 cup of milk
• 3 tablespoons of minced onion
• 1 teaspoon of oil
• 1/2 teaspoon of dry mustard powder
• 1/2 teaspoon of black pepper and salt to taste

Instructions:

Follow the instructions below to make vegetable egg muffins.
1.Preheat your convection oven to 325°F.
2.Chop all vegetables and mix in one teaspoon of oil until excess liquid is evaporated and vegetables turn crispy and tender. Allow cooling.
3.With cooking spray, grease muffin pan.
4.Distribute the onion, Vegetables, and cheeses evenly in muffin cups.
5.In a large-sized mixing bowl, add eggs, seasonings, and milk. Mix well.
6.Over the top of each muffin cup, pour eggs evenly. Bake for 22 to 25 minutes in a preheated convection oven until set.
7.Let it cools down completely before serving.

4.29 TASTY BAKED DUCHESS POTATOES

Total time of cooking

35 minutes
Prep time 20 minutes
Cook time 15 minutes

Serving

6

Nutrition facts

(Per serving)
Calories 137
Fat 7g
Protein 4g
Carbs 14g

Ingredients:

• 1 1/2 pounds of peeled and quartered potatoes
• 2 eggs(separated)
• 3 tablespoons of butter
• 1/8 teaspoon of nutmeg
• Salt and pepper to taste

Instructions:

Follow the instructions below to make baked duchess potatoes.
1.Preheat your convection oven to 400°F.
2.Boil potatoes in salted water for around 15 to 20 minutes, drain and mash potatoes until smooth and creamy. Mix in three tablespoons of butter and seasonings according to your taste, add egg yolks and stir.
3.Put potato batter into a piping bag. Pipe onto a non-stick cookie sheet.
4.Brush egg whites over the top of piped potatoes and bake in a preheated convection oven for around 10 to 15 minutes or until golden in color.

4.30 BUTTERNUT SQUASH ROASTED

Total time of cooking
40 minutes
Prep time 10 minutes
Cook time 30 minutes

Serving
6

Nutrition facts
(Per serving)
Calories 97
Fat 4g
Protein 1g
Carbs 14g

Ingredients:
- 1 butternut (2-1/2 to 3 pounds)
- Fresh parsley
- 2 tablespoons of olive oil
- Salt and pepper to taste
- 1/2 teaspoon of thyme leaves

Instructions:
Follow the instructions below to make butternut squash roasted.
1.Preheat your convection oven to 400°F.
2.Cut Butternut squash in half lengthwise. Remove the pulp and seeds from the center of the butternut squash. Cut into 1-inch slices across. Peel the skin off the edges and dice into 1-inch cubes.
3.Spread the squash on a nonstick baking sheet and pour olive oil, salt, pepper and thyme on top of butternut squash.
4.Toss to mix and roast in a preheated convection oven for 25 to 30 minutes. Once done, broil for 1 to 2 minutes.
5.Sprinkle with parsley when serving.

4.31 MUSHROOMS WITH MARINARA AND WHITE BEANS

Total time of cooking
25 minutes
Prep time 15 minutes
Cook time 10 minutes

Serving
4

Nutrition facts
(Per serving)
Calories 457.55
Fat 15.38g
Protein 25.15g
Carbs 58.15g

Ingredients:
- 8 oz. mushrooms
- 2 15oz. cans of butter beans
- 4 oz. mozzarella
- 2 cups of marinara
- 2 tablespoons of olive oil
- 2 cloves of garlic
- 1 pinch of red pepper crushed
- 1 pinch of salt and pepper
- 1/2 teaspoon of dried basil

Instructions:
Follow the instructions below to make mushrooms with marinara and white beans.
1.Preheat your convection oven at 375°F.Clean and slice mushrooms. In a deep skillet, add olive oil, mushrooms, and a pinch of salt and pepper and sauté until wilted.
2.Add minced garlic to the skillet and cook 2 more minutes with mushrooms.
3.Add the butter beans, basil, marinara, and red pepper to the skillet and stir everything to mix and cook for 2 to 4 minutes. Shred mozzarella on top of the skillet and cover the skillet with a mozzarella layer. Cover the skillet tightly with foil and transfer to a preheated convection oven and bake for around 5 to 8 minutes.
4.Once the cheese melts down, remove foil from skillet and broil in a convection oven for few minutes to brown the cheese's top. Serve warm with garlic bread as a dipping.

4.32 SPINACH AND CHEESE STUFFED MUSHROOMS

Total time of cooking
40 minutes
Prep time 15 minutes
Cook time 25 minutes

Serving
8

Nutrition facts
(Per serving)
Calories 223
Fat 18.8g
Protein 6.1g
Carbs 9.4g

Ingredients:
- 1 package of mushrooms, stems removed(8 ounces)
- 1 package of frozen chopped spinach (10 ounces)
- 1 chopped onion
- 1 package of cream cheese (8 ounces)
- 4 tablespoons of dry bread crumbs
- 4 tablespoons of Italian-style salad dressing
- 4 tablespoons of Parmesan cheese grated
- 4 tablespoons of butter
- 3 cloves of minced garlic

Instructions:
Follow the instructions below to make spinach and cheese stuffed mushrooms.
1.Preheat your convection oven at 325°F.
2.Arrange mushroom on a cookie baking sheet and brush Italian dressing on both sides of each mushroom cap.
3.Bake in a preheated convection oven until mushrooms become tender, for around 12 minutes. Remove mushrooms from the oven and keep the oven on.
4.On medium-high heat, melt butter in a pan, sauté garlic, and onion in hot butter until onion softens,6 to 8 minutes. Add spinach, parmesan cheese, cream cheese, and 3 tablespoons of bread crumbs and stir into onion mixture until fully mixed.
5.Distribute the spinach mixture on each mushroom caps equally, sprinkle the top with remaining bread crumbs. Again, place the baking sheet in the oven.
6.Bake in a preheated convection oven until the top is golden brown and cheese melts down, around 10 minutes, and serve.

4.33 CHEESY SPINACH LASAGNA

Total time of cooking
1 hour 15 minutes

Serving
8

Nutrition facts
(Per serving)
Calories 476
Fat 24g
Protein 29g
Carbs 37g

Ingredients:
- 9 lasagna noodles
- 15 ounces of ricotta cheese
- 4 cups of pasta sauce
- 4 cups of shredded mozzarella cheese(divided)
- 10 ounces of thawed frozen spinach
- 1/2 cup of parmesan cheese shredded(divided)
- 1 large chopped onion
- 1 egg
- 3 cloves of minced garlic
- 1 tablespoon of olive oil
- 1 tablespoon of fresh parsley
- 2 teaspoons of Italian seasoning
- 1/2 teaspoon of salt

Instructions:
1.Preheat your convection oven at 325°F.Boil lasagna noodles and rinse with cold water, pat dry.
2.On medium heat, heat oil in a large-sized skillet. Add garlic and onion together and cook for 5 minutes. Add Italian seasoning and pasta sauce and cook for 5 more minutes until the mixture gets slightly thickens.
3.Meanwhile, squeeze spinach to remove any extra moisture. Mix in 2 1/2 cups of mozzarella, ricotta cheese,1/4 cup of parmesan, egg, and fresh parsley. Combine until incorporated.
4.Spread one cup of sauce in the bottom of the 9x9 inch baking dish—layer with three lasagna noodles. Add 1/2 of the cheese and spinach mixture and 1/3 of the sauce.
5.Layer 3 more lasagna noodles, remaining 1/3 of cheese and spinach mixture, and 1/3 of the sauce again. End with the last 3 noodles and the remaining amount of sauce.
6.Cover tightly with heavy-duty foil to ensure it is fully sealed and bake in a preheated convection oven for around 45 minutes. After 45 minutes, top with remaining parmesan and mozzarella and bake for additional 10 to 15 minutes or until cheese on top become brown.
7.Cool for 10 minutes before eating.

4.34 TASTY AND EASY CARROT CAKE

Total time of cooking
1 hour 10 minutes
Prep time 10 minutes
Cook time 60 minutes

Serving
10

Nutrition facts
(Per serving)
Calories 388
Fat 19.7g
Protein 6.5g
Carbs 48.3g

Ingredients:
- 1 1/2 cups of flour (whole wheat)
- 1 1/4 cups of milk
- 1 1/2 cups of all-purpose flour
- 1 1/2 cups of carrots grated
- 2/3 cup of vegetable oil
- 1/2 cup of walnuts chopped
- 3/4 cup of packed brown sugar
- 3 teaspoons of lemon juice
- 3 teaspoons of vanilla extract
- 2 teaspoons of orange zest
- 1 1/2 teaspoons of baking powder
- 1/2 teaspoon of ground cloves
- 1/2 teaspoon of salt
- 1 1/2 teaspoons of ground cinnamon

Instructions:
Follow the instructions below to make tasty and easy carrot cake.

1.Preheat your convection oven at 325°F.Greased an 8 inches springform baking pan with butter. In a small-sized bowl, mix lemon juice with milk, whisk together, and leave for 5 minutes—mix flour, cinnamon, cloves, baking powder, and salt and set the bowl aside.

2.Cream oil, brown sugar, and orange zest in a large-sized bowl. Add in vanilla and sour milk. Pour flour mixture into it and blend until smooth. Fold in chopped nuts and grated carrots.

3.Pour the cake batter into a prepared springform baking pan and bake in a preheated convection oven for around 1 hour.

4.Check by inserting a wooden skewer; if it comes out dry cake is done, let it cool before serving.

4.35 ROASTED CAULIFLOWER WITH CHEESE SAUCE

Total time of cooking
50 minutes
Prep time 20 minutes
Cook time 30 minutes

Serving
2

Nutrition facts
(Per serving)
Calories 452
Fat 19.7g
Protein 18.95g
Carbs 28g

Ingredients:
- 1 lb. of cauliflower florets frozen
- 1/2 tablespoon of smoked paprika
- 1/8 teaspoon of cayenne pepper
- 1 tablespoon of olive oil
- 1/4 teaspoon of salt
- 1/4 teaspoon of garlic powder
- Freshly cracked pepper

For the cheese sauce:
- 1 tablespoon of butter
- 4 oz. of sharp cheddar shredded
- 1/2 cup of evaporated milk

Instructions:
Follow the instructions below to make roasted cauliflower with cheese sauce.

1.Preheat your convection oven at 375°F.Combine garlic powder, smoked paprika, salt, cayenne, and freshly cracked pepper.

2.Arrange cauliflower florets onto a non-stick baking sheet, then top with olive oil and spices. Mix lightly to coat oil and spices to the cauliflower florets.

3.Roast in a preheated convection oven for around 30 minutes.

4.Meanwhile, in a small saucepan, add milk and butter on medium heat and keep stirring until butter melts down in milk. This will take only a couple of minutes.

5.Turn the heat to low and begin adding shredded cheddar slowly a little amount at a time and keep whisking until cheese melts down completely and the sauce gets thicken.

6.Once roasting is done, Transfer the cauliflower into bowls or platter, pour the cheese sauce over top of roasted cauliflower. Serve warm.

Total time of cooking

40 minutes
Prep time 10 minutes
Cook time 30 minutes

Serving

4

Nutrition facts

(Per serving)
Calories 509
Fat 22.8g
Protein 23.8g
Carbs 55.5g

Ingredients:

- 4 large green bell peppers (seeds, tops, and membranes)
- 1 can of black beans, drained and rinsed (15 ounces)
- 1 package of shredded Mexican cheese blend (8 ounces)
- 1 can of chili-style diced tomatoes (14.5 ounces)
- 2 cups of cooked rice
- 1/2 cup of chopped onion
- 1 tablespoon of olive oil
- 1 tablespoon of salt
- 1 teaspoon of garlic salt
- 1/2 teaspoon of salt
- 1 teaspoon of chili powder
- 1/2 teaspoon of ground cumin

Instructions:

Follow the instructions below to make Mexican-style stuffed peppers.

1. Preheat the convection oven at 325°F.
2. Boil salted water and boil bell peppers in water until slightly softens, about 4 to 5 minutes. Drain.
3. On medium heat in a skillet, heat oil and cook onion in oil until onion softens for 4 to 5 minutes.
4. Add black beans, rice, cooked onion, and tomatoes in a large-sized bowl. Add chili powder, cumin, garlic salt, and 1/2 teaspoon of salt and mix. Into rice mixture, stir in 1 1/2 cups of Mexican cheese.
5. Stuffed each bell pepper with rice mixture; transfer peppers onto 9x9 inches baking dish. Sprinkle the top of peppers with remaining Mexican cheese.
6. Bake for around 30 minutes in a preheated convection oven until cheese melts down and becomes bubbly.

4.37 ACORN SQUASH STUFFED

Total time of cooking

1 hour 15 minutes
Prep time 20 minutes
Cook time 55 minutes

Serving

2

Nutrition facts

(Per serving)
Calories 644
Fat 23.1g
Protein 10.4g
Carbs 111.4g

Ingredients:

- 2 acorn squash (seeded and halved)
- 1 cup of cooked rice
- 1 peeled and thinly sliced red onion
- 1 peeled and grated tart apple
- 4 tablespoons of dried cranberries
- 4 tablespoons of cashews
- 1 tablespoon of butter (cut into small pieces)
- 1 tablespoon of olive oil
- 1 1/2 tablespoons of balsamic vinegar
- 1 tablespoon of panko bread crumbs
- 1/2 teaspoon of ground thyme

Salt and ground black pepper to taste

Instructions:

Follow the instructions below to make acorn squash stuffed.

1. Preheat the convection oven at 325°F.
2. Arrange halves acorn squash cut side down in a baking sheet. Spread few tablespoons of water and cover with aluminum foil tightly.
3. Bake squash in a preheated convection oven for about 30 minutes until squash is soft.
4. while the squash is baking, on medium heat in a skillet, toast cashews for 4 to 5 minutes. Let cashews cool down, and then chop.
5. In a skillet on medium heat, cook onion in hot oil until onion softens for about 10 minutes. Add in balsamic vinegar and mix. Then add apple and cook for 2 more minutes. Remove from stove and allow cooling.
6. Mix onion apple mixture, cranberries, rice, and cashews in a large-sized bowl. Sprinkle thyme salt and pepper on filling mix until fully incorporated.
7. Take out squash from the convection oven and keep the oven on. Divide filling among four squash halves. Sprinkle the top of squash with panko bread crumbs and butter. Bake for 20 to 25 minutes more and serve.

Total time of cooking
55 minutes
Prep time 15 minutes
Cook time 40 minutes

Serving
12

Nutrition facts
(Per serving)
Calories 249
Fat 12g
Protein 14.2g
Carbs 22.1g

Ingredients:
- 4 cups of chopped broccoli
- 9 lasagna noodles
- 3 cups of shredded mozzarella
- 3/4 cup of cottage cheese
- 2 cups of chopped carrots
- 3/4 cup of grated Parmesan cheese
- 2 can of cream of mushrooms (10.75 ounces)
- 2 teaspoons of paprika
- 1 teaspoon of garlic powder
- 1 teaspoon of dried crushed rosemary

Instructions:
Follow the instructions below to make carrot and broccoli lasagna.
1.Preheat the convection oven at 325°F.
1.Steam carrots and broccoli till they become tender.
2.Boil lasagna noodles. In a medium-sized bowl, mix cream of mushroom soup, cottage cheese,1/2 cup parmesan, 2 cups of mozzarella, separate 1 1/4 cup of sauce, and keep it aside. In a remaining sauce, add rosemary, garlic powder, and the cooked veggies and keep them aside
3.In a 9x13 inches baking pan, Layer 3 lasagna noodles at the bottom, pour 1/2 of the veggie mixture,3 noodles, pour the rest of the veggie mixture,3 noodles, and the separated 1 1/4 cup of sauce. Put 1 cup of mozzarella on top of a baking dish. Stir together 1/4 cup of parmesan and paprika and Sprinkle all over the mozzarella.
4.Cover and Bake in a preheated convection oven at 350°F for 1/2 hour. Then remove the lid and bake for additional 10 minutes and enjoy.

Total time of cooking
1 hour 10 minutes
Prep time 20 minutes
Cook time 50 minutes

Serving
6

Nutrition facts
(Per serving)
Calories 298
Fat 23.6g
Protein 8.8g
Carbs 14.5g

Ingredients:
- 6 ounces of chopped mushrooms
- 5 eggs
- 2 chopped leeks, white part only
- 1/2 peeled and diced sweet potato
- 1 chopped onion
- 1 cup of heavy whipping cream
- 1/3 cup of sour cream
- 1 tablespoon of finely shredded Asiago cheese
- 2 teaspoons of olive oil
- 1/2 teaspoon of dried thyme
- 1/2 teaspoon of salt

Instructions:
Follow the instructions below to make mushrooms, leeks, and sweet potatoes quiche.
1.Preheat the convection oven at 325°F.Grease a 9-inch pie dish with cooking spray.
2.On medium heat in a skillet, heat olive oil. Add the onion in heated oil and cook for 2 to 3 minutes. Add leeks, thyme, mushrooms; stir and cook for 5 to 8 minutes.
3.Add in sweet potato and cook until sweet potato gets tender, for around 15 minutes. Put the mixture in a prepared pie pan.
4.Mix sour cream, eggs, cream, and salt in the food processor until smooth and creamy. Spread into a pie dish on top of cooked vegetable mixture and stir slightly. Sprinkle Asiago cheese on top
5.Bake in a preheated convection oven for around 45 to 50 minutes or until the top turn golden brown. Let stand for few minutes before cutting.

4.40 SIMPLE AND DELICIOUS BROCCOLI CASSEROLE

Total time of cooking

1 hour 5 minutes
Prep time 5 minutes
Cook time 60 minutes

Serving

6 to 8 servings

Nutrition facts

(Per serving)
Calories 272
Fat 20.8g
Protein 7.5g
Carbs 13.9g

Ingredients:

- 1 package of frozen chopped broccoli (16 ounces)
- 1 can of condensed cream of mushroom soup (10.75 ounces)
- 1/2 cup of processed cheese sauce
- 1/2 cup of bread crumbs
- 2 beaten eggs
- 1/2 cup of mayonnaise

Instructions:

Follow the instructions below to make simple and delicious broccoli casserole.

1.Preheat the convection oven at 325°F.

2.In a casserole dish, add broccoli, processed cheese, mayonnaise, mushroom soup, and eggs. Mix, top with bread crumbs and bake for around 1 hour. Serve warm.

4.41 CRISPY ONION RINGS BAKED

Total time of cooking

35 minutes
Prep time 10 minutes
Cook time 25 minutes

Serving

4

Nutrition facts

(Per serving)
Calories 147
Fat 3g
Protein 5g
Carbs 26g

Ingredients:

- 2 onions large
- 2 cups of Panko bread crumbs
- 2 cups of buttermilk divided
- 1/2 cup + 2 tablespoons of flour
- 1 tablespoon of Olive Oil
- 2 eggs
- 1/2 teaspoon of each pepper, paprika, seasoning salt, and parsley

Instructions:

Follow the instructions below to make crispy onion rings baked.

1.Peel and slice onions in 1/2 inches thick rings. Transfer sliced onions in a freezer bag with one cup of butter and let stand for at least 30 to 40 minutes.

2.Preheat the convection oven at 400°F

3.Mix eggs, buttermilk, and two tablespoons of flour until combine and smooth. Keep the mixture aside.

4.Combine bread crumbs, seasonings, and olive oil in another mixing bowl.

5.Remove onions from the freezer bag and drain onions well. Put the onion in a 1/2 cup of flour bag and toss well to coat.

6.Arrange the panko mixture into a small-sized bowl, dip onion into the egg mixture, then into the panko mixture one by one to coat.

6.Transfer onion rings into a non-stick baking sheet. Bake in a preheated convection oven for around 20 to 25 minutes until crispy and browned.

7.Top with additional seasoning and serve onion rings with ketchup.

4.42 RED PEPPERS WITH BASIL ROASTED

Total time of cooking
50 minutes
Prep time 10 minutes
Cook time 40 minutes

Serving
6

Nutrition facts
(Per serving)
Calories 84
Fat 5.8g
Protein 1g
Carbs 5.7g

Ingredients:
- 6 halved cherry tomatoes
- 3 red peppers large
- 2 tablespoons of rinsed and drained capers
- 2 tablespoons of balsamic vinegar
- 3 leaves of fresh thyme sprigs
- 3 tablespoons of extra-virgin olive oil
- A handful of fresh basil leaves
- 2 crushed garlic cloves

Instructions:
Follow the instructions below to make red peppers with basil roasted.
1.Preheat the convection oven at 375°F
2.Cut pepper into half lengthwise and scoop out the seeds and discard.
Arrange the red peppers cut side up in the non-stick baking tray and spread the garlic, thyme leaves, tomatoes, and capers between them. Top up with oil, and then sprinkle salt and pepper and roast in a preheated convection oven for around 30 minutes.
3.After 30 minutes, drizzle balsamic vinegar all over the dish and roast for an additional 10 minutes until tender and caramelized. Sprinkle with fresh basil upon serving.

4.43 BLUE CHEESE COURGETTE PIZZA

Total time of cooking
30 minutes
Prep time 15 minutes
Cook time 15 minutes

Serving
Makes 3 pizzas

Nutrition facts
(Per serving)
Calories 834
Fat 39.7g
Protein 36.4
Carbs 79.9

Ingredients:
- 3 x pizza dough bases
- 150g of thinly sliced buffalo mozzarella
- 1 trimmed medium courgette
- 150g of crumbled roquefort
- 3 tablespoons of shelled pumpkin seeds
- Grated zest of 1 lemon
- A handful of fresh mint leaves
- 1 tablespoon of lemon olive oil

Instructions:
Follow the instructions below to make blue cheese courgette pizza.
1.Preheat the convection oven at 375°F.
2.Peel courgette and transfer into a bowl with lemon oil and lemon zest, then sprinkle salt and black pepper. Set aside for around 30 minutes.
3.Arrange pizza dough into a pizza baking pan, top with 1/3 of the toppings, courgette, mint, blue cheese, mozzarella, and pumpkin seeds.
Repeat the procedure with the other two pizza dough as well. Place in a preheated convection oven and bake for 10 to 15 minutes.
4.Transfer to a platter and drizzle the top of pizzas with extra lemon oil and serve.

Total time of cooking
40 minutes
Prep time 10 minutes
Cook time 30 minutes

Serving
6

Nutrition facts
(Per serving)
Calories 88
Fat 0.4g
Protein 3.8g
Carbs 14.3g

Ingredients:
- 12 oz of baby potatoes (cut potatoes in halves or cubes depending on size, you want them to be)
- 2 summer squash or zucchini (cut into 1-inch pieces)
- 8 oz of baby bella mushrooms (ends trimmed and cleaned)
- 12 oz of Campari tomatoes or cherry tomatoes
- 10 to 12 large peeled garlic cloves
- Grated Parmesan cheese for serving
- Extra virgin olive oil
- Red pepper flakes crushed
- 1/2 tablespoon of dried oregano
- Salt and pepper to taste
- 1 teaspoon of dried thyme

Instructions:
Follow the instructions below to make oven-roasted Italian-style vegetables.

1. Preheat the convection oven at 400°F.
2. Add the veggies, mushrooms, and garlic to a large-sized mixing bowl. Coat with olive oil about 1/4 cup of olive oil. Add in the dried oregano, salt, thyme, and pepper. Toss to mix.
3. Arrange the potatoes only in a lightly greased baking pan—roast in the preheated convection oven for around 10 minutes. Take out the pan from the oven after 10 minutes, spread the remaining vegetables and mushrooms, and roast for an additional 20 minutes.
4. Serve straightaway and sprinkle with grated parmesan cheese and red pepper flakes.

Total time of cooking
1 hour 20 minutes
Prep time 10 minutes
Cook time 1 hour 10 minutes

Serving
8

Nutrition facts
(Per serving)
Calories 376
Fat 22g
Protein 13g
Carbs 34g

Ingredients:
- 3 lbs. of Yukon gold potatoes
- 1/4 lb. of grated Parmigiano Reggiano cheese
- 1 cup of heavy cream
- 1/4 lb. of grated gruyere cheese
- 1 cup of milk
- 10 fresh thyme sprigs
- Black pepper
- 3 cloves of minced garlic
- 2 teaspoon salt

Instructions:
Follow the instructions below to make easy and tasty potato gratin.

1. Preheat the convection oven at 375°F.
2. In a large-sized bowl, Mix heavy cream and milk.
3. Using a knife, thinly slice the potatoes and pour the slices into a cream milk mixture. Add the Parmigiano and gruyere cheeses to a cream milk mixture bowl along with thyme sprigs, garlic, salt, and black pepper. Mix well.
4. Spread the potato mixture into an 8x11 inch non-stick baking dish, cover the dish lid tightly with foil.
5. Bake for around 50 hours in a preheated convection oven, remove the lid and bake for an additional 20 minutes until potatoes are golden brown from top. Serve warm and enjoy!

4.46 CLASSIC FRENCH VEGETABLE LOAF

Total time of cooking
1 hour
Prep time 15 minutes
Cook time 45 minutes

Serving
8

Nutrition facts
(Per serving)
Calories 300
Fat 20.3g
Protein 10.7g
Carbs 18.9g

Ingredients:
- 1 1/4 cups of self-rising flour
- 1 1/2 cups of Swiss cheese shredded
- 1 seeded and diced tomato
- 1 chopped shallot
- 1 small diced zucchini
- 1/3 cup of milk
- 1/2 cubed eggplant
- 1/3 cup of olive oil
- 1/2 diced green bell pepper
- 1 clove of minced garlic
- 3 eggs
- 2 tablespoons of olive oil
- Salt and pepper to taste

Instructions:
Follow the instructions below to make a classic French vegetable loaf.

1. Preheat the convection oven at 350°F. Grease and flour non-stick loaf pan of 9x5 inches.
2. On medium heat in a large-sized skillet, heat two tablespoons of olive oil and cook shallot, green bell pepper, garlic, tomato, zucchini, and eggplant until vegetable softens about 10 to 15 minutes. Top the vegetables with salt and pepper.
3. Add self-rising flour with milk and eggs in a large-sized mixing bowl and whisk until fully incorporated. Mix and whisk olive oil, fold cooked vegetables, and swiss cheese into the flour mixture—place batter into greased loaf pan.
4. Bake in a preheated convection oven for about 45 minutes. Check by inserting a wooden skewer in the middle of the loaf; if it comes out clean, your loaf is done.
5. Let it cool down for some time on a wire rack before slicing.

4.47 VEGETABLE ENCHILADA PIE

Total time of cooking
25 minutes
Prep time 15 minutes
Cook time 10 minutes

Serving
2

Nutrition facts
(Per serving)
Calories 609
Fat 22g
Protein 19g
Carbs 76g

Ingredients:
- 400g can of drained mixed beans
- 400g can of chopped tomatoes
- 2 sliced peppers, any color you like
- 4 corn tortillas
- 1 sliced red onion
- 100g of low-fat sour cream
- Small bunch of chopped coriander
- 30g of grated cheddar
- 1 tablespoon of rapeseed oil or vegetable oil
- 2 tablespoons of fajita spice mix

Instructions:
Follow the instructions below to make a vegetable enchilada pie.

1. In a medium-sized pan, heat oil and fry the onion and peppers until soft, for around 10 minutes. Add the beans, chopped tomatoes, fajita spice mix, and seasoning; cook for 5 minutes, then mix the coriander. Warm the tortillas in the microwave and heat the grill.
2. Spread some amount of the onion and pepper mixture on the bottom of the baking dish, top with sour cream and warm tortilla, repeat the procedure three more times, and finish with a final layer of sour cream. Sprinkle cheese on top and grill in a convection oven for around 10 minutes or until bubbly and golden from the top. Serve hot and enjoy!

Total time of cooking
40 minutes
Prep time 15 minutes
Cook time 25 minutes

Serving
4

Nutrition facts
(Per serving)
Calories 553
Fat 36.6g
Protein 18.7g
Carbs 34.1g

Ingredients:
- 1 sliced into 2 cm rounds leek
- 1 large cut into florets cauliflower

For the cheese sauce:
- 6 tablespoons of non-dairy milk
- 400ml tin of coconut milk
- 1 banana shallot
- 2 sprigs of fresh thyme
- 1/2 lemon juice
- 80g of raw cashew nuts (soak in freshly boiled water for 15 minutes)
- 1 tablespoon of white miso paste
- 5 tablespoons of nutritional yeast
- 1 bay leaf
- 1 clove of garlic

For herb topping:
- 100g of dried breadcrumbs
- 3 tablespoons of rapeseed oil
- 2 sprigs of fresh rosemary
- 4 fresh thyme sprigs
- A handful of fresh flat leaf parsley
- A handful of fresh sage leaves

Instructions:
Follow the instructions below to make a leek and cauliflower 'cheese' herb-crusted.

1. Preheat the convection oven at 325°F.Boil water, add leek slices and cauliflower florets and cook for 3 to 4 minutes and drain.

2. Pour all the sauce ingredients, except thyme and bay leaf, into a blender and blend until creamy and smooth.

3. On low heat, add sauce to the saucepan and add bay leaf and thyme.

4. In the blender, blend the herb topping ingredients and set them aside.

5. Mix in drained cauliflower and leek into the hot sauce, stir and then sprinkle with pepper and salt. Pour mixture evenly into a baking dish and top up with herb breadcrumbs—Bake in a preheated convection oven for around 20 to 25 minutes or until golden brown from the top. Keep on checking during baking, so it doesn't get burnt. Serve warm.

4.49 ROASTED SPICY OKRA

Total time of cooking
25 minutes
Prep time 10 minutes
Cook time 15 minutes

Serving
4

Nutrition facts
(Per serving)
Calories 75.1
Fat 5.3 g
Protein 1.9 g
Carbs 7g

Ingredients:
*   12 ounces of small okra
*   4 lemon wedges (for garnishing)
*   1 1/2 tablespoons of olive oil
*   1/4 teaspoon of cayenne pepper
*   1/4 teaspoon of ground coriander
*   1/2 teaspoon of smoked paprika
*   1/2 teaspoon of salt
*   1/4 teaspoon of ground cumin

Instructions:
Follow the instructions below to make roasted spicy okra.
1.Preheat the convection oven at 400°F.
2.Coat the okra with olive oil.
3.In a small-sized bowl, mix cumin, coriander, cayenne pepper, paprika, and salt—Toss okra in the spice mixture.
4.Place coated okra in the non-stick cookie sheet and roast in a preheated convection oven for 14 to 15 minutes.
5.Serve straightaway and squeeze lemon wedges over each serving.

4.50 CRISPY POTATO WEDGES BAKED

Total time of cooking
1 hour
Prep time 15 minutes
Cook time 45 minutes

Serving
4

Nutrition facts
(Per serving)
Calories 256
Fat 12g
Protein 6g
Carbs 32g

Ingredients:
*   4 skin-on small russet potatoes
*   3 tablespoons of olive oil
*   1 teaspoon of garlic powder
*   1/4 cup of Parmesan cheese grated
*   1/2 teaspoon of parsley
*   1 teaspoon of onion powder
*   1/2 teaspoon of seasoned salt

Instructions:
Follow the instructions below to make crispy potato wedges baked.
1.Preheat the convection oven at 400°F.
2.Wash and cut potatoes into wedges. Soak wedges in cold water for approx. 30 minutes. Drain and pat dry.
3.Toss potatoes wedges in the remaining ingredients to coat.
4.Spread coated potatoes wedges on a large non-stick baking pan and bake until crispy and brown, for around 40 to 45 minutes.

4.51 SALT AND VINEGAR ROASTED POTATOES WITH FETA AND DILL

Total time of cooking
55 minutes
Prep time: 15 minutes
Cook time: 40 minutes

Servings
6

Nutrition facts
(per serving)
Calories 218 kcal
Fat 10g
Protein 5g
Carbs 27g

Ingredients
- tablespoons extra-virgin olive oil
- 1 cup distilled white vinegar
- tiny fresh potatoes
- teaspoons sea salt (distributed)
- 1 teaspoon oregano, dry
- cups freshly chopped dill
- garlic cloves, minced
- For serving, a pinch of flaky salt
- 1/2 cup feta cheese, crumbled

Instructions
1.Combine 2 cups of water, the potatoes, vinegar, and 2 teaspoons of sea salt in a big saucepan. Boil, covered, for approximately 10 minutes, or until the potatoes begin to soften but remain firm in the core (depending on the size of your potatoes).
2.Preheat the oven to 425°F and prepare a big sheet pan with parchment paper in the meanwhile.
3.Drain the potatoes and set them aside. Toss them gently with the olive oil, the remaining 14 teaspoon sea salt, and the oregano. Arrange them on the prepared sheet pan and roast for 20 to 30 minutes, or until golden and crisp.
4.Toss the garlic with the heated potatoes. To serve, place the potatoes in a dish and top with feta and dill. If desired, sprinkle a little flaky salt on top.

4.52 MAPLE BALSAMIC ROASTED VEGETABLES

- 1 1/2 tbsp Provence dried herb
- 1 teaspoon rosemary, chopped
- 1 tablespoon balsamic vinegar
- 1 quart of maple syrup

Total time of cooking
1 hour 10 minutes
Prep Time: 20 minutes
Cook time: 50 minutes

Servings
4

Nutrition facts
(per serving)
Calories 158kcal
Fat 3g
Protein 4g
Carbs: 32g

Ingredients
- 1 1/2 pounds peeled sweet potatoes, cut into 1-inch cubes
- 1 1/2 pounds thin rainbow carrots, whole
- 1/2 pound peeled and chopped rutabagas
- tiny red onions, chop into large slices
- 1/3 cup extra virgin olive oil
- 1 1/2 pounds peeled and thinly sliced parsnips
- Half tsp black pepper
- Half tsp sea salt

Instructions
1.Preheat oven to 350 degrees Fahrenheit.
2.Combine the veggies in a mixing basin. Toss in the oil, herbs, salt, and rosemary until completely coated.
3.Place the veggies on a big roasting pan or two baking sheets, leveling them out and not on top of one another.
4.Cook for 45 minutes in the oven, noting that the tip of a sharp knife easily spears the veggies.
5.Put maple syrup and balsamic vinegar in a pan and bring them to a boil while the veggies are in the oven.
6.Reduce heat and continue to cook until the liquid has reduced to roughly half its original volume and is lovely and thick.
7.Return the veggies to the oven for 5 minutes after gently drizzling part of the syrup over them.
8.Serve immediately.

Total time of cooking

: 1 hr 45 mins
Prep Time: 25 mins
Cook Time: 20 mins
Servings
4

Nutrition facts

(per serving)
Calories 288kcal
Fat 9g
Protein 14g
Carbs 38g

Ingredients

To make the pizza base
- 3/4 tsp Yeast
- 1/2 tsp Sugar
- 1 and 1/4 cup flour
- 1/3 cup of water
- 1 teaspoon onion powder (optional)
- Season with salt to taste
- Grease with olive oil
- 1 tbsp. Of butter

Topping
- ½ cup Baby corn
- Carrots
- ½ Green capsicum
- 1 Onion
- Tomatoes
- 1 tsp Oregano
- Butter with garlic and coriander to brush over the crust

Instructions

To make the Pizza base
1. If you're using a microwave, heat the water for 15 to 20 seconds. If you're using another technique, make sure the water is warm to the touch but not boiling, and if you have a food thermometer, the water should be between 120F and 125F.
2. Add sugar to the yeast and mix it in.
3. After that, add the yeast and set it aside. Because we're using instant dry yeast, there's no need to mix the yeast granules because they dissolve quickly in warm water.
4. Sit the yeast mixture for 10 minutes.
5. Your yeast is active when a frothy layer forms on top of the water.
6. Knead the dough for 10 minutes after adding the bubbly yeast mixture to the dry ingredients.
7. Knead in the butter for an extra 5 minutes.
8. Olive oil should be used to grease the bowl and to coat the whole dough.
9. Allow for a 45-minute to an hour rest time for the dough. (If possible, store the dough in the same location as the yeast was proofed.)
10. To determine if your dough is ready, check to see whether it has doubled in size or leave it warm for another 15 minutes.
11. Your dough is ready after it has been proofed (doubled in size). Form a circular foundation for the dough by punching it down.
12. Put the dough in the pan of your choice now. Punch down the pizza base with a knife or fork to prevent it from rising.
To top your Pizza
1. Toss the pizza base with some sauce.
2. After that, top with mozzarella cheese and your favorite toppings.
3. Brush the crust with the coriander garlic butter and sprinkle with oregano.
4. Now comes the convection baking stage. The heat comes straight from the top rods, much as in a convection oven.
5. The pizza should then be kept at 200°C for another 2 to 3 minutes. It's important to check it frequently.

4.54 HUEVOS RANCHEROS BAKE

Total time of cooking
1 hour 45 minutes
Prep Time: 35 minutes
Cook time:1 hour 10 minutes

Servings
5

Nutrition facts
(per serving)
Calories 190kcal
Protein 13g
Fat 11g
Carbs 6g

Ingredients
- 1 chopped red bell pepper
- 1 cup onions, chopped
- 1 pound chorizo sausage in bulk
- 1 can (undrained) organic fire-roasted crushed tomatoes
- 1 packet taco seasoning mix (original)
- 1 can green chiles, chopped
- 1 can drain and rinse black beans
- cups shredded Mexican cheese mix
- 1-gallon milk
- cup avocado, diced
- A quarter teaspoon of salt
- cup blue corn tortilla chips, crushed
- tbsp chopped fresh cilantro leaves
- Lime wedges, for garnish

Instructions
1.Preheat the oven to 350 degrees Fahrenheit. Cooking sprays a 13-by-39-inch (3-quart) baking dish.
2.Cook sausage, bell pepper, and onions in a 12-inch non-stick pan over medium-high heat for 7 to 8 minutes turning periodically until sausage are no longer pink; drain and return mixture to skillet. Reduce to medium heat and add the tomatoes, green chiles, and taco seasoning mix. Bring to a low simmer. Cook, stirring regularly, for 4 to 6 minutes, or until liquid thickens. Remove the pan from the heat. Transfer to baking dish with black beans and 1 cup of cheese.
3.Whisk together the eggs, milk, and salt in a medium mixing bowl until well combined. Add the remaining 1 cup of cheese and mix well. In a baking dish, pour evenly over the sausage mixture.
4.Bake for 40–45 minutes, uncovered, or until eggs are set, and a knife inserted in the middle comes out clean. Allow 5 minutes for cooling. Avocado, chips, and cilantro go on top. Serve with lime wedges on the side.

4.55 ARTICHOKE PIE

Total time of cooking
60 minutes
Prep time: 15 minutes
Cook time: 45 minutes

Servings
4-6

Nutrition facts
(per serving):
Calories 320kcal
Fat 15g
Protein 10g
Carbs 38g

Ingredients
- quail eggs
- crust shells for pies
- 1 cup parmesan cheese, grated
- 1 garlic clove
- 1 can artichoke hearts
- 1 bag shredded mozzarella
- a sprinkle of cayenne

Instructions
1.Preheat the oven to 350 degrees Fahrenheit. Six eggs should be whisked together in a mixing basin. Combine the Parmesan, spicy pepper, shredded mozzarella, and artichokes in a mixing bowl. Black olives or Spanish green olives may also be added (drain and rinse first). Slice or leave whole, but don't add Parmesan cheese if you're using green olives (too salty).
2.Sauté garlic in oil in a skillet, or add garlic powder to beaten eggs instead.
3.Cook for a few minutes with your egg mixture in the pan. Fill one shell with the mixture and cover with the other.
4.Heat oven to 350°F and bake for 45 minutes, or until golden brown on top.

4.56 GREEK STUFFED PEPPERS WITH FETA & MIZITHRA CHEESES

Total time of cooking
40 minutes
Prep time: 15 minutes
Cook time: 25 minutes

Servings
5-6

Nutrition facts
(per serving)
Calories 290kcal
Fat 3g
Protein 10g
Carbs 26g

Ingredients
- 1 cup cubanelle peppers
- ½ cup feta cheese
- Mizithra cheese (half a cup)
- 1/2 cup ricotta cheese
- Sprinkling olive oil
- 1 tablespoon coarsely chopped dill
- 3–4 tablespoons coarsely chopped parsley
- tbsp olive oil for stuffing
- 1 onion, red, coarsely chopped (optional)
- Salt and pepper to taste

Instructions
1.Wash the peppers, remove the caps, and lay them away to use later. Scoop out the seeds with care to avoid breaking or tearing the peppers.
2.Mix and mash the cheeses with a fork in a mixing basin, then add the dill, onion, olive oil, parsley, and pepper to taste. Add additional red pepper flakes if you want them to be a little spicier.
3.Stuff the peppers with the mixture using your fingers. Carefully push down until the peppers are completely filled, about 1/2 inch from the top. To avoid the cheese from melting out of the peppers while cooking, press a little slice of bread into each pepper. Return the tops to each pepper.
4.Glaze the peppers with olive oil and put them in a baking or pyrex dish, one next to the other. Drizzle olive oil over the peppers.
5.Heat the oven to 350° F and cook them for 20 minutes on the top rack. After 10 minutes, flip the peppers. Remove from the oven and serve!

4.57 ROASTED CARROTS

Total time of cooking
55 minutes
Prep time: 20 minutes
Cook time: 35 minutes

Serving
2-4

Nutrition facts
(per serving):
Calories 147kcal
Protein 3g
Fat 14g
Carbs 4g

Ingredients
- 1 tbsp olive oil
- carrots
- 1/2 teaspoon pepper and salt
- A tablespoon of thai chili sauce
- Nutmeg (1/2 teaspoon)
- A half teaspoon of cinnamon
- 1 teaspoon basil, dried or fresh
- 1 teaspoon thyme, dried or fresh

Instructions
1.Preheat the oven to 400°F for 35 minutes (Convection Oven) or 425°F for 40-45 minutes (Conventional Oven).
2.Place the Ziploc bag in a medium dish to keep it stable while you combine the marinade ingredients.
3.Combine chili sauce, olive oil, salt, cinnamon, thyme, nutmeg, basil, and pepper in a Ziploc bag. Close the bag and mix the items together.
4.Remove the top and tip of the carrots with a vegetable peeler, then cut the carrots into broad diagonal slices and add to the marinade, closing the bag and making sure all carrots are coated with the mixture.
5.Spread carrots equally on a baking sheet pan lined with aluminum foil and bake at one of the temperatures listed above.
6.Plate and serve the carrots after they've finished cooking. Enjoy!

4.58 LENTIL AND ROAST VEGETABLES SALAD

Total time of cooking
55 minutes
Prep time: 15 minutes
Cook time: 40 minutes

Servings
4

Nutrition Facts
(Per Serving)
Calories: 158 kcal
Fats: 3g
Proteins 4g
Carbs: 32g

Ingredients
- 350g lentils
- 1 big courgette
- red onions
- 1 cauliflower head
- big carrots
- Vine-ripened cherry tomatoes
- tablespoons balsamic vinegar
- 1 pepper yellow or red
- Olive oil, 1 tbsp
- To taste Himalayan salt

Instructions
1.Preheat the oven to 180 degrees Celsius.
2.Wash the lentils completely, cover them with water, and simmer for 15 to 20 minutes with a pinch of salt; it's best to follow the directions on the package since cooking times vary depending on the variety of lentils.
3.As required, peel and/or wash all of the veggies. Cut/chop as desired, but ideally in large parts.
4.Place all of the veggies on a big tray with enough space between them to prevent them from sticking together; if there isn't enough room, use two trays. Sprinkle some salt and olive oil over the vegetables before placing them in the oven for around 25 minutes. Remove them from the oven, mix them up, and flip them a bit before returning them to the oven for another 13 minutes, depending on how cooked you want them to be. If you want them crispy, keep them in a little longer.
5.Combine the lentils and veggies with balsamic vinegar and toss well. The salad is now ready to eat. It's delicious as a side dish with any meat or seafood, or on its alone.

4.59 SPICED CAULIFLOWER

Total time of cooking
1 hr 30 mins
Prep time: 1 Hr
Cook time: 30 Min

Servings
8

Nutrition Facts
(Per Serving)
Calories 220 kcal
Fat 18g
Protein 5g
Carbs 15g

Ingredients
- A teaspoon of fajita seasoning
- 1 tsp ground cumin
- 1 cauliflower
- 1 teaspoon coriander powder
- 1 teaspoon of salt
- 1 teaspoon of asafoetida
- 1 tablespoon extra-virgin olive oil
- A single lime

Instructions
1.Cauliflower, uncooked, should be broken into little florets.
2.Combine the other ingredients in a mixing basin, and toss the florets in the marinade.
3.While the oven heats up, let the cauliflower in the marinade for roughly an hour. Approx180c
4.Place the marinated cauliflower on a baking dish, sprinkle over any residual marinade, and bake for 30 minutes.
5.Try not to eat everything before anybody else has a chance to. Restraint is very difficult to achieve.

Total time of cooking
4 hours
Prep time: 1 Hour
Cook time: 3 hours

Servings
16

Nutrition facts
(per serving)
Calories 160kcal
Fat 7.9g
Protein 6.9g
Carbs 15.1g

Ingredients
For The Cabbage Rolls
- a tablespoon of sugar
- 1 pound cabbage
- 1 pound ground beef
- 1 tablespoon cooked rice
- 1 teaspoon of lemon juice
- 1 1/2 teaspoon salt, divided
- 1/2 teaspoon paprika, divided
- 1/4 teaspoon pepper

For The Sauce
- 1 tsp pepper
- 1 finely sliced onion
- 1/2 cup boiling water
- a tablespoon of vegetable oil
- 1 tomato sauce can
- a quarter cup of lemon juice
- brown sugar, 1/3 cup

Instruction
1.Wash the cabbage and remove the core. Place the cabbage, core side down, in a large pot of boiling salted water and blanch for 6 minutes until tender. Drain and separate the leaves with care. Alternatively, you may soften the cabbage leaves in the microwave. Remove the softened leaves off the head, then return the cabbage to the microwave to soften the next layer.
2.Rice, meat, sugar, lemon juice, shredded onion, salt, pepper, and paprika are mixed together.
3.Cabbage leaves should be drained. To make the leaf more malleable, trim the firm middle rib. Fill each leaf with a tablespoon of the meat mixture and wrap up from the stem end, leaving the edges slack. Tuck the sides in like a dimple as it's folded up. This eliminates the need for toothpicks to secure the rolls.
4.In a pan or dutch oven, sauté finely chopped onion with remaining tsp salt, paprika, and sprinkle of pepper for approximately 10 minutes in heated oil. Add boiling water to the onion mixture and transfer to a casserole or keep it in the dutch oven. On top of the onions, arrange cabbage rolls.
5.Combine tomato sauce, sugar, and 1/4 cup lemon juice in a mixing bowl; pour over cabbage rolls and cover.
6.Preheat oven till 325° F and cook for two to three hours. Taste and adjust the sweetness and lemon juice as needed. Cook over low heat if using a stovetop.

4.61 ZUCCHINI BOATS

Total time of cooking
45 minutes
Prep time: 15 minutes
Cook time: 30 minutes

Servings
5

Nutrition facts
(per serving)
Calories 309kcal
Fat: 10g
Protein: 51g
Carbs: 6g

Ingredients
- 2-3 zucchini
- A quarter cup of finely chopped onion
- 1 quart of spaghetti sauce (any)
- tbsp butter
- 1 garlic clove, finely chopped
- 1 cup shredded cheddar cheese

Instructions
1.Scoop out the center of the zucchini by cutting it in half long way.
2.For approximately 3 minutes, sauté onion, garlic, and the pulp from the zucchini that you scraped out in a pan. After that, add your spaghetti sauce and simmer for an additional 3 minutes. Fill the zucchini shells equally with the mixture.
3.Butter a 9x13 pan and arrange the filled shells on top. Cook for 18 minutes at 350°F with the lid on. Remove the cover and top with the cheese; simmer for another 5-10 minutes, or until the cheese has melted.

4.62 MEXICAN STYLE EGGPLANT

Total time of cooking
40 minutes
Prep time: 15 minutes
Cook time: 25 minutes

Servings
4-6

Nutrition facts
(per serving)
Calories 80
Fat 7g
Protein 1g
Carbs 5g

Ingredients
- cup tomato sauce
- A half cup of sour cream
- 1 basil leaf for garnish
- 1 eggplant
- 1/4 cup drained mild green chilies
- 1/4 cup finely sliced green onion
- garlic cloves chopped
- Some black olives
- 1-ounce grated jack cheese
- 1 tbsp cumin

Instructions
1.Egg and flour are used to coat the eggplant. Cook till soft in butter or in the oven.
2.Combine green onions, tomato sauce, garlic, chiles, and cumin in a 1 1/2 quart pot and cook for 10 minutes.
3.Spread sauce mixture on top of eggplant in a 9 by 13 baking dish.
4.Place cheese on top of the sauce and bake for 25 minutes at 350 degrees until hot and bubbling.
5.Serve with sour cream with black olives and basil leaves as garnish.

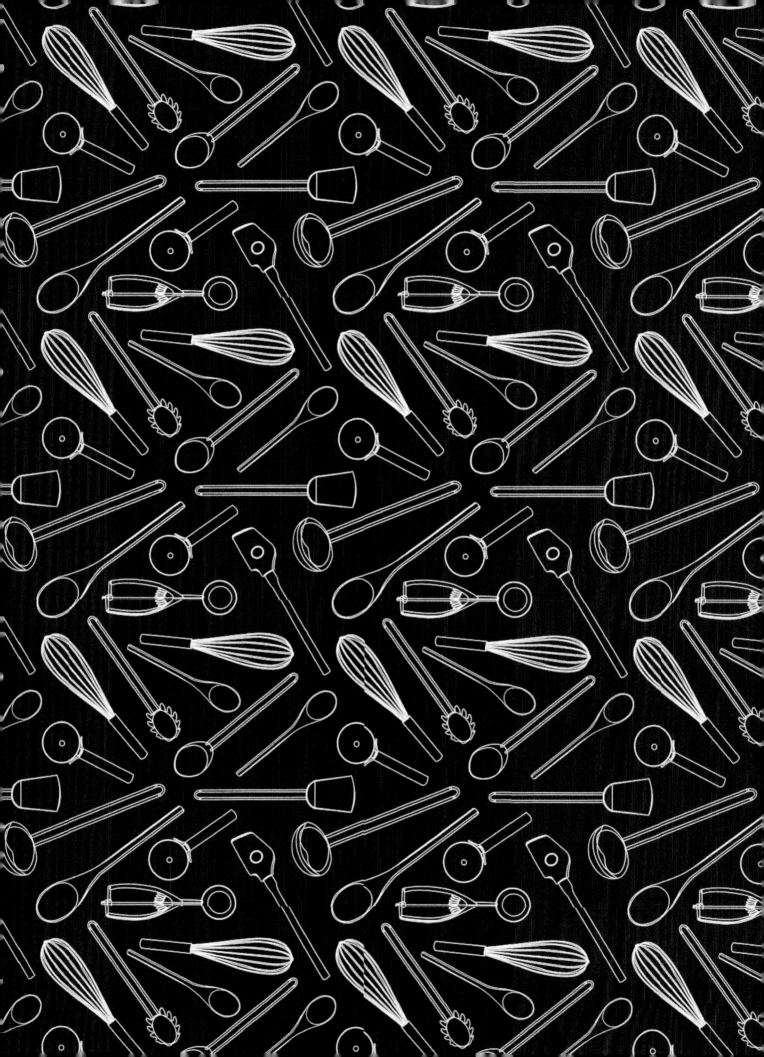

5.1 SIMPLE AND DELICIOUS SEAFOOD PIZZA

Total time of cooking
35 minutes
Prep time 15 minutes
Cook time 20 minutes

Serving
4

Nutrition facts
(Per serving)
Calories 625.6
Fat 44.8g
Protein 47.5g
Carbs 7.8g

Ingredients:
- 1 pizza dough
- 1 1/2 cups of cooked, peeled shrimps
- 1/4 cup of parmesan cheese grated
- 1 cup of crabmeat
- 3 to 4 cloves of minced garlic
- 1 1/2 cups of mozzarella cheese shredded
- Olive oil
- 1 teaspoon of parsley minced

Instructions:
Follow the instructions below to make simple and delicious seafood pizza.
1. Preheat the convection oven at 375°F.
2. Cook garlic in olive oil for few minutes. Add crabmeat and shrimp, mix well, add parsley and cook for few more minutes.
3. Spread 1/2 cup of mozzarella on pizza crust, then place shrimp and crab meat mixture on crust evenly, cover with the remaining amount of cheeses.
4. Bake in a preheated convection oven for around 15 minutes and broil the pizza for 2 to 3 minutes.
5. Cut into slices and serve.

5.2 BAKED HERB-CRUSTED SALMON

Total time of cooking
30 minutes
Prep time 10 minutes
Cook time 20 minutes

Serving
8

Nutrition facts
(Per serving)
Calories 377
Fat 20g
Protein 40g
Carbs 5g

Ingredients:
* 1 salmon fillet (3 to 4 pounds)
* 1 lemon divided
* 2 tablespoons of melted butter
* Salt and pepper to taste

For topping:
* 2 tablespoons of minced fresh parsley
* 3/4 cup of Panko bread crumbs
* 2 tablespoons of shredded parmesan cheese
* 3 cloves of minced garlic
* 1 tablespoon of minced fresh dill

* 3 tablespoons of melted butter
* One lemon zest

Instructions:
Follow the instructions below to make baked herb-crusted salmon.
1. Preheat the convection oven at 375°F.
2. In a small-sized bowl, combine all the ingredients.
3. Greased a baking pan with cooking spray.
4. Arrange salmon on a baking pan and brush melted butter all over the salmon, sprinkle with pepper and salt, and squeeze half of the lemon all over the salmon.
5. Spread crumb mixture over salmon and bake for 14 to 18 minutes or until cooked.

5.3 EASY AND TASTY TUNA NOODLES CASSEROLE

Total time of cooking
40 minutes
Prep time 20 minutes
Cook time 20 minutes

Serving
6

Nutrition facts
(Per serving)
Calories 323
Fat 15g
Protein 19g
Carbs 25g

Ingredients:
* 1 can of tuna drained (5-6 ounces)
* 3 cups of egg noodles
* 10-1/2 ounces of condensed mushroom soup
* 2 stalks of diced celery
* 1 cup of cheddar cheese
* 1 small diced onion
* 1/3 cup of milk
* 2/3 cup of frozen peas defrosted
* 1 tablespoon of butter
* 1 tablespoon of parsley

For the crumb topping:
* 1/2 cup of panko bread crumbs
* 1/2 cup of cheddar
* 1 tablespoon of parsley
* 1 tablespoon of melted butter

Instructions:
Follow the instructions below to make easy and tasty tuna casserole.
1. Preheat the convection oven at 400°F. Mix topping ingredients and set them aside.
2. Boil noodles according to your package directions.
3. Cook celery and onion in butter until softens, for around 5 to 7 minutes.
4. In a large-sized bowl, mix noodles, onion mixture, soup, peas, milk, tuna, cheese and parsley.
5. Spread the mixture into a casserole dish and sprinkle the top with crumb topping.
6. Bake in a preheated convection for 18 to 20 minutes.

5.4 DELICIOUS SEAFOOD STUFFING

Total time of cooking
50 minutes
Prep time 20 minutes
Cook time 30 minutes

Serving
8

Nutrition facts
(Per serving)
Calories 345
Fat 15.7g
Protein 22g
Carbs 28.4g

Ingredients:
- 1 pound of crabmeat
- 1 package of cornbread stuffing mix (6 ounces)
- 1 can of condensed cream of mushroom soup (10.75 ounces)
- 1/2 pound of peeled medium shrimp
- 1 can of chicken broth (14.5 ounces)
- 1/2 cup of margarine
- 1/2 cup of seasoned dry bread crumbs
- 1/2 cup of chopped celery
- 1/2 cup of green bell pepper chopped
- 2 tablespoons of white sugar(divided)
- 1/2 cup of chopped onion

Instructions:
Follow the instructions below to make delicious seafood stuffing.
1.Preheat the convection oven at 400°F.
2.On medium heat, melt the margarine in a large-sized skillet. Add the onion, bell pepper, crabmeat, celery, and shrimp; stir and cook for around 5 minutes. Set them aside. Stir together the stuffing,1 tablespoon of sugar, and bread crumbs in a large-sized bowl. Mix in the cooked seafood and vegetables. Add in cream of mushroom and chicken broth according to your likeness. Spread the mixture into a 9x13 inch baking dish.
3.Bake for around 30 minutes in the preheated convection oven or until toasted from the top.

5.5 CRUSTED PARMESAN TILAPIA

Total time of cooking
20 minutes
Prep time 10 minutes
Cook time 10 minutes

Serving
4

Nutrition facts
(Per serving)
Calories 274
Fat 14g
Protein 36g
Carbs 0.5

Ingredients:
- 4 tilapia fillets
- 1 1/2 tablespoons of mayonnaise
- 1/4 cup of grated parmesan cheese
- 1 tablespoon of lemon juice fresh
- 2 tablespoons of butter
- Salt and pepper to taste
- 1 teaspoon of dill

Instructions:
Follow the instructions below to make crusted parmesan tilapia.
1.Combine all the ingredients except the tilapia in a small-sized bowl and set them aside.
2.Line a baking sheet with heavy-duty foil tightly and place tilapia on it.
3.Broil for 3 to 4 minutes, take out the pan from the oven, flip the tilapia and distribute the parmesan mixture on the uncooked sides of tilapia.
4.Return to the convection oven and broil for an additional 4 to 5 minutes. Make sure not to overcook tilapia.

5.6 STUFFED CRAB MUSHROOMS

Total time of cooking
30 minutes
Prep time 10 minutes
Cook time 20 minutes

Serving
16 mushrooms

Nutrition facts
(Per serving)
Calories 52
Fat 3g
Protein 2g
Carbs 2g

Ingredients:
- 16 large fresh mushrooms
- 6 ounces of crab
- 2 tablespoons of chopped parsley
- 4 ounces of softened cream cheese
- 1/3 cup of Parmesan cheese grated
- 2 thinly sliced green onions
- 1/4 teaspoon of garlic salt

For topping:
- 1 tablespoon of melted butter
- 1/4 cup of bread crumbs

Instructions:
Follow the instructions below to make stuffed crab mushrooms.
1. Preheat the convection oven to 350°F.
2. Whisk cream cheese until smooth and creamy. Stir in the remaining ingredients.
3. Spoon out the insides of the mushroom and discard.
4. Distribute the filling equally among all the mushroom caps. Mix topping ingredients and spread over mushrooms.
5. Bake in a preheated convection oven for around 18 to 20 minutes until fully cooked.

5.7 TASTY FISH CROQUETTES BAKED

Total time of cooking
35 minutes
Prep time 15 minutes
Cook time 20 minutes

Serving
6

Nutrition facts
(Per serving)
Calories 278
Fat 21.6g
Protein 10.1g
Carbs 14.1g

Ingredients:
- 2 cups of cooked steelhead trout
- 1/2 cup of sour cream
- 1 cup of soft bread crumbs
- 1/2 cup of mayonnaise
- 1/2 cup of panko bread crumbs
- 1/2 minced sweet onion
- 1/2 lemon juice
- 1/2 teaspoon of garlic powder
- 1/2 teaspoon of Worcestershire sauce
- Ground black pepper to taste
- 1/2 teaspoon of seasoned salt

Instructions:
Follow the instructions below to make fish croquettes baked.
1. Preheat the convection oven to 400°F.
2. Discard bones, skin, and any crust from trout. Shred with fork. Combine shredded fish with onion, soft bread crumbs, mayonnaise, lemon juice, sour cream, garlic powder, salt, and black pepper in a bowl—form balls out of the mixture coat in panko. Arrange balls on the baking sheet.
3. Bake in a preheated convection oven for 15 to 20 minutes or until croquettes turn light brown.

5.8 SEAFOOD COTTAGE CHEESE LASAGNA

Total time of cooking
55 minutes

Serving
12

Nutrition facts
(Per serving)
Calories 309.6
Fat 16g
Protein 18.8g
Carbs 22g

Ingredients:
- 1 can of drained crabmeat (7 1/2 ounce)
- 8 ounces of uncooked lasagna noodles (9 to 10 noodles)
- 1 can of drained baby shrimp (4 1/2 ounce)
- 2 cups of mozzarella cheese shredded
- 2 cups of milk
- 2 cups of chicken broth
- 1 cup of cottage cheese
- 1/2 cup of parmesan cheese grated
- 1/2 cup of sliced onion
- 1/2 cup of flour
- 1/2 cup of butter
- 1/4 teaspoon of black pepper
- 1/2 teaspoon of dried basil
- 1/2 teaspoon of salt
- 1/2 teaspoon of dried oregano
- 3 cloves of minced garlic

Instructions:
Follow the instructions below to make seafood cottage cheese lasagna.
1. Preheat the convection oven to 325°F. In a sauce, heat butter over medium heat and add garlic, add in flour, pepper, and salt; cook, occasionally stirring, then add milk and broth stir and heat to boiling for about 1 minute.
2. Mix in mozzarella, basil, onions, and oregano. Cook over low, medium heat until cheese melts down.
3. Place 1/4 of the cheese sauce in 13x9 inches baking dish. Layer with 3 to 4 uncooked lasagna noodles. Sprinkle cottage cheese over lasagna noodles. Repeat the procedure one more time and top with shrimp, crabmeat, 1/4 cheese sauce, and 3 to 4 lasagna noodles and cheese sauce. Finish with parmesan cheese.
4. Bake in the preheated convection oven until lasagna noodles are done for around 35 to 40 minutes.
5. Let it stand 10 minutes before eating.

5.9 TASTY BAKED COD FISH

Total time of cooking
30 minutes
Prep time 15 minutes
Cook time 15 minutes

Serving
4

Nutrition facts
(Per serving)
Calories 240
Fat 9g
Protein 35g
Carbs 4g

Ingredients:
- 4 filets of codfish
- 1 1/2 tablespoons of melted butter
- 1/2 lemon

For the topping:
- 1/4 cup of panko bread crumbs
- 1 tablespoon of parsley
- 2 tablespoons of fresh parmesan cheese
- 1/2 teaspoon of paprika
- 1 teaspoon of melted butter
- 1/2 teaspoon of garlic powder

Instructions:
Follow the instructions below to make tasty baked cod.
1. Preheat the convection oven to 375°F.
2. Combine all the ingredients of topping in a small-sized bowl.
3. Rinse cod filets and pat dry. Transfer on a greased pan, spread with butter, and squeeze lemon all over the filets.
4. Top the fillet with panko mixture and cook for around 15 minutes in a preheated convection oven. Broil for 1 minute in the end.

5.10 EASY AND QUICK-ROASTED SALMON

Total time of cooking
40 minutes
Prep time 10 minutes
Cook time 30 minutes

Serving
4

Nutrition facts
(Per serving)
Calories 413
Fat 25g
Protein 35g
Carbs 10g

Ingredients:
- 1 1/2 pounds of salmon fillets
- 3 tablespoons of brown sugar
- 1/4 cup of vegetable oil
- 1/4 cup of soy sauce
- 1 tablespoon of fresh lemon juice
- 1 teaspoon of toasted sesame oil
- 1/2 teaspoon of garlic powder
- 1/4 cup of water

Instructions:
Follow the instructions below to make easy and quick roasted salmon.
1. Preheat the convection oven to 375°F.
2. Except salmon, combine all other ingredients in a small-sized bowl.
3. Pour mixture on salmon and marinate for 1 hour.
4. After 1-hour, transfer salmon to a non-stick baking dish and roast in a preheated convection oven for around 30 minutes. Keep an eye during roasting, so fish don't get burnt.

5.11 DELICIOUS SEAFOOD SALAD BAKED

Total time of cooking
40 minutes
Prep time 10 minutes
Cook time 30 minutes

Serving
4-6

Nutrition facts
(Per serving)
Calories 20.6
Fat 0.1g
Protein 0.7g
Carbs 4.6g

Ingredients:
- 1 cup of chopped green pepper
- 1 cup of crabmeat
- 1/2 cup of chopped onion
- 1 cup of baby shrimp
- 1 cup of chopped celery
- 1 cup of mayonnaise
- 1/2 teaspoon of salt
- 2 tablespoons of soft bread crumbs
- 1 teaspoon of Worcestershire sauce
- 1/2 teaspoon of black pepper
- 1/2 lemon wedge
- 1 teaspoon of butter
- 1/2 teaspoon of paprika

Instructions:
Follow the instructions below to make seafood salad baked.
1. Preheat the convection oven to 325°F.
2. Shred crab meat with a fork. Combine shrimp, crab meat, green pepper, celery, onion, and mayo, add pepper, salt, and Worcestershire sauce.
3. Spread the mixture in a baking dish and top with butter and bread crumbs. Bake in a preheated convection oven for around 30 minutes.
4. While serving, sprinkle paprika on top and side with lemon wedges.

5.12 TASTY BROILED SCALLOPS

Total time of cooking
30 minutes
Prep time 15 minutes
Cook time 15 minutes

Serving
4

Nutrition facts
(Per serving)
Calories 142
Fat 8g
Protein 14g
Carbs 4g

Ingredients:
- 1 pound of sea scallops
- 1 tablespoon of lemon juice
- 1 clove of minced garlic
- 2 tablespoons of olive oil
- Pepper and salt to taste
- Parsley and lemon for garnishing
- 1/4 teaspoons of red chili flakes

Instructions:
Follow the instructions below to make tasty broiled scallops.
1.Combine garlic, olive oil, lemon juice, and red chili flakes and toss scallops in the mixture. Let stand for 10 to 15 minutes.
2.Transfer marinade scallops to the baking pan and sprinkle with pepper and salt. Broil in a convection oven for 5 to 10 minutes.
3.Sprinkle with parsley and side with lemon wedges while serving.

5.13 SCALLOPS. FLOUNDER AND SHRIMP LASAGNA

Total time of cooking
1 hour 10 minutes
Prep time 15 minutes
Cook time 55 minutes

Serving
6

Nutrition facts
(Per serving)
Calories 721
Fat 31g
Protein 39.7g
Carbs 68.3g

Ingredients:
- 2 cans of cream of mushroom (10.75 ounces)
- 1 package of lasagna noodles (16 ounces)
- 1/2 pound of scallops
- 12 ounces of cottage cheese
- 1/2 pound of flounder fillets
- 2 ounces of mozzarella cheese shredded
- 1/2 pound of peeled shrimp
- 1/2 cup of white wine
- 1 chopped onion
- 1/3 cup of milk
- 1 package of cream cheese (8 ounces)
- 1 egg
- 2 tablespoons of grated Parmesan cheese
- 2 tablespoons of butter
- 1/8 teaspoon of ground black pepper
- 2 teaspoons of dried basil
- 1/2 teaspoon salt
- 1 clove of minced garlic

Instructions:
1.In boiling water, cook lasagna, drain, and keep them aside.
2.In a butter cook onion. In a large-sized bowl, combine cream cheese, cottage cheese, salt, basil, pepper, sautéed onion, and egg. Set them aside.
3.Combine milk, mushroom soup, and garlic. Add in the white wine, scallops, shrimp, and flounder and mix. Keep them aside.
4.In a greased lasagna pan, spread a thin layer of seafood sauce on the bottom of the lasagna pan,1/5 of lasagna noodles,1/2 of cheese mixture,1/5 of noodles,1/2 of seafood mixture,1/5 of noodles,1/2 of cheese mixture,1/5 of noodles,1/2 of seafood mixture and remaining lasagna noodles. Spread parmesan and mozzarella cheese on top.
5.Bake in a convection oven at 325°F for around 45 to 55 minutes.

5.14 GRILLED SRIRACHA SHRIMPS

Total time of cooking
30 minutes
Prep time 15 minutes
Cook time 15 minutes

Serving
4

Nutrition facts
(Per serving)
Calories 287
Fat 20g
Protein 23g
Carbs 2g

Ingredients:
- 1 pound of peeled medium shrimp
- 3 tablespoons of sriracha
- 1/4 cup of melted butter
- 3 cloves of minced garlic
- 2 tablespoons of olive oil
- 1 tablespoon of lemon zest
- 1 teaspoon of parsley
- Cilantro for garnish
- 1 teaspoon of honey

Instructions:
Follow the instructions below to make grilled sriracha shrimps.
1.Combine all the ingredients in a large-sized bowl, stir and toss well to coat. Marinate the shrimps for around 30 minutes.
2.Transfer the coated shrimps to a non-stick baking sheet and grill in a convection oven at 325°F for around 10 to 15 minutes until completely cooked.

5.15 CHEESY CRABMEAT DIP

Total time of cooking
50 minutes
Prep time 10 minutes
Cook time 40 minutes

Serving
8

Nutrition facts
(Per serving)
Calories 210
Fat 15.7g
Protein 10.7g
Carbs 6.7g

Ingredients:
- 1 cup of shredded white Cheddar cheese
- 1 cup of meatless spaghetti sauce
- 1 package of softened cream cheese (8 ounces)
- 1 can of drained and flaked crabmeat (6 ounces)
- 2 tablespoons of Worcestershire sauce
- 1/2 teaspoon of salt
- 2 tablespoons of OLD BAY® Seasoning
- 1 teaspoon of ground black pepper

Instructions:
Follow the instructions below to make cheesy crabmeat dip.
1.Preheat the convection oven at 325°F.
2.In the bottom layer of the baking dish spread the spaghetti sauce evenly.
Mix the cream cheese, crabmeat, and cheddar cheese. Season with Worcestershire sauce, old bay, salt, and pepper. Spread over the spaghetti sauce layer evenly.
3.Bake for around 40 minutes in a preheated convection oven. Serve straight away with crackers or baguettes.

Total time of cooking
30 minutes
Prep time 10 minutes
Cook time 20 minutes

Serving
2

Nutrition facts
(Per serving)
Calories 590
Fat 39g
Protein 29g
Carbs 29g

Ingredients:
- 2 halved English muffins
- 1 sliced tomato sliced
- 2 ounces of cheddar cheese
For tuna salad:
- 6 ounces of white flaked tuna (water drained)
- 1 sliced green onion
- 1 teaspoon of Dijon mustard
- 1/3 cup of mayonnaise
- 1 stalk of finely diced celery
- Salt and pepper to taste

- 1/2 teaspoon of lemon juice

Instructions:
Follow the instructions below to make tasty tuna cheesy melts.
1.Preheat the convection oven at 375°F.
2.Combine all the ingredients of tuna salad in a small-sized bowl and mix.
3.Arrange English muffin halves on a non-stick baking sheet and broil for 2 to 3 minutes or until golden brown, then remove from a convection oven.
4.Distribute the tuna mixture equally over English muffins. Top with slices of tomato and cheddar.
5.Bake for 10 to 15 minutes in a convection oven or until cheese melts down. Broil for 1 minute in the end and serve.

5.17 BAKED TROUT FISH IN A FOIL

Total time of cooking
30 minutes
Prep time 10 minutes
Cook time 20 minutes

Serving
2

Nutrition facts
(Per serving)
Calories 213
Fat 10.9g
Protein 24.3g
Carbs 7.5g

Ingredients:
- 2 rainbow trout fillets
- 1 fresh sliced jalapeno pepper
- 2 teaspoons of garlic salt
- 1 sliced lemon
- 1 tablespoon of olive oil
- 1 teaspoon of ground black pepper

Instructions:
Follow the instructions below to make baked trout fish in foil.
1.Preheat the convection oven at 375°F.Rinse the fish fillets and pat dry.
2.Rub trout fillets with olive oil and sprinkle with pepper and garlic salt.
Transfer each fillet on a sheet of aluminum foil. Side with jalapeno slices and squeeze the lemon juice from the lemon's ends over the trout fillets.
Place lemon slices on top of trout fillets and tightly wrap the foil all over the fish and seal the edges. Transfer foil packets on a non-stick baking sheet.
3.Bake for around 15 to 20 minutes in a preheated convection oven and serve.

5.18 BUTTER LEMON BAKED SALMON FETTUCCINE PASTA

Total time of cooking
30 minutes
Prep time 15 minutes
Cook time 15 minutes

Serving
4

Nutrition facts
(Per serving)
Calories 516
Fat 24g
Protein 30g
Carbs 41g

Ingredients:
- 1 pound of skinless and boneless salmon
- 4 tablespoons of butter unsalted
- 3 tablespoons of lemon juice
- 2 finely sliced garlic cloves
- 1 tablespoon of olive oil
- Salt and pepper to taste

For Pasta:
- 1/2 cup of finely chopped dill and parsley
- 1/2 pound of fettuccine pasta

Instructions:
Follow the instructions below to make butter lemon baked salmon pasta.
1. Preheat the convection oven at 370°F.
2. Transfer salmon to a medium-sized baking dish and sprinkle both sides of salmon with pepper and salt.
3. Sprinkle with garlic and butter on top and drizzle over olive oil and lemon.
4. Bake in a preheated oven for around 15 minutes, cool for some time, and then flake into chunks.
5. Add cooked pasta and herbs into the salmon fish pan and toss to coat
fettuccine pasta.
6. Add more lemon if you like and sprinkle with salt and pepper. Serve straight away.

5.19 DELICIOUS GRILLED GARLIC SHRIMP

Total time of cooking
25 minutes
Prep time 10 minutes
Cook time 15 minutes

Serving
8 skewers

Nutrition facts
(Per serving)
Calories 190
Fat 16g
Protein 12g
Carbs 1g

Ingredients:
- 1 pound of peeled shrimp

For marinade:
- 2 teaspoons of lemon juice
- 2 tablespoons of chopped parsley
- 4 cloves of minced garlic
- 1 tablespoon of tomato paste
- 1/3 cup of olive oil
- 1 tablespoon of chopped fresh basil
- 1/2 teaspoon of black pepper
- 1/2 teaspoon of salt

For the garlic butter:
- 1/4 cup of melted butter
- Lemon wedges (for serving)
- 1 clove of minced garlic
- 1 teaspoon of chopped parsley

Instructions:
Follow the instructions below to make delicious grilled garlic shrimp.
1. Combine all the marinade ingredients in a medium-sized bowl and mix them together. Leave shrimps for at least 30 minutes.
2. Arrange shrimps on a skewer and transfer them to a baking sheet.
3. Grill for 10 to 12 minutes at 350°F in a convection oven.
4. Drizzle garlic butter all over the grilled shrimps and serve hot with lemon wedges.

5.20 SIMPLE CRAB TART WITH AVOCADO

Total time of cooking
40 minutes
Prep time 20 minutes
Cook time 20 minutes

Serving
8

Nutrition facts
(Per serving)
Calories 372
Fat 25.5
Protein 18.6
Carbs 18.3

Ingredients:
- 375g pack of ready-rolled puff pastry
- 24 peeled raw king prawns
- 400g of fresh white crabmeat
- 3 sliced small ripe avocados
- 2 tablespoon of crème fraiche
- Unsalted butter knob
- 1 tablespoon of mayonnaise heaped
- 1/2 lime juice
- Pinch of cayenne pepper
- A handful of chopped fresh dill

Instructions:
Follow the instructions below to make a simple crab tart with avocado.
1. Preheat the convection oven at 375°F.Unroll and spread the pastry on a non-stick baking sheet, flatten using your hands and prick holes all over the pastry with a fork. Bake for around 15 to 18 minutes in a preheated oven.
2. Once done, remove from the convection oven, let it cool down for 10 minutes and cut into 8 equal squares. Keep them aside.
3. Mix together mayonnaise and crab meat,crème fraiche, lime juice, cayenne pepper, and chopped dill. Set them aside.
4. In a frying pan, heat butter over medium-high heat and cook prawns until pink in color and slightly golden, cooked well and, set them aside.
5. Divide the sliced avocados evenly between the 8 pastry squares, then top up with a spoon full of the crab mixture and 3 prawns. Sprinkle with dill and serve.

5.21 SHRIMP AND CRABMEAT ENCHILADAS

Total time of cooking
50 minutes
Prep time 20 minutes
Cook time 30 minutes

Serving
6

Nutrition facts
(Per serving)
Calories 607
Fat 36.5g
Protein 26.8g
Carbs 42.6g

Ingredients:
- 1/4 pound of peeled and chopped shrimp
- 1 cup of half-and-half cream
- 1/2 pound of fresh crabmeat
- 1 chopped onion
- 6 flour tortillas (10 inches)
- 1/2 cup of sour cream
- 8 ounces of Colby cheese
- 1/4 cup of melted butter
- 1 tablespoon of butter
- 1/2 teaspoon of garlic salt
- 1 1/2 teaspoons of dried parsley

Instructions:
Follow the instructions below to make shrimp and crabmeat enchiladas.
1. Preheat the convection oven at 325°F.
2. Cook onion in one tablespoon of butter in a large-sized skillet until it softens. Remove skillet from the stove and add in crabmeat and shrimp. Mix half of the shredded cheese into the seafood. Spoon a mixture into each tortilla and roll the tortillas up to cover the mixture. Transfer the rolled tortillas to a 9x13 inch baking pan.
3. On medium heat, in a saucepan, combine sour cream, half and half cream, parsley,1/4 cup of butter, and garlic salt, mix. Pour prepared sauce on enchiladas and top up with remaining cheese.
4. Bake for around 30 minutes in a preheated oven and serve.

5.22 BAKED SALMON WITH HONEY GLAZED

Total time of cooking
30 minutes
Prep time 15 minutes
Cook time 15 minutes

Serving
4

Nutrition facts
(Per serving)
Calories 383
Fat 18g
Protein 35g
Carbs 20g

Ingredients:
• 4 salmon fillets (6 oz each)
• 2 tablespoons of olive oil
• Salt and pepper to taste
For sauce:
• 1/4 cup of honey
• 3 cloves of minced garlic
• 2 tablespoons of fresh lemon juice
• 1 tablespoon of butter
• 1/4 cup of soy sauce
• 1 teaspoon of cornstarch
• 1 teaspoon of red pepper flakes

Instructions:
Follow the instructions below to make baked salmon with honey glazed.
1.Preheat the convection oven at 375°F.With salt and pepper season salmon fillets.
2.Mix all the ingredients of sauce except butter in a small-sized bowl and whisk. Place into a saucepan and bring to boil for 2 to 3 minutes until slightly thickens. Mix in butter and set the sauce aside.
3.In a skillet on medium-high heat, warm olive oil, add salmon and cook for 1 minute from each side.
4.Transfer the salmon fillets into the pan and spoon prepared sauce all over salmon and bake for 8 to 10 minutes in a preheated convection oven or until salmon is cooked. Keep an eye to avoid overcooking.
5.Serve hot with lime wedges.

5.23 WATERCRESS AND CRAB MINI SOUFFLÉ TARTS

Total time of cooking
30 minutes
Prep time 15 minutes
Cook time 15 minutes

Serving
4

Nutrition facts
(Per serving)
Calories 392
Fat 4.2g
Protein 17.2g
Carbs 26.3g

Ingredients:
• 150g of white crabmeat
• Short crust pastry cases (4 x 10cm)
• 140ml of whole milk
• 15g of butter
• 2 eggs(separated)
• 15g of plain flour
• A handful of chopped watercress
• 3 tablespoons of brown crabmeat
• Large pinch of cayenne pepper

Instructions:
Follow the instructions below to make watercress and crab mini soufflé tarts.
1.Preheat the convection oven at 375°F.
2.In a large-sized saucepan on medium heat, melt butter, then mix in the flour and cayenne pepper. Cook and stir for 2 minutes.
3.Slowly add in the milk and whisk until thick paste forms, then mix in the egg yolks (keep whites reserved), watercress and crabmeat.
4.Remove from stove and season.
5.In a bowl, whisk the reserved egg whites until peaks form.
6.Fold in egg whites into crab mixture gently until combined.
7.Distribute the mixture between the pastry cases, arrange cases on a baking sheet and bake in a convection oven for around 12 to 15 minutes. Serve and enjoy!

5.24 ONE-PAN GINGER SESAME SALMON

Total time of cooking

30 minutes

Prep time 15 minutes

Cook time 15 minutes

Serving

4

Nutrition facts

(Per serving)

Calories 387

Fat 15g

Protein 38g

Carbs 23g

Ingredients:

- 4 fillets of salmon
- 2 tablespoons of soy sauce
- 1 pound of broccoli (slice into florets)
- 2 tablespoons of brown sugar
- 1 tablespoon of grated ginger
- 2 tablespoons of rice wine vinegar
- 1 tablespoon of sesame oil
- 1 clove of minced garlic

For glaze:

- 2 tablespoons of chopped green onions
- 2 tablespoons of honey
- 1 teaspoon of soy sauce
- 1/2 teaspoon of sesame seeds toasted
- 1 teaspoon of sesame oil
- 1/2 teaspoon of grated ginger

Instructions:

Follow the instructions below to make one-pan of ginger sesame salmon.

1.Preheat the convection oven at 400°F.

2.Mix all the marinade ingredients and pour in a Ziploc bag with salmon to marinate for 1 hour.

3.On a greased pan, place salmon and discard the remaining marinade. Spread broccoli around the salmon in a pan and sprinkle with pepper and salt.

4.Bake in a preheated convection oven for around 12 to 15 minutes until salmon flakes.

5.Spread the glaze all over the baked salmon and sprinkle with green onions and sesame seeds.

6.Serve with rice.

5.25 DELICIOUS SEAFOOD GRATIN

Total time of cooking

30 minutes

Prep time 15 minutes

Cook time 15 minutes

Serving

8

Nutrition facts

(Per serving)

Calories 397

Fat 19.8g

Protein 44.4g

Carbs 4.2g

Ingredients:

- 1 pound of rinsed and drained bay or sea scallops
- 2 cups of shredded provolone cheese
- 1 pound of peeled fresh shrimp
- 1 pound of crab meat cooked
- 1/2 cup of Parmesan cheese grated
- 1 can of drained button mushrooms (4 ounces)
- 2 cups of hot chicken broth
- 1/2 cup of white wine
- 3 tablespoons of shallots chopped
- 2 tablespoons of fresh parsley chopped
- 3 tablespoons of butter
- 2 tablespoons of olive oil
- 2 tablespoons of all-purpose flour

Instructions:

Follow the instructions below to make delicious seafood gratin.

1.Preheat the convection oven at 375°F.Greased 8 smalls baking dishes with butter.

2.On medium-high heat, in a large-sized skillet, heat olive oil and cook scallops and shrimp until they are firmed, for 5 minutes.

3.Melt butter in a medium-sized saucepan over medium heat. Mix in flour and slowly add chicken broth and turn the heat to high keep stirring until thickened. Add in mushrooms, shallots, and wine; keep cooking for 5 to 10 minutes.

4.Spread scallops, crab, and shrimp in the bottom of greased dishes. Pour the sauce over seafood and top up with cheese.

5.Bake in a preheated convection oven for about 12 to 15 minutes.

6.Upon serving, sprinkle with parsley.

5.26 CRAB FILLED CRESCENT CUPS

Total time of cooking
30 minutes
Prep time 15 minutes
Cook time 15 minutes

Serving
18 crescent cups

Nutrition facts
(Per serving)
Calories 106
Fat 8g
Protein 2g
Carbs 6g

Ingredients:
- 4 ounces of softened cream cheese
- 1/2 cup of mozzarella and 1/3 cup(divided)
- 1 can of Pillsbury Crescent rolls
- 1/4 cup of mayonnaise
- 1 can of crabmeat (6 ounces)
- 1 1/2 teaspoons of lemon juice
- 1 finely sliced green onion
- 1/2 teaspoon of Worcestershire sauce
- 1 clove of minced garlic

Instructions:
Follow the instructions below to make crab-filled crescent cups.
1. Preheat the convection oven at 350°F.
2. Combine mayonnaise, cream cheese, Worcestershire sauce, lemon juice, garlic, 1/2 cup of mozzarella, and green onion. Fold in the crab meat and set them aside.
3. Unfold crescent rolls, spread and cut into 18 even squares.
4. Arrange crescent squares in a muffin pan and press the rolls into the cups. Distribute filling between cups. Sprinkle with the remaining 1/3 cup of cheese.
5. Bake for 12 to 14 minutes in a convection oven and cool for some time before serving.

5.27 TASTY SEAFOOD STUFFED PEPPERS

Total time of cooking
40 minutes
Prep time 15 minutes
Cook time 25 minutes

Serving
8

Nutrition facts
(Per serving)
Calories 411
Fat 24.1g
Protein 31.4g
Carbs 16.3g

Ingredients:
- 4 Cubanelle peppers (hollowed out and cut in half)
- 1 tilapia fillet (bite-size pieces)
- 8 ounces of Cheddar cheese shredded
- 8 ounces of Monterey Jack cheese shredded
- 4 ounces of small bay scallops
- 1 pound of peeled and diced medium shrimp(uncooked)
- 2 cups of white rice cooked
- 1 cup of Tomato Cocktail
- 1 small diced onion
- 1 tablespoon of lemon Juice
- 3 tablespoons of olive oil
- 1 tablespoon of seafood seasoning
- 10 chopped basil leaves
- 3 cloves of minced garlic

Instructions:
Follow the instructions below to make tasty seafood stuffed peppers.
1. Preheat the convection oven at 325°F.On medium-high heat in a pan, heat oil, add garlic and onion, and cook for 3 minutes. Add in tilapia, bay scallops, and shrimp, cook for 4 to 5 minutes until they are halfway done. Mix in tomato cocktail, seafood seasoning, lemon juice, rice, and basil, and cook for 5 minutes more.
2. Remove from stove; mix in Monterey jack cheese. Spoon prepared mixture into peppers and place in a non-stick baking sheet, cover with heavy-duty foil and bake for around 20 minutes in a preheated convection oven. After 20 minutes, remove foil and sprinkle the top of peppers with Cheddar; Bake for additional 5 minutes or until cheese melts down.

Total time of cooking

30 minutes

Prep time 10 minutes

Cook time 20 minutes

Serving

6

Nutrition facts

(Per serving)

Calories 197.9

Fat 8.7g

Protein 22.6g

Carbs 2.9g

Ingredients:

- 1 lb. of haddock fillet (cut into 6 equal pieces)
- 12 peeled jumbo shrimp
- 1 cup of cracker crumbs
- 4 ounces of small bay scallops
- 1/4 cup of melted butter
- 1/2 cup of white wine
- 2 teaspoons of garlic powder
- 2 tablespoons of lemon juice
- 1/2 lemon zest
- 1/2 teaspoon of black pepper

Instructions:

Follow the instructions below to make haddock and seafood baked.

1.Preheat the convection oven at 350°F.Place fish fillets on the bottom of a baking dish in a single layer, then top with shrimp and scallops.

2.Pour the lemon juice and white wine all over the seafood.

3.Mix cracker crumbs, butter, black pepper, garlic powder, and lemon zest in a bowl. Spread over the seafood.

4.Bake for around 15 minutes in a preheated convection oven. Then broil for 2 minutes until browned from the top.

5.29 FISH NUGGETS BAKED

Total time of cooking

25 minutes

Prep time 10 minutes

Cook time 15 minutes

Serving

4

Nutrition facts

(Per serving)

Calories 475

Fat 34g

Protein 26g

Carbs 15g

Ingredients:

- 1 pound of fish fillets
- 1/4 cup of flour
- 1/2 cup of cornflake crumbs
- 2 beaten eggs
- 1/2 cup of panko bread crumbs
- 1 teaspoon of garlic powder
- 1 tablespoon of lemon pepper seasoning
- 1 teaspoon of old bay seasoning

Instructions:

Follow the instructions below to make fish nuggets baked.

1.Preheat the convection oven at 400°F.

2.In a small-sized bowl, Whisk eggs and old bay seasoning and keep it aside.

3.In another separate bowl, mix both the crumbs, lemon pepper seasoning, and garlic powder.

4.Cut fish into bite-sized pieces about 1 to 2 inches.

5.Coat fish in flour. Dip each nugget into the egg evenly and then coat into a crumb mixture from each side.

6.Place on a baking paper-lined cookie sheet and coat with cooking spray.

7.Bake in a preheated convection oven for 10 minutes and broil for 2 minutes.

Total time of cooking
35 minutes
Prep time 15 minutes
Cook time 20 minutes

Serving
6

Nutrition facts
(Per serving)
Calories 349
Fat 33g
Protein 12g
Carbs 3g

Ingredients:
- 1 pound of peeled chopped, and cooked shrimp
- 1 cup of shredded cheddar cheese
- 1/4 cup of diced onion
- 8 ounces of cream cheese
- 2 dashes of hot sauce
- 1/2 cup of mayonnaise
- 1 tablespoon of butter
- 1 tablespoon of lemon juice
- 1/2 teaspoon of dill weed
- 1/4 teaspoon of garlic powder
- 1/2 teaspoon of old bay seasoning

Instructions:
Follow the instructions below to make baked shrimp dip.
1. Preheat the convection oven at 325°F.
2. In 1 tablespoon of butter, cook the onion for 5 minutes until the onion is tender.
3. With a mixer, beat mayonnaise, lemon juice, cream cheese, dill weed, hot sauce, garlic powder, and old bay seasoning until fluffy.
4. Fold in 3/4 cup of cheddar and shrimp meat in the prepared mixture.
5. Spread in a baking dish and sprinkle with remaining cheese. Bake in a preheated convection oven for around 18 to 20 minutes. And serve hot with crackers or baguettes.

5.31 BAKED GARLIC BUTTER LOBSTER TAILS

Total time of cooking
30 minutes
Prep time 15 minutes
Cook time 15 minutes

Serving
2

Nutrition facts
(Per serving)
Calories 515
Fat 36g
Protein 34g
Carbs 17g

Ingredients:
- 1 lobster tails(5oz)
- 4 tablespoons of melted butter
- 1/4 cup of parmesan cheese grated
- 1 teaspoon of Italian seasoning
- 5 cloves of minced garlic
- 1 lemon juice

Instructions:
Follow the instructions below to make baked garlic butter lobster tails.
1. Preheat the convection oven at 375°F. Mix parmesan, lemon juice, garlic, melted butter, Italian seasoning, and a pinch of salt in a medium-sized bowl.
2. Cut the skin off the lobster with sharp scissors and brush the garlic butter seasoning all over the lobster tails.
3. Transfer lobster tails on a non-stick baking sheet and bake lobster tails in a preheated convection oven for 12 to 15 minutes.
4. Serve and enjoy!

5.32 CRABMEAT AND SHRIMP LOAF

Total time of cooking
30 minutes
Prep time 10 minutes
Cook time 20 minutes

Serving
8

Nutrition facts
(Per serving)
Calories 379
Fat 17.1g
Protein 22.7g
Carbs 33.4g

Ingredients:
- 1 loaf of French bread, halved horizontally (1 pound)
- 1 can of crabmeat, drained and flaked (6 ounces)
- 1 package of mozzarella cheese shredded (8 ounces)
- 1 can of small shrimp, drained (6 ounces)
- 1/2 cup of mayonnaise
- 1/4 cup of celery diced
- 1/3 teaspoon of salt
- 1/4 cup of green onions thinly sliced
- 1/3 teaspoon of ground black pepper

Instructions:
Follow the instructions below to make crabmeat and shrimp loaf.
1.Preheat the convection oven at 375°F.
2.In a medium-sized bowl, combine crab, shrimp, green onions, mayonnaise, cheese, celery, pepper and salt together.
3.On the bottom half of the loaf, pour the shrimp mixture and cover with the top half. Wrap with heavy-duty foil tightly around the loaf and bake for around 20 minutes in a preheated convection oven.
4.While serving, cut the loaf into 8 pieces and enjoy!

5.33 SHRIMP AND BROCCOLI ALFREDO BAKE

Total time of cooking
40 minutes
Prep time 20 minutes
Cook time 20 minutes

Serving
4

Nutrition facts
(Per serving)
Calories 577
Fat 32.6
Protein 34.2g
Carbs 39g

Ingredients:
- 1 1/2 cups of Alfredo sauce
- 1 pound of raw peeled and deveined shrimp
- 1 package of angel hair pasta (8 ounces)
- 2 cups of broccoli chopped
- 1/2 cup of grated Parmesan cheese

Instructions:
Follow the instructions below to make shrimp and broccoli alfredo bake.
1.Preheat the convection oven at 325°F.With cooking spray, grease 2-quart casserole dish.
2.Cook angel hair pasta in salted boiling water according to your package instructions.
3.In a skillet on medium heat, cook shrimp for 4 to 5 minutes, then add broccoli and cover the skillet with a lid; about 5 minutes, let broccoli steam. Remove from stove.
4.On the bottom of the prepared baking dish, spread angel hair pasta. Top with broccoli and shrimp. Spread alfredo sauce all over shrimp and broccoli; a top sauce with parmesan cheese.
5.Bake in the preheated convection oven for around 20 minutes until the cheese turns slightly browned.

5.34 CRAB STUFFED MUFFINS

Total time of cooking
50 minutes
Prep time 20 minutes
Cook time 30 minutes

Serving
12

Nutrition facts
(Per serving)
Calories 235
Fat 13.3g
Protein 9.7g
Carbs 18.9g

Ingredients:
- 8 ounces of crabmeat cooked
- 1 cup of cornmeal
- 1 cup of buttermilk
- 1 cup of all-purpose flour
- 1/4 cup of pepper Jack cheese grated
- 1/2 cup of pepper Jack cheese grated
- 1/2 cup of melted butter
- 2 eggs
- 1 1/2 tablespoons of mayonnaise
- 1 tablespoon of green onion minced
- 1 teaspoon of Asian chili paste
- 1/2 teaspoon of baking soda
- 1 teaspoon of grated lemon zest
- 1/2 teaspoon of salt
- 1/4 teaspoon of Worcestershire sauce

Instructions:
Follow the instructions below to make crab-stuffed muffins.
1. Preheat the convection oven at 350°F. Grease 12 cup muffin pan with cooking spray.
2. In a large-sized bowl, combine 1/2 cup pepper jack cheese, crabmeat, chili paste, mayonnaise, Worcestershire sauce, and lemon zest. Sprinkle with salt. Refrigerate with cover.
3. In another large-sized bowl, Mix cornmeal, flour, baking soda, and salt. Whisk in buttermilk, eggs, melted butter, and green onion; whisk until fully incorporated.
4. Distribute the batter in the greased muffin pan evenly. Place 1 to 2 tablespoons of crab mixture in the middle of each muffin. Lightly press and top with 1/4 cup of pepper jack cheese among all muffins.
5. Bake in the preheated convection oven for around 25 to 30 minutes until golden brown from the top.

5.35 BAKED TERIYAKI SALMON

Total time of cooking
35 minutes
Prep time 15 minutes
Cook time 20 minutes

Serving
1

Nutrition facts
(Per serving)
Calories 693
Fat 49g
Protein 39g
Carbs 21g

Ingredients:
- 2 tablespoons of teriyaki sauce
- 1/2 cup of thinly sliced carrot
- 6 oz of skinless salmon (200 g)
- 1 cup of broccoli floret
- Olive oil to taste
- Ground black pepper to taste
- Salt to taste

Instructions:
Follow the instructions below to make baked teriyaki salmon.
1. Preheat the convection oven at 325°F.
2. On parchment paper, place carrots and broccoli. Drizzle olive oil, sprinkle with pepper and salt.
3. Place the salmon over the top of veggies and spread teriyaki sauce over the salmon.
4. Fold the parchment paper over the salmon tightly and seal the edges.
5. Bake for around 20 minutes in a preheated convection oven. Serve warm and enjoy!

5.36 CHEESY SEAFOOD WHITE SAUCE PIZZA

Total time of cooking
40 minutes
Prep time 15 minutes
Cook time 25 minutes

Serving
1 large pizza

Nutrition facts
(Per serving)
Calories 995.4
Fat 60.5g
Protein 83.7g
Carbs 27.4g

Ingredients:
- 2 cups of grated mozzarella cheese
- 1 large pizza dough
- 1 cup of crabmeat
- 2 1/2 cups of mornay sauce
- 12 scallops(halved)
- 1/2 cup of finely chopped red onion
- 1/2 cup of grated grana padano
- 1/2 cup of finely chopped red pepper
- 12 large prawns(halved)
- 1 teaspoon of clarified butter
- 3 cloves of garlic(pressed)
- 1/2 teaspoon of hot paprika
- 1 teaspoon of olive oil

Instructions:
Follow the instructions below to make cheesy seafood white sauce pizza.

1.Preheat the convection oven at 425°F.

2.Place dough in a non-stick pizza pan, sprinkle mozzarella cheese on the bottom, and spread crab meat, scallops and prawns on top of the mozzarella layer. Spread vegetable mixture and then drizzle mornay sauce over the vegetables. Finish with parmesan cheese on top and some hot paprika.

3.Bake in the preheated convection oven for 20 to 25 minutes or until seafood is completely cooked. Allow pizza to cool for 10 minutes before slicing.

5.37 TASTY SEAFOOD RAVIOLI BAKED

Total time of cooking
1 hour
Prep time 15 minutes
Cook time 45 minutes

Serving
6-8

Nutrition facts
(Per serving)
Calories 184.7
Fat 9.7 g
Protein 15.4g
Carbs 4.3g

Ingredients:
- 2 cups of shredded cheddar cheese
- Bag ravioli, cheese-filled (24 ounces)
- 2 cups of chopped crabmeat
- 2 cups of alfredo sauce
- 1 cup of chopped shrimp
- 1 teaspoon Old Bay Seasoning
- 1/4 cup of chopped and roasted red pepper
- 1 teaspoon of ground black pepper
- 2 tablespoons of warm water
- 1/2 teaspoon of salt

Instructions:
Follow the instructions below to make tasty seafood ravioli baked.

1.Preheat the convection oven at 325°F.Grease 9x13 casserole dish with cooking spray. Cook ravioli according to your package instructions and set it aside.

2.Combine in a bowl crab, alfredo sauce, shrimp, pepper, water, salt and pepper, old bay seasoning, and 1 cup of cheese.

3.Fold in the cooked ravioli and the sauce mixture gently, do not break the ravioli. Spread into greased casserole pan.

4.Cover with lid and bake in the preheated convection for around 30 minutes.

5.Sprinkle with remaining cheese on the top and bake without cover for 15 minutes more until cheese melts down.

6.Serve warm and enjoy!

5.38 SIMPLY BAKED SEAFOOD POTATOES

Total time of cooking
45 minutes
Prep time 15 minutes
Cook time 30 minutes

Serving
4-6

Nutrition facts
(Per serving)
Calories 362
Fat 29.8g
Protein 4.1g
Carbs 21.3g

Ingredients:
- 15 to 20 shrimp
- 1 package of Simply Potatoes Diced Potatoes with Onion (20 ounces)
- 1 1/2 cups of mayonnaise(dressing)
- 1/8 ounce of tobiko (flying fish egg)
- 1/2 teaspoon of salt

Instructions:
Follow the instructions below to make baked seafood potatoes.
1.Preheat the convection oven at 375°F.
2.Cut shrimps into bite-sized chunks. Combine mayonnaise, shrimp, tobiko, and salt in a medium-sized bowl. Spread the mixture on the top of diced potatoes layer in the baking dish.
3.Bake for around 20 minutes in the preheated convection oven. Then change the settings to broil and broil for another 8 to 10 minutes.
4.Serve and enjoy!

5.39 QUICK AND SIMPLE SEA BASS OVEN-BAKED

Total time of cooking
35 minutes
Prep time 15 minutes
Cook time 20 minutes

Serving
2

Nutrition facts
(Per serving)
Calories 294
Fat 11.4g
Protein 42.4g
Carbs 3.6g

Ingredients:
- 1/3 cup of white wine vinegar
- 1 lb. scaled and cleaned sea bass
- 2 lemon wedges
- 1 tablespoon of olive oil
- 2 teaspoons of ground black pepper
- 1 tablespoon of Italian seasoning
- 3 cloves of minced garlic
- 1 teaspoon of salt

Instructions:
Follow the instructions below to make sea bass oven baked.
1.Preheat the convection oven at 400°F.
2.Mix garlic, salt, olive oil, and black pepper in a cup.
3.Arrange fish in a baking dish ad rub fish with a prepared oil mixture. Pour white wine vinegar over fish.
4.Bake fish for around 15 minutes in the preheated convection oven. Then sprinkle the fish with Italian seasoning and bake for additional 5 minutes or until the fish is flaky.
5.Upon serving spread the remaining pan juices on top of fish and side with lemon wedges.

5.40 SPICY SEAFOOD PENNE PASTA

Total time of cooking
1 hour 5 minutes
Prep time 20 minutes
Cook time 45 minutes

Serving
6

Nutrition facts
(Per serving)
Calories 563.8
Fat 12.3g
Protein 37.2g
Carbs 78g

Ingredients:
- 16 ounces of penne pasta
- 1 can of whole undrained tomatoes (28 ounces)
- 16 ounces of bay scallops
- Frozen green peas, thawed (10 ounces)
- 8 ounces of large raw shrimp (cut half lengthwise)
- 3 cloves of minced garlic
- 1 cup of parmesan cheese grated
- 1 tablespoon of olive oil
- 1 tablespoon of butter
- 1 tablespoon of fresh basil chopped
- 1/2 onion
- 1 teaspoon of salt
- 1/4 teaspoon of black pepper
- 1/2 teaspoon of crushed red pepper flakes

Instructions:
1.Preheat the convection oven at 325°F.
2.In a large sauce, heat oil and cook onion and garlic for around 2 minutes until onion is soft.
3.Mix in both cans of tomatoes with juice, crushed red pepper. Black pepper and salt. Using a fork, crush tomatoes and bring to boil, low the level heat, and cook uncovered for 30 minutes.
4.Meanwhile, boil penne pasta according to your package instructions. Set it aside.
5.In a large-sized skillet, heat butter and cook shrimp on medium heat for 3 to 4 minutes, add scallops and mix for 10 seconds, and remove skillet from the stove.
6.Add prepared sauce, peas,1/2 cup of parmesan cheese pasta, and basil and mix well until fully incorporated.
7.Pour the mixture into a 13x9 inch greased baking dish and top up with remaining cheese.
8.Cover with lid and bake in a preheated oven for around 35 minutes; after 35 minutes, uncover the dish and bake for additional 10 minutes until the top is slightly browned.

5.41 MAYO-CHEESE MUSSELS DYNAMITE

Total time of cooking
40 minutes
Prep time 20 minutes
Cook time 20 minutes
Serving
2

Nutrition facts
(Per serving)
Calories 367
Fat 34g
Protein 10g
Carbs 5g

Ingredients:
- 12 frozen green mussels on half-shells
- 2 tablespoons of Parmesan cheese
- 1 tablespoon of tobiko fish roes
- 6 tablespoons of mayonnaise
- 1/2 teaspoon of lime juice
- 1 teaspoon of sugar
- 1/2 teaspoon of sriracha

Instructions:
Follow the instructions below to make mayo cheese mussels dynamite.
1.Preheat the convection oven at 325°F.Rinse and clean mussels and dry out with kitchen towels.
2.In a small-sized bowl, combine all the ingredients except mussels and mix well.
3.Spread the mussels on a non-stick baking sheet; spread 1/2 teaspoon of mayo cheese mixture on top of each mussel.
4.Bake the mussels in a preheated convection oven for around 20 minutes until mussels become light brown in color. When baked, top with tobiko fish roes and serve hot.

5.42 GARLIC MAYONNAISE-PARMESAN TOPPING HALIBUT

Total time of cooking
35 minutes
Prep time 15 minutes
Cook time 20 minutes

Serving
2

Nutrition facts
(Per serving)
Calories 237.2
Fat 8.2g
Protein 35.5g

Carbs 3.4g
Ingredients:
- 2/3 lb. halibut fillet
- 1/8 teaspoon of salt
- 2 teaspoons of lemon juice
- 1/8 teaspoon of ground black pepper

For topping:
- 1 teaspoon of tabasco sauce
- 2 tablespoons of light mayonnaise
- 1 tablespoon of parmesan cheese grated
- 1 tablespoon of lemon juice
- 1/2 teaspoon of Dijon mustard
- 1 clove of finely minced garlic
- 1 finely sliced green onion

Instructions:
Follow the instructions below to make garlic mayonnaise parmesan topping halibut.
1.Preheat the convection oven at 400°F.
2.For the topping, combine lemon juice, garlic, mayonnaise, parmesan, mustard tabasco, and green onion.
3.Place fish in a non-stick cookie sheet and sprinkle with salt, lemon juice, and pepper.
4.Bake in the preheated convection oven for around 12 to 15 minutes.
5.Once baking is done, Spread the topping all over the baked fish and broil in a convection oven for around 2 to 3 minutes or until it becomes golden.

5.43 TASTY BAKED TILAPIA PECAN-CRUSTED

Total time of cooking
35 minutes
Prep time 15 minutes
Cook time 20 minutes

Serving
4

Nutrition facts
(Per serving)
Calories 330.4
Fat 12.4g
Protein 38.3g
Carbs 16.9g

Ingredients:
- 4 tilapia fillets (6 ounces)
- 2 tablespoons of chopped pecans
- 3 tablespoons of flour
- 1/2 cup of dry bread crumbs
- 1 tablespoon of oil
- 1/2 cup of buttermilk (low fat)
- 1/2 teaspoon of salt
- 1/2 teaspoon of hot sauce
- 1/4 teaspoon of black pepper
- 1/4 teaspoon of garlic powder
- Lemon wedges for garnishing

Instructions:
Follow the instructions below to make tasty baked tilapia pecan-crusted.
1.Preheat the convection oven at 400°F.Combine pecans, breadcrumbs, pepper, garlic, and salt, in a medium-sized bowl.
2.In another medium-sized bowl, mix in hot sauce and buttermilk.
3.In the third bowl, place flour.
4.Coat fillet into flour, then dip in buttermilk batter, and then finally into breadcrumb mixture.
5.Place fish into a non-stick baking sheet and pour oil all over the fillets. Bake for 15 to 20 minutes in a preheated convection oven. When baking is done, broil for 1 to 2 minutes in a convection oven.
6.Serve hot and side with lemon wedges.

Total time of cooking

35 minutes
Prep time 15 minutes
Cook time 20 minutes

Serving

4-6

Nutrition facts

(Per serving)
Calories 904.1
Fat 46g
Protein 62.7g
Carbs 52.7g

Ingredients:

- 1 1/2 cups of milk
- 1 cup of grated gruyere cheese
- 100g of salad prawns
- 150g of quartered scallops
- 100g of medium prawns
- 650g of white fish fillets (chopped into bite-sized pieces)
- 2 cups of panko breadcrumbs(flakes)
- 3 tablespoons of gruyere extra
- 1 diced onion
- 1/2 cup of dry white wine
- 2 tablespoons of chopped dill
- 1 cup of cream
- 40g of butter
- 2 tablespoons of chopped parsley
- 1 1/2 teaspoons of fish stock granules
- 3 teaspoons of corn flour
- 3 crushed garlic cloves
- Olive oil

Instructions:

1.Preheat the convection oven at 400°F.In a pan, heat olive oil in a small amount, add garlic and onion and cook until translucent; add in white wine and mix well.

2.Combine corn flour with water and add a little amount of corn flour to the garlic onion mixture to thicken the mixture, mix in fish stock, milk, dill, and cheese, keep stirring until cheese melts down, add existing corn flour mix and mix again until mixture thickens.

3.Add in prawns, spinach, fish, and scallops and keep mixing until spinach wilts about 3 to 4 minutes, then pour in the cream and mix to combine and remove from stove.

4.Melt butter in a frying pan, add parsley and panko flakes, mix to combine.

5.Spread fish mixture into a casserole dish and sprinkle with panko mixture and extra cheese on top of the dish.

6.Bake in a preheated convection oven for around 20 minutes or until lightly brown.

7.Garnish with extra dill on top while serving if you like.

5.45 CLASSIC BAKED CATFISH FILLETS

Total time of cooking

30 minutes
Prep time 10 minutes
Cook time 20 minutes

Serving

6

Nutrition facts

(Per serving)
Calories 210.4
Fat 7.4g
Protein 19.1g
Carbs 16g

Ingredients:

- 6 catfish fillets (4 ounces)
- 3/4 cup of yellow cornmeal
- 1 teaspoon of ground red pepper
- 1/4 cup of all-purpose flour
- 1/4 teaspoon of garlic powder
- 2 teaspoons of salt
- Vegetable oil
- 1/4 teaspoon of salt

Instructions:

Follow the instructions below to make classic baked catfish fillets.

1. Preheat the convection oven at 350°F.
2. Combine cornmeal, flour, 2 teaspoons of salt, ground red pepper, and garlic powder in a large-sized bowl.
3. Sprinkle 1/4 teaspoon of salt on both sides of catfish, dip in cornmeal mixture, and coat evenly.
4. Transfer to a non-stick baking sheet and drizzle with a small amount of oil all over the fish.
5. Bake catfish in a preheated convection oven for around 20 minutes until golden in color.
6. Serve and enjoy!

5.46 CRABMEAT ROLL-UPS LASAGNA

Total time of cooking

45 minutes
Prep time 15 minutes
Cook time 30 minutes

Serving

6

Nutrition facts

(Per serving)
Calories 198.4
Fat 3g
Protein 14.3g
Carbs 28.6g

Ingredients:

- 1/4 cup of parmesan cheese
- 8 ounces of crabmeat
- 6 cooked lasagna noodles
- 1 cup of drained 1% fat cottage cheese
- 2 crushed garlic cloves
- 1 egg
- 1 can of Italian tomato sauce (15 ounces)
- 1 tablespoon of dried parsley
- 1 tablespoon of Italian seasoning
- 1/4 teaspoon of onion powder

Instructions:

Follow the instructions below to make crabmeat roll-ups lasagna.

1. Preheat the convection oven at 350°F.
2. For lasagna sauce, combine Italian seasoning tomato sauce and garlic.
3. For filling, mix cottage cheese, parmesan, crabmeat, egg, onion powder and parsley.
4. Place 1/3 cup of filling on each lasagna. Roll each lasagna tightly. In a 9 inches square pan, place the roll seam side down.
5. Drizzle sauce over roll-ups.
6. Covered with lid and bake in a preheated convection oven at 350°F for around 30 minutes.
5. Garnish in the end with grated cheese.

5.47 BROILED STEELHEAD TROUT WITH LEMON GARLIC AND ROSEMARY

Total time of cooking

25 minutes
Prep time 10 minutes
Cook time 15 minutes
Serving
3-4

Nutrition facts

(Per serving)
Calories 45.1
Fat 4.6g
Protein 0.2g
Carbs 1.3g

Ingredients:

- 1 1/2 tablespoons of chopped fresh rosemary
- 1 lb. steelhead fillet (with or without skin)
- 1 lemon zest
- 1/4 teaspoon of salt
- 1 clove of chopped garlic
- 1/2 lemon juice
- 1/2 teaspoon of ground black pepper
- 1 tablespoon of olive and additional for dish greasing

Instructions:

Follow the instructions below to make broiled steelhead trout with lemon, garlic, and rosemary.

1. Preheat the convection oven at 325°F.Line a baking sheet with foil and brush with olive oil.
2. Mix all ingredients except fish into a paste.
3. Place fish into a prepared baking pan, then pour seasoning all over the flesh.
4. Broil fish in a convection oven at 2nd rack for around 5 minutes.
5. Shift baking pan to 3rd or 4th rack and bake for 10 minutes until fish is flaky.
6. Serve with salad or steamed vegetables of your choice.

5.48 CRABMEAT AND PRAWNS SOUTHWESTERN THIN CRUST PIZZA

Total time of cooking

30 minutes
Prep time 10 minutes
Cook time 20 minutes

Serving

1-2

Nutrition facts

(Per serving)
Calories 1185
Fat 69.6g
Protein 81.2g
Carbs 62.6g

Ingredients:

- 1 cup of crab meat shredded
- 3 whole wheat large tortillas
- 18 cleaned and cooked prawns
- 1 1/4 cups of black bean salsa
- 3 cloves of smashed fresh garlic
- 2 tablespoons of butter
- 1 3/4 cups of cheddar cheese
- 1/2 cup of dried fried onion flakes
- 1/2 teaspoon of dried chili pepper flakes

Instructions:

Follow the instructions below to make crabmeat and prawns southwestern thin crust pizza.

1. Brush the butter on top of each tortilla, especially on the outer edges. Place one tortilla on top of the other, press the tortillas together, and transfer to a greased pizza pan.
2. Preheat the convection oven at 375°F.
3. Spread black bean salsa on the bottom of the pizza crust. Place prawns and crab.
4. Sprinkle with garlic and dried onions, then distribute the cheese evenly on top.
5. Bake for around 20 minutes in a preheated convection oven or until cheese is brown and bubbly.

5.49 CRISPY LOBSTER AND CRAB STUFFED MUSHROOMS

Total time of cooking
25 minutes
Prep time 10 minutes
Cook time 15 minutes

Serving
8

Nutrition facts
(Per serving)
Calories 310
Fat 22g
Protein 21.9g
Carbs 6.9g

Ingredients:
- 1 cup of seasoned croutons crushed
- 1 can of crabmeat (6 ounces)
- 1 pound of fresh mushrooms (stems removed)
- 1 pound of cleaned and chopped lobster tail
- 1 cup of mozzarella cheese shredded
- 3/4 cup of melted butter(divided)
- 1/4 cup of mozzarella cheese shredded
- Three tablespoons of garlic minced

Instructions:
Follow the instructions below to make crispy Lobster and crab-stuffed mushrooms.
1.Preheat the convection oven at 350°F.With 1/4 cup of melted butter, grease a large-sized baking sheet. Place mushroom caps over the baking sheet in a single layer.
2.Mix together, remaining 1/2 cup of butter, shredded cheese, crushed croutons, Lobster, crabmeat, and garlic, in a medium-sized bowl. Place filling into mushrooms caps evenly.
3.Bake for 12 to 15 minutes in a preheated convection oven or until golden browned from the top. Sprinkle additional cheeses on top if you like. Serve warm.

5.50 ITALIAN STYLE BAKED OYSTERS

Total time of cooking
20 minutes
Prep time 10 minutes
Cook time 10 minutes

Serving
8 (3 oysters per person)

Nutrition facts
(Per serving)
Calories 76
Fat 2.5g
Protein 5.4g
Carbs 7.7g

Ingredients:
- 24 oysters (on the half shell)
- 1 1/2 slices white bread (1 ounce)
- 1/4 cup of fresh parsley chopped
- 1/4 cup of Italian-seasoned breadcrumbs
- 1/3 cup of green onions sliced
- 1/4 cup of parmesan cheese grated
- 8 wedges of lemon
- 2 cloves of garlic minced
- 1 teaspoon of lemon juice
- 1/8 teaspoon of black pepper
- 1/8 teaspoon of ground red pepper
- Cooking spray

Instructions:
Follow the instructions below to make Italian-style baked oysters.
1.Preheat the convection oven at 425°F.
2.Put bread in a food processor and process until crumbs form.
3.On medium heat, coat a non-stick skillet with cooking spray. Add parsley, garlic, and onions and cook for around 5 minutes; keep stirring. Remove from stove and stir in breadcrumbs, Italian breadcrumbs, parmesan cheese, ground red pepper, lemon juice, and black pepper.
4.Spread oysters on a jelly roll baking pan, Pour breadcrumb mixture on oysters evenly.
5.Bake the oysters for around 8 to 10 minutes or until oyster edges curl. Side with lemon wedges while serving.

5.51 LEMON-HERB BAKED RAINBOW TROUT

Total time of cooking

18 minutes

Prep time: 14 minutes

Cook time: 4 minutes

Servings

3

Nutrition facts

(Per Servings)

Calories: 276 kcal

Fat: 13.6 g

Protein: 35.1 g

Carbs: 2.3 g

Ingredients

- Pepper and salt to taste
- A single lemon (sliced)
- 1 tbsp tarragon
- 1 big rainbow trout fillet
- 1 tbsp olive oil extra virgin
- 1 tablespoon marjoram

Instructions

1.Turn on the oven at 420° F and set the rack in the middle of it. Spread a baking pan with non-stick spray and line it with aluminum foil. Put the fillet on the baking sheet.

2.Season the fish with salt and pepper. Lemon slices should be placed on top of the fish fillet. Top the fish fillets with tarragon and marjoram and lemon wedges. Drizzle olive oil over the fillet of fish.

3.Bake for 14 minutes, or until the fish flakes easily when tested with a fork and is opaque in the middle. Remove the dish from the oven.

4.Serve the fish in three equal portions. It's delicious with wild rice and steamed veggies or in a salad with a balsamic vinaigrette over fresh greens.

5.52 PARMESAN HERB BAKED TILAPIA

Total time of cooking

40 minutes

Prep time: 10 minutes

Cook time: 30 minutes

Servings

4

Nutrition Facts

(Per Serving)

Calories: 223.9 kcal

Fat: 4.8 g

Protein: 35.6 g

Carbs: 7.9 g

Ingredients

- tilapia fillets
- cooking spray
- a quarter cup of fat-free mayonnaise
- 1/3 cup parmesan cheese, grated
- 1/4 cup breadcrumbs, dry
- 1 tablespoon green onions, minced
- 1 teaspoon oregano, dry
- 1 tsp basil (dried)
- a quarter teaspoon of black pepper
- a quarter teaspoon of salt

Instructions

1.Preheat the oven to 400 degrees Fahrenheit. Place the Tilapia on a baking sheet sprayed with cooking spray.

2.Mayonnaise, cheese, and onions are mixed together and sprinkled evenly over the fish. Toss together the breadcrumbs and the additional ingredients; evenly sprinkle over the fish. Spray the fish lightly with cooking spray.

3.Bake for 12 minutes at 400°, or until the fish flakes easily when checked with a fork.

5.53 GRILLED GARLIC SALMON

Total time of cooking
35 minutes
Prep time: 20 minutes
Cook time: 15 minutes

Servings
5

Nutrition Facts
(Per Serving)
Calories: 186.2 kcal
Fat: 12.6 g
Protein: 17.1 g
Carbs: 0.9 g

Ingredients
- cloves garlic
- 1/2 gallon of milk
- 1 fillet of big salmon, sliced to pan size
- 1/2 teaspoon of garlic salt
- 1/2-1 teaspoon of lemon pepper
- 1 tbsp olive oil
- 1 tablespoon of butter

Instructions

1   1/2 cup milk, fine fillet You may soak the fish in milk for up to 5 minutes if it has a stronger odor. Preheat the oven to 350 degrees Fahrenheit.

2   Melt butter and oil in an oven-safe pan until hot. Garlic, finely minced, should be added now. Place the fish skin-side down. Cook for 1 minute. Garlic salt and lemon pepper are the flesh side of the fish. Brown for 2 minute on the other side.

3   Place the fish skin-side down and place it in a 350-degree oven. For medium fish, roast for 5 minutes for every inch of fillet thickness, and for well-done fish, roast for 10 minutes each inch.

5.54 GINGER SOY MAHI MAHI

Total time of cooking
40 minutes
Prep time: 20 minutes
Cook time: 20 minutes

Servings:
4

Nutrition Facts
(Per Serving)
Calories: 190.1 kcal
Fat: 3.1 g
Protein: 33.9 g
Carbs: 8.4 g

Ingredients
- 1 ½ Tbsp brown sugar
- tbsp water
- teaspoons low sodium soy sauce
- 1 tbsp balsamic vinaigrette
- pepper and salt to taste
- 1 tsp. chopped garlic
- 1 tsp. ginger powder
- 1 1/4 pound raw mahi-mahi fillets, sliced into four pieces
- 1 teaspoon extra virgin olive oil

Instructions

1.Stir together the water, garlic sugar, soy sauce, ginger, balsamic vinegar, and olive oil in a shallow glass dish.

2.Season the mahi-mahi with salt and pepper before placing them in the dish.

3.To marinate, cover and chill for 20 minutes (turning after 10 minutes).

4.Preheat the oven to 350 degrees Fahrenheit.

5.Take the fish out of the plate. While the fish is roasting, pour the remaining marinade into a pan and reduce until it reaches a glaze consistency. Set aside until the fish is fully cooked.

6.Place the fish on a baking pan and bake for 10 to 15 minutes, or until it flakes easily with a fork. Check the fish often to prevent overcooking. Transfer the fillets to a serving tray, drizzle the glaze over the fish, and serve right away. To round off your dinner, serve it with wild rice and a vibrant vegetable or salad.

5.55 OVEN-BAKED SEA BASS

Total time of cooking

40 minutes

Prep time: 20 minutes

Cook time: 20 minutes

Servings:

2

Nutrition Facts

(Per Serving)

Calories: 299.0 kcal

Fat: 11.4 g

Protein: 41.6 g

Carbs: 7.3 g

Ingredients

- 1 tbsp olive oil (extra virgin)
- 1 tsp coarsely ground black pepper
- 1 tsp kosher salt
- tsp garlic cloves smashed in a press
- sea bass fillets (cleaned and scaled)
- 1/3 cup white wine vinegar
- Garnish with a lemon wedge
- 1/2 cup fresh parsley leaves

Instructions

1.Preheat the oven to 450 degrees Fahrenheit. Combine the oil, salt, garlic, and pepper in a cup. Fill a shallow 1-quart glass or ceramic baking dish halfway with water. Brush the fish with the oil mixture. Pour wine over the fish and serve.

2.Bake for 15 minutes, uncovered, until opaque throughout and the thickest portion of the fish flakes easily when checked with a fork; sprinkle with parsley and bake for 3 minutes further.

3.Serve the fish with lemon wedges and any pan juices.

5.56 CAJUN TILAPIA

Total time of cooking

30 minutes

Prep time: 25 minutes

Cook time: 5 minutes

Servings

3

Nutrition Facts

(Per Serving)

Calories: 168.1 kcal

Fat: 9.0 g

Protein: 21.0 g

Carbs: 0.0 g

Ingredients

- ¼ Salt
- Talapia Fillets
- ¼ Pepper
- 1 tbsp Margarine

Instructions

1.Preheat the oven to 400 degrees Fahrenheit.

2.Season 3 thawed fish fillets with salt, pepper.

3.Put the fish fillets on a nonstick baking sheet and spread 1 teaspoon of margarine over each fillet.

4.Bake for 22 minutes, or until fish is flaky, with foil covering the whole pan.

5.57 BROILED SWAI WITH SALSA

Total time of cooking
20 minutes
Prep time: 15 minutes
Cook time: 5 minutes

Servings
1

Nutrition Facts
(Per Serving)
Calories 100.0 kcal
Fat: 2.5 g
Protein: 15.0 g
Carbs: 4.0 g

Ingredients
• tbsp Mild One Chunky Salsa
• oz Swai Fillet
• ½ tsp Smokey Paprika
• ½ tsp Garlic Powder
• Use extra Extra Virgin Olive Oil on a paper towel to keep the fish from adhering to the foil.
• Smokehouse Pepper

Instructions
Prep:
1. Rinse and pat dry the filet.
2. To avoid the Swai from adhering to the foil, gently wipe it with EVOO on a paper towel. Place the filet(s) on a baking sheet coated with foil.
3. Season the filet with seasonings.
4. Dollop Distribute 4 tbsp salsa on top of the filet and spread evenly.
Cook:
1. Place a cookie sheet approximately 6" below the heat of the broiler. Set a 15-minute timer.
2. When the timer beeps, inspect the fish. White skin, not transparent flesh, is what you want to see. Increase the time on your timer and keep an eye on the fish to avoid overcooking it.
3. Enjoy the fish and your sides on a plate!

5.58 PARMESAN-CRUSTED WHITE FISH

Total time of cooking
22 minutes
Prep time: 15 minutes
Cook time 7 minutes

Servings
4

Nutrition Facts
(Per Serving)
Calories: 216.4 kcal
Fat: 10.1 g
Protein: 29.0 g
Carbs: 1.3 g

Ingredients
• Paprika (2 teaspoons)
• tilapia fillets (approximately 1 pound total)
• 1/2 cup freshly grated parmesan cheese
• Pepper and salt to taste

Instructions
1. Preheat oven to 400 degrees Fahrenheit. Combine the cheese and paprika in a shallow dish and season with salt and pepper to taste.
2. Drizzle olive oil over the fish before dredging it in the cheese mixture. Place the fish on a foil-lined baking sheet and bake for 10 to 12 minutes, or until opaque in the thickest portion.
3. Serve the fillets with lemon wedges on the side.

5.59 CRUNCHY OVEN FRIED FISH

Total time of cooking
27 minutes
Prep time: 12 minutes
Cook time: 15 minutes

Servings
4

Nutrition Facts
(Per Serving)
Calories: 183.7 kcal
Fat: 1.7 g
Protein: 28.4 g
Carbs: 11.5 g

Ingredients
- 1 beaten egg white
- 1 pound fillets of cod
- 1/4 cup bread crumbs, dry
- A quarter cup of buttermilk
- 1 1/2 tablespoons grated lemon peel
- A quarter cup of cornmeal
- A quarter teaspoon of black pepper
- A half teaspoon of basil

Instructions
1. Preheat the oven to 450 degrees Fahrenheit.
2. Fish should be cut into serving-size pieces.
3. Set aside one egg white that has been beaten with buttermilk until foamy.
4. Combine cornmeal, bread crumbs, basil, lemon peel, and salt and pepper in a mixing bowl.
5. Coat the fish with bread crumbs after dipping it in the egg white mixture.
6. Using non-stick cooking spray, coat a small baking pan.
7. Place the fillets in the baking pan, tucking any thin edges under.
8. Bake for 6 to 12 minutes, or until the fish flakes easily when tested with a fork.

5.60 HONEY DIJON SALMON

Total time of cooking
30 minutes
Prep time: 20 minutes
Cook time: 10 minutes

Servings
4

Nutrition Facts
(Per Serving)
Calories: 302.9 kcal
Fat: 14.9 g
Protein: 31.1 g
Carbs: 9.2 g

Ingredients
- 1 teaspoon mustard
- 1 tsp parsley (dry)
- Salmon filet, 16 oz., deboned and skinned
- 1 oz (20 halves) nuts
- big slices of whole-grain bread, chopped and combined to make crumbs

Instructions
1. Preheat the oven to 425 degrees Fahrenheit.
2. Set aside a small bowl containing nuts, bread crumbs, and parsley.
3. Place the fish in a baking dish that has been buttered. Apply honey dijon on the top of the fish. Toss the bread crumbs on top of the fish.
4. Bake for 24 minutes (until the fish is firm). Serves four people at 4 ounces each.

5.61 PARMESAN BASIL SALMON

Total time of cooking

50 minutes
Prep time: 35 minutes
Cook time: 15 minutes

Servings

4

Nutrition Facts

(Per Serving)
Calories: 153.9 kcal
Carbs: 3.5 g
Protein: 23.0 g
Fat: 4.7 g,

Ingredients

- tbsp breadcrumbs
- tbsp grated parmesan cheese
- paprika, 1/2 teaspoon
- 1 tbsp fresh basil (chopped)
- Salmon, 1 pound
- 1 tsp. pepper
- 1 tbsp parsley, fresh or dried
- 1 tbsp butter spray

Instructions

1. Place the oven rack slightly above the middle of the oven.
2. Preheat the oven to 375 degrees Fahrenheit. Spray a 13 x 9 x 2-inch rectangle pan with cooking spray.
3. Except for the fish, margarine, and parsley, combine all ingredients in a mixing bowl.
4. Brush one side of the fish with margarine and then roll in the crumbs.
5. Place the fish in the pan with the coated sides facing up.
6. Bake 18 minutes, uncovered, or until fish flakes readily with a fork.
7. Garnish with parsley.

5.62 SMOKIN' MAHI MAHI

Total time of cooking

15 minutes
Prep time: 5 minutes
Cook time: 10 minutes

Servings

2

Nutrition Facts

(Per Serving)
Calories: 180 kcal
Fat: 3 g
Protein: 33 g
Carbs: 8 g

Ingredients

- tablespoons smoked paprika
- 6oz Mahi Mahi fillet
- tbsp olive oil
- salt, to taste
- one lemon

Instructions

1. First, infuse a cup of olive oil with a garlic clove and a few red chili peppers. Warm on the burner, then set aside to cool, filter, and pour into a bottle for use.
2. Drizzle olive oil on a cookie sheet, sprinkle paprika on the fish, set on a pan, gently salt, and drizzle with additional oil. Then bake for 9 minutes at 400°, flipping halfway through. Serve with a squeeze of fresh lemon

6.1 QUICK AND EASY ROASTED VEGETABLES TORTILLAS

Total time of cooking
30 minutes
Prep time 10 minutes
Cook time 20 minutes

Serving
8

Nutrition facts
(Per serving)
Calories 309
Fat 7.1g
Protein 13.7g
Carbs 48.6g

Ingredients:
- 8 flour tortillas(8-inch)
- 2 cups of leaf lettuce shredded
- 2 1/2 cups of zucchini julienne-cut
- 2 cups of strips red bell pepper
- 1 can of fat-free refried beans(16-ounce)
- 1 cup of tomato chopped
- 1 cup of reduced-fat cheddar cheese shredded (4 ounces)
- 2 cups of yellow squash julienne-cut
- 1 1/2 cups of red onion vertically sliced
- 1/2 cup of bottled salsa
- 3 tablespoons of dip mix and vegetable soup

Instructions:
Follow the instructions below to make quick and easy roasted vegetable tortillas.
1.Preheat the convection oven at 425°F.
2.In a large-sized zip-loc bag, place zucchini, bell pepper strips, yellow squash, and red onion. Add oil and vegetable soup mix and shake the bag well to coat. Spread vegetable mixture into 13x9 inch baking dish. Bake in a preheated convection oven for around 15 to 20 minutes.
3.Warm-up beans and tortillas according to your package instructions.
4.Place 3 tablespoons of beans on each tortilla and spread 1/2 cup of vegetable mixture and 1/4 cup of lettuce. Sprinkle with 1 tablespoon of tomato,2 tablespoons of cheese, and1 tablespoon of salsa.
5.Roll up and serve.

6.2 EASY BAKED APPLE-SUGAR PUFF PASTRY

Total time of cooking
25 minutes
Prep time 10 minutes
Cook time 15 minutes

Serving
12

Nutrition facts
(Per serving)
Calories 357
Fat 19.7g
Protein 3.3g
Carbs 43.8g

Ingredients:
- 1 package of puff pastry frozen (17.5 ounces)
- 12 pats of unsalted butter
- 6 thinly sliced red apples
- 1/2 cup of preserves apricot
- 1/2 cup of lemonade
- 1/2 cup of sugar superfine
- 1 pinch of sugar crystals coarse

Instructions:
Follow the instructions below to make a quick and easy baked apple-sugar puff pastry.
1. Preheat the convection oven at 325°F.
2. Using a sharp knife, cut puff pastry into 12 squares equally and place on a baking sheet.
3. Dip each one by one into lemonade and diagonally arrange on top of puff pastry square; spread each with 1 pat of butter and sprinkle with sugar-fine sugar in the end.
4. Bake for around 12 minutes in a preheated convection oven.
5. Boil apricot jam into saucepan; cook until jam gets thinned, for around 2 to 3 minutes. Spread jam evenly onto warm pastry; sprinkle top of the pastry with coarse sugar crystals.

6.3 EASY AND QUICK CHEESY BAKED GNOCCHI

Total time of cooking
30 minutes
Prep time 10 minutes
Cook time 20 minutes

Serving
1

Nutrition facts
(Per serving)
Calories 304
Fat 14.6g
Protein 11.2g
Carbs 32g

Ingredients:
- 1/4 cup of mozzarella cheese shredded
- 4 ounces of shelf-stable gnocchi
- 1/3 cup of pasta sauce

Instructions:
Follow the instructions below to make easy and quick cheesy baked gnocchi.
1. In boiling salted water, cook gnocchi for about 3 minutes or according to your package instructions and drain.
2. Preheat the convection oven at 325°F.
3. On the bottom of 5 inches round dish spread 1/2 of pasta sauce. Spread the layer of gnocchi and spread with the remaining sauce over gnocchi and top with shredded mozzarella.
4. Bake for around 20 minutes in the preheated convection oven until cheese melts down.

6.4 QUICK BAKED RED POTATOES WITH BUTTER AND SOUR CREAM TOPPING

Total time of cooking

25 minutes
Prep time 10 minutes
Cook time 15 minutes

Serving

6

Nutrition facts

(Per serving)
Calories 359.7
Fat 11.9g
Protein 7.1g
Carbs 58.9g

Ingredients:

- 5 tablespoons of coarse sea salt
- 6 large red potatoes
- 3 tablespoons of olive oil

For topping:

- 6 teaspoons of butter
- 3 tablespoons of chopped chives (divide into six)
- 6 teaspoons of sour cream
- Pepper and salt

Follow the instructions below to make quick baked potatoes with butter and sour cream topping.

1. Warm-up convection oven at 425°F.
2. Clean potatoes and prick holes in potatoes several times with a fork.
3. Arrange potatoes in a large-sized jelly roll pan and drizzle olive oil on top. Sprinkle with sea salt on both sides of potatoes evenly.
4. Mix all the ingredients of topping in a small-sized bowl and keep them aside.
5. Bake potatoes for around 15 minutes in the preheated convection oven. Once done, take out the pan and cut potatoes into half, spread topping on potatoes evenly, and broil in the convection oven for 1 minute. Serve warm.

Instructions:

6.5 LIME SCALLION FLAVORED SEA BASS

Total time of cooking

25 minutes
Prep time 10 minutes
Cook time 15 minutes

Serving

2-3

Nutrition facts

(Per serving)
Calories 338.9
Fat 13g
Protein 43.7g
Carbs 12g

Ingredients:

- 12 ounces sea bass (cut into sections)
- 2 tablespoons of lime juice
- 5 teaspoons of olive oil
- 3 tablespoons of soy sauce
- 1 bunch of scallions (white and pale green parts only, cut like match sticks)
- 1 tablespoon of minced shallot
- 1 tablespoon of minced ginger
- Salt and pepper to season

Instructions:

Follow the instructions below to make lime scallion-flavored sea bass.

1. Warm-up convection oven at 450°F.
2. Mix lime juice, soy sauce, shallot, ginger, scallions, 3 teaspoons of oil and pepper, and salt in a medium-sized bowl.
3. Brush the glass dish with the remaining oil. Place fish on a dish.
4. Spread sauce over fish. Reserve some amount for drizzling at the time of serving.
5. Bake fish for around 12 to 15 minutes in a convection oven.
6. Top with reserved sauce while serving.

6.6 CLASSIC CHICKEN AND PINEAPPLE CASSEROLE

Total time of cooking
25 minutes
Prep time 10 minutes
Cook time 15 minutes

Serving
4

Nutrition facts
(Per serving)
Calories 335
Fat 12g
Protein 23g
Carbs 30g

Ingredients:
• 1 can of undiluted cream of mushroom soup (10-1/2 ounces)
• 2 chopped celery ribs
• 2 cups of cooked chicken cubes
• 2 cups of pineapple (cut into cubes)
• 1 tablespoon of soy sauce
• 1 tablespoon of chopped green onion
• 1 can of chow mein noodles, divided (3 ounces)

Instructions:
Follow the instructions below to make classic chicken and pineapple casserole.
1. Warm-up convection oven at 350°F.
2. Combine all the ingredients from the list except noodles in a large-sized bowl and mix well. Then stir in 1 cup of chow mein noodles into the mixture.
3. Spread mixture to a casserole greased dish. Place remaining noodles on top and bake for around 10 to 15 minutes.
4. Serve warm and enjoy!

6.7 QUICK PARSLEY AND DILL ROLLS

Total time of cooking
25 minutes
Prep time 10 minutes
Cook time 15 minutes

Serving
4-6

Nutrition facts
(Per serving)
Calories 521.4
Fat 37.6g
Protein 7.4g
Carbs 39.6g

Ingredients:
• 1 can of hungry jack biscuits (12 ounces)
• 1/2 cup of butter
• 2 tablespoons of parmesan cheese grated
• 1 1/2 teaspoons of parsley flakes
• 1 tablespoon of onion powder
• 1/2 teaspoon of dill weed

Instructions:
Follow the instructions below to make quick parsley and dill rolls.
1. Melt butter in a microwave oven.
2. Mix in cheese and herbs into butter. Leave it for 10 to 15 minutes.
3. Using a knife, cut biscuits from the center into halves and dip in butter mixture from all sides to coat evenly.
4. Arrange into 9 inches cake baking pan.
5. Bake in the convection oven at 400°F for around 12-15 minutes.

Total time of cooking

30 minutes
Prep time 15 minutes
Cook time 15 minutes

Serving

8

Nutrition facts

(Per serving)
Calories 596
Fat 40.9g
Protein 19.9g
Carbs 37.3g

Ingredients:

- 1 pound of cooked ground beef
- 2 cups of lettuce shredded
- 2 deep dish pie crusts half-baked (9 inches)
- 1 cup of Cheddar cheese shredded
- 1 can of refried beans (16 ounces)
- 1 cup of tortilla chips crushed
- 1 large diced tomato
- 1 chopped onion
- Black olives
- Sour cream

Instructions:

Follow the instructions below to make beef and cheese taco pies.
1. Preheat the convection oven at 350°F.
2. Spread half refried beans in each pie crust, then layer with cooked ground meat and top up the crust with crushed tortilla chips, onion, and cheese.
3. Bake for around 10 to 15 minutes and then top with tomato, lettuce, black olives, and sour cream.

6.9 SIMPLE AND QUICK TORTILLA CRUST PIZZA

Total time of cooking

30 minutes
Prep time 15 minutes
Cook time 15 minutes

Serving

2

Nutrition facts

(Per serving)
Calories 564.8
Fat 30.6g
Protein 32.7g
Carbs 38.9g

Ingredients:

- 1 can of pizza sauce (15 ounces)
- 1 bag of flour tortillas (10 inches)
- 1 bag of mozzarella cheese shredded (8 ounces)
- Onions, sliced cherry tomatoes, and black olives
- Cooking spray

Instructions:

Follow the instructions below to make simple and quick tortilla quick pizza.
1. Preheat the convection oven at 350°F.
2. With cooking spray, coat the bottom of the first tortilla.
3. Place coated side down on cookie sheet. Sprinkle with a little amount of cheese. Layer up with another tortilla, sprinkle again with cheese, repeat the procedure for 2 more layers, and on the last tortilla, spread pizza sauce and onion, cherry tomato, and olives (or any other toppings of your liking).
4. Bake for around 10 to 15 minutes or until crust is light golden brown and cheese melts down.
5. Slice and enjoy!

6.10 CHOCOLATE CHIPS AND BUTTERSCOTCH BARS

Total time of cooking
30 minutes
Prep time 10 minutes
Cook time 20 minutes

Serving
16

Nutrition facts
(Per serving)
Calories 338
Fat 17.7g
Protein 2.8g
Carbs 42g

Ingredients:
- 2 packages of graham crackers(crushed)
- 1/2 package of butterscotch chips (12 ounces)
- 3/4 cup of melted butter
- 1/2 bag of chocolate chips (12 ounces)
- 1/2 can of condensed milk sweetened (14 ounces)
- Cooking spray
- 1/2 package of miniature marshmallows (10.5 ounces)

Instructions:
Follow the instructions below to make chocolate chips and butterscotch bars.
1.Preheat the convection oven at 350°F.With cooking spray grease square pan of 8x8 inch.
2.Mix in graham cracker crumbs and melted butter together; Spread a layer into the bottom of the greased pan evenly and press. Sprinkle with chocolate chips, butterscotch chips, and marshmallows. Spread with sweetened condensed milk on top of the pan.
3.Bake in the preheated convection oven for around 15 to 20 minutes.
4.Cool it down for a while before cutting it into bars.

6.11 TASTY AND QUICK MEATLOAF

Total time of cooking
30 minutes
Prep time 10 minutes
Cook time 20 minutes

Serving
4

Nutrition facts
(Per serving)
Calories 375
Fat 13g
Protein 27g
Carbs 38g

Ingredients:
- 1/2 cup of bread crumbs dry
- 5 tablespoons of ketchup(divided)
- 1 pound of ground beef
- 2 tablespoons of cider vinegar
- 1/4 cup of sugar
- 1 lightly beaten large egg
- 2 tablespoons of prepared mustard
- 2 tablespoons of onion soup mix
- 2 tablespoons of brown sugar
- 1/4 teaspoon of ground black pepper
- 1/4 teaspoon of salt

Instructions:
Follow the instructions below to make a tasty and quick meatloaf.
1.Preheat the convection oven at 400°F.
2.Combine mustard, egg, bread crumbs, dry soup mix,2 tablespoons of ketchup, pepper, and salt in a large-sized bowl. Stir in beef in the mixture and mix until fully incorporated. Shape into a loaf shape.
3.Place loaf into a shallow baking dish and bake in a preheated convection oven for around 20 minutes or until loaf changes color.
4.Meanwhile, combine vinegar, sugar, and remaining ketchup in a bowl and spread over meatloaf and broil in a convection oven for 1 minute.
5.Let it cool down for a while, then slice and enjoy!

6.12 CHEESY SALSA BEAN BURRITOS

Total time of cooking
30 minutes
Prep time 10 minutes
Cook time 20 minutes

Serving
6

Nutrition facts
(for 2 burritos)
Calories 216
Fat 9g
Protein 9g
Carbs 24g

Ingredients:
- 2 cups of cheddar cheese shredded, divided
- 1 can of refried beans (16 ounces)
- 12 flour tortillas (6 inches)
- 1 cup of salsa
- Lettuce shredded
- 1 cup of long-grain rice cooked

Instructions:
Follow the instructions below to make cheesy salsa bean burritos.
1.Preheat the convection oven at 350°F.Combine together salsa, rice, beans, and 1 cup of cheese. Spread 1/3 cup mixture on the center of each tortilla. Fold and roll up the tortillas
2.In a greased 13x9 inch baking dish, place burritos and spread with the remaining 1 cup of cheese on top. Cover with lid and bake for around 15 to 20 minutes. Before eating, top up with shredded lettuce.

6.13 BANANA OAT AND CINNAMON MUFFINS

Total time of cooking
30 minutes
Prep time 10 minutes
Cook time 20 minutes

Serving
12

Nutrition facts
(Per serving)
Calories 179.4
Fat 6.2g
Protein 4g
Carbs 30.4g

Ingredients:
- 1 cup of oat bran
- 2 large chopped and peeled bananas
- 1 1/4 cups of all-purpose flour
- 3/4 cup of milk
- 1/2 cup of brown sugar
- 1/4 cup of vegetable oil
- 1 tablespoon of baking powder
- 1 large egg
- 1/2 teaspoon of salt
- 1 teaspoon of vanilla
- 1/2 teaspoon of cinnamon

Instructions:
Follow the instructions below to make banana oat and cinnamon muffins.
1.Preheat the convection oven at 375°F.Grease 12 cup muffin pan.
2.Combine flour, oat bran, baking powder, brown sugar, salt, and cinnamon in a large-sized bowl.
3.Pour oil, egg, milk, and vanilla in a medium-size bowl and whisk to mix.
4.Mix in milk mixture with dry ingredients, stir to combine, add banana, and slightly fold.
5.Distribute batter among muffin cups evenly.
6.Bake in the preheated convection oven for around 20 minutes. Keep an eye when baking, so muffins don't get burnt.
7.Cool it down on a rack and serve.

6.14 QUICK BAKED ARTICHOKE AND BRIE

Total time of cooking
30 minutes
Prep time 10 minutes
Cook time 20 minutes

Serving
12

Nutrition facts
(Per serving)
Calories 200
Fat 16.3g
Protein 12.2g
Carbs 1.5g

Ingredients:
- 3 drained and chopped artichoke hearts packed in oil
- 1 Brie round cheese (1 1/2 pound)
- 6 slices of sun-dried tomatoes in oil(minced)
- 2 cloves of garlic minced

Instructions:
Follow the instructions below to make quick baked artichoke and brie.
1.Preheat the convection oven at 350°F.
2.Mix artichoke hearts, garlic, and sun-dried tomatoes in a small-sized bowl.
3.From brie cheese, trim the top part of the rind and discard.
4.Arrange brie in a round-shaped baking dish. Layer tomato mixture on top
5.Bake in the preheated convection oven until cheese softens for around 20 minutes.

6.15 TASTY DIJON-CRUSTED FISH FILLETS

Total time of cooking
25 minutes
Prep time 10 minutes
Cook time 15 minutes

Serving
4

Nutrition facts
(Per serving)
Calories 214
Fat 8g
Protein 28g
Carbs 7g

Ingredients:
- 4 fillets of tilapia (5 ounces each)
- 3 tablespoons of mayonnaise
- 1/4 cup of bread crumbs
- 2 tablespoons of Parmesan cheese grated(divided)
- 2 teaspoons of Dijon mustard
- 2 teaspoons of melted butter
- 1 teaspoon of horseradish prepared
- 1 tablespoon of lemon juice

Instructions:
Follow the instructions below to make tasty Dijon-crusted fish fillets.
1.Preheat the convection oven at 400°F.Mix in mayonnaise, lemon juice, Dijon mustard, horseradish, and 1 tablespoon of cheese. Coat fish in mayonnaise mixture and place on a greased baking sheet.
2.Toss melted butter, remaining cheese, and bread crumbs. Spread over fillets and bake until fish is flaky for around 12 to 15 minutes.

6.16 CINNAMON, BUTTER AND SUGAR STUFFED-APPLES

Total time of cooking

25 minutes
Prep time 10 minutes
Cook time 15 minutes

Serving

4

Nutrition facts

(Per serving)
Calories 270
Fat 11.5g
Protein 0.6g
Carbs 45g

Ingredients:

- 4 tablespoons of butter
- 4 green apples
- 2 teaspoons of cinnamon
- 1/2 cup of brown sugar

Instructions:

Follow the instructions below to make cinnamon, butter, and sugar stuffed-apples.

1.Preheat the convection oven at 325°F.

2.Take out the core of the apple to make a well. Make sure not to cut full; just discard the center part. With 2 tablespoons of brown sugar and 1 tablespoon of butter, stuff each apple and arrange in a baking dish and top up with cinnamon.

3.Bake for around 15 minutes in the preheated convection oven until apple becomes tender and sugar caramelized.

6.17 BEEF AND BROCCOLI BRAIDED BREAD

Total time of cooking

30 minutes
Prep time 15 minutes
Cook time 15 minutes

Serving

2 loaves (8 servings total)

Nutrition facts

(Per serving)
Calories 396
Fat 23g
Protein 20g
Carbs 29g

Ingredients:

- 2 tubes of crescent rolls refrigerated (8 ounces each)
- 1 pound of ground beef
- 3 cups of chopped broccoli frozen
- 1/2 cup of sour cream
- 1/2 cup of onion chopped
- 1 cup of part-skim mozzarella cheese shredded
- 1/4 teaspoon of pepper
- 1/4 teaspoon of salt

Instructions:

Follow the instructions below to make beef and broccoli braided bread.

1.Preheat the convection oven at 325°F.Cook onion and beef in a large-sized skillet on medium heat for 6 to 8 minutes until beef changes color, then stir in cheese, sour cream, broccoli, pepper, and salt and cook for 2 to 3 minutes.

2.Unfold 1 tube of crescent dough and spread it into greased 12x8 inches baking sheet. Spread half of the beef mixture on the center of the rectangle lengthwise.

3.Cut out 1-inch wide strips angle on each side. Fold one strip from each side on filling and pinch ends to close; repeat.

4.Repeat the procedure to make another braid. Bake for 10 to 15 minutes in the preheated convection oven.

5.Serve and Enjoy!

6.18 CLASSIC PEANUT-BUTTER FLAVORED COOKIES

Total time of cooking
30 minutes
Prep time 15 minutes
Cook time 15 minutes

Serving
36 cookies

Nutrition facts
(Per serving)
Calories 135
Fat 8.6g
Protein 2.8g
Carbs 12.6g

Ingredients:
- 1 cup of readymade peanut butter
- 2 eggs
- 1 package of yellow cake mix (18.25 ounce)
- 2 tablespoons of water
- 1/2 cup of vegetable oil

Instructions:
Follow the instructions below to make classic peanut-butter flavored cookies.
1. Preheat the convection oven at 325°F.
2. Pour yellow cake mix, make well in the middle and add in oil, peanut butter, eggs, and water; mix until completely blended. Scoop out tablespoonfuls mixture into non-stick cookie sheets, place cookie batter with a 1-inch gap.
3. Bake in the preheated convection oven for 10 to 12 minutes. Once baking is done, let it cool down on a wire rack before serving.

6.19 CRISPY PORK CHOPS BAKED

Total time of cooking
30 minutes
Prep time 10 minutes
Cook time 20 minutes

Serving
4

Nutrition facts
(Per serving)
Calories 178
Fat 7g
Protein 23g
Carbs 3g

Ingredients:
- 4 pork loin chops boneless (4 ounces each)
- 1/4 cup of milk fat-free
- 1/4 cup of parmesan cheese grated
- 1/4 teaspoon of garlic powder
- 1/4 cup of bread crumbs seasoned
- 1/4 teaspoon of salt
- Cooking spray
- 1/8 teaspoon of ground black pepper

Instructions:
Follow the instructions below to make crispy pork chops baked.
1. Preheat the convection oven at 350°F. In a shallow bowl, pour milk. In another medium-sized bowl, Mix in cheese and seasonings with bread crumbs.
2. One by one, dip chops in milk, then place chops in crumb mixture and coat evenly. Arrange coated chops on a baking sheet greased with cooking spray. Lightly coat chops with cooking spray.
3. Bake for around 10 to 20 minutes in a preheated convection oven. Before serving, let stand chops for around 5 minutes.

6.20 TASTY APPLE SAUCE FLAVORED CORNBREAD

Total time of cooking
30 minutes
Prep time 10 minutes
Cook time 20 minutes

Serving
9

Nutrition facts
(Per serving)
Calories 155
Fat 1.5g
Protein 4.6g
Carbs 30.3g

Ingredients:
- 2 eggs large
- 1 cup of all-purpose flour
- 1/4 cup of applesauce unsweetened
- 1 cup of cornmeal
- 1/4 cup of sugar
- 2 teaspoons of baking soda
- 3/4 cup of skim milk
- 1/2 teaspoon of salt
- 1 teaspoon of baking powder

Instructions:
Follow the instructions below to make tasty apple sauce-flavored cornbread.
1.Preheat the convection oven at 400°F.Grease a baking pan of 8x8 inches.
2.Mix cornmeal, baking soda, baking powder, salt, sugar, and flour.
In another bowl, mix eggs, milk, and applesauce. Fold in dry ingredients and wet ingredients together and mix until fully incorporated.
3.Pour batter into baking pan and bake in the preheated convection oven for around 15 to 20 minutes or until lightly brown and puffed.

6.21 CRISPY AND TASTY TURKEY BURGERS BAKED

Total time of cooking
30 minutes
Prep time 10 minutes
Cook time 20 minutes

Serving
6 burgers

Nutrition facts
(Per serving)
Calories 249
Fat 10g
Protein 24.1g
Carbs 16.7g

Ingredients:
- 1 1/4 pounds of ground turkey
- 1/4 cup of all-purpose flour
- 1 1/4 cups of whole wheat bread crumbs(divided)
- 3 tablespoons of parsley finely chopped
- 2 eggs(divided)
- 3 finely chopped scallions
- 1/2 teaspoon of salt
- Cooking spray
- 1/2 teaspoon of ground black pepper
- 1/2 teaspoon of garlic powder
- 2 dashes of hot sauce

Instructions:
Follow the instructions below to make crispy and tasty turkey burgers baked.
1.Preheat the convection oven at 350°F.With cooking spray, coat a baking sheet.
2.Combine 1 egg, scallions, turkey,1/4 cup of bread crumbs, garlic powder, salt, black pepper, parsley in a medium-sized bowl.
3.Make 6 patties of equal size out of the mixture.
4.Whisk hot sauce and remaining egg in a small-sized bowl. Place flour into a bowl. Place remaining bread crumbs into a bowl.
5.Coat patties first in flour, then dip into the egg mixture, then finish coating with bread crumbs. Arrange patties on the prepared baking sheet, and with cooking spray, coat patties.
6.Bake in the preheated convection oven for around 15 to 20 minutes until crispy.
7.Serve patties in burger buns and enjoy.

6.22 CLASSIC SHEPHERD'S PIE

Total time of cooking
30 minutes
Prep time 20 minutes
Cook time 10 minutes

Serving
6

Nutrition facts
(Per serving)
Calories 516
Fat 25g
Protein 24g
Carbs 49g

Ingredients:
- 1 pound of ground beef
- 1 can of Mexicorn (11 ounces)
- 1 cup of cheddar cheese shredded, divided
- 1 can of ripe olives, sliced and drained (2-1/4 ounces)
- 3 cups of mashed potatoes
- 1 envelope of taco seasoning
- 1/2 teaspoon of salt
- 1 can of diced tomatoes (14-1/2 ounces)
- 1/8 teaspoon of garlic powder
- 1 chopped onion

- 1 1/2 teaspoons of chili powder

Instructions:
Follow the instructions below to make classic shepherd's pie.
1.Preheat the convection oven at 350°F.
2.In a large-sized skillet, on medium heat, cook onion and beef until meat changes color; then drain. Mix the tomatoes, olives, taco seasoning, corn, salt, chili powder, and garlic powder. Boil; stir, and cook for 2 to 3 minutes.
3.Spread to a greased casserole dish. Sprinkle 3/4 cup of cheese and place mashed potatoes on top; top up with remaining cheese. Bake in the preheated convection oven for around 8 to 10 minutes until cheese melts down.
4.Serve straightaway.

6.23 BAKED EGGPLANT LAYERED WITH SEASONING

Total time of cooking
30 minutes
Prep time 10 minutes
Cook time 20 minutes

Serving
6

Nutrition facts
(Per serving)
Calories 54
Fat 3.7g
Protein 2.4g
Carbs 3.2g

Ingredients:
- 1 eggplant (cut into 1/2-inch-thick round slices)
- 1/3 cup of Parmesan cheese grated
- 3 sliced tomatoes
- Salt to taste
- Black pepper to taste
- 1 tablespoon of olive oil
- Cooking spray
- 1 teaspoon of oregano

Instructions:
Follow the instructions below to make baked eggplant layered with seasoning.
1.Preheat the convection oven at 400°F.Grease a baking sheet with cooking spray.
2.Place eggplant slices on a baking sheet top each eggplant slice with tomato slices. Drizzle with olive oil over eggplant and tomato; sprinkle with salt, oregano, and pepper and finish with a layer of parmesan cheese all over the vegetables.
3.Bake in the preheated convection oven for around 15 to 18 minutes until cheese begins to get brown.
4.Switch convection oven to broiler and broil for around 1 to 2 minutes. Serve hot.

6.24 CLASSIC BAKED PINEAPPLE BUTTER CASSEROLE

Total time of cooking
30 minutes
Prep time 10 minutes
Cook time 20 minutes

Serving
6

Nutrition facts
(Per serving)
Calories 424
Fat 19.4g
Protein 6.3g
Carbs 58.8g

Ingredients:
- 1 can of pineapple (20 ounces)
- 1/4-pound softened butter
- 5 slices of bread (remove crusts and break into crumbs)
- 4 beaten eggs
- 1 cup of white sugar

Instructions:
Follow the instructions below to make classic baked pineapple butter casserole.

1. Preheat the convection oven at 350°F.
2. Cream butter and sugar in a medium-sized bowl. Add in eggs. Add drained pineapple, then stir in the bread crumbs. Spread mixture into 10-inch casserole dish.
3. Bake for around 20 minutes in a preheated convection oven or until crispy and browned.

6.25 ITALIAN STYLE SIMPLE BAKED CHICKEN

Total time of cooking
30 minutes
Prep time 10 minutes
Cook time 20 minutes

Serving
4

Nutrition facts
(Per serving)
Calories 554
Fat 39.6g
Protein 31.8g
Carbs 17.1g

Ingredients:
- 4 boneless and skinless chicken breast halves
- 3/4 cup of mayonnaise
- 3/4 cup bread crumbs Italian seasoned
- 1/2 cup of Parmesan cheese grated
- 1/2 teaspoon of garlic powder

Instructions:
Follow the instructions below to make Italian-style simple baked chicken.

1. Preheat the convection oven at 400°F.
2. Mix in parmesan cheese, mayonnaise, and garlic powder in a large-sized bowl. In a separated medium-sized bowl, place bread crumbs. Coat chicken into the mayonnaise mixture, then coats it into bread crumbs evenly. Transfer coated chicken onto a baking sheet.
3. Bake for around 15 to 20 minutes in the preheated convection oven or until chicken coating gets crispy and lightly browned.

6.26 QUICK NUT AND BANANA BREAD

Total time of cooking
30 minutes
Prep time 5 minutes
Cook time 25 minutes

Serving
16 (2 bread loaves)

Nutrition facts
(Per serving)
Calories 306
Fat 17.3g
Protein 3.8g
Carbs 35.4g

Ingredients:
- 2 mashed bananas
- 4 eggs
- 1/2 cup of vegetable oil
- 1 package of yellow cake mix
- 1 package of instant vanilla pudding mix
- 1 cup of pecans chopped
- 1/2 cup of water
- Cooking spray 1 serving

Instructions:
Follow the instructions below to make quick nut and banana bread.
1.Preheat the convection oven at 350°F.Coat two 9x5 inches loaf baking pan with cooking spray.
2.Combine pecans, cake mix, bananas, water, pudding mix, vegetable oil, and eggs and mix in a large-sized bowl with an electric beater until fully incorporated. Distribute batter equally between two loaf pans.
3.Bake in the preheated convection oven for around 20 to 25 minutes or until the top is golden brown.

6.27 TASTY GARLIC AND CHEDDAR BISCUITS

Total time of cooking
25 minutes
Prep time 15 minutes
Cook time 10 minutes

Serving
5 (10 biscuits)

Nutrition facts
(Per serving)
Calories 385
Fat 24.6g
Protein 10.2g
Carbs 31.5g

Ingredients:
- 1 cup of Cheddar cheese shredded
- 1/4 teaspoon of garlic powder
- 2 cups of biscuit mix
- 1/4 cup of butter
- 2/3 cup of milk

Instructions:
Follow the instructions below to make tasty garlic and cheddar biscuits.
1.Preheat the convection oven at 425°F.
2.Combine cheddar cheese, biscuit mix, and milk in a medium-sized bowl with a wooden spoon until the mixture becomes doughy. Arrange spoonfuls of mixture onto greased cookie sheet.
3.Bake in the preheated convection oven for around 8 to 10 minutes or until biscuits are lightly browned.
4.In a saucepan, heat together garlic powder and butter over very low heat until butter fully melts down. Spread garlic butter evenly on biscuits, serve and enjoy.

6.28 CHEDDAR AND CREAM CHEESE STUFFED JALAPENO POPPERS

Total time of cooking
30 minutes
Prep time 10 minutes
Cook time 20 minutes

Serving
4

Nutrition facts
(Per serving)
Calories 137
Fat 10.2g
Protein 5.9g
Carbs 7.7g

Ingredients:
- 1/4 cup of panko bread crumbs
- 12 seeded and halved lengthwise jalapeno peppers
- 2 ounces of Cheddar cheese shredded
- Cooking spray
- 2 ounces of softened cream cheese

Instructions:
Follow the instructions below to make cheddar and cream cheese stuffed jalapeno poppers.
1.Preheat the convection oven at 375°F.With cooking spray, coat a baking sheet.
2.Stuff each jalapeno half with cheddar cheese, cream cheese, and crumbs. Transfer stuffed jalapenos on the greased baking sheet.
3.Bake for around 15 to 20 minutes in the preheated convection oven until cheese melts down. Serve hot and enjoy

6.29 PARMESAN AND BUTTER CHICKEN

Total time of cooking
25 minutes
Prep time 10 minutes
Cook time 15 minutes

Serving
6

Nutrition facts
(Per serving)
Calories 391
Fat 24g
Protein 33g
Carbs 10g

Ingredients:
- 6 skinless and boneless chicken breast halves (6 ounces each)
- 2 cups of bread crumbs soft
- 1/2 cup of Dijon mustard
- 1 cup of parmesan cheese grated
- 1/2 cup of melted butter

Instructions:
Follow the instructions below to make parmesan and butter chicken.
1.Preheat the convection oven at 400°F.
2.In a large-sized bowl, combine bread crumbs, cheese, and butter. Evenly coat chicken in mustard, then dip evenly in bread crumb mixture.
3.Arrange coated chicken in 13x9 inches baking pan.
4.Bake in the preheated convection oven for around 15 minutes or until chicken breasts get crispy and lightly browned.

6.30 QUICK CLASSIC CHOCOLATE CAKE

Total time of cooking
30 minutes
Prep time 10 minutes
Cook time 20 minutes

Serving
15

Nutrition facts
(Per serving)
Calories 216.9
Fat 5g
Protein 3.8g
Carbs 39.7g

Ingredients:
- 1 1/4 cups of buttermilk (mix 1 1/4 cup of water and 5 tablespoons of dry buttermilk)
- 1 3/4 cups of all-purpose flour
- 1 cup of hot boiling water
- 1 3/4 cups of brown sugar
- 2 eggs
- 3/4 cup of cocoa
- 4 tablespoons of vegetable oil
- Powdered confectioner's sugar
- 1 1/2 teaspoons of baking powder
- 1 teaspoon of vanilla extract
- 1 1/2 teaspoons of baking soda
- 1/4 teaspoon of salt

Instructions:
Follow the instructions below to make a quick classic chocolate cake.
1.Preheat the convection oven at 350°F.
2.Place all the dry ingredients in a large-sized bowl.
3.In another large-sized bowl, place all the wet ingredients except hot boiling water.
4.Mix the wet and dry mixtures and add hot boiling water beat until soupy.
5.Pour the chocolate cake batter into 9x13 inches greased baking pan, bake for around 15 to 20 minutes. Sprinkle with powdered confectioner's sugar on top of cake while serving.

6.31 TASTY MEATBALLS CHEESY PIZZA

Total time of cooking
30 minutes
Prep time 10 minutes
Cook time 20 minutes

Serving
8

Nutrition facts
(Per serving)
Calories 321
Fat 16g
Protein 17g
Carbs 28g

Ingredients:
- 12 Italian meatballs fully cooked
- 1 prebaked pizza crust (12 inches)
- 1 cup of cheddar cheese shredded
- 1 can of pizza sauce (8 ounces)
- 1 cup of mozzarella cheese shredded
- 1/4 cup of parmesan cheese grated
- 1 teaspoon of garlic powder
- 1 sliced onion
- 1 teaspoon of Italian seasoning

Instructions:
Follow the instructions below to make a tasty meatballs cheesy pizza.
1.Preheat the convection oven at 325°F.
2.On a nonstick pizza pan, place crust and layer pizza sauce all over the crust, sprinkle with Italian seasoning, garlic powder, and parmesan cheese on top of pizza sauce. Spread meatballs, onion, and remaining cheeses.
3.Bake for around 15 to 18 minutes in a preheated convection oven until cheese melts down. In the end, broil for 1 minute, cut into slices and serve.

6.32 BAKED BEEF AND CHEESE CUPS

Total time of cooking
30 minutes
Prep time 20 minutes
Cook time 10 minutes

Serving
5

Nutrition facts
(Per serving)
Calories 440
Fat 16g
Protein 27g
Carbs 45g

Ingredients:
- 1 tube of buttermilk biscuits refrigerated (12 ounces)
- 1 pound of ground beef
- 1/2 cup of Velveeta cubed
- 1/2 cup of ketchup
- 1 tablespoon of mustard
- 2 tablespoons of brown sugar
- 1 1/2 teaspoons of Worcestershire sauce

Instructions:
Follow the instructions below to make beef and cheese cups.
1. Preheat the convection oven at 400°F.
2. On medium heat in a large-sized skillet, cook beef until it changes color and liquid evaporates. Mix in brown sugar, mustard, ketchup, and Worcestershire sauce. Remove from stove and set them aside.
3. In a greased muffin pan, place each biscuit and press onto the bottom. Put a spoonful of beef mixture into cups equally. Top with Velveeta cheese cubes.
4. Bake in a preheated convection oven for around 8 to 10 minutes or until cups are golden browned.

6.33 QUICK AND CRUNCHY RAISIN OATMEAL COOKIES

Total time of cooking
25 minutes
Prep time 15 minutes
Cook time 10 minutes

Serving
36

Nutrition facts
(Per serving)
Calories 146
Fat 5g
Protein 1g
Carbs 22g

Ingredients:
- 2 cups of raisins
- 2 1/2 cups of quick-cooking oats
- 1 cup of packed brown sugar
- 1 1/2 cups of all-purpose flour
- 1 cup of butter at room temperature
- 1/2 cup of granulated sugar
- 1 tablespoon of fancy molasses
- 1 teaspoon of baking soda
- 2 eggs
- 1/2 teaspoon of cinnamon
- 2 teaspoons of vanilla extract
- 1/2 teaspoon of salt

Instructions:
Follow the instructions below to make quick and crunchy raisin oatmeal cookies.
1. Preheat the convection oven at 325°F.
2. Combine flour, baking soda, cinnamon, oats and salt in a medium-sized bowl and set them aside.
3. Cream brown sugar, white sugar, and butter together. Mix in molasses, eggs, and vanilla and beat until smooth.
4. Slowly add the oats mixture into creamed mixture and fold in raisins.
5. Place 1 1/2 tablespoons of mixture into a non-stick cookie sheet (batter will make 36 cookies in total).
6. Bake in the preheated convection oven for around 8 to 10 minutes until cookies are golden brown from the edges.
7. Transfer to a cooling rack and cool for some time before serving.

6.34 DELICIOUS BAKED JALAPENO CRANBERRY DIP

Total time of cooking
30 minutes
Prep time 10 minutes
Cook time 20 minutes

Serving
40

Nutrition facts
(Per serving)
Calories 46
Fat 3.7g
Protein 1.4g
Carbs 1.9g

Ingredients:
- 1 thin slice of toasted baguette slices
- 10 slices of LAND O LAKES Deli American (cut them into 1/4-inch pieces)
- 2 cups of cranberries frozen
- 1 package of softened cream cheese (8 ounces)
- 2 tablespoons of sugar
- 2 tablespoons of chopped jalapeno pepper

Instructions:
Follow the instructions below to make delicious baked jalapeno cranberry dip.
1.Preheat the convection oven at 350°F.
2.Combine jalapenos and cheeses in a bowl and mix until fully incorporated.
3.In another medium-sized bowl, place sugar and cranberries and toss them to coat. Slowly mix in coated cranberries into cheese mixture.
4.In a 1-quart casserole baking dish, pour the mixture and bake for around 15 to 20 minutes. Keep an eye when baking so it doesn't get burnt.
5.Serve warm with baguette slices.

6.35 QUICK CHEESE SPICY BREAD

Total time of cooking
30 minutes
Prep time 10 minutes
Cook time 20 minutes

Serving
10

Nutrition facts
(Per serving)
Calories 252
Fat 16g
Protein 8.3g
Carbs 18.8g

Ingredients:
- 1 1/2 cups of Cheddar cheese shredded
- 1 3/4 cups of all-purpose flour
- 1/2 cup of cream half-and-half
- 1/3 cup of vegetable oil
- 2 1/2 teaspoons of baking powder
- 1/2 cup of milk
- 1 teaspoon of garlic powder
- 1 teaspoon of Italian seasoning
- 3/4 teaspoon of salt
- 1/2 teaspoon of onion powder
- 1/2 teaspoon of cayenne pepper

Instructions:
Follow the instructions below to make quick cheese spicy bread.
1.Preheat the convection oven at 400°F.Grease 9x5 inch loaf baking pan and set it aside.
2.Combine flour, salt, cayenne pepper, onion powder, baking powder, salt, Italian seasoning, garlic powder, and cheddar cheese in a large-sized bowl and mix. Add in milk, half-and-half cream, vegetable oil, and whisk until fully blended. Spread batter into greased loaf pan.
3.Bake in the preheated convection oven for around 15 to 20 minutes; keep an eye on the loaf during baking so it doesn't get burnt.
4.Cool for some time before slicing.

6.36 TASTY BAKED CHICKEN MUSHROOM

Total time of cooking
30 minutes
Prep time 15 minutes
Cook time 15 minutes

Serving
4

Nutrition facts
(for one chicken breast half)
Calories 311
Fat 16g
Protein 33g
Carbs 8g

Ingredients:
- 1 cup of fresh mushrooms sliced
- 4 skinless and boneless halves of chicken breast (1 pound)
- 1/4 cup of green onions sliced
- 1/4 cup of all-purpose flour
- 1/3 cup of part-skim mozzarella cheese shredded
- 1/2 cup of chicken broth
- 1/3 cup of Parmesan cheese grated
- 3 tablespoons of butter(divided)
- 1/8 teaspoon of pepper
- 1/4 teaspoon of salt

Instructions:
Follow the instructions below to make a tasty baked chicken mushroom.

1.With 1/4 inches thickness, flatten all chicken breast halves. In a medium-sized bowl, place flour and coat chicken in flour from both sides.

2.In 2 tablespoons of butter brown chicken from both sides. Place chicken in 11x7 inches greased baking dish. Sauté mushrooms in the same skillet in remaining butter until it softens, add in chicken broth, pepper, and salt. Boil and cook until liquid remains 1/2 cup, for around 5 minutes. Spread over chicken in a baking dish.

3.Bake at 375°F for around 10 minutes. After 10 minutes, sprinkle with green onions and cheeses and bake for an additional 2 to 3 minutes.

6.37 BAKED BANANA CINNAMON FRITTERS

Total time of cooking
25 minutes
Prep time 15 minutes
Cook time 10 minutes

Serving
4(8 to 10 fritters)

Nutrition facts
(Per serving)
Calories 112
Fat 2.6g
Protein 3g
Carbs 20.8g

Ingredients:
- 2 bananas (cut in bite-size cubes)
- 1/3 cup of dry bread crumbs
- 1 egg white
- 1 teaspoon of white sugar
- 2 tablespoons of dry coconut shredded
- 1/4 teaspoon of ground cinnamon

Instructions:
Follow the instructions below to make baked banana cinnamon fritters.

1.Preheat the convection oven at 375°F.

2.Combine coconut, cinnamon, bread crumbs, and sugar in a medium-sized bowl. Whisk egg white in a medium-sized bowl until creamy. Coat each banana piece in egg white and then coat evenly in a bread crumb mixture. Arrange the bananas on a baking sheet.

3.Bake in the preheated convection oven for around 10 minutes until lightly golden brown.

6.38 BAKED CHEESY LEEKS

Total time of cooking
30 minutes
Prep time 10 minutes
Cook time 20 minutes

Serving
4

Nutrition facts
(Per serving)
Calories 223
Fat 10.9g
Protein 8.9g
Carbs 23.5g

Ingredients:
- 4 medium halved lengthwise leeks
- 1 1/2 cups of skim milk
- 1/2 teaspoon of garlic powder
- 1/4 cup of all-purpose flour
- 1/2 cup of Cheddar cheese shredded
- 2 tablespoons of butter
- Salt and pepper, to taste

Instructions:
Follow the instructions below to make baked cheesy leeks.
1.Preheat the convection oven at 400°F.Coat a 9x12 inches baking dish.
2.On low heat, melt butter. Add in flour until creamy. Slowly add in milk and cheese and mix until cheese melts down. Sprinkle with salt, garlic powder, and pepper. Remove from stove and spread leeks on the bottom of coated baking dish and top with cheese mixture.
3.Bake in the preheated convection oven for around 20 minutes.

6.39 BAKED STEELHEAD TROUT CROQUETTES

Total time of cooking
30 minutes
Prep time 10 minutes
Cook time 20 minutes

Serving
6(8 to 10 croquettes)

Nutrition facts
(Per serving)
Calories 278
Fat 21.6g
Protein 10.1g
Carbs 14.1g

Ingredients:
- 1/2 cup of panko bread crumbs
- 2 cups of cooked leftover steelhead trout
- 1/2 cup of sour cream
- 1 cup of soft bread crumbs
- 1/2 cup of mayonnaise
- 1/2 lemon juice
- 1/2 minced onion
- Ground black pepper to taste
- 1/2 teaspoon of seasoned salt
- 1/2 teaspoon of Worcestershire sauce
- 1/2 teaspoon of garlic powder

Instructions:
Follow the instructions below to make baked steelhead trout croquettes.
1.Preheat the convection oven at 400°F.
2.Remove bones, skin, and any crust from steelhead and flake steelhead with a fork. Mix flaked fish with bread crumbs, mayonnaise, onion, sour cream, Worcestershire sauce, black pepper, garlic powder, and salt in a large-sized bowl. Make balls out of the mixture and coat each ball in panko bread crumbs. Transfer balls on the baking sheet.
3.Bake in the preheated convection oven until croquettes are lightly golden brown, for around 15 to 20 minutes.

6.40 TASTY AND QUICK CAESAR CHICKEN BAKED

Total time of cooking
30 minutes
Prep time 5 minutes
Cook time 25 minutes

Serving
4

Nutrition facts
(Per serving)
Calories 320
Fat 12g
Protein 38g
Carbs 15g

Ingredients:
- 1/4 cup of Parmesan cheese shredded(divided)
- 4 skinless and boneless halves of chicken breast (6 ounces each)
- 1 medium cubed and peeled ripe avocado
- 1/2 cup of fat-free creamy Caesar salad dressing

Instructions:
Follow the instructions below to make quick and tasty Caesar chicken baked.
1.Arrange chicken in 11x7 inches greased baking dish.
2.Combine avocado, salad dressing, and 2 tablespoons of cheese in a medium-sized bowl and spread over chicken. Bake for around 20 to 25 minutes at 375°F in the preheated convection oven. Upon serving, sprinkle with existing cheese.

6.41 QUICK AND EASY HERB BREAD

Total time of cooking
30 minutes
Prep time 5 minutes
Cook time 25 minutes

Serving
1 loaf (16 slices)

Nutrition facts
(Per serving)
Calories 147
Fat 5g
Protein 3g
Carbs 21g

Ingredients:
- 1 cup of fat-free milk
- 3 cups of all-purpose flour
- 1/3 cup of canola oil
- 1 egg at room temperature
- 3 tablespoons of sugar
- 1/2 teaspoon of dried thyme
- 1 tablespoon of baking powder
- 1/2 teaspoon of salt
- 1/2 teaspoon of ground nutmeg
- 3 teaspoons of caraway seeds

Instructions:
Follow the instructions below to make quick and easy herb bread.
1.At 375°F, preheat your convection oven.
2.In a large-sized bowl, Mix in flour, sugar, baking powder, salt, ground nutmeg, caraway seeds, and dried thyme. Whisk together milk, oil, and egg in another large-sized bowl. Combine egg mixture with flour mixture and stir until combined.
3.Spread to 9x5 inches greased loaf pan. Bake for around 20 to 25 minutes.

6.42 BAKED BEANS, TOMATO AND BACON

Total time of cooking
30 minutes
Prep time 10 minutes
Cook time 20 minutes

Serving
12

Nutrition facts
(for 2/3 cup)
Calories 230
Fat 8g
Protein 11g
Carbs 30g

Ingredients:
- 8 cups of lima beans frozen (42 ounces)
- 8 bacon strips (cut into 1-inch pieces)
- 2 cans of diced tomatoes (14-1/2 ounces each)
- 1/2 cup of a green pepper finely chopped
- 1 cup of onion finely chopped
- 2 teaspoons of all-purpose flour
- 2/3 cup of celery finely chopped
- 1/4 teaspoon of pepper
- 2 teaspoons of sugar
- 2 cloves of minced garlic
- 2 teaspoons of salt

Instructions:
Follow the instructions below to make baked beans, tomato, and bacon.
1. At 350°F, preheat your convection oven.
2. In a large-sized saucepan, cook onion, bacon, green pepper, and celery on medium heat until vegetables are soft. Mix garlic and cook for 1 minute. Add in flour, salt, sugar, and pepper. Mix in tomatoes and let boil; keep stirring; cook for 1 to 2 minutes or until thickens. Fold in beans.
3. Spread the mixture to a greased 13x9 inches baking dish. Cover with lid and bake in the preheated convection oven for 15 to 20 minutes or until beans are cooked.

6.43 BAKED CARAMEL OATMEAL BARS

Total time of cooking
30 minutes
Prep time 10 minutes
Cook time 20 minutes

Serving
24 bars

Nutrition facts
(Per serving)
Calories 343
Fat 15g
Protein 3g
Carbs 49g

Ingredients:
- 1 3/4 cups of quick-cooking oats
- 1 cup of milk chocolate chips
- 2 cups of all-purpose flour
- 1 cup of melted butter
- 1 1/2 cups of semi-sweet chocolate chunks
- 1 1/2 cups of packed brown sugar
- 1/3 cup of milk
- 14 ounces of unwrapped caramels
- 1 teaspoon of baking soda

Instructions:
Follow the instructions below to make baked caramel oatmeal.
1. At 350°F, preheat your convection oven. Grease 9x13 non-stick pan very well and set it aside.
2. Combine oats, brown sugar, flour, and baking in a large-sized bowl and mix in butter until fully combined.
3. Spread half oat mixture in the bottom of greased pan. Top with a layer of chocolate.
4. Heat milk and caramels in the microwave until it melts; about 2 to 3 minutes, and mix.
5. Over the chocolate and oat mixture layer, pour the caramel evenly. Sprinkle with the remaining amount of oat mixture press gently to stick.
6. Bake in the preheated convection oven for 15 to 20 minutes. Keep an eye on the bars to avoid burning.
7. Cool down completely before slicing the bars.

6.44 BAKED ASPARAGUS WITH ITALIAN SEASONING CHEESE SAUCE

Total time of cooking
25 minutes
Prep time 10 minutes
Cook time 15 minutes

Serving
8

Nutrition facts
(Per serving)
Calories 113
Fat 7.3g
Protein 7.6g
Carbs 4.9g

Ingredients:
- 1 cup of mozzarella cheese shredded
- 1 pound of trimmed fresh asparagus
- 1/2 cup of Parmesan cheese grated
- 1 cup of cream half-and-half
- 1 teaspoon of Italian seasoning
- 1/4 teaspoon of red pepper flakes
- 2 teaspoons of cornstarch
- 1/2 teaspoon of ground mustard

Instructions:
Follow the instructions below to make baked asparagus with Italian seasoning cheese sauce.
1.Preheat your convection oven at 375°F.In a shallow baking dish, place asparagus.
2.Mix half-and-half cream, Italian seasoning, ground mustard, mozzarella cheese, red pepper flakes, cornstarch, and parmesan cheese. Spread mixture over asparagus in a baking dish.
3.Bake for around 15 minutes in the preheated convection oven until cheese melts down.
4.Serve warm and enjoy!

6.45 QUICK CHEESY POTATO PIZZA

Total time of cooking
30 minutes
Prep time 10 minutes
Cook time 20 minutes

Serving
8 slices

Nutrition facts
(Per serving)
Calories 320
Fat 16g
Protein 12g
Carbs 31g

Ingredients:
- 3 medium baked and cooled unpeeled potatoes
- 1 1/2 cups of mozzarella cheese shredded
- 1 package of pizza crust mix (6 ounces)
- 1/2 cup of cheddar cheese shredded
- 1 cup of sour cream
- 1/4 teaspoon of garlic powder
- 4 to 5 chopped green onions
- 1 tablespoon of melted butter
- 1/4 teaspoon of dried oregano

Instructions:
Follow the instructions below to make quick cheesy potato pizza.
1.Prepare pizza crust according to package instructions. Spread dough into 14 inches greased pizza pan and press, build pizza crust edges slightly. Bake at 375°F in the convection oven for around 4 to 5 minutes.
2.Cut potatoes into cubes of 1/2 inches. Combine garlic powder, butter, and Italian seasoning. Mix in potatoes and toss to coat. In baked pizza crust, spread sour cream evenly; Spread coated potato mixture, onion, and cheeses on top.
3.Bake for around 12 to 15 minutes or until cheese melts down.
4.Slice and enjoy!

6.46 TASTY BAKED CHEESE BREADED SQUASH

Total time of cooking
30 minutes
Prep time 10 minutes
Cook time 20 minutes

Serving
6

Nutrition facts
(Per serving)
Calories 137
Fat 10g
Protein 5g
Carbs 8g

Ingredients:
- 3/4 cup of Parmesan cheese grated
- 4 cups of sliced yellow summer squash (around 3 medium)
- 3/4 cup of panko bread crumbs
- 1 teaspoon of cayenne pepper
- 1/2 teaspoon of salt
- 3 tablespoons of extra virgin olive oil
- 1/2 teaspoon of ground black pepper

Instructions:
Follow the instructions below to make tasty baked cheese breaded squash.
1. Preheat convection oven at 425°F. In a large-sized bowl, add in seasonings and oil and put squash; toss.
2. In another shallow bowl, combine cheese and bread crumbs. Dip in squash slices into crumb mixture and coat all sides evenly. Arrange on nonstick cookie sheets and bake for around 15 to 20 minutes or until light golden brown.

6.47 BAKED BUTTER CREAM ONIONS

Total time of cooking
30 minutes
Prep time 5 minutes
Cook time 25 minutes

Serving
6

Nutrition facts
(Per serving)
Calories 836
Fat 55.9g
Protein 8.4g
Carbs 75.9g

Ingredients:
- 1 1/3 cups of heavy cream
- 4 cups of pearl onions
- 2 1/2 cups of buttery round crackers crushed
- 1/2 teaspoon of salt
- 1/3 cup of melted butter
- 1/2 teaspoon of pepper

Instructions:
Follow the instructions below to make baked butter cream onions.
1. Preheat convection oven at 375°F.
2. In a 2-quart casserole baking dish, place onions and sprinkle with pepper and salt. Spread melted butter all over onions and place crushed crackers on top of onions. Spread the cream over crackers evenly.
3. Bake in the preheated convection oven for around 20 to 25 minutes, serve warm.

6.48 EASY AND QUICK CHICKEN WITH GUACAMOLE AND SALSA

Total time of cooking
30 minutes
Prep time 10 minutes
Cook time 20 minutes

Serving
3

Nutrition facts
(Per serving)
Calories 298
Fat 17.8g
Protein 24.2g
Carbs 9.9g

Ingredients:
- 3 tablespoons of guacamole
- 3 boneless breasts of chicken
- 1/2 cup of Cheddar cheese shredded
- Salt and ground black pepper to taste
- 1/3 cup of salsa

Instructions:
Follow the instructions below to make easy and quick chicken with guacamole and salsa.
1.Preheat convection oven at 350°F.Using cooking spray, grease baking pan.
2.Layout chicken in a baking pan and sprinkle with salt and pepper. Place salsa all over the chicken breasts and spread cheddar cheese on top
3.Bake in the preheated oven for around 15 to 20 minutes until the chicken changes its color to a light golden brown.
4.Once baked, spread with 1 tablespoon of guacamole on each chicken breast when serving.

6.49 QUICK AND TASTY CHEESY BAKED GRITS

Total time of cooking
30 minutes
Prep time 10 minutes
Cook time 20 minutes

Serving
4-5

Nutrition facts
(Per serving)
Calories 223
Fat 13g
Protein 10g
Carbs 16g

Ingredients:
- 1/2 cup of quick-cooking grits
- 1 cup of Monterey Jack shredded (4 ounces)
- 2 cups of chicken broth or water
- 1 egg beaten
- 1 tablespoon of butter

Instructions:
Follow the instructions below to make quick and tasty cheesy baked grits.
1.Boil chicken broth in a large-sized saucepan. Add grits; keep stirring. Slowly mix 1/2 cup of hot mixture with egg. Add egg mixture into a saucepan and mix to combine. Remove saucepan from the stove. Stir in butter and cheese with grits until cheese and butter melt.
2.Take a 1-quart casserole dish and spread grits into the dish. Bake at 325°F in the preheated convection oven for around 15 to 20 minutes. Until golden brown from edges.

6.50 BAKED MUSHROOM BREAD WITH PARMESAN AND ITALIAN SEASONING

Total time of cooking
30 minutes
Prep time 10 minutes
Cook time 20 minutes

Serving
12

Nutrition facts
(Per serving)
Calories 100
Fat 6g
Protein 3g
Carbs 8g

Ingredients:
- 1/2 cup of Parmesan cheese grated
- 1 tube of crescent rolls refrigerated (8 ounces)
- 1 tablespoon of melted butter
- 1/2 teaspoon of Italian seasoning
- 2 cups of fresh mushrooms thinly sliced
- 1/8 teaspoon of pepper

Instructions:
Follow the instructions below to make baked mushroom bread with parmesan and Italian seasoning.
1. Preheat the convection oven at 325°F.
2. Unfold crescent roll dough into a rectangle on an ungreased baking sheet. Press and prick holes using a fork. Bake for around 5 minutes.
3. Meanwhile, mix in mushrooms with melted butter and toss; spread on the baked crust and sprinkle with seasonings and parmesan cheese. Bake in the preheated convection oven for around 12 to 15 minutes until the crust is light brown.
4. Make 12 slices and serve.

6.51 BAKED QUINOA CHICKEN NUGGETS

Total time of cooking
30 minutes
Prep time: 15 minutes
Cook time: 15 minutes

Servings
6

Nutrition Facts
(Per Serving)
Calories: 522 kcal
Fat: 27g
Protein: 29g
Carbs: 48g

Ingredients
- 1 teaspoon powdered garlic
- 3/4 cup flour (all-purpose)
- 3/4 teaspoon black pepper, freshly ground
- 1 1/4 teaspoons kosher salt
- Barbecue sauce (as required for serving eggs)
- ½ cup cooked quinoa
- Pounds boneless, skinless chicken tenders, chopped into bite-size pieces

Instructions
1. Preheat the oven to 400 degrees Fahrenheit. Line a baking sheet with parchment paper.
2. Whisk together the flour, salt, garlic powder, and black pepper in a medium shallow bowl. Whisk the eggs in a second medium shallow basin. In a third medium shallow dish, place the cooked quinoa.
3. Put a piece of chicken in the flour mixture until it is completely covered. Dip it into the egg, letting the excess drop off, and then completely cover it with quinoa. Transfer to the baking sheet that has been prepared. Carry on with the remaining chicken pieces in the same manner.
4. Spray the chicken nuggets with non-stick cooking spray and bake for 12 to 15 minutes, or until golden brown and completely cooked, turning halfway through.
5. If desired, season with extra salt and pepper. On the side, serve the nuggets with honey mustard and barbeque sauce for dipping.

6.52 ROASTED RED POTATOES

Total time of cooking

30 minutes
Prep Time: 5 minutes
Cook Time: 25 minutes

Servings

2

Nutrition facts

(per serving)
Calories: 154 kcal
Fat: 4g
Protein: 3g
Carbs: 28g

Ingredients

- 1 tablespoon extra-virgin olive oil
- tiny red potatoes, 3/4 pound
- 1 tsp. kosher salt
- 1 tsp. garlic, crushed or minced

Instructions

1. To begin, preheat the oven.
2. If using little red potatoes, scrub them and chop them into quarters. Keep the size of the potatoes to around 1 inch or less if using larger potatoes.
3. Combine the potatoes, olive oil, smashed or minced garlic, and kosher salt in a mixing basin.
4. Using a non-stick baking sheet, evenly distribute the mixture. Keep them apart for a while so they can brown properly. If you don't have a non-stick tray, use one that has been greased.
5. Bake for 26 minutes, or until golden brown. The interior temperature should be at least 200 degrees Fahrenheit.

6.53 ROASTED VEGETABLES

Total time of cooking

30 minutes
Prep time: 5 minutes
Cook time: 25 minutes

Servings

4

Nutrition facts

(per serving)
Calories: 220 kcal
Fat: 18g
Protein: 5g
Carbs: 15g

Ingredients

- 1-2 lbs. of your favorite veggies
- salt, pepper, and herbs to taste
- Olive Oil

Instructions

1. Preheat the oven to 425 degrees Fahrenheit. Allow for a complete preheat of the oven. Arrange your rack in the center of the oven room.
2. Vegetables should be washed and dried thoroughly. If desired/needed, peel the potatoes and cut or slice them into reasonably consistent pieces.
3. Arrange the veggies on the baking sheet in a single layer, taking care not to overcrowd the pan. Vegetables that are overcrowded will steam rather than roast.
4. Drizzle or brush olive oil over the veggies and toss well to coat evenly.
5. If desired, season with salt, freshly ground black pepper, and herbs and/or spices.
6. Roast for the specified time in a preheated oven, checking and stirring halfway through.
7. Roast until the veggies are cooked through and caramelized to your liking. Tenderness may be determined by piercing with a knife or fork.
8. Serve right away.

6.54 LEMONY GARLIC TILAPIA

Total time of cooking
30 minutes
Cook time: 10 minutes
Prep time: 20 minutes

Servings
6

Nutrition Facts
(Per Serving)
Calories: 177.3 kcal
Fat: 8.1 g
Carbs: 7.5 g
Protein: 18.1 g

Ingredients
- 1/2 cup bread crumbs
- tbsp lemon juice
- big filets of tilapia
- chopped garlic cloves
- tbsp olive oil

Instructions
1. Preheat the oven to 400 degrees Fahrenheit.
2. Heat the oil in a pan (medium heat).
3. Sauté for 2 minutes with 3 garlic cloves diced.
4. Toss in the lemon juice and bread crumbs, then remove from the heat.
5. Using non-stick cooking spray, coat the baking/casserole dish.
6. Place tilapia fillets in a casserole dish, side by side, in a baking dish that has been treated.
7. Place the bread crumb mixture equally over all of the fish and bake for 15 to 20 minutes, uncovered, until the fish is done.

6.55 SALMON WITH ROSEMARY

Total time of cooking
30 minutes
Prep time: 20 minutes
Cook time: 10 minutes

Servings
4

Nutrition Facts
(Per Serving)
Calories: 227.0 kcal
Fat: 11.5 g
Protein: 28.9 g
Carbs: 0.2 g

Ingredients
- 1 tsp olive oil
- 1 lb of salmon
- A teaspoon of salt
- 1 teaspoon lemon juice
- 1 tbsp garlic, minced
- Pinch of pepper
- Rosemary 1/4 teaspoon

Instructions
1. Cut the fish into four halves of similar size. In a mixing bowl, combine the lemon juice, olive oil, garlic salt, pepper, and rosemary. Apply the mixture to the fish.
2. Grill the fish on a grill rack or on an oven broiler pan at 350 degrees.

6.56 COCONUT CRUSTED MAHI MAHI

Total time of cooking
30 minutes
Cook time: 15 minutes
Prep time: 15 minutes

Servings
4
Nutrition Facts (Per Serving)
Calories: 272.3 kcal
Fat: 10.1 g
Protein: 26.0 g
Carbs: 21.2 g

Ingredients
- 1 cup coconut, finely chopped
- ounce Mahi Mahi
- 1 cup flour, whole wheat
- eggs
- Cayenne pepper, salt, and pepper (To taste)

Instructions
1.Preheat the oven to 375 degrees Fahrenheit.
2.Cut Mahi Mahi into 4 pieces on a baking sheet sprayed with Pam.
3.Put the ingredients in a dish or a plastic bag. Combine the salt, flour, and both peppers in a mixing bowl until well combined.
4.2 eggs, gently mixed in a bowl
5.On a paper plate, spread out the chopped coconut.
6.Put the fish in the flour mixture to coat it completely.
7.To coat the fish, dip it in the egg and then in the coconut.
8.Place on a baking sheet and gently spry the tops with PAM. Bake until the fish flakes easily with a fork and the walnuts are golden.

6.57 BREADED LEMON CHICKEN

Total time of cooking
30 minutes
Prep Time: 15 minutes
Cook Time: 15 minutes

Servings
4

Nutrition facts
(per serving)
Calories: 663 kcal
Fat: 50g
Protein: 48g
Carbs: 2g

Ingredients
- Lemon juice, 1/3 cup
- 3-4 chicken breasts, boneless and skinless
- Veggie oil for pan-frying
- 1 1/2 cup breadcrumbs, seasoned
- Garnish with parsley and/or lemon (optional)
- To taste, lemon pepper

Instructions
1.Make 4 thin chicken breast pieces by slicing the chicken breasts in half horizontally. Place approximately a foot of plastic wrap on the counter and arrange the chicken pieces on top of it. Cover with some plastic wrap and pound out the chicken breasts with a meat mallet until they are 1/4 inch thick.
2.In a big, high-walled pan, heat 1/4 inch vegetable oil over medium heat.
3.Pour or squeeze the lemon juice into a small basin. Breadcrumbs should be placed in a separate shallow dish. Dip each chicken breast slice into the lemon juice one at a time and set aside for 2 minutes at least. Flip the chicken breasts on the other side and cook for another 3 minutes. Transfer to the breadcrumbs and gently press each side to help the breadcrumbs adhere. Remove from the equation. Continue breading the chicken until it is completely coated.
4.2 of the breaded chicken breasts should be added to the oil and thoroughly seasoned with lemon pepper. Overcrowding the pan leads to soggy chicken, so make sure there's enough space between the chicken breasts. Fry until the bottom is dark golden brown, approximately 4 minutes. Carefully flip the chicken with tongs. Continue to pan fry for another 4 minutes after adding more lemon pepper. Repeat with the remaining chicken pieces on a paper towel-lined sheet.Serve with a generous handful of chopped parsley and lemon slices.

6.58 CINNAMON ROLL APPLE PIE

Total time of cooking
45 minutes
Prep time: 15 minutes
Cook time: 30 minutes

Servings
6

Nutrition facts
(per serving)
Calories 250 kcal
Protein: 5g
Carbs: 34g
Fat: 12g

Ingredients
• sliced and cooked huge apples
• 1 croissant pastry pack
• Unrefined sugar, 2-3 tbsp
• 1 tsp cinnamon (optional)
• 1 tsp medium apricots
• 1 tbsp powdered icing sugar
• 3-4 tbsp additional sugar to sprinkle over the top (optional)
• Pomegranate seeds (or any other fresh fruit), 2tbsp

Instructions
1.Turn on the oven to 350° Fahrenheit and gently butter a pan or an ovenproof dish.
2.Cook the sliced apples and sugar in a skillet over medium heat until the sugar is fully dissolved. It will take around 5-6 minutes. Mix in the cinnamon and leave the pan aside to cool.
3.While the apples cool, cut the puff pastry into 2cm (1 inch) thick strips lengthwise.
4.Make a circular design using the pastry strips.
5.Fill up the gaps between the pastry strips with apple slices, leaving some space between each slice. If there are any juices leftover from the apples, drizzle them over.
6.If you want it sweeter, add 3-4 tablespoons more sugar. Apples aren't very sweet, so there's space for more sweetness if you want it.
7.Bake the cinnamon roll apple pie for 20-25 minutes, or until golden brown. Set the pan on a rack in the middle of the oven; if your oven is not fan-assisted, you may need to bake it for 2/3 minutes longer. Simply keep it in until you're happy with the hue.
8.When it's done, pull it out and serve it right away with your topping of choice.

6.59 OVEN ROASTED CORN

Total time of cooking
30 minutes
Prep time: 10 minutes
Cook time: 20 minutes

Serving
6

Nutrition facts
(per serving): Calories: 154kcal
Protein: 3g
Fat: 4g
Carbs: 28g

Ingredients
• 1 pound of butter (1 stick)
• 1 tsp pepper, freshly ground
• 1 1/2 teaspoons of salt
• A quarter teaspoon of onion powder
• Garlic powder (about 3/4 teaspoon)

Instructions
1.Preheat the oven to 400 degrees Fahrenheit.
2.Using softened butter, rub the corn. After roasting, you'll have some butter left over to smear on.
3.Combine ground pepper, garlic powder, sea salt, and onion powder in a small bowl. Sprinkle over the corn and bake.
4.15 minutes in the oven Coat the other side with the remaining butter. Cook for a further 5 minutes.

6.60 ASPARAGUS FRIES

Total time of cooking
30 minutes
Prep time: 5 minutes
Cook time: 25 minutes

Servings
1

Nutrition facts
(per serving)
Calories: 102.2 kcal
Fat: 1.9 g
Protein: 5.5 g
Carbs: 16.1 g

Ingredients
- 8-10 asparagus stalks
- 1 tablespoon ground almonds
- 1 tsp herbs (mixed)
- A single egg
- 1 teaspoon of lemon juice
- 1 tsp garlic powder

Instructions
1. Preheat the oven to 390° F.
2. The asparagus spears' tops should be snapped off.
3. In a mixing dish, crack the egg and whisk it.
4. Coat the asparagus in the egg, then the ground almonds, and arrange on a parchment-lined baking pan.
5. Sprinkle the ground garlic and mixed herbs on top, then pour the lemon juice over everything.
6. Bake 25-30 minutes, flipping halfway through.

6.61 MARINATED PRAWNS

Total time of cooking
30 minutes
Prep time: 20 minutes
Cook time: 10 minutes

Servings
4

Nutrition Facts
(Per Serving)
Calories: 175 kcal
Fat: 8 g
Protein: 18g
Carbs: 7g

Ingredients
- A single lemon
- 1-kilogram raw medium shrimp (peeled and deveined)
- 1 tbsp garlic cloves (minced)
- 1 tsp sesame oil
- 1/4 cup soy sauce
- 1 tablespoon extra virgin olive oil
- ½ cup rice (steamed to serve)
- A third of a cup of coriander (leaves finely chopped)
- ¼ cup peas (steamed)
- ¼ cup broccoli (steamed)

Instructions
1. Combine the garlic, lemon juice, sesame oil, soy sauce, olive oil, and coriander in a small bowl.
2. Place the prawns in ceramic dish, pour the marinade over them, tossing to coat, then cover and chill for 30 minutes.
3. Preheat the oven to 180 degrees Celsius.
4. Remove them from the marinade and set them in an oven-proof dish. Cover with foil and bake for 10 minutes, or until they are pink and cooked through.
5. Serve with snow peas and broccolini rice.

6.62 4 CHEESE FRESH GARDEN STUFFED JALAPENO

Total time of cooking
30 minutes
Prep time: 15 minutes
Cook time: 15 minutes

Servings
5

Nutrition Facts
(Per Serving)
Calories 240 kcal
Fat: 17g
Protein: 4g
Carbs: 19g

Ingredients
- 1 Tbsp parmigiano-reggiano, grated
- 1 softened cream cheese
- fresh jalapenos, cleaned and chopped in half
- 1 tablespoon Italian bread crumbs
- 1 tbsp shredded parmesan cheese
- freshly ground pepper
- 1 tsp chives (fresh)
- 1 tablespoon grated mozzarella cheese
- 1 to 2 slices of yellow American cheese, cut into slices
- 1 green onion or chive bits

- 1-2 slice white American cheese cut in slices
- 1 tomato, thinly sliced

Instructions
1.Cut jalapenos to line an oiled sheet pan. In a mixing bowl, combine the next five ingredients and season with salt and pepper. Fill each pepper halfway. Then add sliced cheeses, tomato, and chive to each pepper.
2.Add additional parmesan, olive oil, and freshly cracked pepper to taste. Preheat the oven to 400 degrees Fahrenheit and bake for 10-15 minutes. Enjoy. Serve with a sprinkle of garlic oil on top of toast.

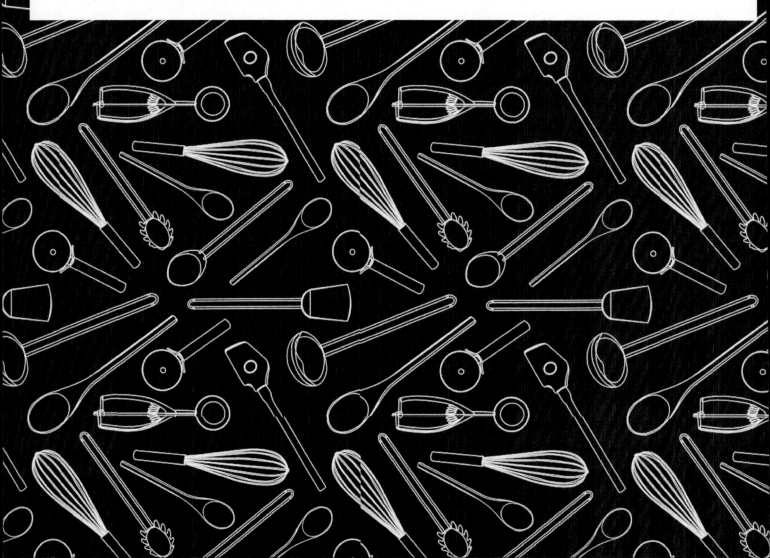

7.1 BEEF CROSTINI WITH BLUE CHEESE

Total time of cooking

20 minutes
Prep time 10 minutes
Cook time 10 minutes

Serving

3 dozen

Nutrition facts

(Per serving)
Calories 48
Fat 1g
Protein 4g
Carbs 5g

Ingredients:

- 1 1/4 pounds of deli roast beef shaved
- 1 French bread baguette (around 10-1/2 ounces)
- 2 tablespoons of chives minced
- 1/3 cup of blue cheese crumbled
- 1 tablespoon of horseradish
- 1/2 cup of sour cream reduced-fat
- 1/4 teaspoon of salt
- Minced chives Additional
- 1/2 teaspoon of ground pepper
- Cooking spray

Instructions:

Follow the instructions below to make beef crostini with blue cheese.

1. Preheat the convection oven at 375°F. Cut the French baguette into 36 equal slices. Arrange on ungreased cookie sheets. Coat with cooking spray. Sprinkle pepper on baguettes, bake for around 4 to 6 minutes until lightly golden brown in color

2. Combine chives, horseradish, sour cream, and salt in a small-sized bowl. Place beef on top of toast. Spread the sour cream mixture on top and sprinkle with additional chives and cheese.

3. Broil in the convection oven for 1 minute and serve.

7.2 GROUND PORK SHEPHERD'S PIE

Total time of cooking
1 hour 15 minutes
Prep time 30 minutes
Cook time 45 minutes

Serving
6

Nutrition facts
(for 1 cup)
Calories 365
Fat 19g
Protein 19g
Carbs 28g

Ingredients:
For Pork Layer:
- 1/2 cup of pork gravy
- 1 pound of ground pork
- 1 cup of rice cooked
- 1 chopped onion
- 1/2 teaspoon of dried thyme
- 2 cloves of minced garlic
- 1/2 teaspoon of salt

For Potato layer:
- 1/4 cup of cheddar cheese shredded
- 2 cups of mashed potatoes

For the Cabbage layer:
- 6 cups of cabbage chopped
- 1 carrot diced
- 1 cup of chicken broth
- 1 chopped onion
- 2 tablespoons of butter
- 1/4 teaspoon of pepper
- 1/2 teaspoon of salt

Instructions:
Follow the instructions below to make ground pork shepherd's pie.

1. Cook pork in a large-sized skillet on medium heat until pork changes color. Add garlic and onion, cook until soft. Mix in pork gravy, rice, thyme, and salt. Spread layer on the bottom of 11x7 inches casserole baking dish.

2. Cook onion and carrot in butter in the same pan on medium heat for around 5 minutes. Mix in cabbage; cook for around 2 minutes. Add chicken broth, pepper, and salt; cover with a lid and cook for around 8 to 10 minutes. Spread evenly over pork mixture layer.

3. Spread mashed potatoes layer over pork and cabbage layer and top up with cheese. Bake for around 40 to 45 minutes in the preheated convection oven at 325°F.

7.3 ARMENIAN-STYLE LAMB AND BEEF PIZZA

Total time of cooking
40 minutes
Prep time 20 minutes
Cook time 20 minutes

Serving
8

Nutrition facts
(Per serving)
Calories 371
Fat 19g
Protein 24g
Carbs 24g

Ingredients:
- 1 pound of ground lamb
- 8 (6 inches) flour tortillas
- 1 pound of ground beef
- 1 can of tomato paste (6 ounces)
- 2 tablespoons of dry red wine
- 1 sliced onion
- 2 diced and seeded jalapeno peppers
- 2 tablespoons of harissa chili paste
- 1 tablespoon of ground sumac
- 1/4 cup of fresh parsley minced
- 1 lemon wedges
- 1/4 teaspoon of salt
- Cooking spray
- 1/2 teaspoon of ground cinnamon
- 1/4 teaspoon of pepper

Instructions:
Follow the instructions below to make Armenian-style lamb and beef pizza.

1. Preheat convection oven broiler.

2. Cook lamb and beef with onion and crumble them in a large-sized skillet on medium-high heat until meat changes its color for around 8 to 10 minutes.

3. Add in all other ingredients except tortillas and lemon wedges to the meat mixture and cook. Keep stirring in between until completely blended. Remove from stove.

4. One by one, coat both sides of tortillas with cooking spray and arrange on a baking sheet. Broil in a convection oven 3 to 4 inches away from heat until crispy 1 minute per side. Top up broiled tortillas with meat mixture and side with lemon wedges upon serving.

Total time of cooking
35 minutes
Prep time 20 minutes
Cook time 15 minutes

Serving
4

Nutrition facts
(Per serving)
Calories 193
Fat 10g
Protein 22g
Carbs 2g

Ingredients:
- 4 pork loin chops boneless (4 ounces each and 3/4 inch thick)
- 2 tablespoons of olive oil
- 1 teaspoon of garlic powder
- 4 teaspoons of fresh lemon juice
- 1 teaspoon of onion powder
- 1 tablespoon of Worcestershire sauce
- 1 teaspoon of salt
- 1 teaspoon of pepper
- 2 teaspoons dried oregano
- 1/2 teaspoon of ground mustard

Instructions:
Follow the instructions below to make Greek-style pork chops.
1. Preheat convection oven broiler.
2. Mix all the ingredients except pork together in a large-sized bowl. Add chops and toss to coat. Refrigerate with cover for around 8 hours or overnight.
3. Discard marinade and shift to baking pan. Broil in the preheated convection oven 4 inches from heat, around for 4 to 5 minutes per side.

7.5 BAKED BUTTERMILK SPICY CHICKEN

Total time of cooking
50 minutes
Prep time 10 minutes
Cook time 40 minutes

Serving
4

Nutrition facts
(Per serving)
Calories 298
Fat 7.5g
Protein 31g
Carbs 27.8g

Ingredients:
- 4 boneless and skinless chicken breast halves
- 2 cups of buttermilk
- 1 clove of minced garlic
- 2 cups of Buffalo wing sauce
- Cooking spray
- 2 tablespoons of Dijon mustard
- 1/4 teaspoon of ground black pepper
- 1/2 teaspoon of salt

Instructions:
Follow the instructions below to make baked buttermilk spicy chicken.
1. Mix buffalo sauce, mustard, buttermilk, salt, garlic, and pepper in a shallow bowl. Add in chicken breasts. Marinate covered in the refrigerator for around 12 to 24 hours.
2. Preheat the convection oven to 350°F. And with cooking spray, grease a 9x13 inches baking dish.
3. Place chicken and marinade into greased baking dish.
4. Bake for around 40 minutes in the preheated convection oven until no juices are left in the pan.
5. Serve and enjoy.

7.6 CLASSIC TURKEY STUFFING

Total time of cooking
45 minutes
Prep time 15 minutes
Cook time 30 minutes

Serving
5

Nutrition facts
(Per serving)
Calories 615
Fat 35.4g
Protein 21.6g
Carbs 52.4g

Ingredients:
- 1 package of thawed frozen green peas (10 ounces)
- 3 cups of stuffing
- 1 1/2 cups of cooked and cubed turkey
- 1 can of cream of celery soup (10.75 ounces)
- 1 can of French-fried onions (6 ounces)
- 3/4 cup of milk

Instructions:
Follow the instructions below to make classic turkey stuffing.
1.Mix 1/2 can of onions and stuffing together. Spread stuffing mixture onto the bottom of a shallow baking dish. To make a shell, press stuffing to the bottom and up sides of the dish.
2.Add in milk, undiluted soup, peas, and turkey into a medium-sized bowl; Spread the mixture into a stuffing shell.
3.Bake, covered with lid at 325°F for around 30 minutes. Sprinkle with remaining onions, bake for an additional 5 minutes uncovered. Serve warm.

7.7 BEEF AND PORK STUFFED PASTA SHELLS

Total time of cooking
1 hour
Prep time 30 minutes
Cook time 30 minutes

Serving
8

Nutrition facts
(3 stuffed pasta shells)
Calories 487
Fat 26g
Protein 22g
Carbs 41g

Ingredients:
- 1/2 pound of lean ground pork
- 2 cans of tomato sauce (8 ounces each)
- 1/2 pound of lean ground beef (90% lean)
- 1 jar of Picante sauce (16 ounces)
- 24 jumbo pasta shells cooked
- 1 cup of water
- 2 cans of green chiles chopped (4 ounces each)
- 1/4 cup of fresh cilantro minced
- 1 shredded carrot
- 1 can of french-fried onions (6 ounces), divided
- 3 cloves of minced garlic
- 2 cups of Mexican cheese blend shredded, divided
- 3 chopped green onions

Instructions:
Follow the instructions below to make beef and pork stuffed pasta shells.
1.Preheat the convection oven at 325°F.
2.On medium heat, in a large-sized skillet, cook pork and beef until they change color, break them into crumbs using a spoon for around 8 to 10 minutes. Add in green onions, garlic, and carrot; cook for 1 minute. Mix in chiles, half of the fried onions,1 cup of cheese, and cilantro. In a large-sized bowl, mix tomato sauce, Picante sauce, and water and mix 1 cup of Picante mixture into a pan.
3.Pour 1 cup of a remaining mixture of Picante into 13x9 inches greased baking dish. Stuff pasta shells with cooked meat mixture. Arrange pasta shells into a baking dish. Sprinkle the top with the remaining sauce. Cover with lid and bake in the preheated convection oven for around 30 minutes. Uncover the dish and sprinkle with remaining fried onions and remaining cheese. Bake for additional 5 minutes until cheese melts down.

7.8 BAKED BEEF MIXTURE UNDER A BUN

Total time of cooking

1 hour
Prep time 35 minutes
Cook time 25 minutes

Serving

8

Nutrition facts

(Per serving)
Calories 423
Fat 23g
Protein 27g
Carbs 26g

Ingredients:

- 2 cups of biscuit/baking mix
- 1 1/2 pounds of ground beef
- 2 cups of cheddar cheese shredded
- 2 beaten eggs
- 1 can of sloppy joe sauce (15-1/2 ounces)
- 1 tablespoon of sesame seeds
- 1 cup of milk 2%

Instructions:

Follow the instructions below to make a baked beef mixture under a bun.
1. Preheat the convection oven at 375°F.
2. Cook beef in a large-sized skillet on medium heat and crumble with a spoon; cook until beef is no longer pink in color. Mix in sloppy joe sauce, spread the mixture into 13x9 inches greased baking dish, and spread cheese.
3. Combine the eggs, milk, and biscuit mix in a large-sized bowl until fully blended. Spread over cheese and top with sesame seeds. Bake for around 25 minutes in the preheated convection oven until light golden brown in color.

7.9 GRILLED SWEET AND SOUR CHICKEN THIGHS

Total time of cooking

35 minutes
Prep time 15 minutes
Cook time 20 minutes

Serving

6

Nutrition facts

(Per serving)
Calories 353
Fat 19.3g
Protein 24.3g
Carbs 19.5g

Ingredients:

- 6 chicken thighs bone-in (5 ounces)
- 1/2 cup of packed brown sugar
- 1/4 cup of apple cider vinegar
- 1 tablespoon of lemon juice
- 1/4 cup of olive oil
- 3 tablespoons of mustard
- 1 teaspoon of seasoned salt
- 1 tablespoon of lime juice
- 1 clove of minced garlic
- 1 teaspoon of ground black pepper

Instructions:

Follow the instructions below to make grilled sweet and sour chicken thighs.
1. In a medium-sized bowl, combine oil, vinegar, brown sugar, lemon juice, mustard, lime juice, seasoned salt, garlic, and pepper, mix until fully combined.
2. Place chicken in a glass baking dish and cover the chicken with sauce. Wrap a glass dish with plastic wrap and keep it in the refrigerator for 8 hours or overnight.
3. Take out marinade chicken from your refrigerator and discard the remaining marinade.
4. Place baking dish in the grill compartment of the convection oven and grill from both sides for around 10 minutes at each side to 300°F.

7.10 GRILLED MARINATED BEEF RIBEYES STEAKS

Total time of cooking
35 minutes
Prep time 15 minutes
Cook time 20 minutes

Serving
4

Nutrition facts
(Per serving)
Calories 570
Fat 40g
Protein 40g
Carbs 8g

Ingredients:
• 4 (8 ounces each) of beef ribeyes steaks (8 ounces each)
• 1/2 cup of barbecue sauce
• 2 tablespoons of steak sauce
• 1 clove of minced garlic
• 3 tablespoons of olive oil
• 1 tablespoon of soy sauce
• 3 tablespoons of Worcestershire sauce
• 2 teaspoons of steak seasoning
• 2 tablespoons of steak sauce

• 1 teaspoon of hot pepper sauce
• 1 tablespoon of red wine vinegar

Instructions:
Follow the instructions below to make grilled marinated beef ribeyes steaks.
1.In a large zip-lock bag, add all the ingredients except steaks mix well and then add steaks, toss to coat. Refrigerate the steaks for 4 hours or overnight.
2.Remove steaks from your refrigerator, discard marinade and transfer to a baking sheet. Place in the convection oven grill compartment and cook for around 5 to 8 minutes from each side at 300°F.

7.11 GRILLED PORK BARBECUED KEBABS

Total time of cooking
35 minutes
Prep time 15 minutes
Cook time 20 minutes

Serving
10 kebabs

Nutrition facts
(Per serving)
Calories 369
Fat 15.8g
Protein 31.1g
Carbs 24.7g

Ingredients:
• 10 bamboo skewers (soaked in water for 20 minutes)
• 5 chopped garlic cloves
• 1 cup of white sugar
• 1 diced onion
• 1 boneless pork loin (4 pounds) (make 1 1/2-inch cube)
• 1 cup of soy sauce
• 1 teaspoon of ground black pepper

Instructions:
Follow the instructions below to make grilled pork barbecued kebabs.
1.Add sugar, onion, black pepper, soy sauce, and garlic in a large-sized bowl and whisk. Add in pork cubes and toss gently to coat. Refrigerate with cover for at least 2 hours or, if possible, overnight.
2.Arrange pork onto soaked skewers and coat with cooking spray. Place in the convection oven grill compartment and cook at 350°F for around 5 to 10 minutes from each side.

Total time of cooking

1 hour
Prep time 25 minutes
Cook time 35 minutes

Serving

8

Nutrition facts

(Per serving)
Calories 931
Fat 56g
Protein 32g
Carbs 73g

Ingredients:

- 1 can of drained and rinsed kidney beans (16 ounces)
- 1 pound of ground beef
- 1 can of ripe olives sliced and drained (2-1/4 ounces)
- 1 can of undiluted condensed bean with bacon soup (11-1/2 ounces)
- 1 can of drained and rinsed black beans (15 ounces)
- 1 cup of sour cream
- 1 jar of thick and chunky Picante sauce (16 ounces), divided
- 2 cups of cheddar cheese shredded, divided
- 1/4 cup of cornstarch
- 3/4 cup of green onions sliced, divided
- 2 to 3 minced garlic cloves
- Double-crust deep-dish pie dough
- 1 tablespoon of fresh parsley chopped
- 1 teaspoon of salt
- 1 teaspoon of paprika
- 1/4 teaspoon of black pepper ground

Instructions:

1.Preheat the convection oven at 400°F.On medium heat, cook beef in a large-sized pan until beef changes its color. Put garlic and cook 1 minute.

2.Combine 1 cup of Picante sauce, soup, parsley, paprika, cornstarch, pepper, and salt in a large-sized bowl. Mix in beans,1/2 cup of onions,1 1/2 cups of cheese, and beef mixture.

3.Roll half dough into a 1/8-inch-thick circle on a floured surface and spread to 9 inches deep-dish pie pan. Pour filling and roll 1/8-inch-thick circle from the remaining half dough and spread over filling extra trim part and seal corners. Mark cuts on top of the pie.

4.Bake for around 30 to 35 minutes until crust is lightly golden browned. Serve with olives, remaining Picante sauce, sour cream, onions, and cheese.

7.13 CHICKEN AND STUFFING MUFFIN CUPS

Total time of cooking

45 minutes
Prep time 20 minutes
Cook time 25 minutes

Serving

6

Nutrition facts

(Per serving)
Calories 243
Fat 9.9g
Protein 12.8g
Carbs 25.8g

Ingredients:

- 1/2 cup of whole berry cranberry sauce
- 2 cups of diced chicken cooked
- 1 can of cream of mushroom soup (10.75 ounces)
- 1 1/2 cups of herb-seasoned stuffing uncooked
- 1/2 cup of Cheddar cheese shredded
- 1 package of chopped broccoli frozen (10 ounces)

Instructions:

Follow the instructions below to make chicken and stuffing muffin cups.

1.Warm up the convection oven at 325°F. Put paper liners into muffin baking pan cups.

2.Mix in stuffing, broccoli, soup, chicken, and cheese in a medium-sized bowl. Place 1/2 cup of chicken mixture into each muffin cup equally.

3.Bake for around 25 minutes in the preheated convection oven or until the muffins are golden browned. Top up each muffin with 1 tablespoon of cranberry sauce while serving.

7.14 CHEESY BEEF STEAK PIZZA

Total time of cooking
35 minutes
Prep time 20 minutes
Cook time 15 minutes

Serving
6

Nutrition facts
(For 2 pieces)
Calories 352
Fat 20g
Protein 21g
Carbs 22g

Ingredients:
- 1 1/2 cups of mozzarella cheese shredded
- 1 tube of crescent rolls refrigerated (8 ounces)
- 2 tablespoons of olive oil
- 1 medium chopped green pepper
- 1/2 pound of deli roast beef thinly sliced
- 1 medium chopped onion
- 1 tablespoon of prepared Italian salad dressing
- 1/4 teaspoon of beef bouillon granules

Instructions:
Follow the instructions below to make cheesy beef steak pizza.
1.Unfold roll dough into a long rectangle; spread on the bottom of 13x9 inches ungreased baking pan and press up the sides and the pan's bottom. Bake for around 8 to 10 minutes at 350°F.
2.Cook onion and green pepper in oil; in a large-sized skillet, add bouillon and cook until vegetables become tender; set them aside.
3.Place beef over crust. Brush salad dressing over and spread with cheese. Bake for around 4 to 5 minutes in the preheated convection oven, and Top the pizza with a green pepper mixture.
4.Make 12 slices and serve.

7.15 BAKED GARLIC AND BUTTER-FLAVORED PORK STEAKS

Total time of cooking
50 minutes
Prep time 20 minutes
Cook time 30 minutes

Serving
6

Nutrition facts
(Per serving)
Calories 353
Fat 25.4g
Protein 26.5g
Carbs 3.9g

Ingredients:
- 6 of pork butt steaks
- 1/4 cup of butter
- 3 cloves of minced garlic
- 1/4 cup of soy sauce
- 1 teaspoon of garlic powder
- 1 bunch of green onions

Instructions:
Follow the instructions below to make baked garlic and butter-flavored pork steaks.
1.Preheat the convection oven to 350°F.
2.In a skillet, melt butter and add soy sauce. Mix in green onions, garlic powder, and garlic, cook until golden browned.
3.Toss pork steaks in the mixture of garlic butter, coat evenly from all sides, and shift to a non-stick baking sheet. Bake in the preheated convection oven for around 25 to 30 minutes until steaks are lightly golden brown. Once baking is done, broil in the convection oven for around 2 minutes. Serve warm and enjoy!

7.16 CHEESY BAKED CHICKEN PENNE PASTA

Total time of cooking
45 minutes
Prep time 20 minutes
Cook time 25 minutes

Serving
4

Nutrition facts
(Per serving)
Calories 449
Fat 14.7g
Protein 42.1g
Carbs 36.6g

Ingredients:
- 2 ounces of Neufchatel cheese
- 1 1/2 cups of penne pasta
- 1 cup of mozzarella cheese shredded
- 1 pound of skinless and boneless chicken breasts (cut into bite-size pieces)
- 1 can of drained diced tomatoes (14.5 ounces)
- 2 tablespoons of Parmesan cheese grated
- 1 cup of pasta sauce
- 1 package of fresh spinach (9 ounces)
- 1 teaspoon of dried basil

Instructions:
Follow the instructions below to make cheesy baked chicken penne pasta.

1.Preheat the convection oven to 350°F.Cook pasta by the direction mentioned on your package, and during the last minute of pasta cooking time, add in spinach and drain, set them aside.

2.In a large-sized skillet, coat the skillet with cooking spray. On medium heat, cook chicken and basil for around 3 minutes. Mix in pasta sauce and diced tomatoes; Let it boil for 1 minute on high heat and 2 minutes on low heat or until chicken is cooked.

3.Add in pasta mixture, Neufchatel cheese, and 1/2 cup of mozzarella cheese. Spread the mixture into a casserole dish. Bake for around 20 minutes in the preheated convection oven and then sprinkle with remaining parmesan and mozzarella cheeses. Bake for additional 3 minutes until cheeses meltdown.

7.17 BAKED CREAMY MUSHROOM CHICKEN

Total time of cooking
1 hour 15 minutes
Prep time 15 minutes
Cook time 1 hour

Serving
3

Nutrition facts
(Per serving)
Calories 754
Fat 57.8g
Protein 40.2g
Carbs 19.7g

Ingredients:
- 1 can of drained whole mushrooms (7 ounces)
- 3 boneless and skinless halves chicken breast
- 4 Swiss cheese slices
- 1 cup of heavy cream
- 1 chopped white onion
- 1/4 cup of buttermilk
- 1 can of cream of chicken soup (10.5 ounces)
- 2 tablespoons of olive oil
- 2 tablespoons of fresh parsley chopped
- 1 teaspoon of salt
- 1 teaspoon of poultry seasoning
- 1/4 teaspoon of ground black pepper
- 1/4 teaspoon of cayenne pepper

Instructions:
Follow the instructions below to make baked creamy mushroom chicken.

1.Preheat the convection oven to 325°F.Sprinkle pepper and salt on chicken breasts and set chicken aside.

2.On medium-high heat, heat olive oil in a large-sized skillet. Cook onion for 5 minutes, add parsley and mix well. In the skillet, place chicken and brown from both sides,5 minutes for each side. Mix in cayenne and poultry seasoning, make sure chicken is completely coated. Arrange chicken into a 9x13 inches baking dish. Cover with mushrooms and set the baking dish aside.

3.In a medium-sized mixing bowl, combine heavy cream, soup, and buttermilk. Add in the onion mixture and mix. Spread the mixture over the chicken. And spread swiss cheese on top evenly.

4.Bake for around 1 hour in the preheated convection oven until chicken is completely cooked. Cool down for 10 to 15 minutes before serving.

Total time of cooking
2 hours
Prep time 30 minutes
Cook time 1 hour 30 minutes

Serving
8

Nutrition facts
(Per serving)
Calories 435
Fat 23g
Protein 23.2g
Carbs 35.1g

Ingredients:
- 3 large thinly sliced potatoes
- 1 pound of ground lamb
- 2 cups of milk
- 2 cups of fresh sliced mushrooms
- 1 package of dry onion soup mix (1 ounce)
- 2 diced carrots
- 1 cup of sharp Cheddar cheese shredded
- 1 diced onion
- 1 cup Havarti cheese shredded
- 2 tablespoons of all-purpose flour
- 1 clove of minced garlic
- 2 tablespoons of butter
- Salt and black pepper (to taste)
- 1 beaten egg

Instructions:
Follow the instructions below to make classic lamb gratin.
1. Preheat the convection oven to 375°F.
2. On medium-high heat in a large-sized skillet, cook lamb; mix in onions, garlic, and carrots. Continue cooking and keep stirring until lamb is crumbly and browned about 6 to 8 minutes. Fold in soup mix into the lamb mixture; remove from stove.
3. On medium heat, melt butter in a medium-sized saucepan. Whisk flour in the heated butter, add 1 tablespoon at a time, make sure no lumps remain. Put milk into butter mixture keep whisking; until the mixture thickens. Switch off the heat and remove the saucepan from the stove. Fold in Havarti cheese and cheddar cheese into milk mixture until cheeses meltdown.
4. Place a small amount of cheese sauce mixture into a beaten egg in a small mixing bowl; whisk well and pour the egg into cheese sauce mixture and fold.
5. In the bottom of the greased casserole dish, place sliced potatoes, sprinkle with pepper and salt. Spread 1/3 of the cheese sauce on the potatoes layer evenly. On top of the cheese, layer spread lamb mixture evenly. Again, spread the remaining potatoes layer on top of the lamb mixture and season with pepper and salt. Pour with remaining cheese over the top sauce. Cover baking dish with lid.
6. Bake for around 60 minutes in the preheated convection oven. After 60 minutes, remove the cover and bake for another 30 minutes until gratin turns golden brown from the top.

7.19 TASTY AND SIMPLE MEATBALL CASSEROLE

Total time of cooking
1 hour 20 minutes
Prep time 30 minutes
Cook time 50 minutes

Serving
6

Nutrition facts
(Per serving)
Calories 641
Fat 39g
Protein 29g
Carbs 43g

Ingredients:
- 1 pound of ground beef
- 3 1/2 cups of spaghetti sauce
- 1 loaf of Italian bread (1 pound) (cut into 1-inch slices)
- 1/4 cup of seasoned bread crumbs
- 1 package of softened cream cheese (8 ounces)
- 1/3 cup of green onions chopped
- 1/2 cup of mayonnaise
- 2 cups of part-skim mozzarella cheese shredded, divided
- 1 cup of water
- 3 tablespoons of Parmesan cheese grated
- 1 teaspoon of Italian seasoning
- 2 minced garlic cloves
- 1/4 teaspoon of pepper

Instructions:
Follow the instructions below to make tasty and simple meatball casserole.
1.Combine bread crumbs, onions, and parmesan cheese in a large-sized bowl and crumble beef in the mixture and mix until completely blended. Make 1-inch balls out of the mixture. Place on a greased baking sheet and bake for around 15 to 20 minutes at 375°F, until meatball changes color.
2.Place bread in a single layer in 13x9 inches baking dish. Combine mayonnaise, Italian seasoning, cream cheese, and pepper. Spread over the bread layer and top with 1/2 cup of mozzarella.
3.Mix water, spaghetti sauce, and garlic and add meatballs. Spread on cheese mixture; top with remaining mozzarella layer. Bake for around 30 minutes at 325°F in the preheated convection oven.

7.20 BAKED TURKEY AND POTATO CROQUETTES

Total time of cooking
35 minutes
Prep time 20 minutes
Cook time 15 minutes

Serving
18 croquettes

Nutrition facts
(Per serving)
Calories 168
Fat 6g
Protein 10.6g
Carbs 19.7g

Ingredients:
- 1 cup of cooked and chopped turkey
- 1 cup of mashed potatoes
- 1/2 cup of panko bread crumbs
- 1 cup of prepared stuffing
- 1 beaten egg
- 1 teaspoon of butter melted

Instructions:
Follow the instructions below to make baked turkey and potato croquettes.
1.Preheat the convection oven at 425°F.
2.Mix panko bread crumbs and melted butter in a medium-sized bowl and set the bowl aside.
3.Combine stuffing, mashed potatoes, and turkey in a medium-sized bowl. Take 1 1/2 tablespoons of turkey mixture and make it into a log shape. Dip into the egg first, then coat in panko bread crumb mixture and arrange on a greased baking sheet. Repeat the procedure with the remaining mixture.
4.Bake for around 15 minutes in the preheated convection oven until crispy and golden in color.

7.21 RUSSIAN-STYLE BAKED BEEF

Total time of cooking

1 hour 20 minutes
Prep time 20 minutes
Cook time 1 hour

Serving

6

Nutrition facts

(Per serving)
Calories 530
Fat 41g
Protein 33g
Carbs 6g

Ingredients:

- 3 tablespoons of mayonnaise
- 1 tenderloin of beef (2 pounds)
- 2 sliced onions
- 1 cup of milk
- Salt and black pepper ground to taste
- 1 1/2 cups of Cheddar cheese grated

Instructions:

Follow the instructions below to make Russian-style baked beef.

1.Preheat the convection oven at 325°F.With cooking spray, grease a baking dish.

2.Slice beef into finger-thick slices. Arrange in 1 layer in the baking dish. Sprinkle with pepper and salt. Spread onion slices and top up with cheddar cheese.

3.Mix mayonnaise and milk and spread evenly over the cheese.

4.Bake for around 1 hour in the preheated convection oven until beef is fully cooked.

7.22 BUTTER LEMON BAKED CHICKEN TENDERS

Total time of cooking

45 minutes
Prep time 15 minutes
Cook time 30 minutes

Serving

8

Nutrition facts

(Per serving)
Calories 81
Fat 3.3g
Protein 11.5g
Carbs 0.9g

Ingredients:

- 8 skinless and boneless chicken tenders
- 1/4 teaspoon of paprika
- 1/3 cup of lemon juice
- Cooking spray
- 4 teaspoons of softened butter
- 1/2 teaspoon of salt

Instructions:

Follow the instructions below to make butter lemon baked chicken tenders.

1.Preheat the convection oven at 400°F.With cooking spray, coat 8x11 inch baking pan.

2.Arrange chicken tenders on coated baking pan in a single layer. Place butter on the tenders and pour lemon juice all over the tenders evenly, sprinkle with paprika and salt.

3.Bake for around 25 to 30 minutes in the preheated convection oven until the pan's juices are dry out.

7.23 TASTY LAMB MEATBALLS BAKED

Total time of cooking
40 minutes
Prep time 20 minutes
Cook time 20 minutes

Serving
21 meatballs

Nutrition facts
(Per serving)
Calories 298
Fat 16.1g
Protein 21.6g
Carbs 16.1g

Ingredients:
- 1/4 cup of yogurt
- 1 pound of ground lamb
- 1/4 cup of raisins
- 2 slices of bread, split into small pieces
- 1 clove of minced garlic
- 1/8 teaspoon of ground black pepper
- 1/4 teaspoon of dried basil
- 1/4 cup of fresh cilantro
- 1/8 teaspoon of salt
- 1/4 teaspoon of dried oregano

Instructions:
Follow the instructions below to make tasty lamb meatballs baked.
1. Preheat the convection oven at 350°F.
2. Combine bread, lamb, raisins, yogurt, garlic, oregano, salt, basil, cilantro, and pepper and mix together in a medium-sized bowl. Make 1-inch balls out of the mixture (mixture will make 21 meatballs).
3. Arrange meatballs on a greased baking sheet and bake for around 20 minutes in the preheated convection oven.

7.24 CLASSIC PORK CHOPS BAKED WITH MUSHROOM SAUCE

Total time of cooking
1 hour 10 minutes
Prep time 20 minutes
Cook time 50 minutes

Serving
6

Nutrition facts
(Per serving)
Calories 231
Fat 11.7g
Protein 17.3g
Carbs 12.9g

Ingredients:
- 1 can of cream of mushroom soup (26.5 ounces)
- 6 pork loin chops (4 ounces)
- 1 can of tomatoes diced (14.5 ounces)
- Cooking spray
- 1 thinly sliced sweet onion
- 1/2 teaspoon of chili powder
- 1/2 teaspoon of paprika
- 1 teaspoon of garlic powder

Instructions:
Follow the instructions below to make classic pork chops baked with mushroom sauce.
1. Preheat the convection oven at 325°F.
2. On medium-high heat, heat a pan. Coat pork chops with cooking spray and sprinkles with paprika, garlic powder, and chili powder. Lightly brown chops in a hot pan, cook for around 5 to 8 minutes in total from both sides. Arrange chops into a casserole baking dish.
3. Combine diced tomatoes and mushroom soup in a large-sized bowl and spread over pork chops, arrange onion slices on top. Cover the baking dish with heavy-duty aluminum foil tightly.
4. Bake for around 40 minutes in the preheated convection oven. After 40 minutes, remove foil and bake for an additional 5 to 10 minutes.

7.25 CHICKEN CHEESE TACO CASSEROLE

Total time of cooking
1 hour
Prep time 20 minutes
Cook time 40 minutes

Serving
8

Nutrition facts
(Per serving)
Calories 508
Fat 29.4g
Protein 32.9g
Carbs 31.2g

Ingredients:
- 1 can of drained and rinsed black beans (15 ounces)
- 4 cups of cooked and shredded chicken
- 1 can of undrained diced tomatoes and green chiles (10 ounces)
- 2 cans of cream of chicken soup (10.75 ounces)
- 1 envelope of taco seasoning mix (1 ounce)
- 2 cups of Cheddar cheese shredded
- Fresh cilantro leaves chopped
- 5 cups of tortilla chips coarsely crushed
- 1 cup of light sour cream
- Green onion sliced
- Tomato chopped

Instructions:
Follow the instructions below to make a chicken cheese taco casserole.

1. Preheat the convection oven at 325°F. Lightly coat a casserole baking dish with cooking spray. Mix the soup, sour cream, chicken, green chiles, tomatoes, seasoning mix, and beans in a large-sized mixing bowl.

2. Spread a layer of half of the chicken mixture on the bottom of the dish, 3 cups of tortilla chips, and half cheese in a casserole dish. Spread with remaining chicken mixture and tortilla chips and cover the dish with a lid.

3. Bake for around 30 minutes in the preheated convection oven. After 30 minutes, uncover the lid and spread with remaining cheese; bake without lid for around 10 minutes or until cheese melts down. Spread with green onion, chopped tomato, and cilantro before eating.

7.26 DELICIOUS LAMB STUFFED PEPPERS

Total time of cooking
1 hour 20 minutes
Prep time 20 minutes
Cook time 1 hour

Serving
6

Nutrition facts
(Per serving)
Calories 273
Fat 16.8g
Protein 12.4g
Carbs 19.3g

Ingredients:
- 8 ounces of ground lamb
- 1 chopped onion
- 6 green bell peppers medium
- 1 cup of rice cooked
- 1 cup of feta cheese crumbled
- 1 cup of cold water
- 2 tablespoons of fresh dill chopped
- 1 tablespoon of olive oil
- 1 cup of tomato sauce
- 1 tablespoon of lemon juice
- 1/2 teaspoon of ground black pepper
- 1 teaspoon of white sugar
- 1/2 teaspoon of ground allspice
- 1 garlic clove minced
- 3/4 teaspoon of salt

Instructions:
Follow the instructions below to make delicious lamb stuffed peppers.

1. Preheat the convection oven at 350°F.

2. On medium heat, heat the oil in a large-sized skillet and add onion; cook for 4 to 5 minutes until translucent. Mix in garlic and cook for another 1 minute.

3. Cut the tops of bell peppers and discard seeds. Arrange bell peppers in 9x12 inches baking dish.

4. Combine cooked onion mixture, salt, allspice, dill, and pepper, in a large-sized bowl. Mix lamb, rice, and fold feta cheese in the mixture. Stuff bell peppers with the prepared mixture.

5. Mix in water with tomato sauce, sugar, and lemon juice. Spread half over the bell peppers and half on the bottom of a baking dish, and cover the dish with heavy-duty foil.

6. Bake in the preheated convection oven for around 45 minutes, remove foil and bake for another 15 minutes. Top up with more sauce if required.

Total time of cooking
6 hours 30 minutes
Prep time 30 minutes
Cook time 6 hours

Serving
3 (3 cups of duck rillettes)

Nutrition facts
(Per serving)
Calories 460
Fat 40.9g
Protein 11.3g
Carbs 9.5g

Ingredients:
For the spice rub:
- 2 teaspoons of dried thyme
- 2 tablespoons of kosher salt
- 2 teaspoons of ground black pepper

For potpourri:
- 2 tablespoons of softened unsalted butter
- 12 cloves of garlic
- 1 duck whole
- 1 tablespoon of brandy
- 6 slices of fresh ginger (1/4 inches thick)
- 3 bay leaves
- 2 teaspoons of fresh parsley chopped
- 1 orange zest (thin strips)
- 1 teaspoon of fresh chives chopped
- 1/2 teaspoon of orange zest grated
- 1 bunch of fresh thyme for garnishing
- 1/2 teaspoon of Dijon mustard
- Salt and ground black pepper to taste
- 1 pinch of cayenne pepper

Instructions:
Follow the instructions below to make tasty duck rillettes.

1. Preheat the convection oven at 225°F. With 2 pieces of heavy-duty aluminum foil, line a 9x13 baking sheet tightly.

2. Mix in 2 teaspoons of black pepper, dried thyme, and kosher salt in a small-sized bowl. Add in ginger, orange zest strips, garlic, bay leaves, and fresh thyme together in another bowl, mix and side them aside.

3. With 2/3 of the kosher salt mixture, season all the duck from inside and out. And fill the cavity of the duck with garlic mixture.

4. With breast side up, Arrange duck into a prepared baking dish and spread the remaining salt mixture. Cover the whole duck and pan tightly with heavy-duty aluminum foil.

5. Roast duck in the preheated convection oven for around 5 to 6 hours until duck meat easily pulls away from bones. Let duck cool down at room temperature after roasting and chill for 12 hours or overnight in the refrigerator.

6. Place meat from duck bones in a bowl and pour all accumulated juices in foil into a large-sized sauced and cook on medium-high heat until hot. Strain the juices into a bowl, let fat and stock separate; shift fat from the top to another bowl.

7. Mash the duck meat, 2 tablespoons of duck stock, butter, 3 tablespoons of duck fat, parsley, chives, brandy, salt, Dijon mustard, cayenne pepper, and black pepper with a wooden spoon or masher in a large-sized bowl. Spread the mixture in a sealable container and press to the bottom. Drizzle the top with little duck fat. Sprinkle with black pepper, orange zest, and thyme leaves on top. Seal and refrigerate for 1 to 3 days to let the flavors blend well.

7.28 SPINACH BEEF AND RICE BAKED

Total time of cooking
1 hour 10 minutes
Prep time 10 minutes
Cook time 1 hour

Serving
4
Nutrition facts
(Per serving)
Calories 440
Fat 14.2g
Protein 24.9g
Carbs 49.5g

Ingredients:
- 1 cup of long-grain rice uncooked
- 1 package of ground beef (16 ounces)
- 1 cup of green bell pepper chopped
- 1 can of diced tomatoes (28 ounces)
- 1 cup of onion chopped
- 1 teaspoon of chili powder
- 1/2 teaspoon of dried thyme
- 1/2 teaspoon of ground black pepper
- 1 teaspoon of browning sauce
- 1 teaspoon of salt

Instructions:
Follow the instructions below to make spinach beef and rice baked.
1. Preheat the convection oven at 325°F.
2. In a hot skillet on medium heat, stir and cook beef until crumbly and golden browned, for around 5 to 8 minutes until no liquid remains. Add rice, onion, tomatoes, bell pepper, salt, chili powder, pepper, browning sauce, and thyme and cover.
3. Transfer skillet into the preheated convection oven and bake for around 1 hour until rice is soft, do stir after 20 minutes of baking.
4. Serve straightaway.

7.29 BAKED LAMB MOROCCAN KEBABS

Total time of cooking
1 hour
Prep time 15 minutes
Cook time 45 minutes

Serving
6

Nutrition facts
(Per serving)
Calories 554
Fat 37.6g
Protein 32.2g
Carbs 22.7g

Ingredients:
- 5 ounces of goat cheese
- 2 pounds of ground lamb
- 1 chopped red onion
- 1 cup of raisins
- 1/3 cup of mayonnaise
- 2 tablespoons of fresh cilantro chopped
- 1/2 teaspoon of ground cumin
- Ground black pepper to taste
- 3/4 tablespoon of cayenne pepper
- Salt to taste
- 2 cloves of chopped garlic
- 1/2 teaspoon of ground coriander

Instructions:
Follow the instructions below to make baked lamb Moroccan kebabs.
1. Preheat the convection oven at 350°F.
2. Mix together raisins, lamb, mayonnaise, red onion, goat cheese, cayenne pepper, cumin, cilantro, salt, coriander, garlic and black pepper in a medium-sized bowl. Distribute mixture into 6 equal parts and press on the skewers.
3. Place skewers on a baking sheet and cook in the preheated convection oven for around 30 to 40 minutes or more until kebabs are browned and completely cooked. In the end, broil for 1 to 2 minutes in the convection oven.

7.30 BAKED HONEY-MUSTARD FLAVORED CHICKEN

Total time of cooking
1 hour 20 minutes
Prep time 10 minutes
Cook time 1 hour 10 minutes

Serving
2

Nutrition facts
(Per serving)
Calories 603
Fat 36.4g
Protein 43.9g
Carbs 28.7g

Ingredients:
- 2 quarters chicken leg with skin
- 3 tablespoons of honey mustard
- 2 large minced cloves of garlic
- 3 tablespoons of oil
- 2 tablespoons of honey
- 2 teaspoons of adobo seasoning
- 1 tablespoon of paprika
- 1 teaspoon of onion powder
- 2 teaspoons of fresh chives chopped
- 1 1/2 teaspoons of dried basil
- 1/2 teaspoon of meat tenderizer

Instructions:
Follow the instructions below to make baked honey-mustard flavored chicken.
1. Preheat the convection oven at 350°F.
2. Combine honey mustard, oil, and honey in a medium-sized bowl until well mixed. Add in paprika, basil, chives, garlic, onion powder, adobo seasoning and meat tenderizer. Mix until completely blended
3. Spread 2 to 3 tablespoons of mustard sauce on the bottom of the glass baking dish. Arrange chicken legs on top and spread the rest of the sauce all over the chicken. Cover the dish with heavy-duty aluminum foil tightly.
4. Bake in the preheated convection oven until chicken changes color and no more juices left in the dish, for around 60 to 70 minutes.
5. Serve warm and enjoy!

7.31 ROASTED BEEF TENDERLOIN SALT-CRUSTED

Total time of cooking
50 minutes
Prep time 25 minutes
Cook time 25 minutes

Serving
4

Nutrition facts
(Per serving)
Calories 467
Fat 34.9g
Protein 35g
Carbs 1g

Ingredients:
- 1 center-cut beef tenderloin roast, trimmed (2 pounds)
- 1 clove of crushed garlic
- 1 egg white
- 3 cups of course-ground sea salt
- 2 teaspoons of ground black pepper

Instructions:
Follow the instructions below to make roasted beef tenderloin salt-crusted.
1. Add pepper, crushed garlic, and egg white in a small-sized mixing bowl and whisk until well blended. Brush all over the beef tenderloin.
2. Spread and fill in about 1/4 inch of a baking dish with coarse salt. Toss tenderloin over salt to coat. Add more salt if required to make sure the baking dish has an even layer of salt. Let stand at room temperature for around 30 minutes.
3. Preheat the convection oven at 450°F.
4. Roast in the preheated convection oven for around 20 to 25 minutes. Remove the salt crust when roasted and shift to the cutting board; cut into slices and serve.

7.32 CLASSIC AND SIMPLE LAMB LOAF

Total time of cooking
1 hour
Prep time 25 minutes
Cook time 35 minutes

Serving
4 (1 loaf)

Nutrition facts
(Per serving)
Calories 409
Fat 29.7g
Protein 22.3g
Carbs 12.2g

Ingredients:
- 1 pound of ground lamb
- 2 slices of diced dry bread
- 2 tablespoons of balsamic vinegar
- 1/4 cup of tomato sauce
- 1/4 cup of milk
- 1/2 teaspoon of vegetable oil, or as required
- 4 cloves of garlic minced
- 1 egg
- 5 leaves of finely chopped fresh mint
- 2 tablespoons of fresh thyme chopped
- 1 tablespoon of lemon zest
- 1 teaspoon of dried and crushed rosemary
- 1/4 teaspoon of ground black pepper
- 1/2 teaspoon of vegetable oil
- 1 tablespoon of Worcestershire sauce
- 1 teaspoon of dried basil
- 3/4 teaspoon of salt
- 1 teaspoon of ground coriander

Instructions:
Follow the instructions below to make a classic and simple lamb loaf.
1.Preheat the convection oven at 375°F.With oil grease a 9x5 inches loaf pan.
2.Add milk and bread to a small-sized bowl and press bread with a spoon to soak up the milk.
3.Combine egg, garlic, lamb, Worcestershire sauce, thyme, coriander, basil, salt, pepper, rosemary and lemon zest in a medium-sized bowl. Mix in soaked bread and discard the milk. Mix using hands until fully combined. Transfer loaf in a greased pan.
4.Mix tomato sauce and mint and spread over the loaf evenly. Drizzle the top of the loaf with balsamic vinegar.
5.Bake in the preheated convection oven for around 35 minutes. Let stand for 5 minutes before serving.

7.33 BAKED ITALIAN-STYLE BREADED PORK CHOPS

Total time of cooking
45 minutes
Prep time 25 minutes
Cook time 20 minutes

Serving
4

Nutrition facts
(Per serving)
Calories 421
Fat 24.1g
Protein 28g
Carbs 20.9g

Ingredients:
- 4 center-cut boneless pork chops, thinly sliced
- 1 cup of dry bread crumbs
- 3 tablespoons of olive oil
- 1/2 cup of milk
- 1 teaspoon of fresh thyme chopped
- Salt to taste
- 1 teaspoon of fresh rosemary chopped

Instructions:
Follow the instructions below to make a baked Italian-style breaded pork chops.
1.Preheat the convection oven at 325°F.Pour oil into the baking dish and coat the whole dish.
2.With a meat tenderizer, pound the chops on a floured surface until they are tender and thin.
3.Place milk in a bowl. Combine thyme, bread crumbs, and rosemary in a second bowl. Dip chops into the milk first and then evenly coat in bread crumbs. Arrange on a baking dish in one layer. Sprinkle with salt.
4.Bake in the preheated convection oven for around 10 minutes on each side until chops are crispy.

7.34 BEEF AND SALSA BAKED TAQUITOS

Total time of cooking
50 minutes
Prep time 15 minutes
Cook time 35 minutes

Serving
6 (12 taquitos)

Nutrition facts
(Per serving)
Calories 480
Fat 22.9g
Protein 25.3g
Carbs 44.1g

Ingredients:
- 1 1/2 cups of Cheddar cheese shredded
- 1 pound of ground beef
- 2 cups of salsa
- 2 cups of white rice cooked
- 12 corn tortillas (6 inches)
- 1 1/2 tablespoons of red bell pepper chopped
- 2 tablespoons of water
- 1 tablespoon of fresh garlic chopped

Instructions:
Follow the instructions below to make beef and salsa baked taquitos.
1.Preheat the convection oven at 350°F.
2.On medium heat, in a large-sized skillet. Stir ground beef and cook until crumbly for around 5 to 8 minutes.
3.Mix in cooked rice, bell pepper, water, and garlic to the beef mixture and cook until mixture is completely heated, for around 3 to 5 minutes. Distribute the mixture between tortillas and close. Arrange tortillas in 8x12 inches baking pan tightly against each other. Drizzle salsa over the tortillas and sprinkle with cheddar cheese.
4.Bake in the preheated oven for around 25 minutes until bubbly.

7.35 BAKED TERIYAKI PINEAPPLE CHICKEN

Total time of cooking
45 minutes
Prep time 15 minutes
Cook time 30 minutes

Serving
6

Nutrition facts
(Per serving)
Calories 433
Fat 19g
Protein 23g
Carbs 42g

Ingredients:
- 1 cup of teriyaki sauce
- 6 skinless and boneless chicken thighs
- 3 green onions (cut to 1/2-inch pieces)
- 2 tablespoons of cornstarch
- 6 rings of Pineapple
- Green onion and sesame seeds for garnish

nstructions:
Follow the instructions below to make baked teriyaki pineapple chicken.
1.Combine chicken thighs with half teriyaki sauce and set aside the remaining teriyaki sauce. Leave the chicken to marinate for around 4 hours or for overnight.
2.In a small-sized saucepan, pour the remaining teriyaki sauce and bring to boil. Mix cornstarch with 2 tablespoons of water and gradually add corn starch into teriyaki sauce stop adding if sauce reaches the desired consistency
3.Take out the chicken and discard the marinade. Arrange chicken, green onions, and pineapple rings into a 9x13 inches baking pan. Top up with prepared thickened teriyaki sauce.
4.Bake in the preheated convection oven at 400°F for around 25 minutes. Garnish with sesame seeds and green onions and broil in a convection oven for 3 to 5 minutes in the end and serve.

7.36 BAKED MEATBALLS STUFFED WITH MAC AND CHEESE

Total time of cooking

40 minutes
Prep time 10 minutes
Cook time 30 minutes

Serving

10 stuffed meatballs

Nutrition facts

(Per serving)
Calories 275
Fat 16g
Protein 18g
Carbs 12g

Ingredients:

- 1 cup of macaroni and cheese prepared
- 1 1/2 pounds of lean ground beef
- 1/2 cup of cheddar cheese grated
- 1 1/2 ounces of cheddar (cut into 10 small cubes)
- 1/3 cup of panko bread crumbs
- 2 tablespoons of barbecue sauce
- 2 tablespoons of chopped onion
- 1 egg
- 1/2 teaspoons of ground black pepper

Instructions:

Follow the instructions below to make baked meatballs stuffed with mac and cheese.
1. Preheat the convection oven at 350°F.
2. Combine egg, onion, beef, panko bread crumbs, pepper, and shredded cheese. Mix until fully combined.
3. Distribute meat into 10 equal portions and make a thin circle out of each portion. Top with 1 tablespoon of macaroni in the center of each circle and place 1 cheddar cube. Fold and close the circle pinch to seal and form a ball. Repeat the procedure with the remaining portions and make 10 meatballs.
4. Transfer meatballs on a non-stick baking sheet and brush the meatballs with barbecue sauce.
5. Bake for around 25 to 30 minutes or until meat is completely cooked.
6. Serve warm and enjoy!

7.37 BAKED CHEESE STUFFED CHICKEN BREASTS WITH SAUCE

Total time of cooking

50 minutes
Prep time 10 minutes
Cook time 40 minutes

Serving

4

Nutrition facts

(Per serving)
Calories 575
Fat 36g
Protein 57g
Carbs 4g

Ingredients:

- 8 mozzarella cheese slices(about 4 ounces in total)
- 2 tablespoons of parmesan cheese grated
- 4 skinless and boneless chicken breasts boneless and skinless(about 7 ounces each)
- 1/2 cup of chicken broth
- 2 cups of fresh spinach
- 1 tablespoon of olive oil
- 3/4 cup of heavy cream
- 1 tablespoon of flour
- 1 clove of minced garlic
- Salt and pepper to taste
- 1 tablespoon of butter

Instructions:

Follow the instructions below to make baked cheese stuffed chicken breasts with sauce.
1. Preheat the convection oven at 400°F.
2. Cut each chicken breast into a butterfly and fill it in with two slices of mozzarella. Sprinkle salt and pepper, season. Fold to close the chicken breasts.
3. In an oven-proof skillet, heat olive oil on medium-high heat. Cook chicken breasts until golden for around 2 to 3 minutes per side. Bake in the preheated convection oven with a skillet for around 18 to 20 minutes.
4. Meanwhile, on medium heat, melt butter. Add in garlic and cook for 1 minute, then add in flour and cook for 1 minute. Slowly add chicken broth and keep whisking. Pour in heavy cream and keep stirring until it thickens about 4 to 5 minutes.
5. Mix in parmesan cheese and spinach and cook for 2 to 3 minutes or until spinach wilts.
6. Add baked chicken to the saucepan and cook them together for around 2 to 3 minutes.
7. Serve with rice or potatoes if you like.

7.38 BAKED BEEF POTATO PIE

Total time of cooking

2 hours
Prep time 20 minutes
Cook time 1 hour 40 minutes

Serving

12

Nutrition facts

(Per serving)
Calories 519
Fat 26.8g
Protein 20g
Carbs 46.1g

Ingredients:

- 2 cups beef stock
- 2 pounds of beef sirloin (cut into cubes)
- 1 cup of carrots chopped
- 2 pie crusts of 10-inch
- 1 can of tomato paste (8 ounces)
- 2 tablespoons of milk
- 2 cubed and peeled large potatoes
- 1 cup of red wine
- 1 teaspoon of Worcestershire sauce
- Salt to taste
- 3 tablespoons of all-purpose flour
- 1/2 teaspoon of ground black pepper
- 1 tablespoon of butter
- 2 cloves of minced garlic

Instructions:

1. Preheat the convection oven at 400°F.
2. Heat butter and oil together in a large-sized saucepan on medium heat. Cook onion and stir until soften for around 10 minutes. Add beef and cook until browned from all sides, for around 5 minutes. Mix in garlic and stir for around 1 minute.
3. Add pepper, flour, and salt into beef mixture; stir for around 2 to 3 minutes to coat beef. Pour wine and wait for 1 boil, turn the heat low and simmer for 4 to 5 minutes.
4. Add in potatoes, beef stock, tomato paste, carrots, and Worcestershire sauce in the beef mixture; Cook until vegetables are tender 30 minutes to 50 minutes. Remove from stove and cool down for a while.
5. Spread pie crust on the bottom of 9x13 inches baking dish and spread beef and potato filling in crust; place the remaining pie crust on top and crimp together the crusts from the edges with a fork or with your fingers. Brush the top of the crust with milk.
6. Bake in the preheated convection oven for around 40 to 45 minutes until crust is lightly browned.

7.39 BAKED MAPLE FLAVORED PORK LOIN ROAST

Total time of cooking

2 hours 20 minutes
Prep time 15 minutes
Cook time 2 hours 5 minutes

Serving

8 (1 loin roast)

Nutrition facts

(Per serving)
Calories 397
Fat 12.8g
Protein 41g
Carbs 28.1g

Ingredients:

- 1 boneless pork loin roast (4 pounds)
- 1 tablespoon of garlic minced
- 1 tablespoon of canola oil
- 3/4 cup of maple syrup
- 1/3 cup of water
- All-purpose flour for dredging
- 3/4 cup of ketchup
- Salt and pepper to taste

Instructions:

Follow the instructions below to make a baked maple-flavored pork loin roast.

1. Preheat the convection oven at 375°F.
2. On medium-high heat in a large-sized skillet, heat oil until oil starts smoking.
   With salt and pepper, season the pork roast and dredge in flour. Dip in hot smoking oil until browned from both sides, around 1 minute per side.
3. Transfer onto a large aluminum foil sheet and arrange on top of the baking sheet; set it aside. Mix the maple syrup, water, ketchup, and garlic. Drizzle 3/4 of the sauce over pork. Wrap the foil over pork and seal from all sides.
4. Bake in the preheated convection oven for around 2 hours. Gently open the foil and broil for around 5 minutes. Serve with the existing sauce.

7.40 CHEESY CHICKEN ROLL-UPS BAKED

Total time of cooking
45 minutes
Prep time 10 minutes
Cook time 35 minutes

Serving
8 rolls

Nutrition facts
(Per serving)
Calories 193
Fat 11g
Protein 16g
Carbs 8g

Ingredients:
- 1 1/2 cups of cooked and shredded chicken
- 10 1/2 ounces of cream of chicken soup
- 1 can of crescent rolls
- 2 cups of steamed broccoli
- 1 1/2 cups of sharp cheddar cheese(divided)
- 1/2 cup of broth
- 1/2 teaspoon of garlic powder
- 1 tablespoon of flour
- 1/2 cup of milk
- Salt and pepper to taste

Instructions:
Follow the instructions below to make cheesy chicken roll-ups baked.
1.Preheat the convection oven at 350°F.
2.In a large-sized bowl, combine milk, broth, flour, salt, garlic powder, soup, and pepper. On the bottom of the 9x13 pan, spread the soup mixture. Separate the triangles of the crescent roll.
3.Distribute all the chicken and broccoli and 1 1/2 cups of the cheddar cheese on crescent rolls.
4.Roll all crescent rolls up and transfer to prepared pan.
5.Bake for around 25 minutes in the preheated convection oven, top up with the remaining cheese, bake for another 5 to 10 minutes.

7.41 CLASSIC CHICKEN PARMESAN MEATLOAF

Total time of cooking
1 hour 10 minutes
Prep time 10 minutes
Cook time 1 hour

Serving
6

Nutrition facts
(Per serving)
Calories 469
Fat 29g
Protein 39g
Carbs 14g

Ingredients:
- 2 pounds of ground chicken
- 1/4 cup of Parmesan cheese grated
- 1/3 cup of diced onion
- 1/2 cup of seasoned bread crumbs
- 3 strings of mozzarella cheese
- 1/4 cup of milk
- 2 minced cloves of garlic
- 1 egg
- 1 teaspoon of Italian seasoning
- 1/2 teaspoon of salt
- 2 tablespoons of chopped fresh parsley

For the topping:
- 1 cup of shredded mozzarella cheese
- 1 1/2 tablespoons of grated parmesan cheese
- 1/2 cup of marinara sauce
- 1 tablespoon of melted butter
- 1 tablespoon of chopped fresh parsley
- 2 tablespoons of panko bread crumbs

Instructions:
1.Preheat the convection oven at 375°F.Spray a loaf pan with cooking spray.
2.On medium heat, cook garlic and onion in olive oil until translucent. Let it cool completely.
3.In a large-sized bowl, add all the meatloaf ingredients and mix until completely fully combined.
4.Spread 2/3 of the mixture into 8x4 inches loaf pan. Make a small well in the middle and add in cheese. Spread the remaining mixture on top of the loaf to seal the cheese layer.
5.Spread marinara sauce on top and bake in the preheated convection oven for around 45 minutes.
6.Mix butter, parmesan cheese, bread crumbs, and parsley together.Top up the meatloaf with bread crumbs and mozzarella topping. Bake for an additional 15 minutes.
8.Cool down for a while, slice, and enjoy!

7.42 ROASTED BEEF TERIYAKI SHISH KEBABS

Total time of cooking
45 minutes
Prep time 15 minutes
Cook time 30 minutes

Serving
8

Nutrition facts
(Per serving)
Calories 306
Fat 5g
Protein 27g
Carbs 38g

Ingredients:
•   2 pounds of beef top sirloin steak (cut into 1 1/2-inch cubes)
•   1 cup of sugar
•   2 cups of fresh pineapple cubed
•   2 to 3 zucchinis (cut into 1-inch slices)
•   1 small onion (cut into 1-inch pieces)
•   1/2 pound of fresh mushrooms
•   1 cup of ketchup
•   1 large green or sweet red pepper (cut into 1-inch pieces)

•   1 cup of soy sauce
•   2 teaspoons of ground ginger
•   2 teaspoons of garlic powder

Instructions:
Follow the instructions below to make roasted beef teriyaki shish kebabs.
1.Preheat the convection oven at 400°F.
2.Combine sugar, ketchup, soy sauce, garlic powder, and ground ginger for the marinade. Mix in half of the marinade with beef in zip loc bag, close, and toss to coat. Keep in refrigerator for overnight. (reserve half of the marinade for later use).
3.Arrange vegetables on soaked wooden skewers, and on another separate skewer, arrange beef with pineapple, and discard the remaining amount of marinade.
4.Transfer the skewers to a baking sheet and roast in the preheated convection oven for around 25 to 30 minutes or until completely cooked.
5.In a small-sized saucepan, boil reserved marinade, keep stirring and cook for 1 minute. Drizzle the sauce over skewers when serving.

7.43 BEEF AND EGG NOODLES BAKE

Total time of cooking
40 minutes
Prep time 15 minutes
Cook time 25 minutes

Serving
6

Nutrition facts
(Per serving)
Calories 474
Fat 27g
Protein 25.8g
Carbs 30.9g

Ingredients:
•   1 pound of (80% lean) ground chuck beef
•   1 1/4 cups of Mexican blend cheese shredded
•   1 can of undrained and diced tomatoes and green chilies
•   6 ounces of uncooked dry extra-wide egg noodles
•   1 can of red enchilada sauce (10 ounces)
•   1/4 cup of green onions thinly sliced
•   1 1/4 cups of water
•   1 teaspoon of Sour cream
•   2 cups frozen mixed vegetables (black beans, corn, red

peppers)
•   Cooking spray

Instructions:
Follow the instructions below to make beef and egg noodles bake.
1.Preheat the convection oven at 375°F.
2.Grease glass baking dish of 13x9 inches with cooking spray. Spread uncooked noodles on the bottom of the baking dish.
3.In a large-sized skillet on medium-high heat. Cook beef for 5 to 8 minutes crumbles with a spoon. Add vegetables, tomatoes, enchilada sauce, and water; boil. Stir and place the mixture over noodles.
4.With heavy-duty foil, cover the whole dish tightly; Bake for around 15 minutes in the preheated convection oven. Uncover, stir and sprinkle cheese all over the top, bake for additional 10 minutes.
5.While serving, sprinkle with green onion and side with sour cream.

7.44 BAKED PESTO-FLAVORED CHICKEN

Total time of cooking
45 minutes
Prep time 15 minutes
Cook time 30 minutes

Serving
6

Nutrition facts
(Per serving)
Calories 448
Fat 22g
Protein 55g
Carbs 4g

Ingredients:
- 1/3 cup of pesto(divided)
- 4 slices of fresh mozzarella cheese
- 4 small chicken breasts (about 5 ounces each)
- 1 tablespoon of balsamic vinegar
- Parsley and fresh basil for serving

For the topping:
- 2 teaspoons of olive oil
- 1 clove of minced garlic
- 1 finely diced Roma tomato
- 1 teaspoon red wine vinegar
- Salt and pepper to taste
- 1/4 teaspoon of dried basil

Instructions:
Follow the instructions below to make baked pesto-flavored chicken.
1.Preheat the convection oven at 375°F.
2.Mix 2 tablespoons of pesto and balsamic vinegar and toss chicken to coat.
3.On medium heat, in a frying pan, heat and brown chicken 2 minutes per side.
4.Transfer chicken to a baking dish and bake in the preheated convection oven for 20 to 25 minutes.
5.Spread remaining pesto all over the chicken breasts, sprinkle the top with cheese and bake for another 5 minutes or until cheese melts down.
6.In a small-sized bowl, combine all the topping ingredients. Drizzle over baked chicken, top with fresh herbs, and serve.

7.45 BAKED SWISS CHEESE AND CORNED BEEF DIP IN BREAD BOWL

Total time of cooking
1 hour 20 minutes
Prep time 15 minutes
Cook time 1 hour 5 minutes

Serving
24

Nutrition facts
(Per serving)
Calories 293
Fat 24.1g
Protein 8g
Carbs 11.8g

Ingredients:
- 3 packages of deli-sliced corned beef(2.5 ounces), diced
- 1 carton of sour cream(8 ounces)
- 1 loaf of Italian bread unsliced(1 pound)
- 2 packages of softened cream cheese(8 ounces)
- 1 cup of Swiss cheese shredded
- 1 1/2 cups of mayonnaise
- 1 tablespoon of vegetable oil or olive oil
- 3/4 chopped onion
- 1 teaspoon of garlic powder

Instructions:
Follow the instructions below to make baked swiss cheese and corned beef dip In Bread Bowl.
1.Preheat the convection oven at 325°F.
2.In a large-sized skillet on medium heat, hot the vegetable oil and cook onion until soft; stir for 5 to 8 minutes.
3.Shit onion into a large-sized mixing bowl. Mix in cream cheese, sour cream, corned beef, swiss cheese, mayonnaise, and garlic powder into the onion, mix until fully blended.
4.From the top of Italian bread, cut the slice of bread and hollow the center, making a long bread bowl in the loaf. Keep at least 1/2 inches of bread on the loaf side; keep bread chunks reserved from the center of Italian bread for dipping if you like.
5.Place the corned beef mixture into the bread bowl. With foil, wrap the bread, boil tightly and transfer on a baking sheet.
6.Bake in the preheated convection oven until dip is bubbly and completely cooked.

7.46 GREEK-STYLE STUFFED LAMB LEG

Total time of cooking
1 hour 55 minutes
Prep time 15 minutes
Cook time 1 hour 30 minutes

Serving
8

Nutrition facts
(Per serving)
Calories 389
Fat 25.7g
Protein 29.6g
Carbs 11.5g

Ingredients:
- 1 package of feta cheese crumbled(8 ounces)
- 1-pound leg of lamb, butter flied (3 1/2)
- 1 jar of drained and chopped marinated artichoke hearts (12 ounces)
- 1 jar of drained and chopped sun-dried tomatoes packed in oil (6 ounces)
- 2 tablespoons of fresh oregano chopped
- 3 cloves of minced garlic
- 2 tablespoons of fresh basil chopped
- Salt and ground black pepper to taste
- Olive oil, as required

Instructions:
Follow the instructions below to make Greek-style stuffed lamb leg.
1.Preheat the convection oven at 325°F.
2.On the chopping board, layout the lamb leg. Pour olive oil all over the lamb evenly. Sprinkle with basil and oregano and top lamb with feta cheese, sun-dried tomatoes, artichoke hearts, and garlic. Season the lamb with pepper and salt.
3.Around stuffing, roll the lamb and wrap the lamb with threads to avoid unrolling. In aluminum foil, wrap the lamb tightly and transfer it to a baking dish.
4.Roast in the preheated convection oven for around 90 minutes, set the lamb aside for 10 to 15 minutes before slicing upon serving drizzle the lamb with pan juices.

7.47 BAKED CHICKEN CHEESY POTATOES RANCH

Total time of cooking
1 hour 10 minutes
Prep time 15 minutes
Cook time 55 minutes

Serving
6

Nutrition facts
(Per serving)
Calories 589
Fat 37g
Protein 37g
Carbs 27g

Ingredients:
- 1 1/4 cup of shredded cheddar cheese(divided)
- 3 cubed chicken breasts
- 1/2 cup of ranch dressing
- 8 slices of cooked, crisp, and crumbled bacon
- 1/2 teaspoon of each garlic powder, pepper, parsley, and dill
- 2 pounds of red potatoes
- 1/2 cup of sour cream
- 4 thinly sliced green onions

Instructions:
Follow the instructions below to make baked chicken cheesy potatoes ranch.
1.Preheat the convection oven at 350°F.
2.Clean potatoes and cut them into 1-inch cubes. Boil potato in salted water for 12 to 15 minutes or until soft.
3.Season the chicken breasts with pepper and salt. Fry chicken on medium heat for about 7 to 8 minutes.
4.Combine sour cream,3/4 cup of cheese, seasonings, and ranch dressing in a medium-sized bowl and mix.
5.Into 9x13 inches greased pan, spread chicken and potatoes. Spread half of the bacon and green onions. Pour sauce over the top. Sprinkle remaining cheese on the top and bake in the preheated convection oven for around 35 minutes or until bubbly and lightly browned.
6.Take out the pan from the convection oven and spread the remaining bacon and green onions on top and side with sour cream when serving.

7.48 ROASTED AVOCADO AND DIJON RUBBED BEEF TENDERLOIN

Total time of cooking
1 hour 5 minutes
Prep time 15 minutes
Cook time 50 minutes

Serving
8

Nutrition facts
(Per serving)
Calories 545
Fat 40.4g
Protein 34.7g
Carbs 8.4g

Ingredients:
- 1 trimmed beef tenderloin (4 pounds)
- 1/4 cup of steak seasoning
- 3/4 jar of Dijon mustard (8 ounces)
- 1 tablespoon of olive oil
- 1 peeled and cubed ripe avocado
- 4 cloves of garlic

Instructions:
Follow the instructions below to make roasted avocado and Dijon rubbed beef tenderloin.
1.Preheat the convection oven at 375°F.With aluminum foil sheet line a roasting pan.
2.On high heat, preheat a large-sized skillet. Heat oil until smoking hot. Cook tenderloin until browned in hot oil from all sides for 5 minutes. Transfer to roasting pan.
3.In the food processor, add avocado, garlic, steak seasoning, and mustard and blend until soft and creamy. Pour the avocado mixture all over the tenderloin and coat evenly.
4.Roast in the preheated convection for around 40 minutes or until tenderloin is done.

7.49 BEEF CHEESE SPAGHETTI PIE

Total time of cooking
1 hour
Prep time 30 minutes
Cook time 30 minutes

Serving
6

Nutrition facts
(Per serving)
Calories 428
Fat 17g
Protein 37g
Carbs 31g

Ingredients:
- 1 cup of mozzarella cheese shredded

For Spaghetti crust:
- 1/2 cup of parmesan cheese
- 6 ounces of spaghetti
- 2 eggs
- 2 tablespoons of butter

For Meat Sauce:
- 14 ounces of diced and drained tomatoes
- 1 pound of ground beef
- 2 cups of pasta sauce
- 1/2 diced small onion

For Cheese layer:
- 1 tablespoon of fresh basil
- 1 cup of ricotta cheese
- 2 tablespoons of parsley

Instructions:
Follow the instructions below to make a beef cheese spaghetti pie.
1.Preheat the convection oven at 375°F.
2.Cook spaghetti according to your package directions. Toss spaghetti with butter.Mix in parmesan cheese and eggs.
3.In a greased deep-dish pan, spread spaghetti on the bottom and press to make a crust. Combine together parsley, ricotta cheese, and basil. Place the cheese mixture layer on the top of the spaghetti layer.
4.Cook onion and beef until beef changes color; stir in pasta sauce and tomatoes. Cook for 10 minutes until thickens. Spread the beef mixture layer on top of the cheese mixture layer.
5.Bake in the preheated convection oven for around 20 to 25 minutes. Sprinkle with mozzarella cheese and bake for another 5 minutes or until cheese melts down.

7.50 OVEN-ROASTED STUFFED DUCK

Total time of cooking
2 hours 50 minutes
Prep time 20 minutes
Cook time 2 hours 30 minutes

Serving
8

Nutrition facts
(Per serving)
Calories 1175
Fat 113g
Protein 33g
Carbs 4g

Ingredients:
- 5-6 pounds of a cleaned whole duck
- 2 chopped onions
- 1/2 lime
- 1 tablespoon of black pepper
- 1 tablespoon of olive oil
- 2 teaspoons of salt
- 1/2 teaspoon of ground cumin

Instructions:
Follow the instructions below to make an oven-roasted stuffed duck.
1. Preheat the convection oven at 325°F.
2. With a clean kitchen cloth, pat dry the duck.
3. Combine all the ingredients and squeeze the half lime over the top and mix well.
4. With the onion mixture, stuff the cavity of the duck. Reserve 2 to 3 tablespoons of onion mixture.
5. Seal duck with toothpicks and take the squeezed lemon rub all over the duck's outer skin. Now with the remaining onion mixture, rub the whole duck.
6. Transfer the duck into the roasting pan and roast in the preheated convection oven for around 2 1/2 hours.
7. Once roasted, let it cool down for some time. Broil in the convection oven until browned.

7.51 SKILLET ROAST CHICKEN WITH SCHMALTZY POTATOES

Total time of cooking
5 hrs 45 min
Prep time: 4 hrs 45 Min
Cook time: 1 hr

Servings
4-6

Nutrition Facts
(Per Serving): Calories: 553 kcal
Fat: 34g
Protein: 38g
Carbs: 23g

Ingredients
- Black pepper freshly ground and salt (to taste)
- Parsley, chopped, to serve as a garnish
- Buttermilk 1½ cups
- 1 whole Chicken
- tbsp olive oil extra-virgin
- 1 1/2 pound halved baby potatoes
- To serve, garnish with fresh parsley.

Instructions
1. Season the chicken well with salt. Allow 30 minutes to rest at room temperature.
2. 1 tablespoon kosher salt, combined with the buttermilk. Pour the buttermilk on top of the chicken in a sealed bag. Seal the bag and press everything together to coat the chicken. Cool it for at least 4 hours and up to a day in the refrigerator.
3. Remove the chicken from the fridge 1 hour before cooking and place it on a platter; discard the brine. Tie the legs together using kitchen thread. Preheat the oven to 425 degrees Fahrenheit.
4. In a large oven-safe pan, arrange the potatoes and sprinkle with olive oil. Season to taste with salt and pepper, then toss to combine.
5. Set the whole chicken on top of the potatoes and bake with the legs pointing to the rear left corner of the oven. After 25 minutes of roasting, reduce the heat to 400°F. Rotate the pan so that the legs face the rear right corner, and roast for another 35 minutes (until the meat reaches 165°F on the inside).
6. Before slicing and serving, let the chicken rest for 10 to 15 minutes. Garnish with chopped fresh parsley.

Total time of cooking

2 hrs 35 minutes
Prep Time: 15 minutes
Cook Time: 2 hrs 20 minutes

Servings

6

Nutrition facts

(per serving)
Calories: 663kcal
Protein 48g
Fat 50g
Carbs 2g

Ingredients

- 1 pound roasting chicken
- 1/4 cup unsalted butter
- 1 tablespoon fresh rosemary
- 3-4 garlic cloves, minced
- 1 tablespoon fresh thyme
- 1–2 rosemary sprigs, fresh
- To taste, freshly cracked black pepper
- 1 teaspoon lemon zest (save 1/2 of the lemon to stuff inside the chicken cavity)
- 1 teaspoon onion powder
- To taste kosher salt
- 1 1/2 teaspoons fresh lemon juice

Instructions

1.Turn on the oven at 375° F. Set for convection baking if you have it. Put a rack in the middle of the oven. Aluminum foil should be used to line the bottom of a roasting pan. Remove from the equation.

Prepare the Garlic Herb-Butter

1.Four of the three garlic cloves should be minced. Combine the minced garlic, butter, herbs, onion powder, and lemon juice and zest in a small saucepan over low heat. To taste, season with salt and pepper.

Prepare the Chicken for Roasting

1.Remove the chicken's neck bone and giblets from the cavity. Using paper towels, pat the chicken dry. Put the meat on a rack in a shallow roasting pan or a deep baking pan, breast side up.

2.To the interior of the hollow wall, sprinkle salt. To liberate the natural oils and taste of the remaining seven garlic cloves, smash them with the side of a chef's knife. Fill the cavity of the bird with these 12 lemon slices and rosemary sprigs.

3.Brush the garlic herb butter on the chicken. Butcher's twine should be used to tie the legs together. If desired, tuck the wings beneath the body. If used, place the cooking thermometer's temperature probe into the thickest section of the chicken.

Roast the Garlic Herb-Butter Chicken

1.Bake for one hour with the roasting pan in the middle of the oven. If you aren't using a cooking thermometer with a probe, check the temperature after an hour using an instant-read thermometer.

2.The interior temperature should be approximately 150 degrees at this stage. Brush the chicken with the juices from the pan's bottom. Put the chicken to the oven to finish cooking. When the chicken starts to brown too much, tent it with foil.

3.Roast chicken for a little longer then bastes it every 30 minutes until it achieves a minimum internal temp of 165 F, approximately 2 hours.

4.Take the chicken out of the oven and baste it one more time. Allow at least 20 minutes for the roasted chicken to settle before cutting.

Total time of cooking
60 minutes
Prep time: 45 minutes
Cook time: 15 minutes

Servings
4

Nutrition Facts
(Per Serving)
Calories: 218.7 kcal
Fat 8.0 g
Protein 8.6 g
Carbs 33.1 g

Ingredients
- lemons
- Season with salt and freshly ground pepper.
- 1 chicken, deboned and chopped into pieces
- 1 tbsp. olive oil
- 1 teaspoon oregano, dry

Instructions
1.Mix the chicken with all of the ingredients (except half of the lemon), in a large mixing bowl. Cut the half lemon in halves and toss it with the chicken and potatoes.
2.Set the meat (skin side up) on the roasting pan. Cook for 45 minutes at 425°F convection, then check for doneness and cook for additional 10 minutes if necessary.

Total time of cooking
1 hr 15 minutes
Prep time: 60 minutes
Cook time: 15 minutes

Servings
10

Nutrition Facts
(Per Serving)
Calories: 376.8 kcal
Fat: 21.1 g
Protein: 21.3 g
Carbs: 24.1 g

Ingredients
- 0.5 cup chopped green peppers
- Onions, raw, chopped, 0.75 cup
- large eggs, fresh,
- Ground beef, 2 lb lean
- Black pepper, 0.75 tsp
- 1 tbsp salt
- 1 can diced tomatoes
- 0.5 cup catsup
- Bread crumbs, dry, 2.25 cup grated, plain

Instructions
1.Mix all of the ingredients (press gently into a loaf pan).
2.Turn on the oven to 350°F and bake for 1 hour.
3.Drain fat and cover with catsup before baking for another 30 minutes.
4.Bake for 60 minutes at 300°F in a convection oven.
5.Remove the loaf from the oven and place it on a wire rack to drain the oil and juices.
6.Cover the bread with 1/2 cup catsup. Cut the meat into pieces.

7.55 DIJON HERB CHICKEN BREASTS

Total time of cooking

60 minutes
Prep time: 15 minutes
Cook time: 45 minutes

Servings

4

Nutrition facts (per serving)

Calories 300 kcal
Fat14 g
Protein 31 g
Carbs 9 g

Ingredients

- 1 tbsp Dijon mustard
- Chicken breasts, skin on, bone-in
- 1/2 sliced yellow onion
- 1 tsp black pepper
- 1 tbsp olive oil
- Chopped parsley leaves
- 1/2 cup chicken stock low sodium
- 1 tsp sugar
- 1 ½ teaspoons chopped garlic
- 1 ½ teaspoons salt
- 1 tsp red chili flakes

Instructions

1.Except for the chicken and onion, combine all ingredients in a large mixing basin. After all of the ingredients have been well mixed, add the chicken and onion. Cover with plastic wrap and let marinate the chicken for at least 45 minutes.
2.Place the chicken on the top rack, skin side down, once it's ready to cook.
3.Cook the meat for 9 minutes (on each side) at 350°F. Allow the chicken to rest for 3-5 minutes after it has been cooked before serving.

7.56 ROAST TURKEY

Total time of cooking

45 minutes
Prep time: 15 minutes
Cook time: 30 minutes

Servings

6

Nutrition Facts

(Per Serving)
Calories 107 kcal
Fat 5.8g
Protein 22.3g
Carbs 2.6g

Ingredients

- 1/4 Cup Extra Virgin Olive Oil
- A (12 To 14-Pound) Turkey
- 1 Teaspoon Freshly Ground Black Pepper
- Paprika (1 Tablespoon)
- Celery Stalks, Chopped
- 1 Teaspoon Kosher Salt
- Big Chopped Onions
- Large Chopped Carrots

Instructions

1.Combine all of the spices and massage them into the turkey along with the olive oil.
2.Combine all of the veggies and fill the turkey with them.
3.To the glass bowl, add the extension ring. Put the turkey (side down) on the bottom rack.
4.Roast the turkey for 13-15 minutes per pound at 350°F. Allow at least 10-15 minutes for the turkey to rest before serving.

7.57 HONEY LIME CHICKEN BREASTS

Total time of cooking
65 minutes
Prep time: 20 minutes
Cook time: 45 minutes

Servings
4

Nutrition Facts
(Per Serving)
Calories 272.9 kcal
Fat 0.5 g
Protein 23.3 g
Carbs 36.5 g

Ingredients
- Half a cup of honey
- chicken breasts, boneless and skinless
- A quarter cup of lime juice
- A third cup of soy sauce

Instructions
1.Mix the soy sauce,honey, and lime juice in a gallon zip lock bag. Set the meat in the bag with the marinate and put it in the refrigerator for at least 30 minutes.
2.After the chicken has marinated, put the breasts on the top shelf of the oven and discard the marinade. Preheat the oven to 350°F and cook for 8-10 minutes on each side.
3.The thickness of the chicken will determine how long it takes to cook. Allow 7 minutes for the chicken to rest before serving.

7.58 CRISPY HONEY GARLIC CHICKEN

Total time of cooking
1 hour 5 minutes
Prep Time: 5 minutes
Cook Time: 1 hour

Servings
4

Nutrition facts
(per serving)
Calories 305 kcal
Protein 40g
Fat 12.6g
Carbs 16.4g

Ingredients
- Half a cup of honey
- 4-5 skin-on bone-in, chicken pieces, 4 pounds
- tbsp rice vinegar
- Pepper and salt to taste
- tbsp minced garlic
- 3-4 teaspoons of water to thin
- tbsp soy sauce

Instructions
1.Turn on the oven at 350 ° F.
2.For easier cleaning, line a roasting pan or a rimmed baking sheet with aluminum foil and spray with cooking spray.
3.Set the chicken (skin-side up) on the hot pan. Season with salt and pepper on both sides.
4.Combine the garlic, rice vinegar, honey, and soy sauce in a small bowl. Thin with water if necessary.
5.Half of the sauce should be spooned over each piece of chicken and thoroughly applied. Set the remainder of the sauce aside.
6.Cover and bake for 50 to 1 hour, or until chicken is cooked through and skin is crispy and golden brown. Spread the chicken with the remaining sauce once or twice while it cooks.

Total time of cooking

2 hr 15 min
Prep Time: 45 minutes
Cook Time: 1 hr 30 minutes

Servings

6

Nutrition facts

(per serving)
Calories 380 kcal
Fat 22 g
Protein 22 g
Carbs 24 g

Ingredients

- 1/3 gallon of milk
- 1 cup bread crumbs (fresh)
- 1 1/2 pounds ground chuck
- 1 pound ground pork
- 1 big sliced onion
- 1 tablespoon butter
- 1 medium carrot
- celery stalks, diced
- eggs, beaten
- 1/2 cup creme fraiche
- garlic cloves, minced
- tablespoons Worcestershire sauce
- Paprika, 1 teaspoon
- 1 teaspoon mustard powder (dry)
- 1 1/2 teaspoons kosher salt
- ¼ cup minced fresh parsley
- 3-4 bacon slices
- 1 tablespoon brown sugar
- 1 teaspoon freshly ground black pepper
- Ketchup, 1 cup
- 1/4 teaspoon nutmeg, freshly grated
- 1 tablespoon mustard (dijon)

Instructions

1.Preheat the oven to 350 degrees Fahrenheit.

2.Put the bread crumbs in a bowl and pour the milk over them. Remove from the equation.

3.Melt the butter and add the celery, onion, and carrot in a large pan,. Season with salt and simmer, turning regularly until the veggies are tender but not browned. Cook for another 4 minutes after adding the garlic. Allow cooling to room temperature after removing from heat and scraping into a small dish (about ten minutes).

4.Whisk together the beaten eggs, crème Fraiche, and Worcestershire sauce in a separate bowl.

5.Place the beef and pork in a large mixing bowl, along with the breadcrumb mixture, veggies, egg mixture, and the other ingredients (except the brown sugar, ketchup, bacon, and mustard). Mix the meatloaf ingredients together with your hands, then transfer them to a large ovenproof baking dish. Five bacon strips should be laid lengthwise over the meatloaf; the remaining bacon strip should be sliced in half and placed at either end of the loaf.

6.Set the timer for 45 minutes in the oven. Meanwhile, whisk together the Ketchup, Brown Sugar, Mustard, and Nutmeg in a separate bowl. Set oven to convection after 45 minutes and cook meatloaf for another 15 minutes.

7.When the meatloaf is cooked, take it out of the oven and pour or brush the glaze all over the bacon. Put in the oven and bake for another 15 minutes, or until the glaze is bubbling. Allow cooling for 15 minutes after removing from the oven. Serve!

Total time of cooking

1 hour 15 mins

Prep Time: 25 min

Cook Time: 50 min

Servings

5

Nutrition facts

(per serving)

Calories 336 kcal

Fat12.8g

Protein 29.3g

Carbs 25.6g

Ingredients

- stalks of celery (diced)
- Butter (2 tablespoons)
- 1 onion (diced)
- 1 carrot (sliced)
- tablespoons garlic chopped
- red potatoes (diced)
- A quarter cup of flour
- ½ cup fresh parsley (finely minced)
- Season with salt and pepper to taste
- 1/2 cup frozen peas

- 1 cup chicken broth
- cups rotisserie chicken (shredded)
- 1 box puff pastry sheets
- 1 egg

Instructions

1. Preheat the oven to 400 degrees Fahrenheit.
2. Melt the butter in a saucepan.
3. Carrots, onion, celery, and potatoes should be added at this point. Cook for 8 minutes, until they are softened.
4. Season with pepper and salt after adding the garlic.
5. Combine the flour, chicken broth, and cream cheese in a mixing bowl. Cook for a further 5 minutes, stirring regularly.
6. Combine the chicken and peas in a mixing bowl.
7. Fill a baking sheet with the mixture and coat it with non-stick cooking spray.
8. Two puff pastry sheets should be rolled out to the width of the sheet pan, cut into 1-inch strips, and layered over the filling.
9. Cut off any extra dough protruding over the edges with a sharp knife.
10. In a small dish, whisk together the egg and brush it over the top of the pot pie.
11. Cook for 35 mins, or until golden brown on top. Remove from the oven and serve with fresh parsley as a garnish.

7.61 CREAMY CHICKEN AND CORN BURRITOS

Total time of cooking

45 minutes

Servings

2-4

Nutrition facts

(per serving)

Calories: 351.0 kcal

Fat 13.0 g

Protein 30.9 g

Carbs 26.0 g

Ingredients

- green onions, cut diagonally (separate 1 out)
- 1 tbsp oil
- 1 garlic clove, grated
- 1 finely chopped tiny poblano chili
- 1/2 teaspoon adobo seasoning
- 1 cup of corn
- Smoked paprika, 1/2 teaspoon
- 1/2 teaspoon powdered ancho chili
- 1 teaspoon oregano
- Kosher salt (1/2 teaspoon)
- Cheddar cheese, grated (1/2 cup)
- Avocado, sour cream, tomato, for serving

- A cup of sour cream
- Some tortillas made with flour
- 1 1/2 cup chopped rotisserie chicken

Instructions

1. Swirl 1 T oil in a small skillet over medium heat. Green onions, poblanos, garlic, maize, chili powders, salt, smoked paprika, and oregano should all be added at this point. Cook until the veggies have softened.
2. Remove the pan from the heat. Combine sour cream, 1 1/2 cup cheese, and chicken in a mixing bowl. To integrate, stir everything together.
3. Fill the tortillas with chicken filling, scooping it toward the bottom edge. Fold in the tortilla's edges and roll it up away from you.
4. Using non-stick spray oil, coat a baking dish. Each tortilla should be rolled in the oil and finished with the seam side down.
5. Preheat oven to 350°F and bake for 30-35 minutes. Alternatively, convect bake for 25-30 minutes at 325°F. Return the burritos to the oven until the remaining cheese has melted, about 5 minutes.
6. Remove from oven and set aside for 5 minutes to cool. Top burritos with the remaining green onion. If preferred, top burritos with sour cream, chopped avocado, and diced tomatoes.

7.62 YUMMY SPICY COCONUT CHICKEN

Total time of cooking
1 hr 45 minutes
Prep time: 1 Hr
Cook time: 45 minutes

Servings
4

Nutrition facts
(per serving)
Calories: 987.8 kcal
Fat 50.3g
Protein 110.8g
Carbs 26g

Ingredients
- coconut milk (200 mL) (tinned)
- chicken drumsticks, or 4-6 chicken breasts
- Optional: 1/2 lemongrass, bruised and chopped
- 1 teaspoon of black pepper (fresh, ground)
- 1 tablespoon ginger (fresh, grated)
- 4-5 onions (spring)
- Optional: 1 tablespoon red chili flakes
- juice of 1 lime or lemon
- 1 teaspoon powdered turmeric

Instructions
1.Preheat the oven for 20 minutes before putting the chicken in.
2.The chicken should be well cleaned. Set it aside and add salt and pepper.
3   Mix the coconut milk with the other ingredients (pepper, ginger, salt, chili flakes, turmeric powder, lemon juice, and spring onions - save a couple for decoration) in a mixing bowl.
4.Combine the chicken in the coconut milk marinade, making sure it is well covered. Cover with clingfilm and chill for 1-2 hours.
5.Place on an oven pan that is big enough to hold all of the chicken, cover with a foil, and bake at 200°C for 28 minutes. Cook for 45 minutes at least. Remove the tray/dish from the oven halfway through cooking, remove the foil, flip each piece of chicken, and return to the oven (uncovered). Cook for another 25 minutes, depending on the size of the meat pieces.

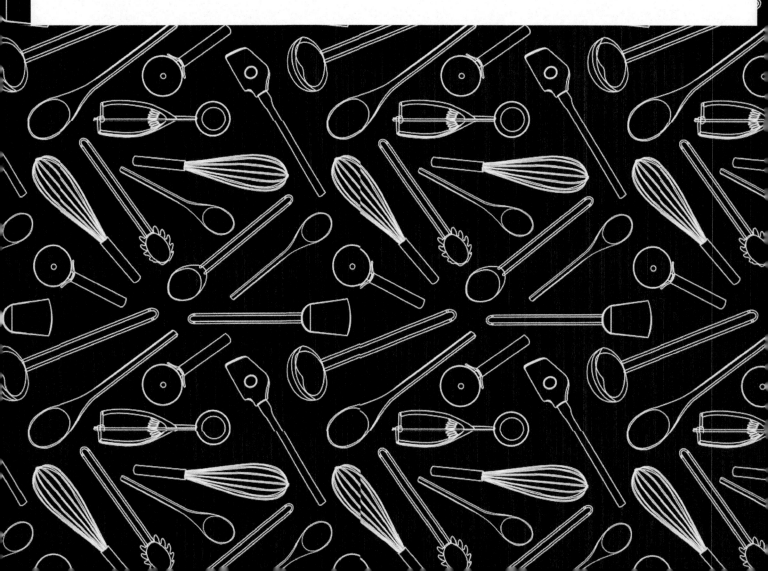

Chapter 8: 5 Ingredients Recipes (Tasty recipes with no more than 5 ingredients)

8.1 EASY COCKTAIL AND SHRIMP DIP

Total time of cooking
25 minutes
Prep time 10 minutes
Cook time 15 minutes

Serving
24 (3 cups)

Nutrition facts
(Per serving)
Calories 54
Fat 3.2g
Protein 4.1g
Carbs 2.2g

Ingredients:
- 1/4 cup of Parmesan Cheese shredded
- 3/4 pound of cleaned, cooked, and chopped shrimp
- 2 sliced green onions
- 3/4 cup of cocktail sauce
- 1 package of softened cream cheese (8 ounces)

Instructions:
Follow the instructions below to make an easy cocktail and shrimp dip.
1.Preheat the convection oven at 325°F.
2.Place cream cheese on the bottom of a shallow oven-proof glass bowl.
3.Toss cocktail sauce and shrimp together and spread over cream cheese mixture.
4.Top with parmesan cheese and green onions and bake in the preheated convection oven for around 10 to 15 minutes.

8.2 EASY CHOCOLATE CHIP COOKIES WITH 5-INGREDIENT

Total time of cooking
25 minutes
Prep time 10 minutes
Cook time 15 minutes

Serving
24 (2 dozen cookies)

Nutrition facts
(Per serving)
Calories 181
Fat 10.3g
Protein 2.5g
Carbs 20.8g

Ingredients:
- 1 cup of chocolate chips semi-sweet
- 2 eggs
- 3 cups of all-purpose flour
- 1 cup of softened butter
- 3/4 cup of brown sugar

Instructions:
Follow the instructions below to make easy chocolate chip cookies with 5-ingredient.
1. Preheat the convection oven at 325°F.
2. In a medium-sized bowl, sift together brown sugar and flour, add eggs and butter into the flour mixture and mix until dough is soft and creamy; fold semi-sweet chocolate chips. Place spoonfuls of dough into the cookie sheet, keep 3 inches gap between each cookie.
3. Bake in the preheated convection oven for around 10 to 15 minutes. Transfer to a wire rack for cooling and then serve.

8.3 BAKED BACON-WRAPPED CHICKEN

Total time of cooking
55 minutes
Prep time 10 minutes
Cook time 45 minutes

Serving
4

Nutrition facts
(Per serving)
Calories 522
Fat 18.8g
Protein 38.4g
Carbs 46.2g

Ingredients:
- 1 pound of sliced bacon
- 4 boneless and skinless chicken breast halves
- 1 bottle of honey barbecue sauce (18 ounces)

Instructions:
Follow the instructions below to make baked bacon-wrapped chicken.
1. Preheat the convection oven at 325°F.
2. Wash the chicken breasts and pat dry with a kitchen cloth, transfer to a 9x12 inches baking dish, spread with 1/2 of the barbecue sauce, and layer with the bacon slices on top crossways. Spread remaining 1/2 sauce on top.
3. Bake for around 45 minutes in the preheated convection oven until no juices remain in the dish.

8.4 CHEESY CAULIFLOWER CRACKERS

Total time of cooking
23 minutes
Prep time 5 minutes
Cook time 18 minutes

Serving
15

Nutrition facts
(Per serving)
Calories 93
Fat 4.7g
Protein 1.5g
Carbs 10.4g

Ingredients:
- 1 package of cauliflower pizza crust (12 ounces)
- 1/3 cup of Parmesan cheese thinly shaved
- 2 tablespoons of olive oil
- 1 1/2 teaspoons of everything bagel seasoning

Instructions:
Follow the instructions below to make cheesy cauliflower crackers.
1.Preheat the convection oven at 425°F.With aluminum foil, line a baking sheet.
2.With olive oil, brush the pizza crust from both sides and transfer it to a baking sheet. Spread parmesan cheese and everything bagel all over the crust.
3.Bake in the preheated oven for around 17 to 18 minutes.
4.Before serving, slice into bite-sized pieces.

8.5 QUICK AND EASY PEANUT BUTTER COOKIES WITH 3-INGREDIENT

Total time of cooking
25 minutes
Prep time 15 minutes
Cook time 10 minutes

Serving
24(2 dozen cookies)

Nutrition facts
(Per serving)
Calories 98
Fat 5.6g
Protein 3g
Carbs 10.5g

Ingredients:
- 1 egg
- 1 cup of peanut butter
- 1 cup of white sugar

Instructions:
Follow the instructions below to make quick and easy peanut butter cookies with 3-ingredient.
1.Preheat the convection oven at 325°F.
2.With an electric mixer, combine sugar, egg, and peanut butter in a large-sized bowl and blend until creamy and soft. Make small balls out of dough and transfer on a baking sheet; flatten each ball using a fork.
3.Bake in the preheated convection oven for around 10 minutes.
4.Before eating, let cookies cool for few minutes.

8.6 PARTY MINI BEEF BURGERS BAKED

Total time of cooking
35 minutes
Prep time 15 minutes
Cook time 20 minutes

Serving
8

Nutrition facts
(Per serving)
Calories 271
Fat 16 g
Protein 11g
Carbs 20g

Ingredients:
- 1 sheet of puff pastry frozen, thawed
- 1/2 pound of ground beef
- 1 egg large
- 4 Havarti cheese slices (4 ounces), quartered
- 1 envelope of ranch salad dressing mix

Instructions:
Follow the instructions below to make party mini beef burgers baked.
1.Preheat the convection oven at 375°F.Combine ground beef and ranch salad dressing together in a small-sized bowl and mix until completely combined. Make 8 thick patties of 1/2 inches each.
2.Cook burgers on medium heat in a large-sized non-stick pan,4 to 5 minutes on each side.
3.Beat an egg in a small-sized bowl. Roll puff pastry on a kitchen-floured surface to make 12 inches square and cut 4 squares of 6 inches out of puff pastry. Cut squares further into half to make 8 rectangles on each rectangle. On one end of each rectangle, arrange burger patty sprinkle with cheese and with egg brush the edges. To enclose, fold the puff pastry around the burger and press the edges using a fork to seal.
4.Shift burgers to a baking sheet and brush the top of all burgers with egg. Bake in the preheated convection oven for 15 to 20 minutes or until lightly browned.

8.7 BAKED CHICKEN WITH LEMON-PEPPER SEASONING

Total time of cooking
35 minutes
Prep time 10 minutes
Cook time 25 minutes

Serving
6

Nutrition facts
(Per serving)
Calories 189
Fat 7.9g
Protein 27.5g
Carbs 0.3g

Ingredients:
- 4 skinless and boneless chicken breasts (7 ounces)
- 2 teaspoons of lemon-pepper seasoning
- 2 tablespoons of avocado oil, or as required
- 1/4 teaspoon of ground black pepper
- 1 teaspoon of dried oregano

Instructions:
Follow the instructions below to make baked chicken with lemon-pepper seasoning.
1.Preheat the convection oven at 375°F.
2.In a small-sized bowl, gather oregano,lemon-pepper seasoning, and pepper and mix. Set the seasoning aside.
3.Heat 1 to 2 tablespoons of oil in a large-sized skillet on medium-high heat until oil shimmers.
4.Dip chicken in the seasonings to coat evenly from both sides and add into shimmering oil. Cook until chicken turns golden in color for 4 minutes on each side and shift to a non-stick baking sheet.
5.Bake in the preheated convection oven until no juices are left in the pan for around 12 to 15 minutes. Serve warm.

8.8 TASTY CABBAGE BAKED STEAKS

Total time of cooking
55 minutes
Prep time 10 minutes
Cook time 45 minutes

Serving
6

Nutrition facts
(Per serving)
Calories 94
Fat 4.7g
Protein 2.7g
Carbs 12.4g

Ingredients:
- 2 tablespoons of garlic minced
- 1 cabbage head
- 1/2 teaspoon of ground black pepper
- 2 tablespoons of olive oil
- 1/2 teaspoon of salt

Instructions:
Follow the instructions below to make tasty cabbage-baked steaks.
1. Preheat the convection oven at 325°F.
2. Cut cabbage into 1-inch thick slices and Spread slices on a casserole dish in a single layer.
3. Spread olive oil over the slices of cabbage and sprinkle with garlic, pepper, and salt. Cover with heavy-duty aluminum foil tightly.
4. Bake in the preheated convection oven for around 45 minutes.

8.9 PINEAPPLE CASSEROLE BAKED

Total time of cooking
1 hour
Prep time 10 minutes
Cook time 50 minutes

Serving
8

Nutrition facts
(Per serving)
Calories 294
Fat 14.6g
Protein 4.8g
Carbs 37.8g

Ingredients:
- 4 eggs
- 1 can of drained and crushed pineapple (20 ounces)
- 1/2 cup of softened butter
- 5 slices of day-old bread (cut the bread into bite-sized cubes)
- 3/4 cup of white sugar

Instructions:
Follow the instructions below to make pineapple casserole baked.
1. Preheat the convection oven at 325°F.
2. Cream butter and sugar together in a bowl with an electric mixer. Mix in eggs and beat until creamy. Fold in pineapple and bread cubes into creamed butter batter, spread the batter into a casserole baking dish.
3. Bake in the preheated convection oven for around 45 to 50 minutes or until eggs are cooked and the top is golden browned.

8.10 UKRAINE-STYLE POTATO BAKED

Total time of cooking
50 minutes
Prep time 10 minutes
Cook time 40 minutes

Serving
6

Nutrition facts
(Per serving)
Calories 414
Fat 21.4g
Protein 13.3g
Carbs 43.3g

Ingredients:
- 1 container of sour cream (16 ounces)
- 6 large boiled, peeled, and sliced potatoes
- 1 sliced onion
- Salt and pepper to taste
- 6 sliced and cooked eggs

Instructions:
Follow the instructions below to make Ukraine-style potato baked.
1.Preheat the convection oven at 325°F.
2.Spread potato slices layer on the bottom of 9x13 inches baking dish. Place onion slices on top of potato slices, layer with sliced eggs, and top with the layer of sour cream. Repeat the layering procedure until ingredients end with the top layer of sour cream and sprinkle with salt and pepper.
3.Bake for around 35 to 40 minutes in the preheated convection oven or until the top is lightly golden brown.

8.11 BARBECUE-STYLE CHICKEN BACON BAKE

Total time of cooking
55 minutes
Prep time 10 minutes
Cook time 45 minutes

Serving
4

Nutrition facts
(Per serving)
Calories 284
Fat 10.1g
Protein 28.8g
Carbs 17.3g

Ingredients:
- 4 boneless and skinless chicken breast halves
- Cooking spray
- 3/4 cup of barbecue sauce
- 8 bacon slices

Instructions:
Follow the instructions below to make a barbecue-style chicken bacon bake.
1.Preheat the convection oven at 325°F.With cooking spray, grease a 9x13 baking dish.
2.On medium heat in a large-sized skillet, cook bacon until edges of bacon get crispy, for around 5 minutes; shift to paper towels and wrap 2 bacon slices over each chicken breast in x-shaped and transfer to a greased baking sheet
3.Bake in the preheated convection oven for around 10 minutes. Spread barbeque sauce all over the chicken breasts and bake for 25 minutes more or until no juices are left in the pan.

Total time of cooking

50 minutes
Prep time 10 minutes
Cook time 40 minutes

Serving

4

Nutrition facts

(Per serving)
Calories 489
Fat 28.8g
Protein 22.4g
Carbs 36.4g

Ingredients:

- 4 parsnips
- 2 chopped red onions large
- 12 chipolatas
- 2 apples
- 1 tablespoon of honey

Instructions:

Follow the instructions below to make baked apples and sausages.

1. Preheat the convection oven at 325°F.

2. On medium-high heat, grease a large-sized pan with cooking spray, cook onions and apple slices, peel parsnips into long strips and add on the top of apple and onions; cook for 1 minute and remove from stove.

3. Transfer the mixture into a casserole dish and layer sausages on top. Bake in the preheated convection oven for around 30 minutes, drizzle honey and bake for another 5 minutes or until golden brown from top.

8.13 BAKED CHEESE SAUSAGE BISCUITS

Total time of cooking

30 minutes
Prep time 10 minutes
Cook time 20 minutes

Serving

10

Nutrition facts

(Per serving)
Calories 227
Fat 16g
Protein 8g
Carbs 16g

Ingredients:

- 1/2 cup of cheddar cheese shredded
- 1 tube of refrigerated buttermilk biscuits (10 counts) (12 ounces)
- 2 beaten eggs
- 1 package of frozen breakfast sausage links fully cooked, thawed (8 ounces)
- 3 tablespoons of green onion chopped

Instructions:

Follow the instructions below to make baked cheese sausage biscuits.

1. Preheat the convection oven at 375°F.On a kitchen floured surface, roll each biscuit into a circle of 5 inches; arrange each biscuit in a muffin cup pan. Split breakfast sausages into fourths. In a medium-sized skillet, brown sausages and distribute sausages between the cups.

2. Combine cheese, onions, and eggs in a small-sized bowl. Spread into cups and bake in the preheated convection oven for around 12 to 15 minutes.

8.14 GARLIC PARMESAN ROASTED CARROTS

Total time of cooking
1 hour 5 minutes
Prep time 10 minutes
Cook time 55 minutes

Serving
4

Nutrition facts
(Per serving)
Calories 98
Fat 5.1g
Protein 3g
Carbs 11.2g

Ingredients:
- 1/4 cup of Parmesan cheese grated
- 1 pound of peeled carrots
- 1/2 teaspoon of garlic salt
- Ground black pepper to taste
- 1 tablespoon of olive oil

Instructions:
Follow the instructions below to make garlic parmesan roasted carrots.
1.Preheat the convection oven at 350°F.With aluminum foil, line a baking pan.
2.Mix garlic salt and olive oil in a small-sized bowl; pour into a zip-lock plastic bag. Place carrots to the zip-loc bag close and toss to coat carrots in oil mixture. Spread coated carrots in a prepared baking sheet.
3.Roast in the preheated convection oven for around 45 minutes. Spread 1/4 cup of parmesan cheese on carrots and continue roasting until cheese melts down for 5 to 10. Garnish with more parmesan cheese while serving.

8.15 CARAMELIZED PECAN BACON BAKED

Total time of cooking
40 minutes
Prep time 10 minutes
Cook time 30 minutes

Serving
12

Nutrition facts
(Per serving)
Calories 142
Fat 12g
Protein 4g
Carbs 4g

Ingredients:
- 1/4 cup of pecans finely chopped
- 12 strips of bacon
- 1/8 teaspoon of pepper
- 1/4 cup of brown sugar packed
- 1/8 teaspoon of ground cinnamon

Instructions:
Follow the instructions below to make caramelized pecan bacon baked.
1.Preheat the convection oven at 350°F.On a baking sheet lined with foil, arrange bacon in a single layer. Bake in the preheated convection oven for around 16 to 18 minutes.
2.Shift bacon strips to a plate and discard the drippings and clean the sheet.
3.Combine remaining ingredients in a medium-sized bowl and coat both sides of baked bacon in a prepared mixture of brown sugar. Return back the coated bacon to a baking sheet. Bake for 8 to 10 minutes more in a convection oven until bacon caramelized. Serve and enjoy!

8.16 MUFFIN WITH A MEAL

Total time of cooking
30 minutes
Prep time 10 minutes
Cook time 20 minutes

Serving
6

Nutrition facts
(Per serving)
Calories 377
Fat 18g
Protein 17g
Carbs 36g

Ingredients:
- 6 large eggs
- 1 package of cornbread/muffin mix (8-1/2 ounces)
- 1 can of corned beef hash (15 ounces)
- Salt and pepper, according to taste

Instructions:
Follow the instructions below to make a muffin with a meal.
1.Preheat the convection oven at 375°F.With cooking spray, grease a 12-cup muffin pan. Distribute beef hash into 6 muffin cups; gently press on the bottom of cups and up sides to form a shell. Crack an egg into each shell; sprinkle with pepper and salt. Combine muffin mix according to your package directions. Place muffin mix batter into 6 cups equally.
2.Bake in the preheated convection oven for around 15 to 20 minutes or until eggs are cooked and muffins are lightly browned.

8.17 AVOCADO FLAVORED CLOUD BREAD

Total time of cooking
45 minutes
Prep time 10 minutes
Cook time 35 minutes

Serving
6

Nutrition facts
(Per serving)
Calories 35
Fat 2.4g
Protein 2.2g
Carbs 0.6g

Ingredients:
- 2 tablespoons of avocado mashed
- 2 eggs, separated
- 1 teaspoon of everything bagel seasoning
- 1/4 teaspoon of cream of tartar

Instructions:
Follow the instructions below to make avocado-flavored cloud bread.
1.Preheat the convection oven at 275°F.With parchment paper, line a baking sheet.
2.Whisk cream of tartar and egg whites in a large-sized bowl and beat until it forms stiff peaks. Mix together egg yolks and mashed avocado. Fold the avocado mixture into an egg whites mixture.
3.Pour 1/4 cupfuls of the prepared mixture on the baking sheet, with a 1-inch gap between each cloud bread. Top with bagel seasoning.
4.Bake in the preheated convection oven until the bottom top becomes firmed for around 30 to 35 minutes. Let stand for at least 25 to 30 minutes before serving.

8.18 TATER-TOT BEEF CASSEROLE

Total time of cooking
1 hour
Prep time 10 minutes
Cook time 50 minutes

Serving
8

Nutrition facts
(Per serving)
Calories 345
Fat 23.8g
Protein 18.5g
Carbs 16.9g

Ingredients:
- 1 package of tater tots frozen (16 ounces)
- 1 pound of ground beef
- 2 cups of Cheddar cheese shredded
- 1 can of condensed cream of mushroom soup (10.75 ounces)
- 1 pinch of salt and ground black pepper to taste

Instructions:
Follow the instructions below to make a tater-tot beef casserole.
1.Preheat the convection oven at 325°F.
2.Cook and mix ground beef in a large-sized skillet on medium heat until beef changes color and browned, for around 8 to 10 minutes; sprinkle with pepper and salt. Mix in cream of mushroom soup into beef mixture. Spread the mixture onto the bottom of 9x13 inches baking dish. Spread a layer of tater tots over the beef mixture layer; sprinkle with cheddar cheese on top.
3.Bake for around 35 to 40 minutes in the preheated convection oven. Serve warm.

8.19 BAKED ONION CHICKEN

Total time of cooking
35 minutes
Prep time 10 minutes
Cook time 25 minutes

Serving
4

Nutrition facts
(For one chicken breast half)
Calories 460
Fat 36g
Protein 23g
Carbs 10g

Ingredients:
- 1 can of crushed French-fried onions (2.8 ounces)
- 1/2 cup of melted butter
- 4 skinless and boneless chicken breast halves (4 ounces each)
- 1 teaspoon of ground mustard
- 1 tablespoon of Worcestershire sauce

Instructions:
Follow the instructions below to make baked onion chicken.
1.Combine Worcestershire sauce, butter, and mustard in a medium-sized bowl. Keep onions in another medium-sized bowl. Dip in chicken breast in butter mixture finish coating with onions evenly.
2.Arrange chicken in 11x7 inches greased baking dish. Drizzle the remaining butter mixture over the chicken.
3.Bake in the convection oven at 375°F for around 20 to 25 minutes.

8.20 PARMESAN GREEN BEANS ROASTED

Total time of cooking

25 minutes

Prep time 10 minutes

Cook time 15 minutes

Serving

4

Nutrition facts

(Per serving)

Calories 43

Fat 1.2g

Protein 3g

Carbs 6.4g

Ingredients:

* 3 tablespoons of Parmesan cheese shredded
* 3/4 pound of trimmed fresh green beans
* 1 pinch of garlic powder
* Olive oil cooking spray
* Sea salt and ground black pepper, according to taste

Instructions:

Follow the instructions below to make parmesan green beans roasted.

1.Preheat the convection oven at 375°F.Grease a baking dish with cooking spray.

2.Arrange green beans into greased baking dish. Sprinkle pepper, sea salt, and garlic powder on top of green beans and mix to coat. Spread parmesan cheese on top.

3.Roast in the preheated convection oven for around 10 to 15 minutes until cheese melts down. Serve straight away.

8.21 PROSCIUTTO-WRAPPED PESTO CHICKEN

Total time of cooking

35 minutes

Prep time 10 minutes

Cook time 25 minutes

Serving

4

Nutrition facts

(Per serving)

Calories 312

Fat 19.3g

Protein 31.5g

Carbs 2g

Ingredients:

* 4 thin slices of prosciutto
* 4 boneless and skinless chicken breast halves
* 1/2 cup of basil pesto prepared(divided)

Instructions:

Follow the instructions below to make prosciutto-wrapped pesto chicken.

1.Preheat the convection oven at 375°F.

2.Place 2 tablespoons of pesto on top of each chicken breast and wrap the entire chicken breast with prosciutto slices completely. Transfer the wrapped chicken onto a baking sheet.

3.Bake in the preheated convection oven until chicken is lightly golden brown and prosciutto is crispy, for around 25 minutes.

8.22 HAM AND CHEDDAR BAKED OMELET

Total time of cooking
50 minutes
Prep time 10 minutes
Cook time 40 minutes

Serving
12 servings

Nutrition facts
(Per serving)
Calories 208
Fat 14g
Protein 15g
Carbs 4g

Ingredients:
- 2 cups of cheddar cheese shredded
- 6 chopped green onions
- 16 eggs large
- 3/4 cup of cubed ham fully cooked
- 2 cups of whole milk

Instructions:
Follow the instructions below to make ham and cheddar baked omelet.
1.Preheat the convection oven at 325°F.Whisk milk and egg in a large-sized bowl. Mix in ham, cheese, and onions. Pour the mixture into 13x9 inches greased baking dish.
2.Bake in the preheated convection oven for around 35 to 40 minutes until eggs are fully set.

8.23 CHOCOLATE-PEANUT MARSHMALLOW BARS

Total time of cooking
35 minutes
Prep time 10 minutes
Cook time 25 minutes

Serving
2 dozen

Nutrition facts
(Per serving)
Calories 175
Fat 8g
Protein 3g
Carbs 24g

Ingredients:
- 2 cups of chocolate-covered peanuts
- 1/2 cup of butterscotch ice cream topping
- 1 package of chocolate chip cookie dough refrigerated (16-1/2 ounces)
- 1 cup of marshmallows

Instructions:
Follow the instructions below to make chocolate-peanut marshmallow bars.
1.Into 13x9 inches baking pan, spread the cookie dough and press onto the pan's bottom. Bake in the preheated convection oven at 325°F for around 14 to 15 minutes or until dough edges are golden brown. Spread peanuts and marshmallows all over the baked dough and drizzle butterscotch ice cream topping on the top.
2.Bake for an additional 6 to 8 minutes. Cool before cutting it into bars.

8.24 OVEN-BAKED ROSEMARY PARMESAN POTATO CHUNKS

Total time of cooking
50 minutes
Prep time 10 minutes
Cook time 40 minutes

Serving
4

Nutrition facts
(Per serving)
Calories 234
Fat 11g
Protein 4.4g
Carbs 29.9g

Ingredients:
- 2 tablespoons of Parmesan cheese grated
- 1 1/2 pounds of new potatoes (cut into bite-sized chunks)
- 1 tablespoon of fresh rosemary chopped
- Salt and pepper, according to taste
- 3 tablespoons of olive oil

Instructions:
Follow the instructions below to make oven-baked rosemary parmesan potato chunks.
1. Preheat the convection oven at 400°F.With aluminum foil, line a baking sheet.
2. Combine olive oil, potatoes, rosemary, and parmesan cheese in a large-sized bowl and toss to coat potatoes with all ingredients. Sprinkle with salt and pepper and toss. Transfer coated potatoes on a baking sheet.
3. Bake for around 40 minutes in the preheated convection oven until potatoes are crispy and golden brown.

8.25 EASY AND CLASSIC MEYER LEMON PIE

Total time of cooking
45 minutes
Prep time 10 minutes
Cook time 35 minutes

Serving
8 (1 pie of 9-inch)

Nutrition facts
(Per serving)
Calories 316
Fat 15.1g
Protein 3.9g
Carbs 42.9g

Ingredients:
- 1 unbaked pastry shell(9-inch)
- 3 eggs large
- 1/4 cup of melted butter
- 1 1/4 cups of white sugar
- 3 3/4 fluid ounces of Meyer lemon juice

Instructions:
Follow the instructions below to make easy and classic Meyer lemon pie.
1. Preheat the convection oven at 325°F.
2. Blend together eggs, sugar, and lemon juice in a blender until creamy.
3. Put melted butter in the mixture and blend for 30 seconds to 1 minute more.
4. Spread the blended lemon filling to the pastry shell.
5. Bake in the preheated convection oven for around 30 to 35 minutes. Allow pie to cool for some time before serving.

8.26 BUTTERMILK FLAVORED MAC AND CHEESE BAKED

Total time of cooking
55 minutes
Prep time 10 minutes
Cook time 45 minutes

Serving
8-10

Nutrition facts
(For 3/4 cup)
Calories 307
Fat 23g
Protein 15g
Carbs 10g

Ingredients:
- 1 package of elbow macaroni (7 ounces)
- 6 large eggs
- 2 1/2 cups of buttermilk
- 3 1/4 cups of cheddar cheese shredded
- 1/2 cup of melted butter

Instructions:
Follow the instructions below to make buttermilk flavored mac and cheese baked.
1. Boil elbow macaroni in salted water according to your package directions. Drain and set macaroni aside.
2. Whisk the eggs in a large-sized bowl. Mix in buttermilk, cheese, and butter, add cooked macaroni, and fold in the mixture to coat.
3. Spread the mixture into 13x9 inches greased baking dish. Bake at 325°F in the preheated convection oven for around 40 to 45 minutes.

8.27 TASTY FRIES AND CHEESEBURGER CASSEROLE

Total time of cooking
1 hour
Prep time 10 minutes
Cook time 50 minutes

Serving
8

Nutrition facts
(For 1 1/2 cups)
Calories 352
Fat 17g
Protein 25g
Carbs 25g

Ingredients:
- 1 package of crinkle-cut French fries frozen(20 ounces)
- 2 pounds of lean ground beef (around 90% lean)
- 1 can of undiluted condensed cheddar cheese soup (10-3/4 ounces)
- 1 can of undiluted condensed golden mushroom soup (10-3/4 ounces)

Instructions:
Follow the instructions below to make tasty fries and cheeseburger casserole.
1. Preheat the convection oven at 325°F. Cook beef on medium heat in a large-sized skillet until beef changes color. Mix in soups and spread the mixture into 13x9 inches greased baking dish.
2. Arrange a layer of fries on top of the casserole. Bake in the convection oven for around 45 to 50 minutes until light brown from the top.

Total time of cooking

35 minutes

Prep time 10 minutes

Cook time 25 minutes

Serving

6

Nutrition facts

(Per serving)

Calories 298

Fat 23g

Protein 16g

Carbs 4g

Ingredients:

- 6 eggs large
- 1/2 cup of Picante sauce
- 1 cup of cheddar cheese shredded
- 1 cup of sour cream
- 1 cup shredded Monterey Jack cheese

Instructions:

Follow the instructions below to make delicious Picante and cheese omelet pie.

1.Preheat the convection oven at 350°F.

2.Spread the Picante sauce into the bottom of 9 inches pie plate. Spread cheeses on top of the Picante sauce layer and set the pie plate aside. Combine sour cream and eggs in a blender and blend until creamy. Pour the mixture over Picante and cheese layer.

3.Bake for around 20 to 25 minutes in the preheated convection oven. Let stand 5 to 10 minutes before slicing.

8.29 MINI GARLIC-HERB CHEESE QUICHES

Total time of cooking

25 minutes

Prep time 10 minutes

Cook time 15 minutes

Serving

45 mini quiches

Nutrition facts

(Per serving)

Calories 31

Fat 2g

Protein 1g

Carbs 2g

Ingredients:

- 3 packages of miniature phyllo tart shells frozen (1.9 ounces each)
- 1 package of garlic-herb spreadable cheese (6-1/2 ounces)
- 2 eggs large
- 2 tablespoons of fresh parsley minced
- 1/4 cup of milk fat-free

Instructions:

Follow the instructions below to make mini garlic-herb cheese quiches.

1.Cream together eggs, milk, and spreadable cheese. Arrange tart shells on a baking sheet and stuff each shell with 2 teaspoons of the mixture. Sprinkle parsley on the top of shells.

2.Bake for around 10 to 15 minutes at 325°F in the preheated convection oven or until shells are golden browned.

8.30 TASTY AND CREAMY SCALLOPED POTATOES

Total time of cooking
1 hour
Prep time 10 minutes
Cook time 50 minutes

Serving
10

Nutrition facts
(For 3/4 cup)
Calories 353
Fat 27g
Protein 4g
Carbs 26g

Ingredients:
•   3 pounds of thinly sliced russet potatoes (about 10 cups)
•   1/2 teaspoon of pepper
•   3 cups of heavy whipping cream
•   1 teaspoon of fresh parsley minced
•   1 1/2 teaspoons of salt

Instructions:
Follow the instructions below to make tasty and creamy scalloped potatoes.
1.Preheat the convection oven at 350°F.Combine together cream, pepper, and salt, in a large-sized bowl. Spread potatoes layer in 13x9 inches greased baking dish. Put cream mixture evenly on top.
2.Bake for around 45 to 50 minutes in the preheated convection oven until golden brown from the top. Sprinkle with parsley while serving.

8.31 CINNAMON-FLAVORED STRAWBERRY BISCUITS

Total time of cooking
30 minutes
Prep time 10 minutes
Cook time 20 minutes

Serving
10

Nutrition facts
(Per serving)
Calories 178
Fat 5g
Protein 3g
Carbs 31g

Ingredients:
•   1 tube of buttermilk biscuits refrigerated (12 ounces) separate into 10 biscuits
•   1/2 cup of sugar
•   10 teaspoons of strawberry preserves
•   1/2 teaspoon of ground cinnamon
•   1/4 cup of melted butter

Instructions:
Follow the instructions below to make cinnamon-flavored strawberry biscuits.
1.Combine cinnamon and sugar in a small-sized bowl. Drench the top and sides of each biscuit in butter and in cinnamon sugar.
2.Arrange biscuits on a baking sheet. Make a deep well in the middle of each biscuit, using the end part of the wooden spoon handle, and stuff each biscuit with 1 teaspoon of strawberry preserves.
3.Bake for around 15 to 20 minutes at 350°F in the preheated convection oven until lightly brown. Cool for around 15 minutes before serving.

8.32 DELICIOUS CHICKEN GRATIN

Total time of cooking
40 minutes
Prep time 10 minutes
Cook time 30 minutes

Serving
6

Nutrition facts
(For 1 1/3 cups)
Calories 709
Fat 54g
Protein 34g
Carbs 19g

Ingredients:
- 1 1/2 cups of Asiago cheese grated, divided
- 3 cups of cooked and shredded chicken
- 1 1/2 cups of mayonnaise
- 2 cans of artichoke hearts water-packed (14 ounces each)
- 3 cups of refrigerated and cooked spinach tortellini

Instructions:
Follow the instructions below to make a delicious chicken gratin.
1. Preheat the convection oven at 325°F.
2. Reserve 1/4 cup of juices from artichoke and discard the remaining juices. Finely chop and mix with tortellini,1 cup of cheese, mayonnaise, chicken, and reserved 1/4 cup of artichoke juice.
3. Pour artichoke mixture in a 13x9 inches greased baking dish and top up with remaining cheese. Bake for around 30 minutes until lightly brown and bubbly from the top.

8.33 SAUSAGE STUFFED JALAPENOS WRAPPED IN BACON

Total time of cooking
30 minutes
Prep time 10 minutes
Cook time 20 minutes

Serving
2 dozen

Nutrition facts
(Per serving)
Calories 97
Fat 9g
Protein 3g
Carbs 1g

Ingredients:
- 12 halved bacon strips
- 3/4 pound of bulk pork sausage
- 24 jalapeno peppers fresh

Instructions:
Follow the instructions below to make sausage stuffed jalapenos wrapped in bacon.
1. Preheat the convection oven at 325°F.
2. Clean peppers. Mark a long cut lengthwise on one side of the pepper and discard seeds.
3. On medium heat, cook sausage in a large-sized skillet until sausage changes color, drain completely. Fill in peppers with sausage and wrap bacon all over the stuffed pepper tightly; insert toothpicks to seal and secure peppers.
4. Roast in the preheated oven for around 20 minutes or until bacon is crispy and tender.

8.34 TASTY RANCH-PARMESAN BREAD ROLLS

Total time of cooking
45 minutes
Prep time 20 minutes
Cook time 25 minutes

Serving
1 1/2 dozen

Nutrition facts
(Per serving)
Calories 210
Fat 8g
Protein 7g
Carbs 26g

Ingredients:
- 1 envelope of buttermilk ranch salad dressing mix
- 2 loaves of bread dough frozen and thawed (1 pound each)
- 1/2 cup of melted butter
- 1 chopped onion
- 1 cup of Parmesan cheese grated

Instructions:
Follow the instructions below to make tasty ranch-parmesan bread rolls.
1.Preheat the convection oven at 325°F.
2.On a kitchen floured surface, separate dough into 18 equal portions and make a ball out of each portion. Combine butter, cheese, and ranch dressing mix in a small-sized bowl.
3.Coat balls in cheese mixture evenly and place in 2 greased square baking pans of 9 inches each. Spread onions on top. Cover with a clean kitchen cloth and leave in a warm place for 45 minutes until rolls doubled.
4.Bake in the preheated convection oven for around 20 to 25 minutes. Cool down on a wire rack before serving.

8.35 QUICK AND EASY HAM STEAKS BAKED

Total time of cooking
55 minutes
Prep time 10 minutes
Cook time 45 minutes

Serving
2

Nutrition facts
(Per serving)
Calories 202
Fat 3.7g
Protein 16.8g
Carbs 24.7g

Ingredients:
- 2 ham steak slices
- 2 tablespoons of Worcestershire sauce
- 1 cup of water, or more as required
- 5 whole cloves of garlic
- 3 tablespoons of brown sugar

Instructions:
Follow the instructions below to make quick and easy ham steaks baked.
1.Preheat the convection oven at 350°F.
2.In a baking dish, combine water, Worcestershire sauce, brown sugar, and cloves and mix. Place ham steaks in a baking dish. Coat evenly in sugar mixture; pour more water if required to cover ham steaks.
3.Bake in the preheated convection oven for around 40 to 45 minutes until steaks are tender.

8.36 BAKED CHICKEN PARMESAN NUGGETS

Total time of cooking

30 minutes

Prep time 10 minutes

Cook time 20 minutes

Serving

8

Nutrition facts

(For 6 nuggets)

Calories 191

Fat 9g

Protein 20g

Carbs 5g

Ingredients:

• 1 1/2 pounds of skinless and boneless chicken breasts (cut into 1-inch bite-sized cubes)

• 1/4 cup of melted butter

• 1/2 cup of Parmesan cheese grated

• 1/2 teaspoon of salt

• 1 cup of panko bread crumbs

Instructions:

Follow the instructions below to make baked chicken parmesan nuggets.

1.Preheat the convection oven at 350°F.

2.Put butter in a bowl and set the bowl aside. Mix in cheese, bread crumbs, and salt in another medium-sized bowl. Drench chicken in butter and then coat in crumbs evenly.

3.Arrange nuggets in a single layer onto two 15x10 inches baking pans. Bake in the preheated convection oven for around 15 to 20 minutes or until nuggets are crispy.

8.37 TASTY HASH BROWNS BAKED

Total time of cooking

1 hour

Prep time 10 minutes

Cook time 50 minutes

Serving

10

Nutrition facts

(Per serving)

Calories 215

Fat 12g

Protein 6g

Carbs 20g

Ingredients:

• 2 cartons of chive and onion cream cheese spreadable (8 ounces each)

• 1 cup of cheddar cheese shredded

• 2 cans of undiluted condensed cream of celery soup (10-3/4 ounces each)

• 1 package of cubed hash brown potatoes frozen (2 pounds)

Instructions:

Follow the instructions below to make tasty hash browns baked.

1.Preheat the convection oven at 325°F.

2.Combine cream cheese and soup in a large-sized oven-proof bowl and microwave for 3 to 4 minutes until cream cheese is completely melted. Stir potatoes in cream cheese mixture to coat.

3.Spread mixture into 13x9 inches greased baking dish. Bake in the preheated convection oven for 35 to 40 minutes. Spread with cheddar cheese on top and bake for additional 4 to 5 minutes until cheese melts down.

8.38 CLASSIC RICE AND CHICKEN CASSEROLE

Total time of cooking
1 hour 25 minutes
Prep time 10 minutes
Cook time 1 hour 15 minutes

Serving
4

Nutrition facts
(Per serving)
Calories 470
Fat 7g
Protein 54g
Carbs 40g

Ingredients:
- 10 ounces of condensed cream of mushroom soup
- 1 1/2 cups of water
- 4 breasts of chicken
- 1 package of onion soup mix
- 1 cup of uncooked long-grain white rice

Instructions:
Follow the instructions below to make classic rice and chicken casserole.
1.Preheat the convection oven at 300°F.
2.With cooking spray, coat 9x13 inches baking pan. Place chicken and sprinkle with pepper and salt to season.
3.Spread uncooked rice layer over the chicken. Put onion soup mix all over the rice layer.
4.Mix in 1 1/2 cups of water and mushrooms soup and Spread on top of the dish.
5.Cover with lid and bake in the preheated convection oven for 1 hour 15 minutes until rice is soft and cooked.

8.39 BAKED SEASONED JICAMA FRIES

Total time of cooking
45 minutes
Prep time 10 minutes
Cook time 35 minutes

Serving
4

Nutrition facts
(Per serving)
Calories 108
Fat 7g
Protein 1g
Carbs 11g

Ingredients:
- 1/2 teaspoon of chili powder
- 2 jicamas large
- 1/2 teaspoon of seasoned salt
- 1/2 teaspoon of garlic powder
- 2 tablespoons of olive oil

Instructions:
Follow the instructions below to make baked seasoned jicama fries.
1.Preheat the convection oven at 400°F.
2.Wash and peel jicama and cut fries. Boil for 5 minutes, drain and pat dry with a clean cloth.
3.Combine all the ingredients in a large-sized bowl and toss jicama in the mixture.
4.Spread coated jicama fries into a non-stick baking pan and bake in the preheated convection oven for around 20 minutes.
5.Stir, flip fries and bake for another 15 minutes or until crispy. Serve hot and enjoy!

8.40 CREAMY QUICK BISCUITS

Total time of cooking
30 minutes
Prep time 10 minutes
Cook time 20 minutes

Serving
1 dozen

Nutrition facts
(Per serving)
Calories 256
Fat 15g
Protein 4g
Carbs 26g

Ingredients:
- 4 teaspoons of sugar
- 3 cups of all-purpose flour
- 2 cups of heavy whipping cream
- 4 teaspoons of baking powder
- 1 teaspoon of salt

Instructions:
Follow the instructions below to make baked creamy quick biscuits.
1.Preheat the convection oven at 350°F.Add baking powder, flour, salt, and sugar, and whisk. Fold in cream.
2.Place 1/4 cupfuls on greased cookie sheets 1 inch apart. Bake for around 18 to 20 minutes until the bottom of the biscuit is lightly brown.

8.41 BAKED EGGS IN AN AVOCADO HOLE

Total time of cooking
25 minutes
Prep time 10 minutes
Cook time 15 minutes

Serving
2

Nutrition facts
(Per serving)
Calories 280
Fat 23.5g
Protein 11.3g
Carbs 9.3g

Ingredients:
- 1 pitted and halved avocado
- 2 teaspoons of chopped fresh chives
- 2 eggs medium
- 2 slices of cooked and crumbled bacon
- 1 pinch sea salt and ground black pepper, according to taste

I

nstructions:
Follow the instructions below to make baked eggs in an avocado hole.
1.Preheat the convection oven at 400°F.
2.In a small-sized bowl, crack two eggs, Be careful not to break the yolks. Keep it intact.
3.Place avocado halves onto a baking sheet. Softly add 1 egg yolk into one halved avocado hole. Pour egg white until the hole is full. Repeat the same procedure for the other avocado. Sprinkle each egg-filled avocado with chives and salt and pepper.
4.Bake in the preheated convection oven for around 15 minutes until eggs are completely set. Top up the avocado with bacon in the end.

8.42 BAKED OATMEAL STUFFED APPLES

Total time of cooking
40 minutes
Prep time 10 minutes
Cook time 30 minutes

Serving
4 stuffed apples

Nutrition facts
(Per serving)
Calories 304
Fat 13.1g
Protein 3.2g
Carbs 46.7g

Ingredients:
- 1/4 cup of butter
- 1/4 cup of brown sugar
- 4 apples
- 1 teaspoon of ground cinnamon
- 1 cup of rolled oats

Instructions:
Follow the instructions below to make baked oatmeal stuffed apples.
1. Preheat the convection oven at 325°F.
2. Discard the center core part of each apple, making a large deep well. Place apples on a baking sheet.
3. Combine brown sugar, oats, and cinnamon in a medium-sized bowl, mix in butter until completely combined. Add 1/4 spoonful of mixture into each apple.
4. Bake in the preheated convection oven for around 30 minutes until apple filling is cooked and bubbly.

8.43 BARBECUE CHICKEN TENDERS BAKED

Total time of cooking
35 minutes
Prep time 10 minutes
Cook time 25 minutes

Serving
4

Nutrition facts
(Per serving)
Calories 175
Fat 2.9g
Protein 23.8g
Carbs 12.1g

Ingredients:
- 1 pound of chicken tenders
- 1/3 cup of barbeque sauce
- 1 tablespoon of caramel sauce
- Cooking spray
- 1 1/2 tablespoons of barbeque seasoning Asian-flavored

Instructions:
Follow the instructions below to make barbecue chicken tenders baked.
1. Preheat the convection oven at 350°F. Grease casserole dish of 8x8 inches with cooking spray.
2. Mix together barbecue seasoning, barbecue sauce, and caramel sauce in a medium-sized bowl and keep 2 tablespoons of mixture reserved.
3. Soak chicken tender one by one into barbecue sauce mixture and coat evenly. Arrange in a greased casserole dish.
4. Bake in the preheated convection oven for around 25 minutes until no juices are left in the pan. Drizzle with reserved sauce and bake for another 5 minutes.

8.44 SIMPLE RAVIOLI CHEESE CASSEROLE

Total time of cooking
50 minutes
Prep time 10 minutes
Cook time 40 minutes

Serving
8

Nutrition facts
(For 1 cup)
Calories 518
Fat 25g
Protein 30g
Carbs 44g

Ingredients:
- 4 cups of mozzarella cheese shredded
- 1 package of cheese ravioli refrigerated (20 ounces)
- 2 cups of small-curd 4% cottage cheese
- 1/2 cup of Parmesan cheese grated
- 3 1/2 cups of pasta sauce

Instructions:
Follow the instructions below to make a simple ravioli cheese casserole.
1.Preheat the convection oven at 325°F.Cook ravioli as per your package directions.
2.Pour 1 cup of pasta sauce on the bottom of 13x9 inches baking dish. Spread a half ravioli layer,1 1/4 cups of pasta sauce,2 cups of mozzarella cheese, and 1 cup of cottage cheese. Repeat the procedure with the remaining ingredients and sprinkle the top with parmesan cheese.
3.Bake in the preheated convection oven for around 35 to 40 minutes until cheese melts down. Allow cooling for at least 5 to 10 minutes before serving.

8.45 TASTY FRESH BLUEBERRY COBBLER

Total time of cooking
1 hour 10 minutes
Prep time 10 minutes
Cook time 1 hour

Serving
8 (1 cobbler of 8 inches)

Nutrition facts
(Per serving)
Calories 310
Fat 12.5g
Protein 3.2g
Carbs 48.5g

Ingredients:
- 4 cups of fresh blueberries
- 1 cup of white sugar
- 1/2 cup of butter
- 1 cup of milk
- 1 cup of self-rising flour

Instructions:
Follow the instructions below to make a tasty fresh blueberry cobbler.
1.Preheat the convection oven at 325°F.Spread butter on the bottom of 8 inches square baking dish and heat butter in preheated oven for 5 minutes.
2.Combine sugar, flour, and milk in a medium-sized bowl. Spread batter all over melted butter evenly. Sprinkle blueberries on top.
3.Bake in the preheated convection oven for around 1 hour. Let cobbler cool down for some time before serving.

8.46 BAKED EGG AND BACON BUNDLES

Total time of cooking
30 minutes
Prep time 10 minutes
Cook time 20 minutes

Serving
6

Nutrition facts
(Per serving)
Calories 311
Fat 28g
Protein 13g
Carbs 1g

Ingredients:
- 6 eggs large
- 12 to 18 strips of bacon
- Freshly ground pepper
- Salt to taste
- 1 teaspoon of butter

Instructions:
Follow the instructions below to make baked egg and bacon bundles.
1.Preheat the convection oven at 325°F.On medium cook, bacon in a large-sized skillet do not crisp just cook partially, drain.
2.Grease 6 muffin cups pan with butter. Cut each bacon strips in half. Place two halves of bacon on the bottom of each muffin cup, and with 1 or 2 whole bacon strips, line the sides of each cup. Crack an egg into each muffin cup.
3.Bake for around 15 to 20 minutes in the preheated convection oven until eggs are completely set. Sprinkle with pepper and salt upon serving.

8.47 BUFFALO CHEESE CHICKEN POCKETS

Total Time of cooking
25 minutes
Prep time 10 minutes
Cook time 15 minutes

Serving
8

Nutrition facts
(Per serving)
Calories 258
Fat 12g
Protein 12g
Carbs 25g

Ingredients:
- 1 tube of large buttermilk biscuits refrigerated(16.3 ounces)
- 3/4 pound of ground chicken
- Blue cheese salad dressing
- 1/3 cup of Buffalo wing sauce
- 1/2 cup of cheddar cheese shredded

Instructions:
Follow the instructions below to make buffalo cheese chicken pockets.
1.Preheat the convection oven at 350°F.Cook chicken on medium heat in large-sized skillet heat until chicken changes color for 5 to 8 minutes, with wooden spoon break into crumbles. Remove from stove and mix in buffalo wing sauce.
2.Roll each biscuit one by one into 6 inches circle on a kitchen-floured surface, spread 1/4 cup of chicken mixture on each circle, and 2 tablespoons of cheese. Fold biscuit dough over the filling and close the edges with a fork to seal.
3.Arrange pockets in a baking sheet and bake in the preheated convection oven for around 12 to 15 minutes. Side with blue cheese dressing while serving.

8.48 SOUTHERN-STYLE TASTY BUTTERMILK BISCUITS

Total Time of cooking
25 minutes
Prep time 10 minutes
Cook time 15 minutes

Serving
8 biscuits

Nutrition facts
(Per serving)
Calories 222
Fat 12g
Protein 4g
Carbs 24g

Ingredients:
- 2 cups of self-rising flour
- Melted butter
- 1/2 cup of cubed cold butter
- 3/4 cup of buttermilk

Instructions:
Follow the instructions below to make southern-style tasty buttermilk biscuits.
1.Knead butter coarsely into the flour until crumbly for 2 to 3 minutes in a large-sized bowl. Add in buttermilk and stir. Place onto kitchen floured surface, Knead 4 to 5 times. Roll out to 3/4 inches thick circle and with a biscuit cutter, cut 2 1/2 inch biscuits.
2.Arrange on a greased baking sheet. Bake in the convection oven at 400°F for around 12 to 15 minutes until lightly golden. Brush butter on top of biscuits and serve.

8.49 CHIVE-GARLIC OVEN-BAKED FRIES

Total Time of cooking
35 minutes
Prep time 10 minutes
Cook time 25 minutes

Serving
4

Nutrition facts
(Per serving)
Calories 200
Fat 4g
Protein 5g
Carbs 39g

Ingredients:
- 4 teaspoons of minced dried chives
- 4 russet potatoes medium
- 1/2 teaspoon of garlic powder
- 1 tablespoon of olive oil
- 1/2 teaspoon of salt

Instructions:
Follow the instructions below to make chive-garlic oven-baked fries.
1.Preheat the convection oven at 425°F.Cut potatoes into julienne strips. Wash with water and rinse.
2.Arrange potatoes in a large-sized bowl. Spread oil and remaining ingredients all over the potatoes and toss with potatoes to coat evenly. Spread into two baking sheets greased with cooking spray.
3.Bake for 20 to 25 minutes in the preheated convection oven until crispy.

8.50 EASY CHICKEN BARBECUED PIZZA

Total Time of cooking

20 minutes
Prep time 10 minutes
Cook time 10 minutes

Serving

4

Nutrition facts

(Per serving)
Calories 510
Fat 18g
Protein 35g
Carbs 52g

Ingredients:

- 1 cup of cooked chicken cubed
- 1 pizza crust prebaked(12-inch)
- 1 chopped red onion
- 2 cups of part-skim mozzarella cheese shredded
- 2/3 cup of honey garlic barbecue sauce

Instructions:

Follow the instructions below to make easy chicken barbecued pizza.

1.Arrange pizza crust on 14 inches pizza baking pan. Place barbecue sauce evenly. Spread with chicken, onion, and cheese. Bake in the convection oven at 325°F for around 10 minutes until cheese melts down.

8.51 CRISPY ROASTED ARTICHOKES

Total Time of cooking

60 minutes
Prep time: 20 minutes
Cook time: 40 minutes

Servings

6

Nutrition facts

(per serving)
Calories: 285 kcal
Fat 27g
Protein 3g
Carbs 10g

Ingredients

- 6-8 split artichokes, quartered
- 3-4 (skin on) garlic cloves
- 1 teaspoon lemon juice
- 1/3 cup olive oil extra virgin
- Mayonnaise (1/2 cup)

Instructions

1.Bring to boil a big saucepan of water, seasoning it with salt and 1 tablespoon of lemon juice.

2.Peel the artichokes' rough outer leaves until you reach the sensitive yellowish leaves in the core. Remove and discard the top third of each artichoke.

3.Remove any leftover stiff leaves and the outside of the stem using a vegetable peeler. Scoop out the fuzzy core of each artichoke and toss it aside.

4.Boil the artichoke hearts for 8 to 10 minutes, depending on their size. After draining, wipe dry with paper towels.

5.Preheat the oven to 400 degrees Fahrenheit. Toss the fried artichoke hearts and garlic cloves with the olive oil in a large mixing dish. Season the artichokes pieces with salt and pepper and arrange them in an equal layer on a baking sheet.

6.Roast for 25 to 30 minutes, stirring regularly, until the artichoke hearts are golden brown and crisp.

7.Peel the garlic cloves from their skins and place them in a small basin. With a fork, mash the cloves until smooth. Mix the mayonnaise with the remaining 1 tablespoon lemon juice in a mixing bowl. Salt & pepper to taste.

8.Serve the crispy artichoke hearts right away with a side of garlic aioli.

8.52 BAKED SWEET POTATO FRIES

Total Time of cooking

: 40 minutes
Prep time: 15 minutes
Cook time: 25 minutes

Servings

6

Nutrition facts

(per serving)
Calories 119kcal
Fat 7g
Protein 1g
Carbs 14g

Ingredients

- garlic cloves
- medium peeled sweet potatoes
- tablespoons of olive oil
- To taste flaky sea salt
- Fresh rosemary sprigs

Instructions

1.Preheat the oven to 400 degrees Fahrenheit. Using a nonstick spray, grease a baking pan.
2.Each sweet potato should be quartered, then sliced into four fat wedges.
3.Mix the potatoes and garlic with the olive oil in a large mixing basin. Set the potatoes in a single layer on the baking sheet that has been prepared. Season with salt and pepper, the rosemary and garlic cloves.
4.Bake for 22 minutes, or until the potatoes are golden brown and crisp, turning halfway through. Serve right away.

8.53 CRISPY SMASHED POTATOES

Total Time of cooking

55 minutes
Prep Time: 30 minutes
Cook Time: 25 minutes

Servings

4

Nutrition facts

(per serving)
Calories: 166 kcal
Protein 4g
Fat: 2g
Carbs: 33g

Ingredients

- tbsp olive oil
- Red potatoes, 4
- Kosher salt & pepper, t0 taste
- Some water

Instructions

1.Add 3-4 cups of water and roughly a teaspoon of salt to a pan large enough to handle the desired number of potatoes.
2.Using a scrubber, scrub some smaller potatoes.
3.Combine the potatoes and water in a large mixing bowl,. Make sure the potatoes are submerged in water. Reduce the heat and cover.
4.Cook for 25 minutes, until they are "fork-tender." This is when you can poke it with a fork, and it comes out effortlessly with barely a little resistance. Turn on the oven at 425°F convection or 450°F standard. Lower the temperature and bake for a little longer.
5.In a baking pan with a rim, drizzle olive oil. Not just a coat, but enough to make it pool a bit. Add the potatoes and mash them to a thickness of approximately 12 inches.
6.More olive oil should be brushed on top. Season with pepper, salt (or anything else you want).
7.Preheat oven to 350°F and bake until golden brown and crisp. It takes around 20-25 minutes. To have them crispier, bake them for 5 minutes longer.

8.54 EASY ROASTED RED POTATOES

Total Time of cooking
35 minutes
Prep Time: 5 minutes
Cook Time: 30 minutes

Servings
2

Nutrition facts
(per serving)
Calories: 154
Protein: 3g
Fat: 4g
Carbs: 28g

Ingredients
- 1 tablespoon extra-virgin olive oil
- tiny red potatoes
- 1 tsp. kosher salt
- 1 tsp. garlic, crushed or minced

Instructions
1. To begin, preheat the oven.
2. If using little red potatoes, scrub them and chop them into quarters. Keep the size of the potatoes to around 1 inch or less if using larger potatoes.
3. Combine the potatoes, olive oil, crushed or minced garlic, and kosher salt in a mixing basin.
4. Using a non-stick baking sheet, evenly distribute the mixture. Keep them apart for a while so they can brown properly. If you don't have a non-stick tray, use one that has been greased.
5. Bake for 30/32 minutes, or until golden brown. The interior temperature should be at least 200 degrees Fahrenheit.

8.55 FISH WITH PARSLEY PESTO

Total Time of cooking
18 minutes
Prep Time: 5 minutes
Cook Time: 12 minutes

Servings
4

Nutrition Facts
(Per Serving)
Calories 157.0 kcal
Fat 5.3 g
Protein 23.8 g
Carbs 5.0 g

Ingredients
Pesto:
- 1 minced garlic clove
- 1 bunch flat-leaf parsley, cut leaves only
- tablespoons bread crumbs (whole wheat or panko)
- teaspoons extra virgin olive oil
- 1 lemon, juiced and zested

Fish:
- fillets, 6-8 ounces each, 16 ounces white-fleshed fish fillet

Instructions
Pesto:
1. Pulse the parsley 6-8 times in a small food processor,.
2. Process until a thick sauce develops with the remaining ingredients.

Fish:
1. Turn on the oven at 400 degrees Fahrenheit (200 degrees Celsius).
2. Preheat a cast-iron skillet to high.
3. Using paper towels, pat the fish dry. Using nonstick cooking spray, lightly sprinkle both sides of the fish.
4. Add the fish to the skillet once it is heated. Cook for a couple of minutes on each side.
5. 1/4 cup pesto on top of each chunk of fish Warm the sauce by placing the pan in the oven (5 minutes).
6. Keep in mind that the handle of the pan will get quite hot in the oven!

8.56 ROASTED GARLIC MAHI MAHI

Total Time of cooking
23 minutes
Prep Time: 3 minutes
Cook Time: 20 minutes

Serving
1

Nutrition Facts
(Per Serving)
Calories 251.4 kcal
Fat 15.0 g
Protein 27.5 g
Carbs 2.7 g

Ingredients
- pieces Mahi Mahi
- 1 tbsp Olive Oil
- 1 Garlic, Roasted
- Dill

Instructions
1.Preheat the oven to 350 degrees Fahrenheit.
2.Take 2-4 filleted Mahi Mahi chunks. Make small slits on the tops of each fish piece.
3.Pour 1/2-1 tablespoon of Garlic Flavored Olive Oil over the fish, then top with Roasted Garlic and Dill.
4.Turn on the oven at 350°F. Put the fish on a pan and set it in the oven for 15-20 minutes.

8.57 SALMON AND ASPARAGUS

Total Time of cooking
27 minutes
Prep time: 15 minutes
Cook time: 12 minutes

Servings
4

Nutrition Facts
(Per Serving)
Calories 236.2 kcal
Fat 11.0 g
Protein 30.3 g
Carbs 3.0 g

Ingredients
- 1 1/2 tablespoons olive oil (extra virgin)
- 1 pound stalks of fresh asparagus, chopped into 2-inch segments
- 1 pound skinless salmon fillets (fresh or frozen)
- To taste, season with coarse sea salt and freshly ground pepper.
- 1 teaspoon fresh parsley, snipped
- 1 teaspoon lemon peel, coarsely shredded

Instructions
1.In a chilly oven, heat two cast-iron skillets (1 medium and 1 big) or oven-safe heavy skillets to 450 degrees F. Combine asparagus and 1/2 teaspoon olive oil in a medium mixing bowl; season with salt and pepper. Brush the remaining 1 teaspoon of olive oil on both sides of the fish and season with salt and pepper to taste.
2.Remove the hot skillets from the oven with care. Place the fish in the big skillet skin side down. In a medium skillet, place the asparagus. Place the skillets back in the oven. Bake for 14 minutes,until fish flakes easily and asparagus is crisp-tender when checked with a fork.
3.To serve, sprinkle lemon peel and parsley over the fish.

8.58 FLOUNDER DIJON

Total Time of cooking
30 minutes
Prep time: 15 minutes
Cook time: 15 minutes

Servings
5

Nutrition Facts
(Per Serving)
Calories 112.1 kcal
Fat 1.5g
Protein 22.0g
Carbs 0.5g

Ingredients
- Cooking spray
- 1 tsp of Dijon mustard
- 16 oz of flounder fillets
- 1 tbsp fresh chopped chives
- 1 tablespoon whipped salad dressing (fat-free)

Instructions
1. Preheat the oven to 350 degrees Fahrenheit.
2. Combine mustard, salad dressing, and chopped chives in a mixing bowl.
3. Brush the fish in a glass baking dish with the dijon mixture. Coat the fish with frying spray.
4. Cook for 12-15 minutes at 350°F.
5. Carrots and brown rice create a fantastic side dish for this delicious fish.

8.59 BROWN SUGAR AND GARLIC CHICKEN

Total Time of cooking
45 minutes
Prep time: 15 minutes
Cook time: 30 minutes

Servings
4

Nutrition Facts
(Per Serving)
Calories: 166.4 kcal
Fat 8.0 g
Protein 19.4 g
Carbs 4.3 g

Ingredients
- 1/4 cup extra virgin olive oil
- Pinch of pepper and salt
- 1 tsp minced garlic cloves
- 3-4 chicken breasts, boneless and skinless
- Brown sugar, 1/4 cup

Instructions
1. On the pan, sauté the minced garlic until golden brown. Remove from heat after gradually adding the brown sugar until it achieves a thick consistency.
2. Season the chicken with salt/pepper and set it in a baking dish. Pour the sauce over the chicken equally.
3. Heat the oven at 500°F and bake for 30 minutes.

8.60 BAKED CHICKEN THIGH

Total Time of cooking

35 minutes

Prep Time: 5 minutes

Cook Time: 30 minutes

Servings

4-6

Nutrition facts

(per serving)

Calories 61 kcal

Protein 2.4g

Fat 3.7g

Carbs 6.2g

Ingredients

- 1 cup of Japanese sake
- chicken thigh, bone-in, skin-on
- Ground black pepper and sea salt, to taste
- 1/2 teaspoon of cayenne pepper
- Tablespoons of soy sauce

Instructions

1.Preheat the oven to convection mode at 220°C (425°F).

2.Using a paper towel, thoroughly dry the chicken thighs.

3.In a large baking dish, combine Japanese sake and soy sauce. Stir everything together well. Place them skin-side up chicken thighs in the pan. Arrange them such that more flesh is shown and that they don't overlap.

4.Season the chicken skin with a generous amount of sea salt and black pepper. Cayenne pepper should be evenly distributed.

5.Bake for 30 minutes.The skin must be crisp and the thermometer inserted near the bone must register 165 degrees F.

6.Allow for a 5- to 10-minute cooling period. As the main course, serve warm.

7.To reheat the leftover chicken, bake it with the remaining pan sauce at 180 degrees Celsius (350 degrees Fahrenheit) until warm. The chicken will maintain its moisture.

8.61 BAKED SALMON

Total Time of cooking

20 minutes

Prep Time: 5 minutes

Cook Time: 15 minutes

Servings

2

Nutrition facts

(per serving)

Calories: 376

Protein: 23

Fat: 30g

Carbs: 3g

Ingredients

- 1 filet of salmon
- Tablespoons fresh dill, coarsely chopped
- Melted 1/2 cup butter salted
- ½ tbsp crushed garlic cloves
- tablespoons lemon juice fresh

Instructions

1.Preheat the oven to 375°F. Line a four-sided baking pan with aluminium foil. Place the fish in the foil's center.

2.Combine garlic, lemon juice, melted butter, and dill in a glass measuring cup. Combine all ingredients in a mixing bowl.

3.Immediately pour the butter mixture over the fish. Pull the edges and ends of the aluminum foil up and crimp them together to thoroughly cover the fish.

4.Bake for 18 minutes, until the salmon flakes easily with a fork, in a preheated oven.

8.62 BAKED CHICKEN TERIYAKI

Total Time of cooking
12 hrs 30 minutes
Prep Time: 12 hours
Cook Time: 30 minutes

Servings
6

Nutrition facts
(per serving)
Calories: 316 kcal
Protein 39g
Fat 8g
Carbs 19g

Ingredients
- 3-4 teaspoons of sake
- 10-12 chicken thighs
- A tablespoon of mirin
- A spoonful of sugar
- A tablespoon of chopped ginger and garlic
- A tablespoon of soy sauce

Instructions
1.In a large Tupperware or Ziploc bag, combine all of the ingredients.
2.Marinade for at least 30 minutes, but 12-24 hours is preferable.
3.Spread foil over the pan and, if preferred, spray with cooking/canola oil spray.
4.Place the chicken on foil and pour the remaining marinade over it.
5.Turn on the oven at 400°F ,when hot, bake for 25-30 minutes.
6.Place the chicken on a dish after it's a little crispy and done cooking.
7.Pour the remaining pan juices into a cup, skim off the fat, and pour the sauce over the chicken.

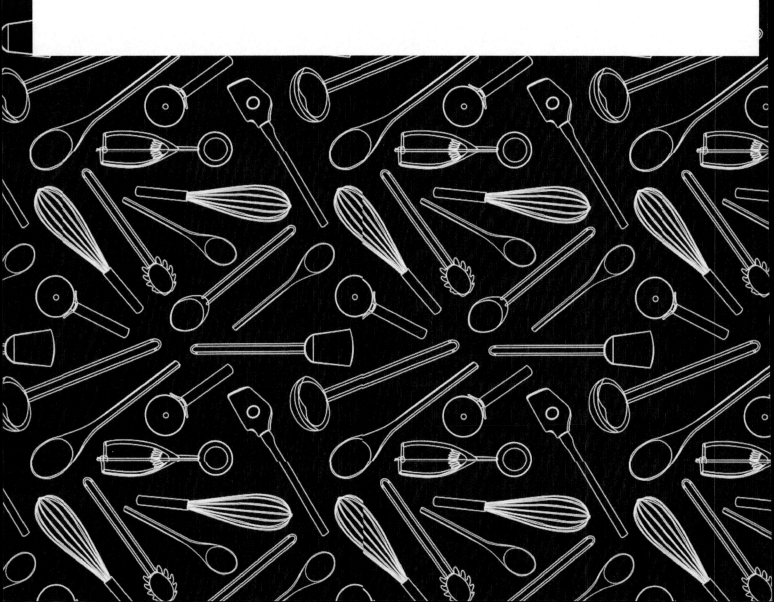

9.1 CREAM CHEESE AND STRAWBERRY COBBLER

Total Time of cooking
55 minutes
Prep time 10 minutes
Cook time 45 minutes

Serving
12

Nutrition facts
(Per serving)
Calories 106
Fat 4g
Protein 1g
Carbs 17g

Ingredients:
• 2 cups of fresh strawberry halves
• 1 cup of all-purpose flour
• 1 package of cream cheese (4 ounces), cut into small cubes
• 1 cup of white sugar
• 1 cup of milk
• 2 teaspoons of baking powder
• 1/2 teaspoon of salt
• 1/2 cup of melted butter

Instructions:
Follow the instructions below to make cream cheese and strawberry cobbler.
1. Preheat the convection oven at 375°F.
2. Into the bottom of 9x13 inches baking dish, spread a layer of melted butter.
3. In a small-sized bowl, combine sugar, milk, baking powder, flour, and salt together. Layer on top of butter in the baking dish. Place strawberry halves on top of the baking dish and put cream pieces on top of the strawberries.
4. Bake in the preheated convection oven for around 35 to 45 minutes.

9.2 CLASSIC MOLASSES COOKIES WITH COFFEE-GLAZED

Total Time of cooking

30 minutes

Prep time 20 minutes

Cook time 10 minutes

Serving

3 dozen

Nutrition facts

(Per serving)

Calories 106

Fat 4g

Protein 1g

Carbs 17g

Ingredients:

- 1 cup of confectioners' sugar
- 1/3 cup of molasses
- 3/4 cup of softened butter
- 1/3 cup of heavy whipping cream
- 1/2 cup of brown sugar packed
- 2 1/4 cups of all-purpose flour
- 1/2 cup+1/3 cup of sugar
- 1 1/2 teaspoons of ground cinnamon
- 1 teaspoon of vanilla extract
- 1 1/2 teaspoons of instant coffee granules
- 2 teaspoons of baking soda
- 1/2 teaspoon of salt
- 1 teaspoon of ground ginger
- 1/4 teaspoon of ground allspice
- 1 egg at room temperature
- 1/2 teaspoon of ground cloves

Instructions:

Follow the instructions below to make classic molasses cookies with coffee-glazed.

1.Preheat the convection oven at 325°F.

2.Cream brown sugar, butter, and 1/2 cup of granulated sugar until fluffy in a large-sized bowl,5 to 8 minutes. Mix in molasses, vanilla, and egg. In another medium-sized bowl, mix flour, spices, salt, and baking soda. Slowly mix into creamed mixture until completely combined.

3.Make rounded tablespoonfuls out of dough, coat in remaining sugar, and arrange on ungreased cookie sheets 2 inches apart. Bake for around 8 to 10 minutes in the preheated convection oven. Transfer to wire rack and cool for some time.

4.Mix cream, confectioners' sugar, and coffee granules until completely mixed. Spread over cookies and serve.

9.3 WALNUT AND CRANBERRY LOAF

Total Time of cooking

55 minutes

Prep time 10 minutes

Cook time 45 minutes

Serving

16

Nutrition facts

(Per serving)

Calories 238

Fat 8g

Protein 5g

Carbs 37g

Ingredients:

- 2 cups of buttermilk
- 3 cups of all-purpose flour
- 1 1/2 cups of fresh cranberries
- 3/4 cup of white sugar
- 1/2 cup of chopped walnuts
- 1/4 cup of melted butter
- 1 tablespoon of baking powder
- 1 teaspoon of baking soda
- 1 teaspoon of salt
- 1 beaten egg

Instructions:

Follow the instructions below to make walnut and cranberry loaf.

1.Preheat the convection oven at 325°F.

2.Gather all the dry ingredients and mix.

3.Add egg and milk to the dry mixture. Mix until soft and creamy, add butter, and mix until fully combined; do not over mix. Fold in the walnuts and cranberries in the mixture.

4.Spread batter evenly into two 8x4 inches greased loaf pans.

5.Bake for 40 to 45 minutes in the preheated convection oven until the loaf is completely baked.

6.Cool for some time before slicing. Make 8 slices out of each loaf.

9.4 BASIC OATMEAL AND PEANUT BUTTER BARS

Total Time of cooking
30 minutes
Prep time 10 minutes
Cook time 20 minutes

Serving
9 bars

Nutrition facts
(Per serving)
Calories 293
Fat 3g
Protein 9g
Carbs 37g

Ingredients:
- 1 cup of all-purpose flour
- 1 cup of rolled oats
- 1/3 cup of chocolate chips
- 3/4 cup of creamy peanut butter
- 1/2 cup of milk
- 1/2 cup of brown sugar
- 1 teaspoon of baking soda
- 1 teaspoon of vanilla
- 1/2 teaspoon of salt

Instructions:
Follow the instructions below to make basic oatmeal and peanut butter bars.
1. Preheat the convection oven at 325°F.
2. Combine peanut butter, oats, and brown sugar in a mixer until fully incorporated. Add in vanilla and milk until completely combined.
3. Mix in flour, salt, and baking soda in a small-sized bowl and add in the prepared mixture. Fold in chocolate chips in the mixture.
4. Spread mixture into 8x8 inches lined baking pan and bake in the convection oven for around 18 to 20 minutes.
5. Cool completely before slicing the bar.

9.5 SIMPLE AND CRISPY SUGAR COOKIES

Total Time of cooking
30 minutes
Prep time 20 minutes
Cook time 10 minutes

Serving
8 dozen

Nutrition facts
(For 2 cookies)
Calories 117
Fat 4g
Protein 2g
Carbs 18g

Ingredients:
- 5 cups of all-purpose flour
- 1 cup of softened butter
- 2 eggs at room temperature
- 1/4 cup of 2% milk
- 2 cups of sugar
- 1 teaspoon of baking soda
- 1 teaspoon of vanilla extract
- 1 1/2 teaspoons of baking powder
- 1/2 teaspoon of salt

Instructions:
Follow the instructions below to make simple and crispy sugar cookies.
1. Preheat the convection oven at 325°F.
2. Cream sugar and butter in a large-sized bowl until fluffy. Mix in vanilla and eggs. Add baking powder, flour, salt, and baking soda and combine with creamed mixture. Pour milk into the mixture and whisk. Cover with plastic wrap and refrigerate for 20 to 30 minutes.
3. Roll out dough into 1/8 inches thickness on a floured surface, with 2 inches cookie cutter cut dough into desired shapes. Arrange onto greased cookie sheets 2 inches apart.
4. Bake for around 10 minutes in the preheated convection oven until the edges of cookies are golden brown.

9.6 CAKE MIX CHEESECAKE DESSERT WITH RASPBERRY TOPPING

Total Time of cooking
1 hour 20 minutes
Prep time 20 minutes
Cook time 1 hour

Serving
24

Nutrition facts
(Per serving)
Calories 356
Fat 17.7g
Protein 4.6g
Carbs 42.1g

Ingredients:
•   1 container of whipped topping frozen (8 ounces), thawed
•   1 package of vanilla flavored cake mix (18.25 ounce)
•   2 packages of raspberries frozen (10 ounces), thawed
•   4 packages of cream cheese (8 ounces)
•   1 1/3 cups of white sugar
•   4 eggs
•   1/2 cup of kirschwasser
•   4 teaspoons of vanilla extract
•   1/2 cup of white sugar

Instructions:
Follow the instructions below to make a cake mix cheesecake dessert with raspberry topping.
1.Preheat the convection oven at 325°F.With cooking spray, grease and flour 9x13 inches baking pan.
2.Ready cake mix according to your package directions. Spread into 9x13 inches greased pan and set the pan aside. Beat eggs, cream cheese,1 1/3 cups of sugar, and vanilla in a large-sized bowl until fluffy. Pour over cake batter layer.
3.Bake in the preheated convection oven for around 1 hour.
4.For the topping: In blender or bowl, mix in 1/2 cup of sugar, raspberries,1/2 cup of kirschwasser, and blend until creamy. Drizzle over baked dessert.

9.7 PUMPKIN PIE MINI MUFFINS

Total Time of cooking
45 minutes
Prep time 20 minutes
Cook time 25 minutes

Serving
12 mini muffins

Nutrition facts
(Per serving)
Calories 125
Fat 3g
Protein 3g
Carbs 23g

Ingredients:
•   15 ounces of pumpkin puree
•   1/2 cup of flour
•   1/2 cup of brown sugar
•   10 ounces of evaporated milk
•   1/4 cup white sugar
•   2 eggs
•   1 1/2 teaspoons pumpkin pie spice
•   1/4 teaspoon of baking soda
•   1/2 teaspoon of salt
•   1/4 teaspoon of baking powder

•   Whipped cream for serving

Instructions:
Follow the instructions below to make pumpkin pie mini muffins.
1.Preheat the convection oven at 350°F.Grease a 12-muffin cup pan.
2.Combine baking soda, flour, salt, and baking powder in a small-sized bowl.
3.Add in white sugar, eggs, spice, brown sugar, pumpkin puree, and evaporated milk in a medium-sized bowl and mix well. Put dry ingredients and combine well. Distribute batter evenly between muffin cups.
4.Bake in the preheated convection oven for 24 to 25 minutes. Let it cool down for 10 minutes.
5.Remove muffins from the pan and keep them in the refrigerator for at least 3 hours or overnight. Spread whipped cream on top of muffins and serve.

9.8 COCONUT PINEAPPLE CAKE WITH LIME FROSTING

Total Time of cooking
50 minutes
Prep time 20 minutes
Cook time 30 minutes

Serving
12

Nutrition facts
(Per serving)
Calories 398
Fat 14g
Protein 4g
Carbs 23g

Ingredients:
- 1/3 cup of packed brown sugar
- 2 cups of all-purpose flour
- 1 cup of undrained crushed pineapple
- 1/2 cup of flaked sweetened coconut
- 1/2 cup of white sugar
- 1/2 cup of chopped pecans
- 1/4 cup of oil
- 2 mashed bananas
- 1 lime
- 1 1/4 teaspoon of baking powder
- 1 1/4 teaspoon of baking soda
- For the lime frosting:
- 2 cups of powdered sugar
- 4 ounces of softened cream cheese
- 1 lime (juice and zest)
- 2 ounces of softened butter

Instructions:
Follow the instructions below to make coconut pineapple cake with lime frosting.

1.Preheat the convection oven at 350°F.Coat 9x9 inches pan with cooking spray.

2.Combine flour, baking soda, lime zest, coconut, pecans, baking powder, and a pinch of salt in a small-sized bowl.

3.Mix together eggs, pineapple, bananas, brown sugar, oil, white sugar, and 1 teaspoon of lime juice in a medium-sized bowl.

4.Combine wet ingredients with dry ingredients until completely mixed(don't over mix). Spread the batter into greased pan and bake for 25 to 30 minutes in the convection oven.

5.Beat all the frosting items together with an electric mixer and spread over cooled cake, slice, and enjoy!

9.9 EASY AND QUICK OATMEAL BANANA COOKIES

Total Time of cooking
25 minutes
Prep time 10 minutes
Cook time 15 minutes

Serving
12

Nutrition facts
(Per serving)
Calories 127
Fat 6g
Protein 2g
Carbs 17g

Ingredients:
- 1 cup of bananas mashed
- 1 3/4 cups of all-purpose flour
- 1 cup of chocolate chips
- 1 1/4 cups of large flake oats
- 1/2 cup of brown sugar
- 2/3 cup of softened butter
- 1/2 cup of sugar
- 1/2 cup of walnuts chopped
- 1 teaspoon of cinnamon
- 1 teaspoon of vanilla
- 1/2 teaspoon of baking powder
- 1/2 teaspoon of baking soda
- 1/4 teaspoon of salt
- 1 egg

Instructions:
Follow the instructions below to make easy and quick oatmeal banana cookies.

1.Preheat the convection oven at 375°F.With baking paper, line a cookie sheet.

2.Mix flour, baking soda, cinnamon, salt, baking powder, and oats together.

3.Cream together sugar and butter until soft. Whisk in the egg.

4.Stir in vanilla and mashed bananas. Mix in the flour mixture slowly at a time until fully incorporated. Add in chocolate chips and nuts and lightly fold in the mixture.

5.Place tablespoonfuls onto lined cookie sheets. Bake in the preheated convection oven for 12 to 15 minutes or until golden brown from the edges.

9.10 DOUBLE CHOCOLATE AND MACADAMIA BISCOTTI

Total Time of cooking
30 minutes
Prep time 10 minutes
Cook time 20 minutes

Serving
2 dozen

Nutrition facts
(For 2 Biscotti)
Calories 267
Fat 15g
Protein 3g
Carbs 31g

Ingredients:
- 1/2 cup of white chips or vanilla
- 1 tube of chocolate chip cookie dough refrigerated (18 ounces)
- 1/2 cup of macadamia nuts coarsely chopped

Instructions:
Follow the instructions below to make double chocolate and macadamia biscotti.
1.Preheat the convection oven at 350°F.
2.Combine dough, nuts, and chips in a large-sized bowl. Knead with your hands until well mixed. Separate dough into two equal parts.
3.Spread each piece into 13 inches greased baking sheets with 2 inches thickness. Bake at 350°F in the convection oven for around 12 to 15 minutes until light brown.
4.Cut biscotti diagonally into 1-inch slices; after cutting, separate each piece about 1/4 inches. Bake 4 to 5 minutes more. Cool biscotti for some time before serving.

9.11 TASTY POPPY SEEDS LEMON CAKE

Total Time of cooking
45 minutes
Prep time 10 minutes
Cook time 35 minutes

Serving
15

Nutrition facts
(Per serving)
Calories 320
Fat 12g
Protein 3g
Carbs 51g

Ingredients:
- 1 package of instant vanilla pudding mix (3.4 ounces)
- 1/4 cup of poppy seeds
- 1 package of lemon cake mix
- 4 eggs at room temperature
- 1/2 cup of canola oil
- 1 cup of water

For the drizzle:
- 2 tablespoons of lemon juice
- 2 tablespoons of water
- 2 cups of confectioners' sugar

Instructions:
Follow the instructions below to make tasty poppy seeds lemon cake.
1.Combine pudding mix, eggs, cake mix, oil, and water in a large-sized bowl and beat on low speed using an electric mixer for around 1 minute. Beat the butter on medium speed for around 2 minutes. Mix in poppy seeds and shift the batter to 13x9 inches greased and floured baking pan.
2.Bake in the convection oven for around 30 to 35 minutes at 325°F. Once baked, transfer to a cooling rack.
3.Combine the confectioner's sugar, water, and lemon juice in a small-sized bowl, pour over the cake, and serve.

9.12 CRISPS ALMOND COFFEE COOKIES

Total Time of cooking
25 minutes
Prep time 10 minutes
Cook time 15 minutes

Serving
6 dozen

Nutrition facts
(Per serving)
Calories 168
Fat 8g
Protein 2g
Carbs 23g

Ingredients:
- 1 cup of toasted and chopped almonds
- 2 cups of brown sugar packed
- 1/2 cup of brewed coffee at room temperature
- 1 cup of shortening
- 3 1/2 cups of all-purpose flour
- 3 tablespoons of sugar
- 1 1/2 teaspoons of ground cinnamon, divided
- 1 teaspoon of salt
- 2 eggs at room temperature
- 1 teaspoon of baking soda

Instructions:
Follow the instructions below to make crisps almond coffee cookies.
1. Cream together brown sugar and shortening until fluffy in a large-sized bowl. Mix eggs, one at a time, and keep beating after adding each egg. Whisk in coffee. Stir together baking soda, flour, 1 teaspoon of cinnamon, and salt; slowly add the flour mixture into the creamed mixture and combine well. Fold in almonds.
2. Place teaspoonfuls into cookie sheet 2 inches apart. Mix in remaining cinnamon and sugar; Sprinkle the cinnamon-sugar mixture on top of cookies and slightly press with hands to flatten.
3. Bake in the convection oven for 10 to 15 minutes at 350°F.

9.13 RASPBERRY JAM DESSERT BARS

Total Time of cooking
40 minutes
Prep time 10 minutes
Cook time 30 minutes

Serving
20

Nutrition facts
(Per serving)
Calories 405
Fat 19.5g
Protein 3.3g
Carbs 55.7g

Ingredients:
- 4 cups of all-purpose flour
- 2 cups of white sugar
- 1 1/2 cups of raspberry jam
- 2 cups of softened butter
- 4 egg yolks

Instructions:
Follow the instructions below to make raspberry jam dessert bars.
1. Preheat the convection oven at 325°F.
2. Whisk together sugar and butter in a medium-sized bowl until creamy.
Mix in egg yolks, slowly stir in the flour to make a dough.
3. Press half of the dough onto the bottom of 9x13 inches greased baking pan. Spread a layer of raspberry jam evenly. Flat the remaining dough and arrange it over the raspberry layer, evenly cover the top.
4. Bake for around 30 minutes in a convection oven until lightly golden brown from top. Let cool down for a while before slicing.

9.14 ORANGE-ZEST BLACKBERRY CAKE

Total Time of cooking
55 minutes
Prep time 10 minutes
Cook time 45 minutes

Serving
10

Nutrition facts
(Per serving)
Calories 405
Fat 12g
Protein 4g
Carbs 38g

Ingredients:
- 1 1/2 cups of all-purpose flour
- 2 cups of blackberries fresh
- 1 cup of sugar, divided
- 1/2 cup of sour cream or plain yogurt
- 1/2 cup of softened butter
- 1 teaspoon of orange zest grated
- 1/8 teaspoon of salt
- Confectioners' sugar(optional)
- 1/2 teaspoon of baking soda
- 1 tablespoon of all-purpose flour
- 1 egg large

Instructions:
Follow the instructions below to make an orange-zest black-berry cake.

1.Preheat the convection oven at 325°F.

2.Cream together 3/4 cup of sugar and butter in a large-sized bowl until fluffy,5 to 8 minutes. Whisk in orange zest and egg. In another medium-sized bowl, combine 1 1/2 cups of flour, salt, and baking soda. Mix in gradually to creamed mixture with sour cream, keep beating, and spread the batter to 9 inches greased and floured springform baking pan.

3.In a small-sized bowl, stir together 1 tablespoon of flour with blackberries and toss gently to coat. Spread blackberries all over the batter and sprinkle with remaining sugar on the top of the batter.

4.Bake in the convection oven for around 40 to 45 minutes. While serving, dust the top of the cake with confectioners' sugar.

9.15 BASIC AND SOFT RAISIN APRICOT COOKIES

Total Time of cooking
35 minutes
Prep time 15 minutes
Cook time 20 minutes

Serving
18

Nutrition facts
(Per serving)
Calories 232
Fat 10.5g
Protein 2.8g
Carbs 33.7g

Ingredients:
- 1 cup of raisins
- 1 cup of apricots dried
- 1 cup of pecans chopped
- 2 cups of all-purpose flour
- 1 cup of white sugar
- 1 tablespoon of warm water
- 1 teaspoon of baking powder
- 1 teaspoon of baking soda
- 1 teaspoon of ground allspice
- 1/2 teaspoon of ground cinnamon
- 1/2 cup of shortening
- 1/2 teaspoon of salt
- 1 egg

Instructions:
Follow the instructions below to make basic and soft raisin apricot cookies.

1.Preheat the convection oven at 350°F.

1.In a blender, grind apricots. Combine flour, spices, baking powder, and salt in a small-sized bowl.

2.Cream together sugar and shortening in a large-sized bowl. Mix in baking soda with warm water and dissolve. Add it to creamed mixture, beat until smooth. Whisk in the egg.

3.Gradually mix in the dry ingredients, keep mixing until fully combined. Stir in raisins, apricots, and pecans. Cover tightly and chill for at least one hour.

4.Place teaspoonfuls in a cookie sheet,2 inches apart, and bake for around 18 to 20 minutes.

9.16 CLASSIC BANANA CHOCOLATE CAKE

Total Time of cooking
45 minutes
Prep time 15 minutes
Cook time 30 minutes

Serving
8

Nutrition facts
(Per serving)
Calories 391
Fat 16g
Protein 6g
Carbs 60g

Ingredients:
- 1 1/2 cups of flour
- 1/2 cup of chocolate chips mini
- 4 mashed bananas
- 1/2 cup of cocoa powder
- 1/2 cup of butter at room temperature
- 1/4 cup of brown sugar
- 2 eggs
- 1 teaspoon of baking soda
- 1/2 cup of white sugar
- 1/2 teaspoon of baking powder

Instructions:
Follow the instructions below to make a classic banana chocolate cake.
1.Preheat the convection oven at 325°F.
2.Whisk together sugars and butter until creamy. Mix in the eggs and mashed bananas.
3.In a large-sized bowl, combine cocoa powder, flour, baking powder, and baking soda.
4.Mix in the chocolate chips and flour mixture to the banana mixture and whisk until completely combined.
5.Spread the batter into 9 inches greased and floured round cake pan.
6.Bake for around 25 to 30 minutes in the preheated convection oven.

9.17 IRISH–STYLE CUPCAKES WITH IRISH CREAM FROSTING

Total Time of cooking
40 minutes
Prep time 15 minutes
Cook time 25 minutes

Serving
2 dozen

Nutrition facts
(Per serving)
Calories 273
Fat 9g
Protein 2g
Carbs 45g

Ingredients:
- 2 1/2 cups of all-purpose flour
- 1 1/2 cups of sugar
- 1/2 cup of Irish cream liqueur
- 3/4 cup of applesauce unsweetened
- 1/2 cup of softened butter
- 3 teaspoons of baking powder
- 2 teaspoons of vanilla extract
- 1/2 teaspoon of salt
- 2 eggs at room temperature
- For the frosting:
- 6 tablespoons of Irish cream liqueur
- 1/3 cup of softened butter
- 4 cups of confectioners' sugar
- 4 ounces of cream cheese reduced-fat

Instructions:
Follow the instructions below to make Irish-style cupcakes with Irish cream frosting.
1.Preheat the convection oven at 325°F.Cream sugar and butter in a large-sized bowl until fluffy for around 5 to 8 minutes. Beat eggs, add one at a time and beat well. Whisk in vanilla and applesauce.
2.In another large-sized bowl, combine flour, salt, and baking powder; Mix the dry ingredients with the prepared creamed mixture and Irish cream liqueur.
3.Pour batter into paper-lined muffin cups evenly. Bake in the preheated convection oven for around 20 to 25 minutes. Cool completely on wire racks.
4.For Irish cream frosting: whisk together cream cheese and butter until creamy. Add in Irish cream liqueur and beat. Mix in confectioners' sugar; whisk them together until soft and creamy. Arrange Irish cream frosting on top of cupcakes with a piping bag and serve.

9.18 TASTY PECAN BUTTER COOKIES

Total Time of cooking

30 minutes

Prep time 15 minutes

Cook time 15 minutes

Serving

24

Nutrition facts

(Per serving)

Calories 179

Fat 12.8g

Protein 2g

Carbs 14.9g

Ingredients:

- 2 cups of all-purpose flour
- 1 ½ cups of pecan halves
- 1 cup of softened butter
- 1 egg
- 1/2 teaspoon of salt
- 2/3 cup of brown sugar packed

Instructions:

Follow the instructions below to make tasty pecan butter cookies.

1.Preheat the convection oven at 350°F.

2.Cream together egg, brown sugar, and butter in a large-sized bowl. Mix until completely combined.

3.Gradually add salt and flour to the mixture and whisk well. Refrigerate with cover for at least an hour.

4.Separate one-inch pieces from the dough and make them into balls. Arrange on baking sheets 2 inches apart. Using hands, press down balls to flatten. Put pecan on the top of a cookie and lightly press.

5.Bake for around 10 to 15 minutes in the preheated convection oven until light golden brown from the edges.

9.19 EASY AND DELICIOUS GINGERBREAD CAKE

Total Time of cooking

1 hour

Prep time 15 minutes

Cook time 45 minutes

Serving

16 slices

Nutrition facts

(Per serving)

Calories 177

Fat 3g

Protein 3g

Carbs 35g

Ingredients:

- 2 cups of all-purpose flour
- 1 cup of sugar
- 1 cup of hot boiling water
- 1 cup of vegetable oil
- 1 cup of molasses
- 2 tablespoons of warm water
- 3 eggs
- 2 teaspoons of baking soda
- 1 1/2 teaspoons of cinnamon
- 1 1/2 teaspoons of ginger
- 1 teaspoon of cloves

Instructions:

Follow the instructions below to make an easy and delicious gingerbread cake.

1.Preheat the convection oven at 325°F.

2.Add sugar, molasses, spices, eggs, and oil and mix with a hand mixer until fully combined. Mix in flour gradually.

3.Combine together 2 tablespoons of water and baking soda. Mix into the batter and whisk well. Add hot boiling water and mix until fully incorporated.

4.Shift the batter into a 9x13 inches grease cake pan line with baking paper and spread evenly.

5.Bake for around 35 to 45 minutes in the preheated convection oven. Allow to cool completely and pipe whipped cream over the cake while serving.

9.20 CHERRY CRACKER DESSERT

Total Time of cooking
15 minutes
Prep time 15 minutes
Cook time 5 minutes

Serving
9

Nutrition facts
(Per serving)
Calories 448
Fat 34.6g
Protein 3.5g
Carbs 32.1g

Ingredients:
- 1 can of cherry pie filling (12 ounces)
- 1 1/4 cups of graham cracker crumbs
- 1 package of cream cheese (8 ounces)
- 1 cup of heavy cream
- 3/4 cup of melted margarine
- 1 dash of almond extract
- 1/2 cup of white sugar
- 1 dash of vanilla extract

Instructions:
Follow the instructions below to make a cherry cracker dessert.
1.Preheat the convection oven at 325°F.Mix in melted margarine and graham cracker crumbs together in a small-sized bowl. Spread on the bottom of 9x9 inches baking dish and press to set. Bake for around 5 minutes in the convection oven. Keep it aside.
2.Combine sugar, vanilla, cream cheese, and almond extract in a large-sized bowl. Stir well. In another medium-sized bowl, beat cream with an electric beater until fluffy. Stir whipped cream into cream cheese mixture. Place over cooled baked crust. Spread cherry pie filling and smooth the layer with a spatula to cover the top. Keep in the refrigerator and let chill for some time before serving.

9.21 TASTY AND SOFT BAKED LEMON CHEESECAKE BITES

Total Time of cooking
40 minutes
Prep time 20 minutes
Cook time 20 minutes

Serving
12 cheesecake bites

Nutrition facts
(Per serving)
Calories 216
Fat 8g
Protein 3g
Carbs 17g

Ingredients:
- 16 ounces of softened cream cheese
- 4 Viennese cookies
- 2 eggs
- 4 teaspoons of blackcurrant jam
- 1/3 cup of honey
- 4 teaspoons of orange marmalade
- 4 teaspoons of lemon curd
- 1 tablespoon of melted butter
- 1/2 teaspoon of vanilla extract
- 1 teaspoon of lemon juice

Instructions:
Follow the instructions below to make tasty and soft baked lemon cheesecake bites.
1.Preheat the convection oven at 325°F.
2.Process melted butter and cookies in a food processor until crumbly. Distribute the mixture over 12 cups muffin pan lined with foil liners and press gently on the bottom of each cup to form crust.
3.In a medium-sized using electric beater, whisk cream cheese until fluffy. Put lemon, eggs, honey, and extract and beat until soft and creamy on medium speed.
4.Spread cream cheese mixture over each cookie crust. Spread one teaspoon of orange marmalade and then layer with black currant jam and lemon curd on top of the cheesecakes. Swirl the top layers of cheesecake bites with a toothpick.
5.Bake in the preheated convection oven for around 20 to 22 minutes. Allow cooling for some time before serving.

9.22 MEXICAN-STYLE SUGAR CHOCOLATE CRISPS

Total Time of cooking
30 minutes
Prep time 20 minutes
Cook time 10 minutes

Serving
4 1/2 dozen

Nutrition facts
(Per serving)
Calories 85
Fat 4g
Protein 1g
Carbs 11g

Ingredients:
- 1 1/4 cups of sugar(divided)
- 1 3/4 cups of all-purpose flour
- 2 ounces of melted and cooled unsweetened chocolate
- 1 cup of chocolate chips semisweet
- 1/4 cup of light corn syrup
- 3/4 cup of shortening
- 1 1/2 teaspoons of ground cinnamon
- 1 egg at room temperature
- 1/4 teaspoon of salt
- 1 teaspoon of baking soda

Instructions:
Follow the instructions below to make Mexican-style sugar chocolate crisps.

1.Preheat the convection oven at 325°F.Cream 1 cup of sugar and shortening together until soft, for 5 to 8 minutes, whisk in the egg, melted chocolate, and corn syrup. In another medium-sized bowl, mix together flour, baking soda, salt, and cinnamon. Slowly add into creamed mixture and mix together until fully incorporated. Fold in chocolate chips.

2.Make 1-inch balls out of dough and coat in remaining sugar. Arrange on cookie sheets 2 inches apart. Bake in the preheated convection oven for around 8 to 10 minutes until the top of the crisps cracks and puff.

9.23 PECAN AND CHOCOLATE PIE DESSERT BARS

Total Time of cooking
1 hour
Prep time 15 minutes
Cook time 45 minutes

Serving
40 bars

Nutrition facts
(Per serving)
Calories 194
Fat 9.9g
Protein 2.1g
Carbs 26.9g

Ingredients:
For the Crust:
- 2/3 cup of margarine
- 1/3 cup of white sugar
- 2 cups of all-purpose flour
- 1/3 teaspoon of salt

For the filling:
- 1 package of chocolate chips (11 ounces)
- 1 1/2 cups of light corn syrup
- 4 eggs
- 1 1/2 cups of pecans chopped
- 1 cup of brown sugar
- 3 tablespoons of margarine
- 1/8 teaspoon of salt
- 1 1/2 teaspoons of vanilla extract

Instructions:
Follow the instructions below to make pecan and chocolate pie dessert bars.

1.Preheat the convection oven at 325°F.Mix white sugar, flour, and salt in a large-sized bowl. Mix in margarine to the mixture until crumbly. Spread mixture on the bottom of 10x15 inches greased jelly roll pan and press to make a crust.

2.Bake the crust in the preheated convection oven for around 20 minutes.

3.Meanwhile, make the filling by combining together brown sugar, margarine, corn syrup, vanilla extract, eggs and salt in a large-sized bowl until soft and creamy. Fold in pecans.

4.Sprinkle chocolate chips on cool baked crust and place filling over the chocolate chip evenly.

5.Bake in the preheated convection oven for around 20 to 25 minutes. Allow to cool for some time before cutting into bars.

9.24 BAKED CROISSANT CREAMY PUDDING WITH DELICIOUS KAHLUA SAUCE

Total Time of cooking
1 hour 5 minutes
Prep time 20 minutes
Cook time 45 minutes

Serving
9

Nutrition facts
(Per serving)
Calories 894
Fat 51g
Protein 10g
Carbs 99g

Ingredients:
- 1 1/2 cups of half-and-half cream
- 6 croissants (cut into bite-sized pieces)
- 2 eggs large
- 2 1/4 cups of sugar
- 4 egg yolks large
- 1 1/2 teaspoons of salt
- 3 cups of heavy whipping cream
- 4 1/2 teaspoons of vanilla extract

For the sauce:
- 1 cup of sugar
- 2 ounces of chopped unsweetened chocolate
- 1/2 cup of evaporated milk
- 3 tablespoons of Kahlua (coffee liqueur)
- 2 tablespoons of butter
- Pinch of salt

Instructions:
Follow the instructions below to make baked croissant creamy pudding with delicious Kahlua sauce.

1. Place croissant pieces in 9 greased ramekins evenly and arrange ramekins on baking sheets.

2. Mix in eggs, cream, sugar, half-and-half, vanilla, salt, and egg yolks in a large-sized bowl. Spread the mixture over croissant; set aside for 10 minutes until croissants are soaked and softened. Bake for around 40 to 45 minutes at 300°F until completely cooked.

3. On medium-low heat in a small-sized sauce, melt butter and chocolate together. Put milk, sugar, and salt and stir for 4 to 5 minutes or until the mixture thickens. Remove from stove and drizzle Kahlua sauce over warm pudding when serving.

9.25 ZUCCHINI-FLAVORED CHOCOLATE COOKIES

Total Time of cooking
25 minutes
Prep time 15 minutes
Cook time 10 minutes

Serving
4 dozen

Nutrition facts
(Per serving)
Calories 59
Fat 2.5g
Protein 0.9g
Carbs 8.5g

Ingredients:
- 2 1/4 cups of all-purpose flour
- 1 3/4 cups of zucchini grated
- 1/3 cup of unsweetened cocoa powder
- 1/2 cup of white sugar
- 1 egg
- 1/2 cup of shortening (butter flavored)
- 1/2 cup of brown sugar
- 1 teaspoon of baking soda
- 1 teaspoon of vanilla extract
- 1/2 teaspoon of salt

Instructions:
Follow the instructions below to make zucchini-flavored chocolate cookies.

1. Preheat the convection oven at 325°F. Cream white sugar, brown sugar and shortening together in a medium-sized bowl. Mix in egg and vanilla. Whisk together flour, baking soda, cocoa powder and salt; slowly mix into creamed mixture. Stir in the zucchini. Place tablespoonfuls of batter onto the prepared baking sheets.

2. Bake for around 8 to 10 minutes in the preheated convection oven. Cool the cookies on a wire rack before serving.

9.26 CARAMEL APPLE CINNAMON CRISPS

Total Time of cooking

1 hour
Prep time 15 minutes
Cook time 45 minutes

Serving

12

Nutrition facts

(Per serving)
Calories 564
Fat 20g
Protein 7g
Carbs 94g

Ingredients:

- 1 package of caramels (14 ounces), halved
- 3 cups of oats
- 8 cups tart apples thinly sliced and peeled
- 2 cups of all-purpose flour
- 1 cup of cubed cold butter
- 1 1/2 cups of brown sugar packed
- 1 cup of apple cider, (divided)
- 1 teaspoon of ground cinnamon

Instructions:

Follow the instructions below to make caramel apple cinnamon crisps.

1.Preheat the convection oven at 325°F.Combine flour, brown sugar, oats, and cinnamon in a large-sized bowl; mix in butter until the mixture is crumbly. Press half mixture on the bottom of 13x9 inches greased baking dish. Layer half of the caramels, apples, and remaining oat mixture. Repeat the procedure of layers. Spread 1/2 cup of cider vinegar on top.

2.Bake in the preheated convection oven for around 30 minutes. Spread remaining cider; bake 15 minutes more.

9.27 DELICIOUS PUMPKIN CAKE WITH CREAM CHEESE AND BUTTER FROSTING

Total Time of cooking

50 minutes
Prep time 15 minutes
Cook time 35 minutes

Serving

12

Nutrition facts

(Per serving)
Calories 621
Fat 26g
Protein 6g
Carbs 94g

Ingredients:

- 2 1/2 cups of canned pumpkin
- 2 cups of flour
- 1 3/4 cups of white sugar
- 1 cup of mini chocolate chips
- 1/2 cup of vegetable oil
- 2 teaspoons of baking soda
- 1 teaspoon of pumpkin pie spice
- 1 teaspoon of vanilla
- 1 teaspoon of cinnamon
- 4 eggs
- 1 tablespoon of baking powder

For the frosting:
- 3 1/4 cups of powdered sugar
- 8 ounces of softened cream cheese
- 1 teaspoon of vanilla extract
- 1/3 cup of softened butter

Instructions:

Follow the instructions below to make delicious pumpkin cake with cream cheese and butter frosting.

1.Preheat the convection oven at 325°F.Combine baking powder, flour, baking soda, pumpkin pie spice and cinnamon in a large-sized bowl.

2.Combine oil, vanilla, pumpkin, sugar and eggs in a separate medium-sized bowl.

3.Add in flour mixture with pumpkin mixture and combined completely. Don't over-mix the batter. Fold in chocolate chips.

4.Pour batter into 9x13 inches greased and floured pan and bake for 30 to 35 minutes in the preheated convection oven.

5.Beat together butter and cream cheese. Mix in powdered sugar and vanilla and beat on medium speed for few minutes.

6.Spread the frosting on the cool baked cake evenly. Slice and enjoy!

Total Time of cooking
25 minutes
Prep time 15 minutes
Cook time 10 minutes

Serving
36

Nutrition facts
(Per serving)
Calories 156
Fat 7.8g
Protein 2.1g
Carbs 20.4g

Ingredients:
- 1 1/2 cups of pitted and chopped dates
- 3 cups of all-purpose flour sifted
- 1 1/3 cups of white sugar
- 1 cup of pecans chopped
- 1 cup of softened butter
- 2 teaspoons of water
- 1 teaspoon of baking soda
- 1/2 teaspoon of ground cinnamon
- 3 eggs
- 1/4 teaspoon of ground cloves

Instructions:
Follow the instructions below to make a date and pecan cookies.
1.Preheat the convection oven at 350°F.Beat together sugar and butter until fluffy. Put in eggs one at a time and keep beating after each addition. Mix together flour, cinnamon, baking soda and cloves; slowly add into creamed mixture and stir well. Combine dates and water and fold into dough. Add chopped pecans and fold. Cover tightly and chill for around 1 hour.
2.Place spoonfuls of dough onto the prepared cookie sheet.
3.Bake for 8 to 10 minutes in the preheated convection oven. Let cookies cool before eating.

9.29 MARSHMALLOW BUTTERSCOTCH BROWNIES

Total Time of cooking
40 minutes
Prep time 15 minutes
Cook time 25 minutes

Serving
12

Nutrition facts
(Per serving)
Calories 448
Fat 21.4g
Protein 5.1g
Carbs 57.5g

Ingredients:
- 2 cups of milk chocolate chips
- 1 cup of butterscotch chips
- 2 cups of marshmallows
- 1 1/2 cups of all-purpose flour
- 2 eggs
- 1/2 cup of butter
- 2/3 cup of brown sugar packed
- 1 teaspoon of vanilla extract
- 2 teaspoons of baking powder
- 1/2 teaspoon of salt

Instructions:
Follow the instructions below to make marshmallow butterscotch brownies.
1.Preheat the convection oven at 325°F.
2.Heat butterscotch and butter in a large-sized oven-proof bowl in the microwave until it completely melts. Set the liquid mixture aside for cooling.
3.Meanwhile, combine brown sugar, flour, baking powder, vanilla, salt and eggs into another medium-sized bowl. Mix with the butterscotch mixture until fully incorporated. Stir in chocolate chips and marshmallows.
4.Pour batter into 9x13 inches greased baking pan.
5.Bake for around 25 minutes in the preheated convection oven. Keep an eye on brownies while baking, do not overcook.

9.30 SOFT FRUIT COCKTAIL AND NUT COOKIES

Total Time of cooking
30 minutes
Prep time 15 minutes
Cook time 15 minutes

Serving
36

Nutrition facts
(Per serving)
Calories 196
Fat 9.5g
Protein 2.9g
Carbs 26.1g

Ingredients:
- 1 1/2 cups of walnuts chopped
- 1 can of drained fruit cocktail (15.25 ounce)
- 1 cup of shortening
- 4 cups of all-purpose flour
- 1 cup of raisins
- 1 cup of brown sugar packed
- 3 eggs
- 1 teaspoon of baking powder
- 1 teaspoon of ground cloves
- 1/2 cup of white sugar
- 1 teaspoon of ground cinnamon
- 1 teaspoon of baking soda
- 1 teaspoon of vanilla extract

Instructions:
Follow the instructions below to make soft fruit cocktail and nut cookies.
1.Preheat the convection oven at 325°F.Cream together brown sugar, white sugar and shortening in a medium-sized bowl. Mix in eggs one by one and then mix in vanilla. Combine baking soda, flour, baking powder, cloves and cinnamon; whisk into creamed mixture. Gently fold in the raisins, nuts and fruit cocktail. Make sure not to crush the fruits.
2.Place spoonfuls of batter on to greased cookie sheet. Bake for around 13 to 15 minutes in the preheated convection oven.

9.31 CLASSIC COCONUT MACAROONS WITH CHOCOLATE GLAZE

Total Time of cooking
25 minutes
Prep time 10 minutes
Cook time 15 minutes

Serving
36

Nutrition facts
(Per serving)
Calories 154
Fat 10g
Protein 3g
Carbs 14g

Ingredients:
- 14 ounces of sweetened condensed milk
- 5 1/2 cups of flaked coconut
- 1/8 teaspoon of salt
- 2 teaspoons of vanilla extract
- 2/3 cup of flour

For the chocolate glaze:
- 1/2 teaspoon of coconut oil
- 1 cup of semi-sweet chocolate chips

Instructions:
Follow the instructions below to make classic coconut macaroons with chocolate glaze.
1.Preheat the convection oven at 325°F.With baking paper, line a cookie sheet.
2.Mix in flour, coconut and salt together. Stir in vanilla and condensed milk.
3.Place spoonfuls of 1-inch balls onto a lined cookie sheet.
4.Bake for around 12 to 15 minutes in the preheated convection oven. Cooldown macaroons completely.
5.Melt coconut oil and chocolate chips in the microwave, stir well and coat the bottom of all cooled macaroons into chocolate glaze and spread remaining chocolate on top on top if you like. Keep in the refrigerator to set glaze and chill.

9.32 MOIST AND TASTY BASIC CHOCOLATE CAKE

Total Time of cooking
45 minutes
Prep time 10 minutes
Cook time 35 minutes

Serving
12

Nutrition facts
(Per serving)
Calories 248
Fat 10g
Protein 2g
Carbs 39g

Ingredients:
- 1 3/4 cups of flour
- 1 cup of hot boiling water
- 2 cups of sugar
- 3/4 cup of cocoa powder
- 1 cup of milk
- 2 eggs
- 1/2 cup of vegetable oil
- 2 teaspoons of baking soda
- 1 teaspoon of vanilla extract
- 1 1/2 teaspoons of baking powder

- 1/2 teaspoon of salt

Instructions:
Follow the instructions below to make a moist and tasty basic chocolate cake.
1.Preheat the convection oven at 325°F.
2.Combine flour, cocoa, baking powder, salt, sugar and baking soda in a large-sized bowl.
3.Mix in eggs, oil, vanilla and milk to dry ingredients mixture and mix with an electric beater on medium speed for 2 minutes. Gently add in hot boiling water mix until fully incorporated.
4.Spread batter into 3x8 inches greased and floured round cake pan and bake in the preheated convection oven for 25 to 35 minutes. Cool for some time before slicing. Serve with your favorite frosting and drizzle with a topping of your choice.

9.33 PERSIMMON AND WALNUTS COOKIES

Total Time of cooking
25 minutes
Prep time 10 minutes
Cook time 15 minutes

Serving
72 (6 dozen)

Nutrition facts
(Per serving)
Calories 42
Fat 2.1g
Protein 0.4g
Carbs 5.9g

Ingredients:
- 1 cup of white sugar
- 1 cup of persimmon pulp
- 1/2 cup of walnuts chopped
- 1 cup of all-purpose flour
- 1/2 cup of raisins
- 1/2 cup of shortening
- 1 egg
- 1/4 teaspoon of ground cloves
- 1/2 teaspoon of baking soda
- 1/2 teaspoon of salt

- 1/2 teaspoon of ground cinnamon
- 1/2 teaspoon of baking powder

Instructions:
Follow the instructions below to make a moist and tasty basic chocolate cake.
1.Preheat the convection oven at 325°F.
2.Beat together sugar and shortening in a large-sized bowl. Mix in the persimmon pulp and egg. Combine together baking soda, cloves, flour, baking powder, salt and cinnamon; mix into persimmon mixture. Stir in raisins and walnuts. Place teaspoonfuls of mixture onto greased cookie sheets 1 1/2 inches apart.
3.Bake in the preheated convection oven for around 14 to 15 minutes or until cookies edges are golden brown.

9.34 LEMON AND RICOTTA CHEESE DESSERT CAKE

Total time of cooking
1 hour
Prep time 10 minutes
Cook time 50 minutes

Serving
8

Nutrition facts
(Per serving)
Calories 314
Fat 16g
Protein 7.6g
Carbs 36.6g

Ingredients:
- 1 cup of ricotta cheese
- 1 cup of cake flour
- 1/4 cup of milk
- 1/2 cup of softened butter
- 3 eggs
- 3/4 cup of white sugar
- Zest and juice of 1 large lemon
- 2 teaspoons of baking powder
- 1 teaspoon of vanilla extract

Instructions:
Follow the instructions below to make a lemon and ricotta cheese dessert cake.
1. Preheat the convection oven at 300°F.
2. Combine flour and baking powder together in a small-sized bowl.
3. In a large-sized bowl, beat softened butter and sugar together using an electric beater. Mix in vanilla and eggs one at a time beat until completely combined. Put the lemon zest, ricotta cheese and lemon juice into the mixture and beat for 2 to 3 minutes on medium speed. Pour in milk and beat the mixture on low speed just to combine everything.
4. Spread batter into round 8 inches greased and lined springform pan.
5. Bake in the preheated convection oven for around 45 to 50 minutes; keep checking when a cake is baking, so it doesn't get burnt.

9.35 CREAM CHEESE CHOCOLATE CHIP BROWNIES

Total time of cooking
40 minutes
Prep time 10 minutes
Cook time 30 minutes

Serving
24

Nutrition facts
(Per serving)
Calories 275
Fat 14.9g
Protein 3.9g
Carbs 32.2g

Ingredients:
- 2 packages of frozen cookie dough (16 ounces)
- 2 packages of softened cream cheese (8 ounces)
- 3 eggs at room temperature
- Cooking spray
- 1 cup of white sugar
- 1 tablespoon of vanilla extract

Instructions:
Follow the instructions below to make cream cheese chocolate chip brownies.
1. Preheat the convection oven at 325°F. With cooking spray, coat the sides and bottom of the jelly roll pan.
2. Beat together sugar, cream cheese and eggs in a large-sized bowl with an electric mixer and beat until soft; put vanilla extract and beat for another minute.
3. Cut 1 roll of cookie dough and arrange it on the bottom of greased jelly roll pan. Spread cream cheese mixture over cookie layer. Cut and adjust the second roll layer on top of the cream cheese mixture layer.
4. Bake for around 30 minutes in the preheated convection oven until cookies are lightly browned. Cool down completely before slicing.

9.36 LEMON-FLAVORED BUTTERMILK PIE

Total time of cooking

40 minutes
Prep time 10 minutes
Cook time 30 minutes

Serving

8

Nutrition facts

(Per serving)
Calories 400
Fat 19g
Protein 4g
Carbs 51g

Ingredients:

- 1 pie crust unbaked (9 inches)
- 1 1/2 cups of white sugar
- 1 cup of buttermilk
- 1/2 cup of softened butter
- 3 tablespoons of all-purpose flour
- 2 teaspoons of vanilla extract
- 1/4 teaspoon of fresh nutmeg grated
- 3 eggs at room temperature
- 1 tablespoon of lemon juice

Instructions:

Follow the instructions below to make lemon-flavored buttermilk pie.
1.Preheat the convection oven at 325°F.
2.Spread Pie crust on a 9-inch pie plate.
3.Whisk eggs until fluffy. Beat in flour, butter and sugar until creamy. Stir in lemon, buttermilk, nutmeg and lemon juice, beat until mixed.
4.Spread the mixture into pie crust evenly and bake in the preheated convection oven for around 40 to 50 minutes until fully cooked.
5.Cool down the pie before serving.

9.37 CHIA SEEDS AND OATMEAL COOKIES

Total time of cooking

25 minutes
Prep time 10 minutes
Cook time 15 minutes

Serving

12

Nutrition facts

(Per serving)
Calories 262
Fat 8.2g
Protein 3.4g
Carbs 47.4g

Ingredients:

- 1 cup of cranberries dried
- 2 cups of rolled oats
- 1/4 cup of unsweetened coconut shredded
- 2/3 cup of applesauce
- 1 cup of brown sugar
- 1/2 cup of chocolate chips
- 2/3 cup of whole wheat flour
- 3 tablespoons of coconut oil
- 2 tablespoons of chia seeds
- 1/2 teaspoon of baking powder
- 1 teaspoon of ground cinnamon
- 1/2 teaspoon of salt
- 1 teaspoon of baking soda

Instructions:

Follow the instructions below to make chia seeds and oatmeal cookies.
1.Preheat the convection oven at 325°F.With baking paper, line a cookie sheet.
2.In a large-sized bowl, stir in brown sugar, chia seeds, baking soda, oats, cinnamon, baking powder, flour and salt. Mix coconut oil and applesauce with oat mixture until dough is fully incorporated. Gently fold in chocolate chips, coconut and cranberries into prepared dough. Place dough onto a baking paper-lined cookie sheet.
3.Bake in the preheated convection oven for around 10 to 15 minutes until edges are lightly brown.

9.38 TASTY AND MOIST LIME–WHITE CHOCOLATE MUFFINS

Total time of cooking
35 minutes
Prep time 10 minutes
Cook time 25 minutes

Serving
12

Nutrition facts
(Per serving)
Calories 295
Fat 12.6g
Protein 4.3g
Carbs 40.9g

Ingredients:
- 2/3 cup of white chocolate chips
- 2 cups of all-purpose flour
- 1/4 cup of coconut-flavored rum
- 1/2 cup of brown sugar(divided)
- 1/2 cup of lime juice
- 1/2 cup of white sugar
- 1/2 cup of melted butter
- 2 teaspoons of baking powder
- 3/4 teaspoon of salt
- 2 eggs
- 1/4 teaspoon of baking soda

Instructions:
Follow the instructions below to make tasty and moist lime white chocolate muffins.
1.Preheat the convection oven at 325°F.
2.Mix together white sugar, baking powder, salt,1/4 cup of brown sugar, flour and baking soda in a medium-sized bowl.
3.In another small-sized bowl, combine melted butter, eggs, lime juice and rum together. Gradually add into the flour mixture and mix until all ingredients are fully blended into each other. Stir in white chocolate chips.
4.Place batter evenly into greased muffin baking pan. Spread remaining brown sugar over the top of muffins.
5.Bake in the preheated convection oven for around 25 minutes or until light golden brown from top.

9.39 SIMPLE AND CRUNCHY CORNMEAL COOKIES

Total time of cooking
25 minutes
Prep time 10 minutes
Cook time 15 minutes

Serving
24

Nutrition facts
(Per serving)
Calories 122
Fat 6.8g
Protein 1.3g
Carbs 14.3g

Ingredients:
- 1/2 cup of cornmeal
- 3/4 cup of shortening
- 1 egg
- 1 1/2 cups of all-purpose flour
- 3/4 cup of white sugar
- 1 teaspoon of butter flavored extract
- 1/4 teaspoon of salt
- 1 teaspoon of vanilla extract
- 1 teaspoon of baking powder

Instructions:
Follow the instructions below to make simple and crunchy cornmeal cookies.
1.Beat together the sugar and shortening. Crack an egg and beat. Whisk baking powder, cornmeal and flour together. Put butter flavored extract, vanilla and salt and mix all ingredients together until fully incorporated.
2.Place spoonfuls onto coated cookie sheet. Bake in the convection oven to 350°F for around 12 to 15 minutes or until cookies are lightly golden brown.

9.40 APRICOT AND NUT SQUARE BARS

Total time of cooking
1 hour 10 minutes
Prep time 15 minutes
Cook time 55 minutes

Serving
32 bars

Nutrition facts
(Per serving)
Calories 105
Fat 4.4g
Protein 1.3g
Carbs 15.5g

Ingredients:
- 1 cup of all-purpose flour sifted
- 2/3 cup of apricots dried
- 1 cup of brown sugar packed
- 1/4 cup of white sugar
- 1/3 cup of confectioners' sugar for garnish
- 1/2 cup of softened butter
- 1/2 cup of walnuts chopped
- 2/3 cup of all-purpose flour sifted
- 1/2 teaspoon of vanilla extract
- 1/2 teaspoon of baking powder
- 2 eggs large
- 1/4 teaspoon of salt

Instructions:
Follow the instructions below to make apricot and nut square bars.
1. Preheat the convection oven at 325°F.
2. Boil apricots in the small-sized saucepan and boil for around to 10 minutes drain and set apricots aside, then thoroughly chop.
3. Cream 1/4 cup of sugar, butter and 1 cup of flour together until the mixture is crumbly. Spread the mixture into an 8x8 inch greased square pan, press down to make a crust. Bake in the preheated convection oven for around 20 to 25 minutes until crust is firm and light golden in color.
4. Combine brown sugar and eggs together in a large-sized bowl until completely blended. Mix baking powder, 1/3 cup of flour and salt together. Add into the egg mixture and mix. Fold in walnuts, apricots and vanilla. Place mixture over baked crust layer.
5. Bake in the preheated convection oven for around 25 to 30 minutes or until topping is set. Cool it down on a wire rack. Cut into bars and dust confectioners' sugar on top of bars.

9.41 DELICIOUS AND CHEWY CHOCOLATE CHIP COOKIES

Total time of cooking
27 minutes
Prep time 15 minutes
Cook time 12 minutes

Serving
45 cookies

Nutrition facts
(Per serving)
Calories 138
Fat 6g
Protein 1g
Carbs 17g

Ingredients:
- 1 3/4 cup of semisweet chocolate chips (additional for garnishing)
- 2 3/4 cups of all-purpose flour
- 1 1/4 cup of packed brown sugar
- 2 teaspoons of cornstarch
- 1 cup of melted unsalted butter
- 1/2 cup of sugar
- 1 1/2 teaspoon of vanilla extract
- 1 teaspoon of baking soda
- 1 egg large+1 egg yolk (at room temperature)
- 3/4 teaspoon of salt

Instructions:
Follow the instructions below to make delicious and chewy chocolate chip cookies.
1. In a large-sized bowl, combine both sugars and melted butter and mix. Stir in egg and egg yolk. Put vanilla mix until fully combine and set the bowl aside.
2. Whisk cornstarch, flour, baking soda and salt together in a medium-sized bowl. Slowly add in flour mixture to wet ingredients bowl and mix until fully incorporated. Fold in chocolate chips in the dough.
3. Cover and keep the dough in the refrigerator to chill for around 20 minutes.
4. Preheat the convection oven at 325°F. With baking paper, line the baking sheets.
5. Place dough on the lined baking sheets with rounded tablespoonfuls, 2 inches apart and sprinkle chocolate chips on top of cookies, and press slightly on the dough.
6. Bake for around 12 minutes; make sure cookies should be a little bit soft in the centers; they will cook on baking sheets completely. Do not bake too much otherwise; cookies will become hard.
7. Let stand for few minutes before serving.

9.42 TASTY AND MOIST RED VELVET CHEESECAKE

Total time of cooking
40 minutes
Prep time 15 minutes
Cook time 25 minutes

Serving
12

Nutrition facts
(Per serving)
Calories 499
Fat 36g
Protein 5g
Carbs 44g

Ingredients:
For Red velvet:
• 1/2 cup of vegetable oil
• 1 box of red velvet cake mix
• 1/3 cup of milk
• 1 egg

For Cheesecake(no-bake):
• 1 1/2 cups of heavy cream
• 12 ounces of cream cheese
• 1 teaspoon of vanilla

• 1 1/2 cups of powdered sugar
For topping/decorating:
• Whipped cream
• Raspberries

Instructions:
1.Preheat the convection oven at 350°F.Take 10 inches springform pan and grease bottom and sides of the pan with cooking spray.
2.Add egg, oil, dry cake mixes and milk and mix using an electric beater on medium speed for 2 minutes.
3.Pour the batter into the greased pan and bake in the preheated convection oven for around 20 to 25 minutes or check by inserting a wooden skewer or knife in the center if it comes out dry cake is done.
4.Whisk together powdered sugar, cream cheese and vanilla using an electric beater until smooth and fluffy. Mix in heavy cream and keep beating until the mixture is thick.
5.To loosen the cake, run a knife around the edges of the cake. Pour cheesecake mixture all over the cooled red velvet cake evenly. Cover with plastic wrap and keep in the refrigerator for at least 4 hours or overnight.
6.While serving, spread whipped cream on top of the cake and evenly layer out with cake knife place raspberries on top of the cream, slice and enjoy!

9.43 BUTTER BARS WITH BAKED LEMON CURD FILLING

Total time of cooking
50 minutes
Prep time 10 minutes
Cook time 40 minutes

Serving
16

Nutrition facts
(Per serving)
Calories 179
Fat 8g
Protein 2g
Carbs 25g

Ingredients:
For the butter crust:
• 1/2 cup of powdered sugar(plus 2 tablespoons of additional powdered sugar)
• 10 tablespoons of butter at room temperature
• 1/4 teaspoon of salt
• 1 1/4 cups of flour
For the lemon filling:
• 1/3 cup of lemon juice
• 3 eggs large at room temperature
• 1 tablespoon of lemon zest

• 1 cup of granulated sugar
• 1/2 teaspoon of baking powder
• 3 tablespoons of flour

Instructions:
Follow the instructions below to make butter bars with baked lemon curd filling.
1.Preheat the convection oven at 325°F.Combine together powdered sugar, salt and flour. Add in butter and mix until the mixture gets crumbly. Shift the mixture to 9x9 inches greased pan and press down on the pan to make a crust.
2.Bake in the preheated convection oven for around 15 to 20 minutes until crust is lightly browned.
3.Beat together all the filling ingredients until thick and creamy.
4.Spread over the baked crust evenly and Bake in the convection oven for another 18 to 20 minutes.
5.Cool the bars fully, sprinkle powdered sugar all over and cut into bars.

9.44 THE BEST BANOFFEE PIE

Total time of cooking
3 hour 10 minutes
Prep time 10 minutes
Cook time 3 hour

Serving
8

Nutrition facts
(Per serving)
Calories 321
Fat 22g
Protein 2g
Carbs 30g

Ingredients:
* 1 1/2 cups of heavy cream
* 1 can of sweetened condensed milk (approx. 14oz)
* 2 tablespoons of sugar
* 3 bananas peeled and sliced
* 1 graham cracker crust
* 1 teaspoon of vanilla

Instructions:
Follow the instructions below to make the best banoffee pie.
1.Spread one can of condensed milk into a small-sized casserole dish and wrap the dish with heavy-duty foil tightly.
2.Adjust the casserole dish to a larger baking pan and fill the pan with 3/4 inches of water. Bake in the preheated convection oven at 400°F for 60 to 90 minutes or until condensed milk becomes golden brown in color. Set the casserole dish aside to cool.
3.Place sliced bananas into the bottom of the crust and spread cooled condensed milk all over the top.
4.Beat sugar, cream and vanilla in a large-sized bowl until fluffy. Spread whipped cream on top of the pie and refrigerate for 2 to 3 hours. Once chilled, serve and enjoy!

9.45 STARBUCKS INSPIRED SWIRL RASPBERRY POUND LOAF WITH FROSTING

Total time of cooking
1 hour 30 minutes
Prep time 30 minutes
Cook time 1 hour

Serving
16 slices

Nutrition facts
(Per serving)
Calories 135
Fat 8g
Protein 2g
Carbs 14g

Ingredients:
* 1/3 cup of raspberry fruit spread seedless
* 2/3 cup of milk
* 1 box of pound cake mix
* 2 eggs
* 6 drops of red food coloring
* 1/4 cup of butter
* 1 teaspoon of lemon juice
* For the frosting:
* 1 cup of powdered sugar
* 1 teaspoon of lemon juice
* 8 ounces of softened cream cheese

Instructions:
Follow the instructions below to make Starbucks inspired swirl raspberry pound loaf with frosting.
1.Preheat the convection oven at 325°F.Combine butter, eggs, pound cake mix and milk. With an electric mixer, beat on medium speed for around 2 to 3 minutes.
2.Separate 1/3 of the cake batter and mix in food coloring and raspberry spread.
3.Mix in lemon juice in the white batter.
4.First, spread the white batter in greased and floured 9x5 inches loaf pan, then spread layers of red and white until the batter finishes. Using a wooden skewer, swirl the batter lightly.
5.Bake in the preheated convection oven for around 50 to 60 minutes. Once baked, let the loaf cool down for some time.
6.Whisk cream cheese on medium-high speed using an electric beater until soft. Mix in lemon juice and powdered sugar, keep beating until just creamy. Pipe the frosting on the loaf.

9.46 LEMON-HONEY GLAZE CHEESECAKE BAKLAVA

Total time of cooking
1 hour
Prep time 25 minutes
Cook time 35 minutes

Serving
36

Nutrition facts
(Per serving)
Calories 147
Fat 10g
Protein 2g
Carbs 14g

Ingredients:
- 2 cups of chopped walnuts
- 16 ounces of softened cream cheese
- 2 cans of Pillsbury crescent refrigerated (8 oz each)
- 1 1/2 cups of sugar
- 1/4 cup of honey
- 1/2 teaspoon of lemon peel grated
- 1 teaspoon of fresh lemon juice
- 1/2 teaspoon of ground cinnamon

Instructions:
Follow the instructions below to make lemon-honey glaze cheesecake baklava.
1.Preheat the convection oven at 325°F.Unroll and spread 1 can of crescent into 9x13 inches ungreased pan.
2.Beat together 1 cup of sugar, lemon peel and cream cheese with an electric mixer on medium speed until foamy. Pour the batter over the prepared dough and set it aside.
3.Mix in remaining 1/2 cup of sugar, cinnamon and walnuts together in a small-sized bowl. Place over cream cheese layer.
4.Spread the second crescent sheet over the first to cover the filling completely.
5.Mix in honey and lemon juice and brush the top of the dough with honey lemon glaze.
6.Bake in the preheated convection oven for around 30 to 35 minutes or until lightly browned. Cool and then keep in the refrigerator for around 3 hours or overnight. Slice and enjoy!

9.47 BEST-EVER PLUM PUDDING DESSERT BAKED

Total time of cooking
55 minutes
Prep time 15 minutes
Cook time 40 minutes

Serving
12

Nutrition facts
(Per serving)
Calories 265
Fat 13.4g
Protein 4.6g
Carbs 34.5g

Ingredients:
- 3 cups of bread cubes
- 1 cup of golden raisins
- 1/2 cup of butter
- 1 cup of currants dried
- 1/2 cup of pecans chopped
- 3/4 cup of white sugar
- 1 tablespoon of all-purpose flour
- 2 teaspoons of ground cinnamon
- 1/2 teaspoon of pumpkin pie spice
- 1/2 teaspoon of ground allspice
- 5 eggs
- 1/2 teaspoon of ground cloves

Instructions:
Follow the instructions below to make the best-ever plum pudding dessert baked.
1.Preheat the convection oven at 325°F.
2.Cream sugar and butter together. Crack egg one at a time and keep beating until completely incorporated. With flour, mix currants, pecans and raisins in a separate medium-sized bowl. Fold the flour mixture into the butter mixture. Stir in cinnamon, bread, cloves, allspice and pumpkin pie spice. Spread the mixture into an 8x8 inches baking dish.
3.Bake in the preheated convection oven for around 35 to 40 minutes.

9.48 EASY AND MOIST RED VELVET COOKIES

Total time of cooking
20 minutes
Prep time 10 minutes
Cook time 10 minutes

Serving
24 cookies

Nutrition facts
(Per serving)
Calories 161
Fat 10g
Protein 1g
Carbs 17g

Ingredients:
- 1 cup of white chocolate chips
- 1 box of red velvet cake mix
- 1/2 cup of vegetable oil
- 2 eggs

Instructions:
Follow the instructions below to make easy and moist velvet cookies.
1. Preheat the convection oven at 325°F.
2. Mix in eggs, cake mix and oil together until completely blended. Fold in white chocolate chips.
3. Place heaping tablespoonfuls on a baking paper-lined sheet.
4. Bake for around 8 to 10 minutes in the preheated convection oven. Cool down for some time on the wire rack before serving.

9.49 THE PERFECT BAKED RAISIN RICE PUDDING

Total time of cooking
1 hour 30 minutes
Prep time 30 minutes
Cook time 1 hour

Serving
10-12

Nutrition facts
(Per serving)
Calories 155
Fat 2.4g
Protein 4.5g
Carbs 28.9g

Ingredients:
- 2 cups of milk
- 1 cup of white rice uncooked
- 1/3 cup of raisins
- 1/2 cup of white sugar
- 2 cups of water
- 1 teaspoon of vanilla extract
- 3 beaten eggs
- 1 pinch of ground nutmeg
- 1/2 teaspoon of salt

Instructions:
Follow the instructions below to make the perfect baked raisin rice pudding.
1. Preheat the convection oven at 300°F.
2. Put uncooked rice and water in 3 quarter saucepans, boil for some time, reduce the heat and keep boiling for 25 to 30 minutes.
3. Mix in milk, vanilla extract, sugar, beaten eggs and salt in a large-sized bowl. Add in rice and raisins and stir. Spread the mixture into a casserole dish.
4. Bake in the preheated convection oven for around 30 minutes. After 30 minutes, mix pudding and sprinkle the top with nutmeg. Bake for another 30 minutes.

9.50 ALMOND CHOCOLATE AND COCONUT CAKE

Total time of cooking
1 hour
Prep time 30 minutes
Cook time 30 minutes

Serving
16

Nutrition facts
(Per serving)
Calories 486
Fat 34.5g
Protein 6.2g
Carbs 44.1g

Ingredients:
- 1 cup of chocolate chips
- 1 bag of coconut shredded (14 ounces)
- 1 package of chocolate cake mix
- 1 cup of evaporated milk
- 26 marshmallows large
- 1/2 cup of butter
- 1/2 cup of whole almonds
- 1/2 cup of white sugar
- 1 cup of white sugar
- 1/3 cup of vegetable oil
- 1/2 cup of evaporated milk
- 1 cup of water
- 3 eggs

Instructions:
1.Preheat the convection oven at 325°F.
2.Mix in chocolate cake mix, eggs, water and oil in a large-sized bowl; beat on medium speed with an electric mixer until creamy, for around 2 minutes. Spread mixture into 9x13 inches greased pan.
3.Bake for around 25 to 30 minutes in the preheated convection oven. Check by putting a wooden skewer in the cake if it comes out clean; the cake is done.
4.Combine 1 cup of sugar, marshmallows and 1 cup of evaporated milk together in a large-sized pot; on medium heat, stir and cook until marshmallows are completely melted for 5 minutes. Mix in coconut and spread coconut mixture evenly over hot cake.
5.Add butter,1/2 cup of evaporated milk and 1/2 cup of sugar in a medium-sized saucepan; bring to 1 to 2 boils and keep stirring for few minutes. Remove from stove and fold in almonds and chocolate chips in the mixture. Pour the mixture over the coconut layer evenly.
6.Cool the cake until the chocolate and coconut layers are fully set, for around 30 minutes.

9.51 TOASTER OVEN PEANUT BUTTER COOKIES

Total time of cooking
51 minutes
Prep time: 10 minutes
Cook time: 11 minutes

Serving
8 Cookies

Nutrition Facts
(Per Serving)
Calories 126kcal
Fat 7.3g
Protein 3.3g
Carbs 12.8g

Ingredients
- Natural creamy peanut butter (1 tbsp.)
- tablespoons softened unsalted butter
- 1/8 teaspoon vanilla extract (pure)
- 1/4 cup organic brown sugar
- 1/3 cup whole wheat flour
- 1 egg white (big)
- A quarter teaspoon of baking powder
- A quarter teaspoon of baking soda
- Coarsely sliced tiny dark chocolate
- 3-4 peanut butter cups
- 1/8 teaspoon sea salt (need more for sprinkling)

Instructions
1.Cream the peanut butter, butter, and sugar together in a medium mixing basin with a hand mixer until light and fluffy. Whisk the egg white and vanilla extract in a separate bowl. Reduce the mixer's speed to low and add the baking powder, baking soda, flour, and salt.
2.Refrigerate dough for 30 minutes after mixing in chopped peanut butter cups.
3.Preheat your toaster oven to 375°F and gently oil or line your cookie sheet with a toaster oven silicone baking mat while the dough chills.
4.Roll dough into 8 balls and space them at least 1 inch apart on the prepared cookie sheet. If using, season the dough with salt.
5.Bake for 13 mins, or until the edges are gently brown and the cookies are set.
6.Cool on baking sheet (at least for 5 mins) before moving to wire shelf to cool completely.

Total time of cooking

2 hrs 45 minutes
Prep Time: 2 hrs
Cook Time: 45 minutes

Servings

8

Nutrition facts

(per serving)
Calories 382 kcal
Fat 19g
Protein 4g
Carbs 50g

Ingredients

Strawberry pie crust
*   1 tablespoon granulated sugar
*   1/2 cup freeze-dried strawberries
*   1/2 teaspoon fine sea salt
*   1/2 cups flour (more will be needed for dusting)
*   1/4 cup ice water, plus more as needed
*   sticks cold unsalted butter (remember to cut it into 1/2 inch cubes)

Filling and finishing
*   1 cup halved fresh strawberries
*   1 tsp fine sea salt
*   1 tablespoon lemon juice, freshly squeezed
*   1/2 teaspoon vanilla extract (pure)
*   tsp granulated sugar
*   Corn starch, 1/3 cup
*   1 egg white (big)
*   Sugar for sanding and finishing

Instructions

Make the pie crust:

1. Pulse the strawberries and granulated sugar into a fine powder in a food processor. Continue to process until the flour and salt are thoroughly mixed.

2. Pulse in the butter in a kitchen robot until the mixture looks like tiny peas. Place in a medium mixing basin.

3. Make a hole in the flours mixture and put in in the ice water. Hand-mix until the mixture comes together consistently but isn't sticky or crusty. If required, add one tbs of water at a time.

4. Half the pie dough and roll out each half into a 1-inch-thick disk. Refrigerate for 30 minutes (at least) or up to overnight after wrapping each disk snugly in plastic wrap.

Prepare the filling:

1. Toss the strawberries, lemon juice, vanilla, and salt together in a large mixing dish.

2. Mix together the sugar and the corn starch in a separate small dish. Toss the strawberries with the mixture and toss well to incorporate.

3. Whisk together the egg white and 1 tablespoon water in a separate small dish, to produce an egg wash. Reserve.

Assemble the pie:

1. Create disk of dough to 1/4 inch thickness on a lightly floured board. Set in a 9-inch pie plate and use scissors to cut the extra crust around the edge so that just 1/2 inch drapes over the plate's edge.

2. Fill the pie crust with the mixture and place it in the refrigerator while you work on the lattice.

3. Roll out another dough disk to a thickness of 1/4 inch. Cut the dough into 1.5-inch-wide strips. Lay 5 pieces vertically and equally spaced on top of the pie to produce the lattice crust.

4. Fold the other strips back to uncover the pie filling, then place one of the remaining pieces horizontally over the pie. Fold the vertical strips over the pie, then the opposite vertical strips over the horizontal strip.

5. Place a fresh horizontal stripe on top of the previous one, then fold the vertical strips over the new horizontal strip once again. Continue weaving over and under with the remaining strips until you have a lattice. Roll up the overhanging bottom crust and crimp the pie crust's edge as desired.

6. Preheat the oven to 425°F and chill the pie for 20 minutes. Brush the surface of the pie with the egg wash and sprinkle with the sanding sugar after the oven is preheated. Bake for 45 minutes (at least), until the top starts to brown slightly and the filling is bubbling. Before slicing and serving, allow the cake to cool fully.

9.53 CHOCOLATE CHIP COOKIE FOR MODERN TIMES

Total time of cooking
45 minutes
Prep Time: 15 minutes
Cook Time: 30 minutes

Servings
36 cookies

Nutrition facts
(per serving)
Calories 205 kcal
Fat 11g
Protein 3g
Carbs 27g

Ingredients
- 1 1/2 cups all-purpose flour
- 1 cup almond flour
- 1 1/2 cups light brown sugar
- 1/2 cup granulated sugar
- 1 tbsp baking soda
- 1 tbsp flaky sea salt
- A dozen big eggs, room temperature
- 15 ounces bittersweet chocolate, chopped
- tablespoons pure vanilla extract
- 1 cup unsalted butter, melted

Instructions
1.Preheat the oven to about 375° F for 25 minutes. Use parchment paper or silicone cooking mats to line two baking sheets.
2.Whisk all together with the baking soda, sugars, salt and flours in a medium mixing basin. Whisk the melted butter, eggs, and vanilla together quickly in a separate small basin. Mix dry and wet ingredients in a bowl. Make sure the chocolate chunks are uniformly spread throughout the dough, keeping a little amount for the tops.
3.Take a heaping spoonful of dough and shape it into balls between your palms. Arrange the cookies on the prepared baking pans, leaving plenty of room between them. Reserve the chocolate bits and press them into the tops of the cookies. Bake for 10 to 12 minutes, one sheet at a time, until crispy on the outer edges and soft and slightly underbaked on the interior.
4.Pull out the pan from the oven and season with salt, or leave it out if salt isn't your thing. Allow cooling for at least 2 minutes on the pan before transferring to plates to serve warm.

9.54 CHRISTMAS MAGIC COOKIE BARS

Total time of cooking
35 minutes
Prep Time: 10 minutes
Cook Time: 25 minutes

Servings
25

Nutrition facts
(per serving)
Calories 150 kcal
Fat 7g
Protein 1g
Carbs 20g

Ingredients
- 1 1/2 cups baking crumbs (chocolate)
- 1/3 cup salted butter, melted
- 1 1/2 cups unsweetened flaked coconut
- 1 can of condensed dulce de Leche, 300 mL (sweetened)
- 1 cup chocolate chips (semi-sweet)
- 1 cup chopped Christmas cherries (red and green)

Instructions
1.Preheat the oven to 350 degrees Fahrenheit.
2.In an 8x8 pan, melt the butter. If desired, line the pan with tinfoil to make removal simpler.
3.Make a uniform layer of baking crumbs on top of the butter.
4.Drop spoonfuls of condensed milk on top of the crumbs to make an equal layer.
5.Over the condensed milk, sprinkle the following three ingredients in the order listed. Gently press down.
6.Bake for 90 minutes, until the coconut is golden brown.
7.Remove from the oven.
8.Let it cool fully in the pan before slicing. To remove it, pull it out with tinfoil and then slice it.

Total time of cooking

25 minutes
Prep time: 15 minutes
Cook time: 10 minutes

Servings

25

Nutrition facts

(per serving)
Calories: 388
Fat: 19g
Protein: 4g
Carbs: 52g

Ingredients

- 3/4 cup sugar (dark brown)
- 1 cup cold, diced butter
- A single huge egg
- 1/2 cup sugar (granulated)
- tbsp vanilla extract
- 1 cup chocolate chips
- 1 ½ cup flour (all-purpose)
- 1 egg yolk
- 1 pound of cake flour
- 1 tsp. Salt (kosher)
- 1 teaspoon powdered baking soda
- 1 teaspoon bicarbonate of soda

Instructions

1.Preheat the oven to 400 degrees Fahrenheit. Use parchment paper or silpats to line two baking sheets.
2.Add brown sugar cubed butter and granulated sugar to the bowl of a stand mixer fitted with the paddle attachment.
3.Mix at low speed with your appliance for a few seconds, then gradually raise to medium-high for approximately 3-4 minutes, or until thoroughly combined and fluffy.
4.Reduce the speed of the mixer and put in the egg and egg yolk, followed by the vanilla extract. Mix on medium for approximately 30 seconds, scraping down the sides and bottom with a rubber spatula as required, until thoroughly combined.
5.Combine salt, baking soda, both flours, and baking powder in a mixing bowl with the mixer turned off. Reduce to a moderate speed and stir until just blended. Don't overmix the ingredients.
6.Add chocolate chips to the mix. Turn off the mixer,remove from it and knead the dough a little to make sure the chocolate chips are uniformly distributed.
7.Roll the dough into 2 oz. Balls between your hands to produce a smooth surface. Place approximately 2 inches apart on baking sheets that have been prepped.
Bake:
1.Bake for 4-5 minutes in a preheated oven with convection, then flip baking trays and bake for another 4-5 minutes with convection.
2.Allow cooling on trays for a few minutes before transferring to wire racks.

9.56 MERINGUE COOKIES.

Total time of cooking
55 minutes
Prep time: 40 minutes
Cook time: 15 minutes

Servings
24

Nutritional facts
(Per Serving)
Calories 22.8 kcal
Fat 0.0 g
Protein 0.3 g
Carbs 5.5 g

Ingredients
- 2/3 cup sugar, granulated
- egg whites
- 1/2 teaspoon of your favourite seasoning (strawberry vanilla, almond, rum, etc.)
- A quarter teaspoon of cream of tartar

Instructions
1.Whip cream of tartar with whites egg on high speed until thick and frothy. Slowly add the sugar to the bowl and whip until the mixture holds firm, glossy peaks.

2.Stir in the flavouring extract and any other ingredients using a spatula. Spoon 1/2-tablespoon quantities onto cooking parchment-lined 12- by 15-inch baking sheets, forming 1-inch-wide mounds approximately 1 inch apart.

3.Bake meringues until dry and firm to the touch on the surface and practically dry on the inside, 30 to 35 minutes in a 275° conventional or convection oven; if baking two sheets at once in one oven, rotate their positions midway through baking. Allow to set on sheets for 5 minutes before sliding a spatula beneath the meringues and transferring to racks to cool entirely.

9.57 LEMON SQUARES

Total time of cooking
45 minutes
Prep time: 20 minutes
Cook time: 25 Min

Servings
12

Nutritional facts
(Per Serving)
Calories 83.3 kcal
Fat 1.4g
Protein 1.6g
Carbs 16.3 g

Ingredients
- 1 pound of sugar
- 1 tablespoon of butter
- 1/4 cup powdered sugar
- 1 teaspoon lemon peel grated
- 1-1/4 cup flour
- 1 egg
- 1 teaspoon powdered baking soda
- 2-3 teaspoons of lemon juice

instructions
1.Mix the butter and powdered sugar in a large mixing bowl and beat until light and fluffy. 1 cup flour, gradually added until well combined. Fill a small casserole baking dish halfway with the mixture. Heat the oven to around 350 ° F and bake the dish for 10 minutes.

2.Combine the leftover flour and baking powder in the medium-sized mixing bowl, then add the eggs one at a time. Slowly incorporate the other ingredients into the mixture. Pour the mixture on top of the cake crust.

3.Heat the oven to 350°F and bake the dish for 15 minutes. Allow for thorough cooling before cutting into squares.

9.58 OVEN CHOCOLATE FUDGE CAKE

Total time of cooking
1 hour 30 minutes
Prep Time: 15 minutes
Cook Time: 15 minutes

Servings
4

Nutritional facts
(Per Serving)
Calories 379
Fat 30g
Protein 5g
Carbs 30g

ingredients
- 3-4 teaspoons of butter
- 1 ½ cups semi-sweet chocolate chips
- eggs
- 1 teaspoon espresso powder
- 1 teaspoon of flour
- A quarter teaspoon of vanilla extract

Instructions
1. Preheat the toaster oven to 400 degrees using the "Bake" feature.
2. Using parchment paper, line the bottoms of four separate tartlet pans and gently brush the sides with oil. Place the prepared pans on a quarter sheet pan or another size suitable for your toaster oven. If your oven is tiny; you may need to bake in two batches.
3. Melt the chocolate and butter in a medium microwave-safe dish in 20-second intervals, stirring after each, until smooth. Check to see whether all of the chocolate has melted and is smooth.
4. Remove from the microwave once melted and put aside.
5. While the chocolate cools, whisk the eggs on low speed until foamy, then increase to high speed and whip until the eggs are light and fluffy and have tripled in volume.
6. In a separate bowl, combine the flour and espresso powder.
7. Combine the chocolate and the egg mixture in a large mixing bowl.
8. Pour the batter into the tartlet pans, divide it equally, and bake for 15 minutes. The top should be solid, while the center should be soft, like a mousse, and the sides should be hard.
9. Wait 30 minutes (at least) for the cake to cool in the tartlet pans before removing it. Before serving, let it cool somewhat.

9.59 OVEN CHOCOLATE COOKIES

Total time of cooking
27 minutes
Prep time: 10 minutes
Cook time: 7 minutes

Servings
6

Nutrition Facts
(Per Serving)
Calories 104 kcal
Fat 5.6g
Protein 1.7g
Carbs 14g

Ingredients
- 1 1/2 tablespoons unsalted butter, melted
- teaspoons brown sugar
- 1 big egg yolk
- 1/4 teaspoon Vanilla Extract
- tablespoons Chocolate Chips, divided
- 1/2 teaspoons unsweetened baking powder
- 1/4 cup white whole wheat flour
- 1 tsp. Cocoa powder
- 1 tsp. fine sea salt
- Baking Soda, 1/4 teaspoon

Instructions
1. Mix sugar and butter until fluffy in a medium mixing dish with a hand-held mixer, (about two minutes).
2. Combine the egg yolk and vanilla extract in a mixing bowl.
3. Add the baking soda, flour, cocoa powder, and salt to the mixer at the lowest speed. Mix just until everything is well blended. 2 tablespoons chocolate chips 2 teaspoons
4. Refrigerate cookie dough for at least 10 minutes.
5. Heat your toaster oven to 350°F as the dough chills. Use a silicone baking mat to line your cookie sheet or lightly grease it.
6. Make tablespoon-sized balls out of cooled dough. On the prepared pan, space them at least 2 inches apart. On the top of the dought Place the remaining chocolate chips on top of the dough and gently push them in.
7. Bake them for 7 minutes, until they are set, but the centers are still puffy and soft.
8. Allow for a few minutes of cooling on the pan before transferring to a cooling rack.

6.60 EASY CINNAMON SUGAR BAKED APPLES

Total time of cooking
60 minutes
Prep time: 15 minutes
Cook time: 45 minutes

Servings
4-8

Nutrition Facts
(Per Serving)
Calories 90 kcal
Protein 2g
Carbs 18g
Fat 2g

Ingredients
- Tbsp butter
- A tablespoon of cinnamon sugar
- red apples
- 1 Tbsp cinnamon
- 1/3 cup brown sugar

Instructions
1.Preheat the oven to 400° F for convection baking. The apples should be washed and chopped on the top and bottom. Cut around the core in the apple's center using a paring knife.
2.Take your fingers and push the apple's core out. If removing the core proves difficult, cut a little deeper around the core. Cut the apples in half along the center to make a shallow baking dish. Each apple should resemble a barrel sliced in half with two cut edges.
3.Place the apples cut side up and cut side down in the dish.
4.Melt the butter in a saucepan. Brown sugar should be added when the butter is still hot. Once the brown sugar has dissolved, pour the mixture over the apples and roll them around in it to fully cover each piece.
5.Cover with alluminium foil and bake at 400°F for 26 minutes on convection.
6.Remove the foil and sprinkle the cinnamon and cinnamon sugar on top of each piece. The dish is made using pure cinnamon.
7.Cook for 15 minutes at 400°F convection oven, uncovered, or until golden brown on top. Remove the apples from the oven and spread the liquid from the pan over them.
8.Put ice cream on top of the hot apple for a fast and simple dessert.

9.61 OVEN BAKED PEARS

Total time of cooking
30 minutes
Prep Time: 5 minutes
Cook Time: 25 minutes

Servings
2

Nutrition Facts
(Per Serving)
Calories 118 kcal
Fat 7g
Protein 1g
Carbs 14g

Ingredients
- 1/8 teaspoon cinnamon powder
- 1 teaspoon maple syrup (pure)
- 1 Red Anjou Pear
- tbsp. pecans, chopped
- Chocolate Chips (Semisweet)

Optional Toppings:
- Ice Cream with Vanilla Flavor
- Greek Yogurt
- Whipped Cream

Instructions
1.Heat the toaster oven to 350 degrees F with the cooking rack in the lowest position. A baking dish or cookie sheet should be lightly oiled.
2.Cut the pear in half and scoop out the seeds with a teaspoon. Slice a tiny bit from the rear of the halves if they don't lie flat.
3.Sprinkle cinnamon over the pear halves in the baking dish, then fill with chocolate chips and pecan bits. Drizzle maple syrup over both pieces of the sandwich.
4.Bake for 25/35 minutes, or until pears are softened. The baking time may vary based on the pear type and maturity.
5.Serve warm with a ball of vanilla ice cream or yogurt on top.

Total time of cooking

55 minutes
Cook time: 40 minutes
Prep time: 15 minutes
Servings: 12

Nutrition facts

(per serving)
Calories 283 kcal
Fat 14g
Protein 6g
Carbs 37g

Ingredients

- 230 g white all-purpose plain flour
- 180g sugar
- 180 g full-fat yogurt
- 1 tsp turmeric medium eggs
- 100ml oil
- 1 pinch of salt
- 1/2 orange (medium)
- 1 tbsp orange and lemon zest
- 1/2 teaspoon bicarbonate of soda
- a half teaspoon of baking powder

Instructions

1. Heat the oven to 375°F
2. Grease the baking pan (mine is 12cm X 20cm). Use a little veil of oil or butter. The spray might also suffice.
3. Whisk together the eggs and sugar with a hand electric whisker until frothy. Pour in the oil a bit at a time, constantly whisking until all of it is incorporated.
4. Toss in the yogurt and stir to combine. Don't over whisk the mixture. Combine the zest and salt in a bowl.
5. Add the baking powder, soda bicarbonate, and orange juice to a small container, such as a coffee cup or something similar, and stir to combine.
6. Mix in the flour and turmeric powder quickly with a spatula until the flour is almost completely absorbed into the cake batter. Maybe there are lumps in the batter, but don't worry; what matters is that you don't overmix it.
7. Take about 1/3 of the cake mix (batter) and place it in a separate bowl. Toss in the cacao powder and stir lightly to incorporate it.
8. Pour the cacao mix into a centerline over the turmeric cake mix in the prepared pan and pour the 2/3 cake mix into the prepared tin. Make swirling motions with a chopstick or the handle of a wooden spoon to give the cake a marble look. You don't want to make too many since you want the marble patterns instead of combining and homogenizing the two batters.
9. Heat the oven at 350°F and bake the marble cake for 40 minutes. If the skewer test comes out clean and the cake has shrunk somewhat, it's ready.
10. Pull out from the oven and set aside to cool for 5 minutes. Allow it to cool entirely on a cooling rack after removing it from the tin.
11. It'll be ready to eat in 30-40 minutes. If desired, serve with a chocolate drizzle or a scoop of ice cream.

9.63 FRESH HOMEMADE PEACH PIE

Total time of cooking
2 hrs 10 minutes
Prep time: 2 hrs
Cook time: 10 minutes

Servings
5

Nutrition facts
(per serving)
Calories 262.1 kcal
Fat 11.7g
Protein 2.2g
Carbs 38.5g

Ingredients
- 1 package room temperature cream cheese
- A quarter cup of lemon juice
- 1/2 cup peeled and sliced firm ripe peaches
- A quarter cup of sugar
- A quarter cup of corn starch
- A quarter cup of orange juice

Instructions
1. Prick sides and bottom of the unbaked dough in the pan at 1-inch intervals using a fork, 15 to 20 minutes until brown in a 375° conventional or convection oven; cool on a rack.
2. Whisk cream cheese and 1/2 cup sugar until smooth. Spread evenly over the cold puff pastry's bottom.
3. In a blender, combine 1 cup sliced peaches, the remaining 3/4 cup sugar, orange juice, and corn starch until smooth. Pour into a 3- to 4-quart saucepan and cook, constantly stirring, for 4 minutes, or until the mixture boils and thickens. Pull out the pan off the heat and squeeze in the lemon juice.
4. To coat the slices, stir the remaining 5 1/2 cups of peaches into the hot peach glaze. Allow for a 25-minute cooling period before scraping the cream cheese mixture into the crust.
5. Chill for at least 3 hours, until stiff enough to cut. Cut into wedges and serve.

9.64 ORANGE BUTTER COOKIES

Total time of cooking
2 hrs 10 minutes
Cook time: 10 minutes
Prep time: 2 hrs

Servings
10

Nutrition facts
(per serving)
Calories 82.9 kcal
Fat 2.2 g
Protein 0.8 g
Carbs 15.2 g

Ingredients
- 1 cup all-purpose flour
- 1 stick sweet cream butter, no salt
- 1 valencia orange, peeled and zested
- 1/2 cup sugar, granulated
- 1 teaspoon vanilla extract
- A single egg
- 1–2 cups powdered sugar
- A tablespoon of orange juice

Instructions
1. Preheat the oven to 350 degrees Fahrenheit. Combine the butter, 1/2 cup sugar, and orange zest in a mixing bowl. Orange to be saved for juice later in the recipe.
2. Then add the eggs and vanilla extract. Remember to gently scrape down the sides of the bowl and stir slightly.
3. Mix in the flour until it's completely combined. Turn out onto the counter and knead once or twice to ensure a cohesive mass has formed.
4. Dividing the dough into thirds. Place the dough in a food plastic bag and seal it.
5. One-third at a time should be used. Other dough portions should be chilled until ready to use. Roll out to a thickness of approximately 1/4 inch. Cut out using cookie cutters.
6. 10 minutes in the oven When you take it out of the oven, the edges should be gently browned. Allow cooling on a wire rack.
7. Make a glaze using the Valencia orange juice that has been set aside. Begin with 2 tablespoons of juice. Using roughly a cup of powdered sugar, make a thick glaze.
8. Using a butter knife, spread the glaze on cookies. Allow to air-dry overnight. Keep the container sealed.

Total time of cooking

60 minutes
Cook time: 40 minutes
Prep time: 20 minutes

Servings

6

Nutrition facts

(per serving)
Calories 150 kcal
Protein 7g
Fat 4g
Carbs 30g

Ingredients

- Spelled flour (200 g)
- 275 g flour
- 1 tbsp sugar
- 1 tbsp orange
- 1 tbsp lemon zest
- 25 g of live yeast
- 1 cup lukewarm milk
- 80 g melted butter
- tbsp chia seeds
- tbsp icing sugar
- 1 softly beaten medium egg

For the filling

- 1/2 cup of jam
- 1 tbsp chia seeds
- 1/2 cup chopped and roasted mixed nuts

Instructions

1.Blend the two kinds of flour, chia seeds, and salt in a larger mixing basin and stir to combine. Add the eggs, lemon, and orange rind/zest at the center of the flours. Set it aside.

2.Combine the yeast, 4 tbsp sugar, and 100 mL warm milk in a cup. Mix vigorously until the yeast and sugar are fully dissolved. Pour this mixture into the well and set it aside for 10-15 minutes, or until it starts to boil.

3.Knead the dough with the remaining milk, room temperature butter, or melted butter. Knead until your hands are free of any dough that was originally quite sticky.

4.Take the dough and give it the shape of a ball and place it in a basin to rest until it doubles or triples in size, covered with a cloth.

5.Roll the dough into one or two rectangles on a lightly floured or oiled board.

6.Spread the jam evenly with the back of a spoon, then top with the roasted nuts and chia seeds.

7.Roll out the dough on a table, cut it into 1 inch or 2.5 cm thick rolls, and set them on an oiled pan with minimal space between them.

8.Preheat the oven to 185 degrees Celsius (375 degrees Fahrenheit).

9.Allow the buns to rise for another 10-15 minutes while the oven warms up.

10.Place the buns in the oven after softly biting the egg and egg washing them. Bake for 30/35 minutes, or until a beautiful light brown color has developed.

Conclusion

On the planet of recipes, the convection oven is one of the best inventions. It is like a savior for cooking freaks, those who want to save their time by cooking quickly and without much effort. The convection oven has a heating element and inside fan, which flow air in such a miraculous way that heat is divided among the whole dish.

You can keep the dishes wherever you want in the oven. However, avoid putting too many dishes simultaneously as this can affect the performance of a convection oven; you don't have to move the dishes for specific cooking styles. You can adjust temperatures and other features according to your needs. It is brittle because it has both a heating element and a fan.

A convection oven of high classification can last for like eternity. Gives the best outcome when used for certain functions like roasting vegetables and meats or browning etc. On the contrary, common complaints are that they don't let the dough rise completely. If you want to make the most of baking, always opt for a convection oven in which the fan can be shut down. The convection oven's best function is to use less power than any other regular or traditional ovens.

Because of its rapid outcome, convection ovens are commonly used in commercial bakery uses Because they provide tremendous results in crispness and browning. Automated and manual, both options are available in the convection oven, but they usually crackdown effortlessly. But still can function for ample of great recipes. A convection oven mostly a great option when you want to buy an up-to-date appliance for your kitchen that can give a huge amount of interest, ease and help.

RECIPES INDEX

Acorn Squash Stuffed...103
aked Mixed Berries Oatmeal.......................................37
aked Peach French Toast...37
aked Zucchini Slice (Gluten-Free)................................35
Almond Chocolate And Coconut Cake.........................274
Apple Caramel French Toast Casserole.........................33
Apple Granola Crisp..46
Apricot And Nut Square Bars......................................269
Armenian-Style Lamb And Beef Pizza...........................184
Artichoke And Hot Collards Dip...................................56
Artichoke Pie..113
Asparagus Cheesy Snack..74
Asparagus Fries...181
asty And Easy Carrot Cake...102
Avocado Flavored Cloud Bread...................................225
Bacon And Cheese Round Potatoes..............................71
Bacon and Eggs Dutch Baby Pancakes.........................44
Bacon Wrapped Stuffed Mini Peppers...........................81
Baked Apple And Sausages...223
Baked Asparagus With Italian Seasoning Cheese Sauce.....173
Baked Bacon-Wrapped Chicken...................................218
Baked Banana and Nuts French Toast...........................38
Baked Banana Cinnamon Fritters.................................169
Baked Beans, Tomato And Bacon.................................172
Baked Beef And Cheese Cups......................................167
Baked Beef Mixture Under A Bun.................................187
Baked Beef Potato Pie...203
Baked Breakfast Apple Butter Biscuit............................27
Baked Breakfast Italian Eggs......................................39
Baked Butter Cream Onions..174
Baked Buttermilk Spicy Chicken..................................185
Baked California Vegetable...95
Baked Caramel Oatmeal bars......................................172
Baked Cheese Sausage Biscuits...................................223
Baked Cheese Stuffed Chicken Breasts With Sauce..........202
Baked Cheesy Leeks...170
Baked Chicken Cheesy Potatoes Ranch.........................207
Baked Chicken Parmesan Nuggets...............................235
Baked Chicken Teriyaki..248
Baked Chicken Thigh...247
Baked Chicken With Lemon-Pepper Seasoning................220
Baked Creamy Mushroom Chicken...............................191
Baked Croissant Creamy Pudding With Delicious Kahlua Sauce.....261
Baked Egg And Bacon Bundles....................................240
Baked Eggplant Layered With Seasoning........................162
Baked Eggs In An Avocado hole...................................237
Baked French Toast With Stuffed Apples........................26

Baked Garlic And Butter-Flavored Pork Steaks................190
Baked Garlic Butter Lobster Tails.................................134
Baked Herb-Crusted Salmon.......................................120
Baked Honey-Mustard Flavored Chicken.......................199
Baked Italian-Style Breaded Pork Chops........................200
Baked Lamb Moroccan Kebabs....................................198
Baked Maple Flavored Pork Loin Roast.........................203
Baked Meatballs Stuffed With Mac And Cheese..............202
Baked Mushroom Bread With Parmesan And Italian Seasoning.....176
Baked Oatmeal Stuffed Apples....................................238
Baked Onion Chicken..226
Baked Parmesan Chicken Slider....................................51
Baked Pesto-Flavored Chicken....................................206
Baked Quinoa Chicken Nuggets...................................176
Baked Salmon...247
Baked Salmon With Honey Glazed................................130
Baked Seasoned Jicama Fries......................................236
Baked Steelhead Trout Croquettes...............................170
Baked Sweet Potato Fries...243
Baked Swiss Cheese And Corned Beef Dip In Bread Bowl...206
Baked tater tots..21
Baked Teriyaki Pineapple Chicken................................201
Baked Teriyaki Salmon...136
Baked Trout Fish In A Foil..127
Baked Turkey And Potato Croquettes...........................193
Banana Bread Inspired Brownies...................................65
Banana Oat And Cinnamon Muffins..............................157
Barbecue Chicken Tenders Baked.................................238
Barbecue-Style Chicken Bacon Bake............................222
Basic And Soft Raisin Apricot Cookies..........................256
Basic Oatmeal And Peanut Butter bars..........................251
Bbq Chicken Wings...82
Bean And Tuscan Sausage Dip......................................55
Beef And Broccoli Braided Bread.................................159
Beef And Cheese Taco Pies..155
Beef And Egg Noodles Bake..205
Beef And Pork Stuffed Pasta Shells..............................186
Beef And Salsa Baked Taquitos...................................201
Beef Cheese Spaghetti Pie...208
Beef Crostini With Blue Cheese...................................183
Beet and goat cheese appetizers...................................80
Best Artichoke And Spinach Dip....................................76
Best breakfast toast with egg and cheese........................17
Best-Ever Plum Pudding Dessert Baked.........................272
Blue Cheese Courgette Pizza......................................106
Blueberry Breakfast French Toast..................................26
Breaded Lemon Chicken..179

Breakfast Apple omelet...18
Breakfast Baked Oatmeal..42
Breakfast Burrito Casserole..43
Breakfast Cranberry and Orange Bread......................39
Breakfast Danish Buns...32
Breakfast Egg In A Hole Bagel......................................35
Broiled Crab Snacks...72
Broiled Steelhead Trout With Lemon Garlic And Rosemary....143
Broiled Swai with Salsa..148
Brown Sugar and Garlic Chicken................................246
Brunch Bacon Pizza...18
Brunch Bake..47
Brunch Baked Strawberry Rolls...................................19
Brunch Florentine Pizza..30
Brunch Onion Tart..28
Buffalo Cheese Chicken Pockets...............................240
Buffalo chicken bites with spinach and parmesan cheese....79
Butter Bars With Baked Lemon Curd Filling..............270
Butter Lemon Baked Chicken Tenders.......................194
Butter Lemon Baked Salmon Fettuccine Pasta........128
Buttermilk Flavored Mac And Cheese Baked............230
Butternut Squash Roasted..100
Cabbage Rolls...116
Cabbage Wedges Roasted..85
Cajun Tilapia..147
Cake Mix Cheesecake Dessert With Raspberry Topping....252
Caramel Apple Cinnamon Crisps...............................262
Caramelized Onion, Spinach, And Bacon Strata.........21
Caramelized Pecan Bacon Baked...............................224
Carrot And Broccoli Lasagna......................................104
Cauliflower Mac And Cheese Baked.............................95
Cheddar And Cream Cheese Stuffed Jalapeno Poppers....165
Cheddar Bacon Garlic Bread...75
Cheddar Chile Cornbread...71
Cheese 'n' Ham Biscuit Stacks......................................55
Cheese And Mushroom Strata.......................................97
Cheese Bread Sticks...61
Cheese Fresh Garden Stuffed Jalapeno.....................182
Cheese Olives Baked..75
Cheeseburger Bacon Bombs...66
Cheesy Baked Chicken Penne Pasta..........................191
Cheesy Beef Steak Pizza..190
Cheesy Cauliflower Crackers.......................................219
Cheesy Chicken Roll-Ups Baked.................................204
Cheesy Crabmeat Dip...126
Cheesy Easy Pizza Flavored Dip...................................70
Cheesy Salsa Bean Burritos..157
Cheesy Sausage & Egg Bake...47
Cheesy Seafood White Sauce Pizza...........................137

Cheesy Spinach Lasagna...101
Cherry Cracker Dessert...259
Chevre And Roasted Veggies Quiche...........................19
Chia Seeds And Oatmeal Cookies..............................267
Chicken And Stuffing Muffin Cups.............................189
Chicken Cheese Puffs...53
Chicken Cheese Taco Casserole.................................196
Chive-Garlic Oven-Baked Fries...................................241
Chocolate Chip Cookie for Modern Times..................276
Chocolate Chip Cookies...277
Chocolate Chips and Butterscotch Bars....................156
Chocolate-Peanut Marshmallow Bars........................228
Christmas Magic Cookie Bars......................................276
Cinnamon roll apple pie...180
Cinnamon Roll Smokies..80
Cinnamon Sweet Potato Chips......................................82
Cinnamon, Butter, And Sugar Stuffed-Apples............159
Cinnamon-Flavored Strawberry Biscuits....................232
Classic And Simple Lamb Loaf....................................200
Classic And Simple Oven Omelet..................................28
Classic Baked Catfish Fillets.......................................142
Classic Baked Pineapple Butter Casserole................163
Classic Banana Chocolate Cake..................................257
Classic Chicken And Pineapple Casserole.................154
Classic Chicken Parmesan Meatloaf..........................204
Classic Coconut Macaroons With Chocolate Glaze...264
Classic Egg Casserole..22
Classic French Vegetable Loaf....................................108
Classic Giant Pretzels..62
Classic Italian Parmesan Eggplant...............................87
Classic Lamb Gratin..192
Classic Molasses Cookies With Coffee-Glazed..........250
Classic Peanut-Butter Flavored Cookies....................160
Classic Pork Chops Baked With Mushroom Sauce.....195
Classic Rice And Chicken Casserole..........................236
Classic Sausage Italian Bruschetta..............................53
Classic Shepherd's Pie...162
Classic Turkey Stuffing...186
Cocoa Peanut Butter Granola..42
Coconut Crusted Mahi Mahi..179
Coconut Pineapple Cake With Lime Frosting.............253
Corn Mini Muffins with Cheddar Spicy Filling..............52
Cornish Vegetable Pasties...96
Crab Filled Crescent Cups...132
Crab Stuffed Muffins..136
Crabmeat And Prawns Southwestern Thin Crust Pizza....143
Crabmeat and Shrimp Loaf..135
Crabmeat Roll-Ups Lasagna..142
Cracker Barrel Meatloaf...211

Cranberry, Garlic And Cheddar Mini Breads 29
Cream Cheese And Strawberry Cobbler 249
Cream Cheese Chocolate Chip Brownies 266
Creamy Chicken and Corn Burritos 215
Creamy Quick Biscuits 237
Crescent Sausage Rolls 40
Crisps Almond Coffee Cookies 255
Crispy And Tasty Brussels Sprouts 89
Crispy And Tasty Turkey Burgers Baked 161
Crispy Baked French Fries 77
Crispy Honey Garlic Chicken 213
Crispy Lobster And Crab Stuffed Mushrooms 144
Crispy Onion Rings Baked 105
Crispy Pork Chops Baked 160
Crispy Potato Wedges Baked 110
Crispy Roasted Artichokes 242
Crispy Smashed Potatoes 243
Crispy Tofu Bites 84
Crumpet Butter And Caramel Pudding 31
Crunchy Oven Fried Fish 149
Crusted Parmesan Tilapia 121
Cucumber And Tomato Bruschetta 98
Date And Pecan Cookies 263
Date And Walnut Quick Bread 36
Delicious And Chewy Chocolate Chip Cookies 269
Delicious Baked Jalapeno Cranberry Dip 168
Delicious Chicken Gratin 233
Delicious Grilled Garlic Shrimp 128
Delicious Lamb Stuffed Peppers 196
Delicious Mediterranean Vegetable Sandwich Grilled 93
Delicious Picante And Cheese Omelet Pie 231
Delicious Pumpkin Cake With Cream Cheese And Butter Frosting 262
Delicious Rutabaga Gratin 98
Delicious Seafood Gratin 131
Delicious Seafood Salad Baked 124
Delicious Seafood Stuffing 121
Delicious Spinach And Seafood Mornay 141
Delicious Vegetable Pot Pie 94
Delicious Zucchini Casserole 92
Dijon Crispy Smashed Potato 86
Dijon Herb Chicken Breasts 212
Double Chocolate And Macadamia Biscotti 254
ealthy And Tasty Oatmeal Blueberry Bread 38
Easy And Classic Meyer Lemon Pie 229
Easy And Delicious Gingerbread Cake 258
Easy and Delicious Mushrooms Roasted 91
Easy And Moist Red Velvet Cookies 273
Easy And Quick Baked Shrimp Dip 134
Easy and Quick Broiled Tomatoes 57

Easy And Quick Cheesy Baked Gnocchi 152
Easy and Quick Chicken With Guacamole And Salsa 175
Easy And Quick Crostini 61
Easy And Quick Oatmeal Banana Cookies 253
Easy And Quick-Roasted Salmon 124
Easy And Tasty Potato Gratin 107
Easy And Tasty Tuna Noodles Casserole 120
Easy And Yummy Brunch Reuben Bake 24
Easy Baked Apple-Sugar Puff Pastry 152
Easy Breakfast Bake 48
Easy Chicken Barbecued Pizza 242
Easy Chicken Buffalo Dip 54
Easy Chocolate Chip Cookies With -Ingredient 218
Easy cinnamon rolls with homemade jam 283
Easy Cinnamon Sugar Baked Apples 280
Easy Cocktail And Shrimp Dip 217
Easy Granola Cookies 72
Easy Pumpkin Breakfast Bread 34
Easy Roasted Red Potatoes 244
Egg And Bacon Breakfast Lasagna 41
Egg And Potato Cheesy Bake 25
Egg Cheese And Bacon Breakfast Bread 22
Egg Sausage-Vegetable Bake 29
Farmer's Breakfast Casserole 20
Feta And Roasted Pumpkin Tarts 20
Fish Nuggets Baked 133
Fish with Parsley Pesto 244
Flounder Dijon 246
Fresh Homemade Peach Pie 282
Garlic Mayonnaise-Parmesan Topping Halibut 140
Garlic Parmesan Roasted Carrots 224
Ginger Soy Mahi Mahi 146
Greek Stuffed Peppers with Feta & Mizithra Cheeses 114
Greek-Style Pork Chops 185
Greek-Style Stuffed Lamb Leg 207
Grilled Chicken Hawaiian Pizza 68
Grilled Garlic Salmon 146
Grilled Marinated Beef Ribeyes Steaks 188
Grilled Pork Barbecued Kebabs 188
Grilled Potato Packets (Potato in A Foil) 96
Grilled Sriracha Shrimps 126
Grilled Sweet And Sour Chicken Thighs 187
Ground Pork Shepherd's Pie 184
Haddock And Seafood Baked 133
Ham And Broccoli Cheese Quiche 24
Ham And Cheddar Baked Omelet 228
Homemade Chicken Nuggets 78
Homemade Fish Sticks 78
Homemade pizza in a convection oven 112

Honey Dijon Salmon..149
Honey Lime Chicken Breasts......................................213
Huevos Rancheros Bake..113
Irish-Style Cupcakes With Irish Cream Frosting.............257
Italian Style Baked Oysters..144
Italian Style Simple Baked Chicken.............................163
Jalapeno Crescent Cups...67
Leek And Cauliflower 'Cheese' Herb-Crusted.................109
Lemon And Ricotta Cheese Dessert Cake.....................266
Lemon Garlic Roasted Chicken and Potato Wedges.........211
Lemon Squares..278
Lemon-Flavored Buttermilk Pie..................................267
Lemon-herb Baked Rainbow Trout..............................145
Lemon-Honey Glaze Cheesecake Baklava.....................272
Lemony garlic tilapia...178
Lentil and roast vegetables salad................................115
Lime Scallion Flavored Sea Bass................................153
Loaded Nachos Tater Tot..63
Low-Carb Garlic Bread...31
Mac And Cheese Jalapeno Bites.................................58
Maple Balsamic Roasted Vegetables............................111
Marble cake with cacao and turmeric..........................281
Marinated Prawns...181
Marshmallow Butterscotch Brownies............................263
Mayo-Cheese Mussels Dynamite................................139
Meringue cookies..278
Mexican Style Eggplant..117
Mexican Style Stuffed Peppers...................................103
Mexican-Style Sugar Chocolate Crisps.........................260
Mini Brie And Cranberry Bites....................................60
Mini Garlic-Herb Cheese Quiches...............................231
Mini Zucchini Bites..62
Moist And Tasty Basic Chocolate cake..........................265
Muffin With A Meal..225
Mushrooms Leeks and Sweet Potatoes Quiche...............104
Mushrooms With Marinara And White Beans..................100
Old Meatloaf...214
One-Pan Ginger Sesame Salmon................................131
Orange Butter Cookies...282
Orange-Zest Blackberry Cake.....................................256
Oven Baked Pears...280
Oven Chocolate Cookies...279
oven chocolate fudge cake..279
Oven Roasted Corn...180
Oven Roasted Italian Style Vegetables.........................107
Oven-Baked Parmesan Tomatoes................................89
Oven-Baked Rosemary Parmesan Potato Chunks............229
Oven-Baked Sea Bass..147
Oven-Baked Zucchini Fries..66

Oven-Roasted Stuffed Duck.......................................209
Parmesan And Butter Chicken....................................165
Parmesan Basil Salmon..150
Parmesan Green Beans Roasted.................................227
Parmesan Herb Baked Tilapia....................................145
Parmesan-Crusted White Fish....................................148
Party Mini Beef Burgers Baked...................................220
Party Savory Bread..64
Pattypan Squash Roasted...97
Pecan And Chocolate Pie Dessert Bars.........................260
Pecan cookies with rye and barley flakes......................43
Pecan Pear and Pancetta Puffs..................................56
Pepperoni Pizza Bread Loaf.......................................52
Pepperoni Pizza Cheesy Puffs....................................73
Pepperoni Pizza Rolls..57
Persimmon And Walnuts Cookies................................265
Pineapple And Carrot Muffins.....................................67
Pineapple Casserole Baked.......................................221
Pistachio Puff Pastry Twists.......................................69
Popper Cups With Jalapeno.......................................70
Potato Egg and Beef Bake...40
Prosciutto-Wrapped Pesto Chicken.............................227
Pumpkin Pie Mini Muffins...252
Quiche Brunch Cups..32
Quick And Crunchy Raisin Oatmeal Cookies..................167
Quick And Easy Ham Steaks Baked.............................234
Quick And Easy Herb Bread......................................171
Quick And Easy Peanut Butter Cookies With -Ingredient....219
Quick And Easy Pistachio Bread.................................41
Quick And Easy Roasted Vegetables Tortillas.................151
Quick And Simple Sea Bass Oven-Baked......................138
Quick And Tasty Cheesy Baked Grits...........................175
Quick And Tasty Peanut Butter Bread...........................36
Quick Baked Artichoke And Brie.................................158
Quick Baked Red Potatoes With Butter And Sour Cream Topping.........153
Quick breakfast Pizza slices with quail eggs...................45
Quick Cheese Spicy Bread...168
Quick Cheesy Potato Pizza..173
Quick Classic Chocolate Cake....................................166
Quick Nut And Banana Bread.....................................164
Quick Parsley And Dill Rolls.......................................154
Raspberry Jam Dessert Bars......................................255
Red Peppers With Basil Roasted.................................106
Roast Turkey..212
Roasted Avocado And Dijon Rubbed Beef Tenderloin.......208
Roasted Beef Tenderloin Salt-Crusted..........................199
Roasted Beef Teriyaki Shish Kebabs............................205
Roasted Brown Sugar Rutabaga..................................87
Roasted Carrots..114

Roasted Cauliflower With Cheese Sauce 102
Roasted Chicken with Garlic and Herb Butter 210
Roasted Garlic Mahi Mahi 245
Roasted Mixed Nuts 77
Roasted Parmesan Garlic Potatoes 90
Roasted Red Potatoes 177
Roasted Spicy Okra 110
Roasted Vegetables 177
Roasted Yams with Ginger, Miso and Scallions 93
Root Vegetables Roasted 88
Russian-Style Baked Beef 194
Salmon and Asparagus 245
Salmon with Rosemary 178
Salt and Vinegar Roasted Potatoes with Feta and Dill 111
Sausage Bites 49
Sausage Stuffed Jalapenos Wrapped In Bacon 233
Scallops, Flounder And Shrimp Lasagna 125
Scrambled Egg Muffins 48
Scrumptious bacon and egg cupcake omelet 46
Seafood Cottage Cheese Lasagna 123
Seasoned Oyster Crackers 83
Sheet Pan Chicken Pot Pie 215
Shrimp And Broccoli Alfredo Bake 135
Shrimp And Crabmeat Enchiladas 129
Simple And Classic Breakfast Pizza 34
Simple And Crispy Sugar Cookies 251
Simple And Crunchy Cornmeal Cookies 268
Simple And Delicious Broccoli Casserole 105
Simple And Delicious Seafood Pizza 119
Simple and Easy Pinwheels 54
Simple And Quick Tortilla Crust Pizza 155
Simple And Tasty Vegetable Frittata 91
Simple Crab Tart With Avocado 129
Simple Ravioli Cheese Casserole 239
Simply Baked Seafood Potatoes 138
Skillet Roast Chicken with Schmaltzy Potatoes 209
Smokin' Mahi Mahi 150
Soft Fruit Cocktail And Nut Cookies 264
Southern Style Pastry Puff For Brunch 25
Southern-Style Tasty Buttermilk Biscuits 241
Southwest-Style Bake Sausage 27
Spiced cauliflower 115
Spicy Beef And Bean Pie 189
Spicy Seafood Penne Pasta 139
Spinach And Cheese Stuffed Mushrooms 101
Spinach Beef And Rice Baked 198
Spinach Chips 83
Squares Cheese Appetizer 74
Starbucks Inspired Swirl Raspberry Pound Loaf With Frosting 271

Strawberry Pie with Strawberry Crust 275
Stuffed Baked Cherry Peppers 73
Stuffed Crab Mushrooms 122
Stuffed Pizza Mushrooms 76
Tasty And Creamy Scalloped Potatoes 232
Tasty And Easy Cheesy Vegetable pizza 94
Tasty And Moist Lime-White Chocolate Muffins 268
Tasty And Moist Red Velvet Cheesecake 270
Tasty And Quick Caesar Chicken Baked 171
Tasty And Quick Meatloaf 156
Tasty And Quick Vegetable Pasta Salad 90
Tasty And Simple Meatball Casserole 193
Tasty And Soft Baked Lemon Cheesecake Bites 259
Tasty Apple Sauce Flavored Cornbread 161
Tasty Baked Cheese Breaded Squash 174
Tasty Baked Chicken Mushroom 169
Tasty Baked Cod Fish 123
Tasty Baked Duchess Potatoes 99
Tasty Baked Tilapia Pecan-Crusted 140
Tasty Broiled Scallops 125
Tasty Cabbage Baked Steaks 221
Tasty Cheese And Ham Croissant 30
Tasty Cheese And Ham Sliders 69
Tasty Dijon-Crusted Fish Fillets 158
Tasty Duck Rillettes 197
Tasty Fish Croquettes Baked 122
Tasty Fresh Blueberry Cobbler 239
Tasty Fries And Cheeseburger Casserole 230
Tasty Garlic And Cheddar Biscuits 164
Tasty Grilled Pineapples 64
Tasty Hash Browns Baked 235
Tasty Lamb Meatballs Baked 195
Tasty Meatballs Cheesy Pizza 166
Tasty Pecan Butter Cookies 258
Tasty Pizza Bagels 58
Tasty Pizza Bubble 60
Tasty Poppy Seeds Lemon Cake 254
Tasty Potato Skins Baked 68
Tasty Ranch-Parmesan Bread Rolls 234
Tasty Seafood Ravioli Baked 137
Tasty Seafood Stuffed Peppers 132
Tasty Snickers Flavored Croissants 23
Tasty Streusel Blueberry Coffee Cake 23
Tasty Stuffed Mushrooms (Stuffed Sausage Mushrooms) 59
Tasty Tuna Cheesy Melts 127
Tasty Vegetable Casserole 92
Tasty Vegetable Lasagna 88
Tater-Tot Beef Casserole 226
The Best Banoffee Pie 271

The Perfect Baked Raisin Rice Pudding 273

Toaster Oven Peanut Butter Cookies 274

Ukraine-Style Potato Baked 222

umpkin Cookies Sandwich With Frosting Of Maple Cream Cheese 33

Vegetable Cheesy Casserole 86

Vegetable Egg Muffins 99

Vegetable Enchilada Pie 108

Walnut And Cranberry Loaf 250

Watercress And Crab Mini Soufflé Tarts 130

Wrapped Bacon Scallops 59

Yummy And Easy Pizza Rolls 63

Yummy spicy coconut chicken 216

Zucchini Boats 117

Zucchini-Flavored Chocolate Cookies 261

The Perfect Baked Raisin Rice Pudding 273

Toaster Oven Peanut Butter Cookies 274

Ukraine-Style Potato Baked 222

umpkin Cookies Sandwich With Frosting Of Maple Cream Cheese 33

Printed in Great Britain
by Amazon